Paula Radcliffe was born in Northwich, Cheshire, in 1973, but grew up in Bedford. She joined Bedford and County Athletics Club at the age of eleven, and competed in the world cross-country championships at sixteen. After graduating from Loughborough University with a first-class degree in modern languages in 1996 she devoted herself full-time to her running, and is now acknowledged as one of the finest athletes of the modern era.

As well as her medals at 5,000 and 10,000 metres, Paula has now established herself as the master of the ultimate distance race, the marathon. She holds the world record and won the London Marathon in 2002, 2003 and 2005. In November 2004 she won the New York Marathon in breathtaking style and in 2005 she took the gold medal at the World Championships in Helsinki for the same distance.

She was awarded an MBE in June 2002, and later that year was voted the BBC's Sports Personality of the Year. She lives in Loughborough with her husband and manager, Gary Lough.

David Walsh, who worked with Paula on her autobiography, has been judged Sports Writer of the Year in Britain three times and is chief sports writer with the *Sunday Times*.

There are so many people deserving of this dedication, it is impossible to include them all. How to choose from so many? I have chosen one from each end of the Radcliffe family spectrum.

To my grandmother, Olive, the best grandmother anyone could have. Your zest for life influences us all. You showed us how to go after what you want while always treating others fairly. You taught me that life is for living, you only get one shot at it, so live it to the full and enjoy every minute.

To my beautiful niece, Maya, who with her parents will soon be moving to Australia. We will miss you all so much. Of course we'll still see you as much as possible but maybe through this you'll get to know your Auntie Paula a little better. You'll never know how your cuddles, smiles and innocent love helped to remind me what really matters after Athens. Live your life to the full. Remember the story of the five balls, have the courage to go after your dreams and always fight for what you believe in.

PAULA

My Story So Far

PAULA RADCLIFFE

with David Walsh

POCKET
BOOKS

LONDON • SYDNEY • NEW YORK • TORONTO

First published in Great Britain by Simon & Schuster UK Ltd, 2004
This edition published by Pocket Books, 2005
An imprint of Simon & Schuster UK Ltd
A CBS COMPANY

3 5 7 9 10 8 6 4 2

Simon & Schuster UK Ltd
1st Floor
222 Gray's Inn Road
London WC1X 8HB

www.simonandschuster.co.uk

Simon & Schuster Australia
Sydney

A CIP catalogue record for this book is available
from the British Library.

ISBN 978-074347-869-4

Typeset in Perpetua by M Rules
Printed and bound in Great Britain by
Cox & Wyman Ltd, Reading, Berks

Acknowledgements

There are so many people whose love, support and friendship have enriched my life and without whom I wouldn't have achieved all that I have.

My amazing husband Gary. I love you so much and am so lucky I get to spend my life with you. From the moment I met you I've known how special you are to me. You are my lover and best friend above all else but so much more besides. You are my pillar of strength who unselfishly gives so much. You are always there for me and give me the extra confidence and belief that helps me get so much more from myself.

My wonderful parents, Peter and Pat. Someone once said to me that if you could choose your parents, I couldn't have done a better job. That is so true. You are the best there could be. You taught us to give the best of ourselves, in all that we do, but always to enjoy life and keep the perspective. You are always there with your unshakeable love and unconditional support.

All of my family and friends. Thank you so much for your unending love and support. With you I am always just Paula, and that is what I love so much. You are all such special people. I am so lucky to have the chance to spend time and have fun with you all.

My coach, Alex Stanton. I was so lucky to join your group at the age of eleven. You are so much more than a coach. You and Rosemary are always there for me, giving so much of yourselves to all you do. Your knowledge, intuition and calm reassurance are so strong and unwavering. Together we have come such a long way and still have a long way to go. Thank you for everything.

My physiotherapist, Gerard Hartmann. Thank you so much for your support and dedication to keeping my body healthy and in one strong piece. You are such a strong, kind and skilled person. More than a physiotherapist, you are also a great friend and motivator and have brought so much to my career and life.

So many others have helped keep my body healthy and strong: Mark Buckingham, Vaughan Cooper, Bruce Hamilton, Bryan English and Brian Welsby; Pipsa, Rone and Mark in Loughborough; Michel Riff and Daniel Hardelin in Font-Romeu; and Dana Paine in Albuquerque. Thank you all so much. Dr Andy Jones, my physiologist, thank you for your gruelling tests, excellent advice and confidence bolstering enthusiasm.

Thanks also to Max Jones, my weights coach, and all those at UK Athletics, Loughborough University and High Performance Centre, and Bedford & County Athletics Club for all your help and support.

Sian Masterton, Abi Tordoff and Clifford Bloxham at Octagon. Thank you for your hard work and support and also for your great friendship.

Thanks to Nike, it is a pleasure to work with a company so committed to helping sport and athletes, listening to our thoughts and needs, and to Vittel and Cadbury for their support.

Finally thanks to Simon & Schuster and to David Walsh.

Much of my adult life has been consumed by running, resting, racing and recovering. When I first began to write this book, I wondered what else could I write about? But the detail of my life has shaped me as an athlete and a woman. Others will see many parallels with their lives. My races may be faster, the public interest greater, but the emotions I feel are those experienced by countless people. Who doesn't have achievements and disappointments in their life, successes and failures? Maybe through reading my story some people will be inspired to work harder to develop their talents and realise their dreams. If that were to happen, the writing of the book would be all the more worthwhile. Principally, though, this book is my opportunity to tell my story, to show how so many others have affected my life and to tell of their contributions. Without them it would be a very different story.

If there is one message I want to get across, it is that I am passionate about the importance of sport in our lives and what it can bring to us. Without sport I would not be the person I am today. It isn't the level at which I race that is important because at any level sport teaches us. Athletics has taught me about myself, both my strengths and weaknesses. I have learned to respect and be more aware of my body, how it must be looked after and what must be done to get the best out of it. What I have learned in sport is applicable to everyday life and it has helped me to make more of my life and, especially, to have more fun. Because of athletics I am more self-confident and outgoing than I would otherwise have been. Sport has also shown me how to be more understanding and respectful of the achievements of others. I've learned how better to handle and cope with the stresses that life can throw at us.

I think of the many, many interesting people I have met through athletics, the places I have seen, the cultures I have marvelled at. It has shown me the value of getting along with people, the results that can be achieved through teamwork, the fun that can come from camaraderie. My closest friends now are people first encountered on the sport's trail. We first shared an interest in running, then we shared experiences in life. For all of these reasons I would encourage everyone to make time for sport and to remember that it isn't the level that matters.

At a time when obesity levels are rising and posing an ever greater danger to health, the importance of sport has rarely been so obvious. Everyone, but especially children, needs to be more active. It is why I was so keen to support Cadbury's Get Active Campaign aimed at getting children more involved in sport. I don't believe kids today eat any more or any worse than we did, but in my view they don't take enough exercise. By not getting out there, they hurt themselves and society in general, and they also miss out on so much.

Essentially, this book tells how running has affected my life. It is about the things that are important to me: the ideals, the goals and the dreams. I may not have achieved all these yet, but my ambition is to be able to say at the end of my career, 'I believe I have achieved all that I was capable of achieving.' Then I will move on to my life after athletics and there will be new aspirations, fresh dreams. How much longer will my career last? I don't honestly know, but hopefully for a good while yet and certainly to Beijing and another shot at my Olympic dream. Who knows, maybe I'll stay around long enough to be part of what could be an amazing experience for everyone at London 2012. All we need is the chance to show what we could do as hosts. I believe London would do an outstanding job and put on a Games to treasure forever. Whatever the duration of my career, my plan now is to keep going as long as I still enjoy training and competing. When it becomes a chore, when my body and mind no longer enjoy the grind, when racing is no longer my first love, then that will be the time to hang up the racing shoes. However, I can never see myself hanging up my running shoes because I can't imagine a time when I would not want to run; it is too much a part of me. I love to get out there and be at one with my body, feel the wind against me, see how fast I can go. It is my stress relief, my thinking time. The act of running has been and will always be something that I love and cannot imagine being unable to do.

I know that I am extremely lucky in being able to make my living doing something that I would be doing anyway. It is a privilege I have never taken for granted. When my career is over I won't push my body to the limits like I do today but I will always want to get out there and run. And when the racing days are over, that will be the time to give something back to the sport that has given me so much.

There were occasions, particularly in the aftermath of Athens and the endless dissection and criticism, when I wondered if I wanted to share a very personal story with the world. Then I thought of all the wonderful support and compassion I had received and how all the people who have backed me deserved to know what happened in Athens and everywhere else along the way. Also to know that I am okay, that I've picked up the pieces and am back to being me. I still love my running and am relishing the prospect of future races and contemplating new goals and dreams and how best to achieve them. Above all I'm back to being happy and I'm enjoying life.

Yes, I had a disaster – a big one. Yes, I was devastated for a while and the scars will probably always remain there somewhere, but writing this book has made me think about what I have already achieved in my career, what I have to be grateful for in my life and what is still there for me to achieve. Often the biggest setbacks and the cruellest disappointments are what make us stronger and in the course of this book you may notice that setbacks and disappointments have always worked out that way for me.

This is also an opportunity for me to thank countless people for their support. Not just the people who have directly helped me but also all of those who watch my races and cheer me on. The support has been amazing; nothing that I could write here would do it justice but I want people to know how appreciative I am. Experiences like the Flora London Marathons, the Commonwealth Games, the Great North events and the British Grand Prix are made special because of the tremendous atmosphere that surrounds them. These are memories that will stay with me and I feel so grateful for having experienced them. Without the people, the occasions would be nothing.

Neither will I ever forget winning the BBC Sports Personality of the Year in 2002. The number of people who took the trouble to vote astounded me – at first I was convinced I had misheard. It touched me deeply and as an award, it has a particular meaning for me because it was decided by votes from the general public. From the bottom of my heart, thank you.

When I decided to write this book, I had intended to tell my story so far and obviously I hoped that Athens would be a happy place to end it. Life doesn't always work out the way we would like but I did not need Athens to deliver that message. However, one deep disappointment is not a reason to change long-term plans or give up on my dreams. What happened at the Olympics makes me all the more determined to keep working and inspires me to try even harder.

This doesn't mean the time immediately after Athens wasn't

difficult for me. I had faced the biggest failure of my career and didn't fully understand why it had happened. There were reasons, plenty of them, but I still couldn't understand what happened to make me feel *so* bad and *so* weak. However, it never once crossed my mind that my career might be over or even that I was no longer the athlete I once was. I didn't believe the marathon had beaten and broken me. Yet, I had to face all of these things and more in the media and public reaction to Athens. Facing up to what happened forced me to be hard on myself; to question myself and not be afraid of the answers. The process has been good for me.

I know that I am not a quitter. In Athens I had to fight against very challenging circumstances; I made some mistakes, didn't handle some things well and paid the price for that. I will learn from the experience and come back tougher. I still have so much left to achieve and have not become a lesser athlete.

After a devastating emotional experience, you seek comfort and inspiration from wherever you can. Something I read after the Olympics made real sense to me. It was in a James Patterson novel and I found it uplifting because it explained something I have long felt but never worked out into words. It is, I believe, relevant to everyone's life. It was about five balls: life is about juggling five balls in the air. They are health, family, friends, integrity and career/achievement. These balls are not the same; the important thing to remember is that the career ball is made of rubber but the others are more fragile. You can take more risks with the rubber ball. You may try to throw it through higher and higher hoops because if you do drop it, it will eventually bounce back. Normally, this ball does not suffer long-term damage. The other four balls need to be looked after more carefully. If you drop one of these it will be damaged and it may even shatter. To me it is a valid analogy because it symbolises what is important in life and should be remembered. So long as we have our health, integrity, family and friends we can overcome life's hurdles.

In sport, it is especially true that we take risks with that achievement ball. I throw it higher and higher and push myself to achieve all that I am capable of. The last place I ever wanted to drop that ball was in the most important race of my life. Unfortunately it happened and now I have to recover. However, what is most important is that the other balls are safe and unharmed: I still have the best family and friends, they still love me as much as ever and they have been invaluable in helping me to come to terms with, and then move on from, the disappointment of Athens. Equally, my health and integrity are still intact. People may have questioned my integrity for stopping in two races but I know that I ran as far as my body could go in that marathon. I could go no further.

I do not doubt my ability to push past the pain barrier in future races. With a healthy body, you can achieve amazing things. When it is not healthy it will let you know and if you persist, it will shut down. It is important to heed these warnings and my body gave me no choice. For the 10,000m I did what was important to me: I gave myself the chance to run well so that I would never have to wonder 'what if?' Although it didn't come off, at least I found out the answer and can live with that. I did what I felt was right, even though I knew if it didn't work out it would be criticised. When I knew there was nothing left, I didn't risk long-term injury or inflict further damage on a battered body.

While obviously not 100 per cent healthy in Athens, I didn't do lasting damage to my health and drop that very important ball. I have recovered now and am already able to consider how I am going to bring that achievement ball back into play. That was one of my worries immediately after Athens: had I damaged my body long term? I felt so awful that I was concerned there was something seriously wrong with me. Fortunately the tests revealed nothing that I have to worry about but I learned a great lesson about anti-inflammatory tablets and stress levels. I will be staying away from them in the future.

It took time for the leg injury that caused so much stress in the two weeks before Athens to clear fully and it took time for my stomach to settle down. But as I write this I am again feeling completely well and very thankful for that fact. There will be plenty more races and championships in the future. Athens was devastating but I will get over it and move on.

Without family and friends that would have been impossible. After Athens, Gary and I spent time with my parents. It was in the immediate aftermath and we were too raw emotionally to return home alone; we needed their support and the chance just to talk. We talked and talked, tried to make sense of what had happened and to put it into perspective. We wanted to learn from it and move on. I cried a lot on their shoulders, and they made me see that it had happened and that it wasn't my fault. Circumstances did conspire and I am grateful for the chance to be able to fully explain it further on in this book.

Being with Mum and Dad made me see that although regrettable, painful and witnessed by millions, Athens was just a couple of weeks. One event that went horribly wrong. I walked around the garden with them and knew there was no way I was going to let this beat me, and it would only change me for the better. I am inspired that those who have always been there for me remain ever loyal.

My coach Alex Stanton is still there everyday, the same, constant reassuring presence. He helped in rebuilding my fitness and now he's working with me on the return to competition.

'You have to stop thinking you're Superwoman,' he tells me. 'Not many could have come through what you faced in Athens and got to the start-line. You have to accept you're human like the rest of us. Forgive your body, get strong again and then carry on working for what you want.'

Alex's wife, Rosemary, has got the all-clear from colon cancer which is wonderful – and more important than anything that happened in Athens.

My physiotherapist, Gerard, has been in constant contact and has taken a very well-earned break to recover from all the stress he suffered on my behalf. I am so grateful for the sacrifices he has made and all his hard work in trying to help me realise my goals. His help and friendship have made me a better person and athlete and will continue to be invaluable. All of my friends have been there for me. Texts, emails, phone calls that mean so much, hugs that reassured me.

As he always has been, Gary remains by my side. Supporting, caring and above all helping us to get back to normal. We stayed in England until all of the health tests were completed and then we went away. Not to escape but just to be together. A great deal of our life is spent away in different training venues in far-flung places. We have always been relaxed spending day after day together, doing the things we enjoy doing.

By putting ourselves into this routine we gave ourselves the opportunity of getting back to normal. It is what makes us happy. We have also had the chance to visit and explore somewhere new and we have really enjoyed our time in Arizona. The town of Flagstaff is quite small and very friendly, the countryside beautiful. I explored new trails, saw lots of deer, elk, snakes and even came across a tarantula. Not that I had been seeking that encounter! Of course, I have trained and worked hard while all the time listening to my body and my heart. If on occasions I was too tired or didn't want to train, I didn't. But those days have actually been very few. When I went for a run in a freezing snowstorm and saw not a soul out there, I knew I was better and back to normal!

Every time I visit the hot sulphur baths in Dorres, near Font-Romeu in the Pyrenees, I see, engraved in the rocks, the words: '*Notre plus grand gloire n'est pas de ne jamais tomber mais de se relever à chaque fois que l'on tombe.*' 'Our greatest honour is not that we never fall down, but that we pick ourselves up again each time we fall.' This is so important in life. We should never be afraid to go after something that we want for fear of failure. We all need the courage to try, we may not get there straight away, sometimes we may never get there, but we must never be afraid to give all that we can to go after our goals and dreams.

The things you have to work the hardest to achieve are often the achievements you most treasure. For me this is true of the World Cross-Country and Championship medals on the track. I also know that by aiming for the highest peaks, you may not reach them but by aiming so high you can achieve far more than you originally thought possible. 'Aim for the moon; even if you miss, you'll land among the stars,' Alex would say to me as a child. To me, as an ambitious 11-year-old who had just watched the LA Olympics and Ingrid Kristiansen setting a world record in the London Marathon, this meant I had to have the courage to go after my dreams.

Unless you put yourself on the line and give it your best shot you'll never know what you could achieve. I can tell you that the 11-year-old who wanted to go to the Olympics and win in world record time, win the London Marathon and be the fastest in the world, never thought that at the age of 30 she'd have ticked off two out of three of those dreams. And she is still working on the third. More importantly I am happy with my life and with the woman I have become.

I still have so much left to do. Next year's World Championships are a definite goal and I still want that world track title. Longer term, the Olympic gold remains a goal. Yet, as well as the medals and titles, I also simply want to compete in different races and different places. It is what I enjoy doing, getting out there and racing. And I will continue to do it as long as I am able. Winning isn't everything to me but running and giving my all is.

2

I don't remember a time in my life when I didn't run. Running to tell my mum that Martin, my younger brother, had disappeared with his friends from Larch Tree Close in Barnton, near Northwich, where we first lived – 'Mum, Mum, he's escaped again . . .' Running down the lane behind our house to meet Dad as he returned from his training run. Mum would have calculated the time and known when he was due to come into view on the lane. 'Okay, there he is; go now.' Aged 4, I would scamper off, not stopping or slowing until I reached him. Without drawing breath I would then turn and run alongside him all the way back to the house. Even then running was fun.

I can still see Mum raising her eyes to heaven when she saw my medal from the village sports day: 'I don't know how you won that egg-and-spoon race. You're forever dropping things round here.' Calamity Jane, she called me. On summer holidays at the beach we would go for a swim and afterwards Martin and I would run on the sand. Martin is two years younger than me and spent much of his early life just trying to keep up. Then he grew tall and got faster, and it was me who struggled to stay with him. It was always fun, but it was never just for the fun of it: we both wanted to outdo the other. Not easy, but it was the way we both wanted it.

At primary school in Kingsley, my friend Germaine Hilditch and I would go running together. She wanted me to join the Frodsham Harriers in the next village, but they didn't let you in until you were nine. Another full year: that seemed forever.

My first competitive experiences came in a series of inter-schools races when I was nine. In the first race, I finished second. The next event was over a short loop in Delamere Forest where Dad used to train for his marathons and half-marathons. On Saturday afternoons for a few weeks before the race he took me to the forest and we practised the course. There was a big hill on the circuit and over the following two years he would teach me how to run downhill. 'Running downhill is a technique,' he said. 'It's about relaxing, letting your legs do the work and concentrating on keeping your body relaxed and balanced. You mustn't force it; you take your speed from the gradient. People can get too tense going downhill, they hurt their knees and they end up fighting the gradient. Remember that when people get to the top of the hill, they like to catch their breath, so if you go hard on the downhill, you have a chance of breaking away.' Ah, breaking away. Yes. Years later I would use this advice down a snowy hill in Boston to win the World Junior Cross-Country.

I won that inter-schools race, but not without it causing a little angst. Jonathan Ollier was my boyfriend, or as much of a boyfriend as a nine-year-old girl can have. He ran in the boys' race but didn't win. His friend came to me with the bad news: 'Jonathan's not very happy because you've done better than him.' Even at that point in my life, there was no way I would have run differently to keep some boy happy. At home I talked it over with Mum, told her about Jonathan and said there was no way I was going to lose just to please someone else. Mum said that was right. Luckily the friendship survived.

My favourite runs were with Dad in Delamere Forest. He would do his long run there most weekends. Mum, Martin and I would leave a half an hour later in the car, Mum taking a Mars bar and a carton of orange juice for his snack at halfway. Martin and I would play in the forest while we waited for Dad to get to the rendezvous. That forest is a children's paradise – close to where we would meet up, there was a big hole that Martin and I called 'the polar bear hole'. We would go to the hole to see if any polar bears had been caught. There was also a rope tied to the branch of a tree and we would swing on it.

Then Dad would come along and I would run with him for as long as I could. It seemed to me we ran a long way together before exhaustion overtook me. It was probably only a kilometre or so but the run was a high point for me. One time Dad and I ran a charity race through the forest, staying side by side for the entirety of the race, 6 miles. Martin, of course, didn't want to run alongside his sister and set off with friends. I was 10, he was 8 and somewhere along the way, he got ahead and finished before us. I was really annoyed and felt cheated because we had not seen him go past. The competitive streak was always there.

But it isn't just the competition that appeals to me. Running is something I enjoy, full stop. Being out in a nice part of the countryside, running fast, the breeze in your face, feeling free and just seeing how long you can keep going. There is the sense of escape from the real world, the exhilaration that comes when you run hard, the search to see how far you can push yourself, just being at one with yourself: they are all part of what I love about running. Mum and Dad might have thought it was a healthy pastime but I didn't do it because of them. A year or so after moving to Bedford and joining the local club there, my coach Alex Stanton wanted to put me in his squad for the National Inter-Club Cross-Country, but that meant training two nights a week instead of one. He went to my mum.

'Would Paula be able to come to training on Tuesdays and Thursdays?'

'It's not up to me,' she replied. 'It's her sport. You've got to ask her.'

When he asked I thought it was a big honour and was so happy. That was the end of my Thursday evenings with the judo club: outside of school and home, running became my life. Bedford & County Athletic Club became my sporting and my social life.

Years and years later, long after we left Cheshire for Bedfordshire, I was visiting my grandmother in Liverpool and went back to Delamere Forest for a run. I tried to find the trail Dad and I had used. After spending a long time looking, I never found it. Trees had got bigger, some had been cut down, there were many new young trees and parts of the forest had been flooded. Delamere is very much a living forest. Things weren't the same as they had been to a 10-year-old girl. But that early experience left its mark and I still enjoy running in a forest more than any other kind of setting. Not that I complain about where I run.

Give me a sunny morning, a nice country road, park or trail, and that's where I want to be, even though it may hurt at the end because of the speed. That run is my time, no one else is there and my mind can be where I want it to be. At times when I was preparing for an exam or bothered about something in my personal life, running freed me up. It was my reward for hard work. I would study all day then escape it all in the evening for a run. Quite often if I was stuck on a maths problem, the best thing was to leave it, go for a run and then in the middle of a run, I would just get it. Nothing sorts the mental clutter as effectively as a good run.

Even though I want to win every race – European and World titles, Olympic medals and to continually improve my times – success and the material rewards are not why I run. I do this sport because I love the act of running. My greatest fear is not missing out on a medal, but the injury that might stop me from doing this very basic activity. It was a passion for running that drew me into the sport and after the races are finished and competitive challenges are no more, the desire to run will still be there. I can't imagine living and not running.

I was conceived in Sandal, Wakefield, in Yorkshire, and was then born and raised for seven years in the village of Barnton, near Northwich in Cheshire. My parents then moved to nearby Kingsley and stayed there for five years before finally moving south and settling in the village of Oakley, just outside Bedford. We moved because Dad's job changed. He was qualified in human resources and worked for different companies before becoming a Personnel Director with Whitbread. Pat, my mum, was a primary school teacher who gave up her job when Martin and I were young and then returned to teaching when the time was right. She would never have taught at a school where my brother and I were pupils. It's not fair, she says – children have the right to enjoy school on their own without mum spying on them, and they sometimes get picked on if one of their parents is a teacher at the school.

How can I begin to explain what my parents did for Martin and me? Once, when I was about 13 or 14, I remember noticing that except for one item, every piece of furniture in my bedroom was made by Dad. Okay, it was a hobby of his, but it was also by saving money on things like bedroom furniture that we had the money to go on a continental holiday in the summer. To us, that was a high point of the year. Similarly, Mum would make a lot of our clothes and even though we weren't rich, we were always able to do things and go places. Most of all we had lots of fun.

Peter, my dad, came from Liverpool. As we lived the first eleven years of my life in Cheshire, we spent a lot of time around Dad's family, especially my grandparents, Bill and Olive. Granddad died ten years ago but Grandma is still with us. They played an important part in my life and Grandma still does. Granddad's father, my great granddad William Radcliffe, had an interesting life. He was an engineer on whaling boats and was once in South Georgia, a small British island not that far from Antarctica.

Boats on which he sailed were twice torpedoed, once in each war, and though it did affect his health, he was mentally tough and I am sure some of his qualities found their way into succeeding generations of the Radcliffe family. His father, my great, great grandfather, was a committed road-walker and would do the London to Brighton walk. Endurance definitely ran in the genes: his son, my great granddad William, finding himself out of work in the 1930s, once walked from Liverpool to Hull just to get a job.

William and my great grandmother had three children, a boy and two girls. Partly because her husband was away at sea so often, my great grandmother was close to her son and when he came back from the Second World War with a wife, she reacted cautiously.

Granddad, who was also called William, had been promoted through the ranks to be an officer in the Army Medical Corps after surviving Dunkirk. He was based in Cairo when he met my grandma, who was a QA nursing officer with the army. They fell in love, got married in the Egyptian city of Alexandria and spent their honeymoon at Kyrenia in Cyprus. They came home and bought a house in Woolton, not far from my great grandmother and great-grandfather, who died shortly afterwards.

Athletics was in the family, and Granddad used to compete in the army. He was a sprinter and often told me stories of how he would sharpen his spikes before races. Once Martin and I began to race, his enthusiasm was infectious. He liked nothing better than to watch us race and was very proud of what we did. The incident that really caught his imagination was one of Martin's earliest races, an 800m. Martin was very talented – without having the same passion that I had for the sport – but his real difficulty was his size. He became very tall, he is now 6 foot 5, and his thin physique never really filled out. When he trained hard, he became susceptible to injury. You don't see many top-class athletes of his size and there are good, physiological reasons for that.

In the particular race that Granddad loved, Martin was well clear of the pack when with 200 metres to go he stopped, removed his tracksuit top, folded it neatly and placed it on the ground. He then started off again and still won the race. Granddad thought that was hilarious and would laugh heartily every time he retold the story.

But the most distinguished member of the sporting Radcliffe family was Dad's great aunt Charlotte, who won a silver medal in the 4 x 100m freestyle relay at the 1920 Paris Olympics. Although she was my great great aunt, I knew Charlotte Radcliffe as Aunt Lottie. I have no particular memory of what she was like but I do remember being round at her house when I was about 4 or 5. She died shortly after that. Mum and Dad have photographs of Lottie in her bathing suit, and the story was often told in our house of the swimming events in Paris taking place in the river Seine, with poor Aunt Lottie and her team-mates having to share the water with toads and frogs. When Martin and I told the story, the toads and frogs were joined by rats.

After winning her silver medal, Aunt Lottie worked on the *Queen Elizabeth* as a fitness consultant, though I don't imagine that was her job title in those days. She was away at sea for long periods but Dad has very definite memories of her. He says she was a strong and handsome woman who always looked like she had been an athlete. Sadly she had a stroke when she was in her fifties and that affected her for the rest of her life.

Thinking maybe that I had inherited some of Lottie's prowess in the water, Mum took us to swimming lessons, which I enjoyed, but never as much as running. The story of the rats stayed in my mind and I used it to justify my preference for running.

My grandparents' home at Woolton in Liverpool was a fun house. Grandma was from Carmarthen in Wales and has always known how to live life to the full. We would spend hours playing games like hide and seek and I'm sure Grandma was disappointed when we grew out of them! After getting married, she became Casualty sister at Sefton Hospital in the city and Granddad worked in a camera shop. They also had a sweet shop for a number of years. Holidays were as important to them as they would be to my parents. Grandma once queued for hours to buy two tents in an army surplus sale.

'Don't know what you're doing that for,' Granddad said. 'That'll be no good to us because I'm not going camping. I spent all my years in the army in a tent and I hated it.'

That didn't put Grandma off, nothing did. Grandma and I share the same birthday and are very alike. Once we make up our minds to do something we both do all that we can to achieve it. She bribed Granddad with the promise that when they eventually went camping in Europe, they would return to many of the places he had been stationed during the war. First they experimented in Wales and Grandma prayed the weather would be good. It was perfect. Grandma loved it, my dad and his sister Susan loved it, and even Granddad was won over. 'Oh, all right,' he said, 'we can take it on the continent next year.' That began their holidays around France, Spain and other European countries. This was the 1950s and there weren't that many English families who put their car on a ferry and headed off to Europe on a camping holiday. They often got themselves lost but Granddad was a good linguist and spoke fluent French and German. Whatever talent I have for languages came from him and my mum, who is also an excellent linguist.

Those trips to the continent were as much adventures as holidays. Dad tells stories about the places they saw, the people they met. How when he and his parents first visited the Costa Brava, they travelled on dirt roads and if you wanted petrol, you drove inland and queued in some town square for your fuel. Dad was a boy through all of this but the experiences remained with him and he was very keen that his children would have the same opportunities to see other countries and experience other cultures. Our family holidays to France and Spain and many other European countries were direct descendants of the adventures he had enjoyed in his youth.

Granddad and Grandma lived next door to the Davis family in Woolton, whose son Rodney played in a group called the Quarrymen, which eventually evolved into the Beatles. The Quarrymen, according to Dad, started out as a skiffle group with a washboard, a tea chest, a guitar and a few other things. John Lennon was a member, and much to Grandma's annoyance, he and Rod used to practise a lot in Davis's back garden. 'That's a right racket they're making,' Grandma would say, unaware that what she was hearing would evolve into the greatest band in the history of pop music.

In their very early days the Beatles performed at a local church fête, and a few years ago the *Daily Mail* reproduced a photograph from that long-ago gig. In the front row, sitting cross-legged and looking well pleased with himself, is Dad. He actually went to school with John Lennon's stepsister, the same school John had attended some years before.

Pat, my mum, was an only child from Rawmarsh in Yorkshire, where her parents had a pet shop and Grandpa was a transport inspector. She was very close to her first cousins, who lived nearby, although the effect of being an only child meant she was determined to have at least two children of her own. Whenever Martin and I fought, Mum would say, 'Don't be horrible to each other, I used to cry for a brother or sister when I was small, it was all I ever wanted.' Maybe that didn't lead to an immediate cessation of hostilities but we got the message. Because they lived in Yorkshire, we didn't see Mum's parents as often as Dad's, but we did often go and stay at Rawmarsh and they would come and stay with us.

My most vivid memory is getting up early in the morning and having breakfast with Grandpa. He would make me toast with blackberry jam and we would talk. Grandpa had acute bronchitis most of his life and his chest was never the best. He passed away when I was 11.

Mum went to the local Methodist Church and her social life revolved around the youth club associated with the church. They would go to the club on Thursday evenings and play tennis, table tennis and darts. This was the West Riding of Yorkshire in the 1960s. In her early teens, Mum was encouraged to help with the teaching of the little ones at the church and from that experience she realised she loved being around young children. Consequently she never wanted to be anything other than a teacher. After doing A-levels she went to teacher training college at Thornbridge Hall, at Ashford-in-the-Water near Bakewell in Derbyshire. One of her dormitory friends, Dilys, was engaged to Steve, a friend of Dad's. At that time Dad was doing a degree in Economics and Business at Sheffield University, and to make up a foursome he went on a blind date with Mum to the local pub in Great Longstone, near to the college.

Mum asked Dilys, who had already met Dad through Steve, what her blind date was like. She said, 'He's got beautiful eyes, but he's not tall enough for you.' Mum is 5 foot 11 and that made her taller than Dad, something that didn't bother her as much as Dilys thought it would. 'I do remember thinking he was a lovely person,' Mum says, 'and when, a week after our first meeting, he rang up and asked me to go out, I wasn't going to refuse. And Dilys was right about his eyes.' They had their first date in Monsal Dale, a small village not far from Thornbridge Hall, and went for a walk by the river Wye. Steve and Dilys didn't survive but they helped make a match that did.

Mum and Dad continued seeing each other through their college days, which Dad claims as the reason his degree wasn't as good as it should have been. Mum tells stories about those early days, how Thornbridge was an all-girls college and quite strict. There were curfews and mad dashes to get back before doors were locked at 10.30 in the week. One midweek evening, Dad took Mum to watch his team Liverpool play Derby County at the old Baseball Ground and, of course, traffic was terrible after the game and it was well past curfew when they got back to Thornbridge. Making the best of a difficult situation, Dad eased Mum through the window of a friend's room on the other side of the building to the warden, but when she had tip-toed to the safety of her bedroom, the warden was there to meet her!

After graduating, Dad worked as a general management trainee near Mansfield and Mum taught at Rawmarsh Monkwood Infant School in Yorkshire. They saved their money and eighteen months later, they married. Dad's first job was with Rank Hovis McDougall in their bakeries division. Their first home was in Wigan; after that Wakefield, where I was conceived, and then Northwich where I was born. Dad worked in personnel and training, stayed with the bakery for eight years and then moved to a wine merchants called Ashe & Nephew, which was eventually taken over by Whitbread and became Thresher. After working in three of the Whitbread divisions he became human resources director of Whitbread Beer Company. They sold that business to one of the biggest breweries, Interbrew, and he became human resources director for Interbrew UK. He took early retirement in June 2003. Mum went with the flow of Dad's career, finding a teaching post in whatever area his job took him. Eventually in Bedfordshire her career had the chance to progress; she became a deputy head, then headteacher of rural Eileen Wade Lower School at Upper Dean in north Bedfordshire. She too took early retirement at the same time as Dad and they are now making the most of it and living life to the full.

Our first home was 10 Larch Tree Close in Barnton, near Northwich, and even though we spent just seven years there, I have vivid memories. We lived at the end of the Close and did all of our playing there. I had no intention of being my brother's keeper but if Martin left the Close, it was up to me to tell Mum immediately. There were big windows at the front of the house that went all the way to the ground and, according to Mum, I was 'the eyes and ears of the Close'. 'Nothing gets past you,' she would say. Vera Metcalfe, a lovely lady who lived at the other end of the Close, was similarly watchful and ours had to be the safest little cul-de-sac in Cheshire. Years and years later I had a very nice letter from Vera – I think it was after the world marathon record in London – and it was good to hear from a person who went all the way back to my childhood in Barnton.

I went to Little Leigh Primary in the next village. It was a small country school that had two pet sheep, Esther and Ruth. We would comb the sheep and then spin the yarn and make things out of wool. Mum had been taught in a similarly small country school which was also environmentally aware, and she wanted her children to go to a school that had a similar emphasis. Mum would drive us to school and Martin and I would fight about where we sat because the floor of Mum's old Morris 1300 had rusted, allowing water to spray upwards and create a very wet patch on the back seat.

We moved to Kingsley when I was 6. Kingsley was another Cheshire village, about 10 miles away, but the house was bigger and that was the reason for the move. The sadness of leaving the Close was lessened by still being near enough to Barnton for trips back and forth to see friends. At Kingsley, we lived in Beech View Drive and were allowed to ride our bikes to school. Mum rode with us until we were big enough to be allowed to ride on our own. Kingsley had its advantages. We had a bigger garden and soon after we arrived, Dad built us a climbing frame. The estate itself was full of families with young children and we soon had lots of new friends. We were the kind of family that got into things. Mum joined the local drama group, Martin and I saw a leaflet advertising the judo club in the next village, Frodsham, and we persuaded Mum to let us join. At the weekends, we would often do things with our grandparents.

Even though running would soon become an important part of my life and was destined to become my career, my parents encouraged us to do everything and to see what we did in perspective. Running was just one more hobby, another activity to be enjoyed. From Mum's point of view, our music lessons were just as important and each week my brother and I went to Mary Kearns and later John Bromley for piano lessons. Mary later went on to become a nun – she had to have been saintly to persevere with me as a pupil.

Whereas Martin wasn't bad, I was tone deaf. Mum would walk with Martin and me to our lesson and on the way back she would stop at the newsagents to pay her weekly newspaper bill. At the shop Mum would buy us a treat. It was a reward for our commitment to the piano. I always chose a bar of Orkney fudge that could be broken into eight pieces. Then each day, after my 30 minutes' piano practice, I would allow myself one square of fudge. It was a way of motivating myself to do the practice: 'When it's over, you'll have some fudge.' On Sundays, after the last piano practice for that week, I allowed myself two squares. Martin's treat never survived the journey home.

Music was such a struggle for me. I got to Grade 4 and remember once doing the exam with a sprained wrist, as if my lack of talent wasn't enough of a handicap. One hundred was the pass mark and over the four exams I got 107, 100, 108 and 100. After moving from Cheshire to Bedford, the piano was abandoned in favour of the flute, and I got to Grade 3 in that. It wasn't that I hated music, but my lack of talent frustrated me. Eventually Mum realised it just wasn't there. What I knew was that it was much easier to put on your running shoes and go training. That was something I was a lot better at and, anyway, it was far more enjoyable.

Dad had been into running and cycling in his youth, and was quite good. But he eventually gave it up. At university he smoked and continued to until he got married. For a short time he became a really heavy smoker, getting up to fifty a day. He gave up before I was born, vowing he would never smoke again. Without cigarettes, he put on a lot of weight, and that encouraged him to go back running. For as long as I can remember, he has been a runner. His weekend morning runs in Delamere Forest were sacrosanct, and it also became an important outing for Martin and me.

There are two stories told by my parents that make people laugh, but one of them conveys more than a grain of truth. It concerns Dad's marathon-running days. From running to get some exercise and lose weight, he started running half-marathons and finally progressed to the full marathon. He was not that competitive about his running, just another person who loved going for a run. Of the three marathons he ran, the first was his quickest, as he managed to finish in a fraction under 3 hours 50 minutes. Times and finishing positions may not have mattered to him but they did to me, even though I was little more than a toddler. At one of the drinks stations on the marathon route, Mum, Martin, our grandparents and I waited to hand Dad his Mars bar and drink. With all of us there, he stopped to talk for a few seconds and other runners were naturally overtaking him. I was outraged. 'Dad, what are you doing stopping? There are people passing you! Get going, get going. Now! Now!' To me, at the age of five or six, it was unfathomable that he would just stand there and let people pass him by.

The other story, I suppose, shows a softer side. My parents say I was two at the time; my memory is that I was three or four. It was when Dad worked for Ashe & Nephew in Liverpool. One Saturday morning he took Mum, Martin and me into his office which was in an old Victorian warehouse in Stone Street. After we got there, he and Mum were inside the office leaving me playing in the outer office where the secretary had her desk. They thought it would be fun to ring the secretary's phone and see if I would pick it up. I did.

Dad: 'Hello, who is that?'

Me: 'I'm my Daddy's little girl, my daddy isn't here right now but I can take a message.'

The only time he ever got cross with me over running was the first time I qualified to represent the South of England in an inter-region competition involving the South, the North, the Midlands, Scotland

and Wales. It was in Mansfield and I got so nervous before the race that it made me physically sick, which is not the ideal pre-race preparation. My performance suffered as a result and Dad, who knew what had gone wrong, was not impressed.

'Right,' he said, 'if you're going to be that nervous, then it's not fun and you can't do it any more.' Dad didn't often react instinctively and he rarely got angry with me. That day he did. In his youth, he used to get nervous before competing and it hurt his performance. No one told him there were ways of dealing with pre-race nerves and he continued to be badly affected by them. He was determined his old problem would not become mine, and he was adamant I should never lose sight of the fact that it was my hobby, something I voluntarily chose to do. Along with the downhill running and never looking behind in a race, it was another important lesson he taught me.

Most of the rules in our house were devised and implemented by Mum. We couldn't go out to play until our homework was done. A certain time was allotted for our reading and it had to be done, something that was easy for me because I loved books. We were not allowed to have a digital watch until we first learned to tell the time the old-fashioned way. Sensible rules but, of course, we disagreed over the television. *Grange Hill* was a popular series about a secondary school when we were young but Mum's view was that we should not watch until we were old enough to understand it. 'It is fiction and it does reflect real life, but until you are mature enough to see it for what it is, you can't watch it,' she would say. Martin and I would turn down the sound as the opening credits came on and turn it back up when the programme actually began. Mum now says she used the same ploy to watch *Coronation Street* when she was growing up.

A girl that Mum taught once said to me, 'Thank God she's your mum and not mine.' That puzzled me because ours wasn't an overly strict house, and with Mum you could talk about anything. I've always been really close to her, I love her to bits, but along the way, I did learn she was not a woman you wanted to get on the wrong side of. I would never cross her, Martin would never cross her. Some of my friends would answer back to their parents and the thought would always run through my mind, 'Wouldn't have got away with that in our house.' Yet my recollections of growing up are of how much fun and happiness there was and still is in our family.

As for Mum being a woman you didn't want to cross, I learned that at a very young age. It was my last year at Little Leigh Primary School and there was a test at school I didn't want to do.

'Not feeling very well this morning,' I said to Mum, 'I've got a sore throat and feel terrible.'

Mum was sympathetic and agreed there was no way I should go to school feeling like that. Great. But it was a long boring morning and by lunchtime, I was telling Mum I felt okay to go to school in the afternoon. She immediately guessed something was up, told me to get ready and frog-marched me into school. Speaking with the teacher, she asked if there had been anything on that morning. 'Oh, they had a test, that's all.' 'That's okay,' said Mum, 'Paula's feeling much better now and she'll do hers in the afternoon.'

I never tried anything like that again.

3

There are two sides to my personality. One is stubborn and intensely competitive. The other is sensitive, self-conscious; a little vulnerable. Part of that is a yearning to be liked and accepted, which has always been there. The emotional woman is as much a part of me as the determined athlete. You have to be emotional about things, things have to matter to you, otherwise why would you invest so much of yourself in something? With no guarantees about the outcome, this is especially true of elite sport. Yet it is my sport that has given me the self-confidence to handle these insecurities and the emotional vulnerability. The love and support of family and friends, and especially Gary, has also played a part in that.

It wasn't so straightforward in my teens – but then at that age, it never is. I lacked a lot of the self-confidence that would come as I grew up and with my success in running. There was also a time, in my mid-teens, when I felt very insecure and had more than the usual amount of heartache. My best friend Liz Yelling, or Lizzie Talbot as I knew her then, and I have been closer than sisters since I was twelve. We would spend all our free time hanging out together and were always at either her house or mine. Mostly we just did teenage things, but there were also more serious discussions. What's wrong with me? I remember asking her. Why didn't I have a boyfriend? Liz said I intimidated them. 'No,' I said, 'it's because I'm not pretty.' I had a brace on my teeth at the time and a low opinion of how I looked.

At one stage I also had a few problems with some of the other girls at Bedford & County Athletic Club. Though it all seems minor when viewed in hindsight, it was a big thing to me at the time. We had always been a close group and got on really well. Then I started to improve in my running, and one day I beat one of the other girls who had always been the best. She didn't take it well and it changed my whole relationship with the rest of the group. Liz was also ostracised simply because she stood by me. It went on for about a year, a period when the atmosphere in our age group was terrible. It was teenage bitchiness rather than bullying, but was particularly aimed at me, and it upset me a lot.

I don't want to exaggerate this unhappy episode in my life – I recall it only because it reminds me of the kind of person I was then and still am to a great extent: vulnerable, but obstinate. I would ask Mum and my coach Alex Stanton why the girls were nasty to me, and they would say it wasn't my fault and not to let it upset me. Mum said it was better to turn the other cheek. This was more or less what I did, but no matter what happened or how upsetting things got for me, the other girls were not going to stop me from being as good a runner as I could be. So I would put even more effort into my training, and if by doing that I beat them in races, so much the better. No one was going to make me try less hard.

As I mentioned, it was my friend Germaine Hilditch who first got me into an athletics club. We were at Kingsley primary school in Cheshire and we used to run a bit together, the kind of running around one does at school, playful rather than competitive. Germaine and her older sister Julia were members of Frodsham Harriers, a club in the neighbouring village of Frodsham. 'You should come along,' she said. It didn't take much persuading to get me and later my brother Martin to join up. We were that kind of family. As a teacher, Mum knew schools weren't in a position to provide as much sport as kids need and we were encouraged to get involved in clubs outside school. So if there was a notice looking for people to do judo or badminton or whatever, we were the first to sign up. Mum herself was involved in the amateur drama club, Dad ran almost every day and Martin and I were game to try any sport. Though they wanted us to get involved in sport, Mum and Dad always let Martin and I decide for ourselves. They would drive us there but we chose where we wanted to go.

Martin and I had a typical brother/sister relationship. Because there were just two of us, we were very close, and when push came to shove, we stuck up for each other. When we changed schools or moved from our first home in Barnton to Kingsley, I would make sure Martin settled in with his new classmates. He would look out for me in different ways. One memory stands out. We were holidaying in Austria and even though it was August, it was wet. The river alongside our campsite was almost breaking its banks, something that didn't stop Martin and I from messing around and fishing for frogs. I was leaning out from the bank, holding on to a branch of a tree when it snapped and I fell fully clothed into the river. As we were ready to leave and everything was packed away, there was going to be real trouble. Before I did anything, Martin went running off to Mum and Dad. 'It wasn't her fault. Honestly, it wasn't her fault. Don't be angry with her. It was an accident, it wasn't her fault.' You remember moments like that.

There were other sides – maybe I should say friendly edges – to our relationship. We were always very competitive. From the day Martin went past Dad and I without us noticing him and then finished in front of us at a charity race in Delamere Forest, I never wanted to be beaten by him. In my mind, it didn't matter that he was a boy and I was a girl, my two-year age advantage offset that. We used to go to races together; ordinary league races or Sunday league races on the track, and his race would often follow mine. Even though I was trying to beat my PB (personal best) for a particular distance, I was also conscious of Martin's PB for that distance and wanted to beat his as well. One time I ran a race and beat his PB and then, 15 minutes later, he went out and set a faster time which pleased him no end because he had put me in my place. Martin was conscious of staying ahead of me and was a talented athlete. He trained with Alex Stanton in Bedford for about two years and that meant we trained together quite a bit.

That competitive edge was always there. Martin was quick, but endurance was my strength and when we did interval training, I would try to lessen the recovery time after each individual repetition. 'Come on,' I'd say and then jog back to the start and make sure he had less time to recover. He would walk. 'Come on, a bit quicker,' I'd say. Anything that could be done to make it harder for him and reduce the impact of his greater speed in our 200- or 400-metre reps, I would do. That's the way I am. When Gary and I first trained together, one of us would be half a stride ahead of the other.

'Why are you pushing it?'

'I'm not.'

'Yes you are. Look, you're just ahead of me.'

As both of us are stubborn, no one would give an inch and the pace would just get faster and faster. I would like to say we have both matured and are far more sensible now, but that wouldn't be entirely true.

When Martin and I played tennis, a game we would play around the time of Wimbledon or on holiday, it was never just for the fun of it. We both had to win. Usually it meant my working on his temper; if teased in the right way, he would lose his cool, hit the ball too hard and it would fly out of court. You couldn't say it was a very nice way to win, but when you had your competitive little brother on the other side of the net, niceness didn't come into it.

Dad always admired Martin for the way he coped with having a smart-arse big sister. Though I never saw it like this, Martin could easily have been intimidated by me, but he never was. He just got on with doing his own thing and he still does. There were times in our youth when it wasn't easy for him; days when my very single-minded approach to things would just mortify him. For example, we might be staying in some nice campsite in France and I would have training to do; some drills or some bounds. He would say, 'Do you have to do that here? Everyone's looking at you.' He was sensitive to what people thought, whereas it was more important to me to get the training done.

Frodsham Harriers was run by George Bunner, and for a small, rural athletics club, it was light years ahead of its time. In summer we raced and trained at Frodsham Park, where the lines were painted on the grass. We thought of it as our track. When the days shortened and the evenings got dark, we moved indoors to the local hall where we used turnaround boards in order to continue our training. This was a big wooden board placed against the end of the hall; we would run up it, put a foot on it, turn around and run back. It allowed us to do proper training indoors. George was the pioneer of sports hall athletics.

My memory is of the fun we used to have. At the end of each training session we would do a 'paarlauf', or 'pair run', where the entire group was divided into relay teams. There might be three or four teams, little kids paired with much bigger teenagers, maybe eight or ten people in each team, and we would run and run, cheering each other on, shouting, cajoling, desperately wanting your team to win.

Whether we trained indoors or outdoors, George never needed a bull-horn or any kind of amplification to make himself heard. From the other end of the hall or even the far side of the grass track we used in summer, he never failed to be understood. He dealt mostly with the older kids – I was one of the youngest and he wouldn't remember me. Mrs Briggs was the lady in charge of my group. She would say, 'Right, you're going up to the Pike today,' or 'Today, we're doing 200-metre reps.' If we went to a cross-country race, she would get our numbers, organise us, tell us where we needed to be. Frodsham was an athletics club in the fullest sense, as we tried all sorts of different disciplines. I did the high jump and quite enjoyed it. But, and this is a big 'but', it was clear I wouldn't be any good at it and I didn't get the same buzz I got from running. The long run to Overton Pike, a huge sandstone ridge above the floodplain of the river Mersey, was my favourite. It's got tracks and paths and is very steep. We would leave from Frodsham Park and maybe it wasn't quite as far as I remember it, but when you're 10 or 11, a little seems a lot. It was a tough climb up to the Pike, on some parts you had to use steps, but it was the severity of the climb that attracted me. When you run, the pain can be your friend or your enemy. It was always my friend.

It was at Frodsham Harriers that the running bug bit me, and though I would spend just two years with the club before moving with my family to Bedford, the connection with the people and the area has remained. This year George Bunner asked my grandmother, Olive Radcliffe, to start one of the races at Kingsley Carnival. My grandma is 86 years of age but she is well and has always had a wonderful zest for life. At first she said yes but then thought about it and told George she would rather not. We were all a little surprised because it wasn't like her to say no. She later confided that she thought she was a little too old to run in a race at Kingsley Carnival. When George had asked her 'to start' a race at Kingsley, she took him to literally mean she had to run. When it was explained she would just be the race's official starter, she immediately agreed. What I love about Grandma is that when she believed she had to run, she thought about it for a few days before feeling she had to say no. At 86, that's not bad.

*

Days you remember: the move to our new home in Oakley, just outside Bedford. There was sadness at leaving Cheshire because it was home and it had so many happy memories. But change is also exciting and we were looking forward to it, and the new experiences it would bring – in fact it was while house-hunting that my brother and I stayed in a hotel for the first time. Martin and I thought it hilarious that our rabbits had to spend the night in the bath.

They survived it. The next day we arrived in Oakley, though we didn't make the best of starts. We had barely opened the door of our new home when a swarm of flying ants descended on our kitchen. They were everywhere, and though no one said anything, we were thinking, 'Oh, this is a horrible place, this isn't going to work out.' We had never seen anything like it and no one knew what to do. Mum sat on a step and cried. 'Mum,' I said, 'it won't be that bad, we'll get rid of them.'

I hated to see her unhappy and always wanted to make things better. I've always been the peacemaker in the family – Dad says I am a bridge-builder, a reputation that probably comes from long-ago days on holiday in France or Spain when he and Mum would have a row over a missed exit off a motorway or a wrong choice at a big roundabout. Mum would be in the front passenger seat trying to read the map while we were getting lost. 'You're holding the map the wrong way,' Dad would say. 'Well, you do it yourself then,' she would say, throwing it at him, and the arguing would begin. They would shout at each other and I would be sitting in the back, doing my best to calm them down. 'Please don't fight. Don't shout. It's all right.' I hated it when Mum and Dad argued, especially over such a stupid thing.

After winning our battle with the flying ants, we realised Oakley was a nice village. It's got one little shop, a post office, two churches and the Great Ouse river is nearby. To help us settle in, Dad built a big run in the back garden for our rabbits, Cotton Tail and Flopsy. With a bigger garden, I was allowed to keep some guinea pigs. Dad also made us another tree house. We had enough grass in the back garden to have a sort of tennis court, and we had a nice orchard at one end. During the summer holidays Martin and I would have fun climbing the trees, collecting fruit to put into bags and sell at the end of our drive. Cooking apples, plums, classic English produce. It was our pocket money and one summer we made quite a lot. So we settled pretty quickly into our new home.

Dad wasted little time in checking out the athletics clubs in Bedford. There were two clubs in the town, Bedford & County and Bedford Harriers, but the choice was really no choice at all. Bedford Harriers was more of an adult road-running club, while Bedford & County catered more for children. On the first night Dad took us down to the Bedford & County club and I was put straight into the group looked after by Alex and Rosemary Stanton. My first impressions were that Alex was a really nice man but that Rosemary was stricter. With Alex you could get away with things, but you would be on your best behaviour around Rosemary. However, Alex can be tough when he needs to be. They were a very good team. Alex took responsibility for the coaching while Rosemary maintained discipline and supported Alex. Parents helped out too, and when we went on our longer runs or ran by the river, adults would be stationed at 150-metre intervals or follow in cars to ensure we were always safe. Once when we were on a run I was out on my own and a car kept tooting its horn at me. After a couple of hoots I got fed up, thinking it was a carload of lads, and I turned round and stuck my finger up at it. The car pulled alongside, Rosemary leaned out and said, 'Don't ever do that to me again, young lady, and ease off a bit!'

Alex and Rosemary had a really good group of girls. There was great camaraderie among us and, as I've said, we were a really tight group to begin with. My best friends were at the club rather than school. I trained once a week in that first year, and raced at weekends, but the club quickly began to play a much bigger part in my life. In that first year we had a good strong team: Kate Foster, Clare Wilson, Emily Williams, Elinor Caborn, Lisa Richardson, Rosie Mallarkey and Claire Peet. Kate, Clare, Emily, Eli and I were the same year, Lisa and Rosie were a year younger. Claire Peet was a year older. After training, we would hang around at the club, talking and having fun because it was as much a social club as a sports club for us.

I went to my first National Cross-Country Championships as an innocent 11-year-old without any expectations. We had been in Bedford for about five months and my training had been relatively light. It was just a thrill to be there. They were held in Leicester, not a million miles from where we lived, but we still got there late. Mum and Dad had no idea what happened when you arrived at a big race and thought if they got there half an hour before the start that would give us plenty of time. From that day onwards I would tell Mum and Dad my race began half an hour before it actually did because they were always late. For those first Nationals at Leicester I spent 20 minutes queuing for the loo and had just enough time to get my number, put on my spikes and run the race. Apart from the fact that it snowed and my finishing place was 299th, I remember little else from what was then the biggest race of my life. Dad, I remember, was well pleased with my performance. 'Two hundred and ninety-ninth out of six hundred and six, you got in the first half,' he said. Even though I wouldn't let on, I was quite pleased too, because it was all such a new experience for me and even then I realised that with proper preparation, I could do much better.

It was typical of Alex that he watched us perform that day and came away with the belief that the team title was winnable the following year. It meant a very significant improvement but he believed we could do it and inspired faith in us. He could see that Kate, Clare and Emily were strong, and that with more training, I could develop into his 4th scorer. To get me up to speed, he asked Mum if it would be okay for me to train twice a week. As was the custom in our house, the decision was left up to me – and so it was training twice a week. For me it was a big honour to be asked to join the top girls' group, and judo was immediately dropped to leave more time for athletics. For Mum it was a bit of a nightmare as Martin's judo and my training were on at the same time but at very different locations in Bedford.

During my second year it was obvious we were improving and growing as a team. We would all travel on the team coach to races and that journey became part of our build-up. We were team-mates but we were also friends. After races we might have a sleepover in one house where we would talk about races and other things into the early hours. Everything that year was geared towards the National Cross-Country Championships, and the belief that we could win the team title grew over time. When the big day came, we were all excited and nervous. Going on the bus to the race, Alex had a pen and notebook and was estimating where he thought everyone would finish. I was intrigued to know where he thought I would place and whether he believed we would get enough points to win. He had me down as the team's 3rd or 4th place scorer, maybe getting into the top 15. After 299th the previous year, that would represent a huge improvement, but I was now a different athlete from the complete novice who had done well to break into the top 300.

As things turned out, I did better than Alex anticipated. Kate Foster finished 2nd in the race and was our leading scorer. I was 4th and our 2nd best scorer. We actually had six athletes in before any other team had four and the team title was ours. That night we all went back to one of the girls' houses and had a big party. There was a local cross-country race the next day and after being up for most of the night, we weren't at our sharpest the following morning. There was still so much to talk about and as we basked in the glory of our victory the previous day, the whistle went to start the race. Maybe we expected a gun-start, maybe we just weren't paying attention but as all the other girls set off, we were standing there looking at each other. 'We're national champions, they'll stop it and start again.' Except they didn't come back and we had to chase off after them.

We did that and still ended with the first four across the finish line. As we neared the end, Kate and I were clear. She had finished two places in front of me in the Nationals and though I wanted to beat her if I could, she was a stronger runner. With about 150 metres to go, she took a wrong turn and that left me alone at the front. It wasn't the way I wanted to win and rather than kick on, I waited for her, and she ended up beating me in the sprint. There were no regrets because, for me, to win in that way would have been worse than finishing second. To me it wasn't fair to take advantage of someone's misfortune. If I was ever going to beat Kate it had to be fair and square. I still think that would hold today, although it's unlikely someone could go the wrong way in a major championship. Certainly the ethic of winning fairly is still uppermost for me. Victory has to count where it means the most, in my heart, and for me to believe in myself and my achievements those victories must be won fairly.

A year or so after our move to Bedford I became good friends with Liz Yelling. She had lived in Bedford but when her parents separated, Liz went with her mum to Cornwall. Then one evening at the club, the girls were all talking about her. 'Oh, Lizzie's come back, yeah she's back, she's going to be back on the team.' Soon I saw her at the club and we got to know each other. Good friends from the beginning, best friends in no time at all; we have stayed best friends ever since. I would sleep over at her house, she practically lived at our house, and Mum used to say Lizzie was 'like an adopted daughter'. She's still someone I can always turn to. No matter what, she is there for me and I am there for her.

It wasn't just Liz and me; all the girls on the team were good friends. We were a successful team and even though we wanted to win, the atmosphere nurtured by Alex and Rosemary made it easy for us to enjoy the experience. We hung around together after training, gossiping and talking about boys, and if it was someone's birthday, she got thrown into the big bath.

The atmosphere changed a little, though, when I began competing at Under-15 level.

How can I tell this without presenting a one-sided story? With more training came increased strength and endurance. I could run harder and further. The advantage that others had over me became less and then, when we were on the Under-15 team, the balance shifted. I started to improve. That changed the chemistry of our relationship. Before that Kate had been the best runner in our group and was totally accepted as that. I might have imagined beating her one day, but through my first two or three years, she always beat me, and even though she might get beaten by someone at the Nationals or the English Schools competition, she was still our leading scorer.

We were also good friends for much of that time – our birthdays were within a few days of each other in December, her mum and my mum were joint team managers at the club and I spent a lot of time at her house. Partly because she went to private school, she got more homework than we did – she would sometimes have to do it at races and I would help her. In fact we would all help so she could get it done and out of the way.

I had upset what had been the accepted order and that led to resentment. With hindsight it is easy to dismiss the division that followed as an example of the trials and tribulations common among teenage girls. At the time it was an enormous issue in our lives and caused a lot of stress and upset. Liz was on my side and because she supported me, she too was picked on. We would be excluded from the other girls' conversations, we would be made fun of and generally it became obvious that we were no longer considered part of the inner circle. The girls who had been at the club longer were the natural leaders of the group. Many of the other girls followed. I was quieter, maybe timid by comparison, but would never blindly follow someone else. I liked to do my own thing, and would do it stubbornly, but without ever wanting to stand out from the crowd.

Of course Liz and I would moan about them when we were together. There was a stage where another girl, if they got beaten by someone else on the team, had something bought for her so that she wouldn't act up. We thought it was unfair that she should receive a present to improve her mood after a disappointing result. The undercurrent of animosity led to tough times. There was the day Liz and I had to hide under our coats at the back of the bus because they were pelting peanuts at us. Seen from the outside, it was nothing, a bit of fun. Alex would have looked down from the front of the bus and thought, 'Kids, they're only kids.' That's how it would have seemed. Another time we were on a training run and Liz got pushed into a rose bush. The other girls said it was an accident but we knew it wasn't. We're now good friends with the girl who did that and now that the scars have healed we can all laugh about it.

Without trying to upset the other girls or even doing anything wrong, I brought some of it on myself. One little incident has stayed in my mind. One New Year's Eve we all had a sleepover at one girl's house and because there was a Southern Inter-Counties Cross-Country race two days later, I didn't want to stay up very late. Sometime after midnight I tried to get to sleep but as the other girls were still talking and having fun, they were annoyed with me. They went on about how boring I was and generally tried to make me feel guilty for not wanting to stay up with them. When I won the race two days later, that didn't go down too well, but it proved to me that the effort to get some sleep on New Year's Eve had been right. It was little things like this that contributed to the division.

They were never going to change me and, in hindsight, the angst it caused was an important test of my attitude. If there were weaknesses, they would have come to the surface during this time and encouraged me to compromise. The opposite was the case. Training harder and being even more competitive was my way of getting back at the other girls, but most of all, it was what I wanted to do. Though that might have made things worse, it didn't matter to me because what was important was giving myself every chance to do as well as I could.

There is no way in sport of concealing your competitive instinct or disguising your ambition: your performance reveals your attitude as much as your talent. It is different in the classroom because there it was possible to sit back and let others take centre stage. When the teacher asks a question, you might know the answer but you don't have to be the one with your hand in the air going, 'Please Miss, please Miss!' Not being the one to give the answer doesn't hurt you in the exams at the end of the year and, with the exception of language classes, I stayed pretty quiet in the classroom.

I wanted to be as good as I could be, but without standing out or drawing attention to myself. Sport is different; to be the best you have to accept that you might stand out. You do the best you can do in every race. The competitive instinct means giving your best effort every time. For some people the fame and the attention is a motivation in itself. For me this isn't important. I want to be the best that I can, to get the most that I can from my talent and hard work. I love the buzz of running fast and winning. However, I have had to learn how to accept and deal with the attention that comes with it.

As a family we discussed most things. I would come home after training and over the evening meal Mum would ask how things were and soon the tears would start to flow. I would explain how the girls were being horrible, maybe I had got the silent treatment or had been belittled in some other way. I just wanted to be liked by the other girls. It was an impossible situation for Mum. As joint team manager she couldn't interfere. We were also a hugely successful team and no one wanted to jeopardise that. Mum had to be totally impartial.

Once she did speak to Alex Stanton but that put him in a no-win situation because he, too, could not come down on one side over another. As a teacher, Mum has always felt it is better to let young people sort out their own differences. She gave me lots of advice, told me to stick to my guns and be true to myself. 'Paula,' she would say, 'if this is how they behave, are they really your friends? What you mustn't do is behave in the same way; don't give like for like. Neither should you let them put you down or stop you doing what you want to do.' Martin would see me crying at the table and say, 'Is there anything I can do?' There was nothing any of us could do. We just had to wait for time to pass so we could move on to the next phase of our lives.

There was only one occasion when Mum got involved and part of the reason for that was because the problem did not involve me. It was a local cross-country race. I had twisted my ankle, so was on crutches and just watching the action. Liz and another girl were ahead and had the race between them when, close to the finish, the girl's mum sent Liz the wrong way. I was really infuriated and screamed at Liz to make sure she quickly got back on the right course. She did get back and she won the race.

This couldn't be allowed to pass and so Mum spoke to the lady, saying the differences between the girls should be left to the girls to sort out and that adults should not get involved. Because it was for Liz and not her own daughter, Mum felt comfortable making the case. I admired her refusal to get involved on my behalf. 'Adults,' she would say, 'only make things worse.' On the other hand, when I was feeling down and in need of a cuddle, she was always there.

Teenage girls eventually grow up and now, fifteen years later, those wounds have long healed and the scars are no longer visible. Liz and I are still best friends and we're again good friends with all our old team-mates. We shared an important time in our lives and had a lot of fun together. There were ups and downs along the way, but we were still the best team in the country.

4

From the moment running became a serious part of my life, Alex
Stanton has been by my side. People say to me now, 'Oh yeah, he was
your coach at Bedford & County Athletic Club, are you still with
him?' They imagine I must have moved on since then, found someone
else. This will never be the case as long as he still wants to help me.
Some things have changed, we've all got a lot older and there is now
a small group of people that I rely on, but Alex remains a very
important part of the team. He is my first coach and my only coach.
We speak on the telephone most days; we talk about how training is
going and discuss my schedule for the following days. He listens,
offers his take on things and, invariably, he makes sense. His
calmness, his encouragement, his modesty, his willingness to learn
new things and – maybe most of all – his friendship have contributed
more to my career than any words here can properly explain. All of
these things make him a great coach. He understands me as an athlete
but also as a person. From the day that a skinny 11-year-old finished
299th in her first National Cross-Country Championships, Alex and
his wife Rosemary have been there for me.

It is funny now to think back to those first championships. There was snow in the air and it was bitterly cold. When we got stripped off, Mum thought it was lunacy but then when I came in 299th, we were all so pleased. From my point of view, there were 607 runners in the race and that meant that over 300 girls had finished behind me. Mum and Dad saw it the same way and we were all in great spirits afterwards. Alex was also pleased because all he ever expects is that we do our best, and if we do, that is what matters to him. But in his quiet and unassuming way, Alex can be a determined tower of strength. A number of the other girls had run well and after the race, he said we would come back the following year and win the national team title. That was beyond what we thought possible but Alex was right: we were capable of rising to that challenge and a year later we did become national champions.

That first year at Bedford, Alex didn't always remember my name and used to call me 'Poppet' or something that sounded like that. There were lots of girls in the group but he was the kind of man who made time for each one, regardless of what standard they were. He would get as much satisfaction from some girl running a personal best in a lowly race as he would from another girl in his group winning a national title. What he never does is make judgements about anyone; instead he just tries to help us get the best out of ourselves, but without pushing too hard or demanding too much. There is so much that I like about his approach. When it came to a choice between homework and athletics, he would say homework had to come first. If someone missed training because of homework, that was fine. He and Rosemary took the time to be interested in us as human beings. If I did well in my exams, he would be as pleased or more pleased for me than if I had run well in a race.

I guess they became like second parents to me. During my first year at university in Loughborough, I would return home at the weekends to train with Alex, and he would come up to watch my training on Wednesday afternoons. I developed a good system: I would leave my washing with Mum at the weekend and Alex would bring it back clean on a Wednesday! This saved me a huge amount of time and hassle queuing for the only two washing machines in the university residence halls where I stayed for the first two terms.

Alex has always been there for me in ways that transcend my running. He wanted to know how my studies were going, whether or not I was settling in at Loughborough. Whenever I had any sort of problem or something that was bothering me, I was always comfortable speaking to Alex about it. It's the way he listens without judging that I find so reassuring.

'Don't worry,' Alex would say, 'everything will sort itself out in its own time.' And, of course, he was usually right.

In 1994 I got a serious stress fracture injury that went undiagnosed for a long time, and which meant a long period on the sidelines. Well, not exactly the sidelines, because it was still possible to do cross-training sessions in the swimming pool. Sessions in the pool are boring and even though he couldn't really do anything while he was there, Alex would come along to encourage me. Although he ended up giving me a lot of his time, he continued to work with the other girls at the club, and that has never changed. Look at how much of his and Rosemary's lives have been devoted to the club in Bedford, the travelling he has done on behalf of so many young athletes, the financial cost of getting to faraway places and all the sacrifices he has made for the benefit of others. He does all this for the love of it, and says he gets his reward when any of us girls runs well. However, it was important to me that I made sure that he and Rosemary were properly recompensed for all of their hard work and support. As soon as I was able to I made sure that this happened, as I felt that they were and still are such an important part of whatever I achieve. As Alex says, we're in this together. I also feel that it is an important issue. In order to have successful professional athletes we need the support of skilled coaches. We cannot expect them to be committed to doing this job properly and give up their own time voluntarily. Their hard work should be recognised as the full-time job it is. By properly supporting our coaches we are more likely to have a support structure there to bring through sporting champions for the future.

There are so many memories of Alex's selfless commitment.

How many times did Mum drive me to the park in Bedford to find Alex waiting, his bicycle packed into the boot of his car? He took the bike so he could follow me on my training runs. Once he came to our house in Oakley because that day's run was from the village into Bedford, around Bedford for a bit and then back to the house. It was a really windy day – I remember the elements were so severe I had to run with my head down to keep going. We were on this long road in Bedford, into the teeth of the wind, and Alex couldn't keep up on his bike. Left a little behind, he took a short cut to get back up to me. This happened while my head was down and I was battling into the wind. Glancing behind eventually, I realised Alex wasn't there. 'What's happened?' I thought and instinctively doubled back in search of him.

Surely he hadn't had an accident? He was nowhere to be seen. I retraced my route for another bit but still no sign of him. By now I had come to the conclusion that there had been an accident and panic overtook me. Running to the school in Bedford where Mum taught, I told her how Alex had gone missing. 'We've got to find him in case he's had an accident.' Mum and I got into her car and drove over our running route, looking for signs of an accident. There was nothing. Frustrated, we just drove back home and there he was waiting for us.

'Where have you been?' I asked.

'Where have you been?'

'Out looking for you.'

What has helped to keep us close is that Alex still treats me exactly the same as any of the other girls that he coaches, and I would never want it any other way. To him and Rosemary, as with all my family and friends, I am always just Paula, and with them I always know that I am accepted and loved no matter what happens in the world of professional athletics. I can always turn to any of them for a true, honest perspective on things. He is there for me now as much as he's ever been and he understands that with greater experience and understanding of my own physiology, I can now take more responsibility for my training and general preparation. So we now discuss the training a lot more, although as the coach he has the final say. Sometimes we don't agree, usually because I might want to do a bit more, and we will talk it out for a while. Sometimes he says I can wrap him around my finger but in truth I always respect his opinion and instincts. One thing has always been true: I never go out and do anything behind his back — either I persuade him first or it doesn't happen. Alex also knows how central Gary's role has become — now things are often a three-way discussion, and Alex will get feedback from Gary on how I look in training as he is with me all the time. He also understands the importance of my physiotherapist, Gerard Hartmann, in keeping my body healthy, and gets on well with him. In the early days, we worked one-on-one most of the time, but now we are a team and everyone plays an important part. The thing about Alex is that in his mind, it is not about him, it is about all of us working together.

After the crushing disappointment of finishing 4th in the 10,000 metres at the Sydney Olympics in 2000, he expressed to Gerard a feeling of having let me down and how he thought it was time for him to bow out. What he was suggesting was that I could get someone else who might do a better job and he was totally willing to stand aside. My failure to win a medal in Sydney was not Alex's fault, I simply wasn't strong enough or good enough on the day. There was no way I wanted him to end his involvement or could envisage carrying on without him. For me that wasn't an option, but it was typical of Alex to offer to step aside. The part he finds difficult is the media attention; he would be happy if he never had to speak to a journalist and he hates going on television. From the beginning, he made clear his complete indifference to the spotlight and that is as much the case now as it was ten or fifteen years ago.

Typically, when we made the decision to try the marathon, Alex did a lot of extra research and thinking because he had little experience of helping runners prepare for the marathon. For me that wasn't a problem. Our relationship worked, so why change? Of course it has evolved from him telling me exactly what to do, to a situation where we now discuss my training schedule together. In terms of coaching, he knows me better than anyone could ever know me. But he just doesn't rely on that. One of his great strengths is his willingness to learn new things and embrace new ideas. He has never been afraid to speak to other coaches with greater experience, and before I ran my first marathon, he talked to several coaches who had worked with elite marathon runners. He noted what he felt was worthwhile, chucked away the rest and gave me lots to think about. Because he has been so prepared to listen to other points of view, we have been able to grow together.

And maybe we are bound together because he was my original mentor, the person who first believed in me. In his own quiet way he can also be very inspiring. One of the first things he said to me was, 'Aim for the moon; even if you miss, you'll land among the stars.' Alex and I have always aimed for the top. If he sets times for a session, he always knows I'll try to beat those times! As our relationship has matured and changed over the years, he has always been strong and supportive without ever wanting to control me too much or to change the way I run. 'I will get a couple of the guys to run seven-minute miles with her,' the Loughborough coach George Gandy once said to Alex. 'You'll do well if you can get her to slow down enough to run seven-minute miles,' Alex replied. Our emphasis has always been quality over quantity. He has always appreciated that I have a mind of my own, just as I have always respected his opinion.

At the age of 17 I had my first experience of a World Championship. This was the 1991 World Junior Cross-Country at Antwerp in Belgium. It was a big event in my young life. Although junior was Under-20, it meant you had to be 19 in the year of the race and even though I had just had my birthday on 17 December, I would have just two chances at the World Junior title. In truth nothing much was expected of me in Belgium as Andrea Duke had beaten me in that season's English Schools, so this was very much a step into the great unknown. All I wanted was to run as well as I could there and to enjoy the experience. Mum and Dad travelled by car to Antwerp, taking Alex and Rosemary with them. At the team hotel on the morning of the race I felt sick with nerves, a situation that improved only when we got to the course and the warm-up began. 'This is what you've worked so hard for. This is where you want to be,' I reminded myself. 'Just run your race, do your best, no one can ask any more than that.'

It was nerve-wracking. This was the next level for me and an entirely new experience. When the Bedford & County team travelled to a race, we were among our own friends and the club officials were often people we had known for years. Being used to making friendly chat, I spoke to one of my team-mates as we were about to begin the warm-up. 'Um,' she said, 'would you mind not talking so much? I don't like to be around people when I am warming up.' One of our national coaches spoke to me and said that the race would begin at a frantic pace but then settle down. He was right about the first part, wrong about the second.

Starting at a sprint, the race continued at an unbelievable pace. It never eased. I started as fast as I could and then picked my way through the field during the second half, eventually finishing a respectable 15th. For me it was a reasonable effort, but not as good as the Scottish girl Hayley Haining, who was our leading scorer in 7th place and also the first European home. Andrea finished 27th – an indication to me that I had performed pretty well.

None of us, not Mum or Dad, nor Alex or Rosemary, had known what to expect. Lydia Cheromei from Kenya won the race and even though I was pleased with how I'd done, the gap from 15th to 1st seemed enormous. But Alex is such a logical man. He took Cheromei's time, worked out she had run between 3.05 and 3.10 for each kilometre, and decided we would train for the following year's World Junior Championships by learning to run at that speed. That was just what I needed, a target that gave our training a real edge. We would go down to the club on Monday evenings, just Alex and I, and we started with a set of three 1-kilometre runs at 3.10 to 3.15 for each kilometre with minimal recovery time. Then we moved it up to 4 × 1km and all the time, we tried to lower the time for each kilometre.

The 1992 World Junior Cross-Country Championships in Boston, Massachusetts, were the target and we were determined to get there fitter and better prepared than I had ever been in my life.

It was an unusually vivid dream, made all the more plausible by the fact that in it everything happened as it should. The race started at a mad sprint with everyone jostling and trying to get a place near the front. That didn't bother me because the National Cross-Country Championships were always the same, you just had to deal with it. This year it was the Under-17 race, my sixth 'Nationals', and though I had never placed lower than 4th, I had never won one. This was to be my year and in the dream, I was propelled forward by the desperation to make the race hard and burn off my biggest rival, Jeina Mitchell.

Back then I didn't have any hang-ups about not being able to win in a sprint, but Jeina was the Schools 1,500m champion on the track, and there was no way I wanted her on my shoulder turning into the finishing straight. Somewhere along the way, she lost contact and I kept pushing to make sure she never got back. At the finish line I was alone and well clear. It was so real that I lay in my bed, semi-conscious, and thought, 'Yes, that's it: I've done it at last.' But as I became fully conscious, reality replaced illusion and I thought, 'Oh my God, I have to go and do that again.'

Perhaps it was the fact of my sleeping in the spare double bed of my grandparents' home in Liverpool that allowed me to sleep so soundly. The '91 National Championships were in Liverpool, Dad and I travelled up from Bedford the day before while Mum travelled up with the other girls on the team bus. Getting up there the night before the race meant I could have a full night's sleep and Dad insisted I sleep in the double bed while he slept in one of the two bunk-beds that Martin and I habitually used. My routine before dropping off to sleep is to mentally rehearse how I intend to run the next day's race. Once that's done my mind then thinks of something relaxing, such as lying on a beach, and then allowing natural tiredness to take over. They say dreams come to those in deep sleep and that night in Liverpool, I must have been in the deepest slumber.

Next morning Grandma cooked my special pre-race breakfast: toast, tinned tomatoes with cheese melted on top and bacon on top of that. Mum always wanted us to have a hot breakfast in our systems before setting off on a day of cross-country running and I had grown up on big pre-race breakfasts. As I walked into the kitchen, the smell of the bacon was in the air and the thought struck me again: yes, this race has definitely not been won. Remarkably, the actual race was identical to the race in the dream. I ran really hard to break away from Jeina and got clear before the finish. It was a huge victory for me. After years of near misses and always finding one or two girls too good for me, this was my turn to be national champion and to achieve this in Liverpool with Grandma and Granddad out on the course made it particularly special. Granddad had so much fun watching Martin and I race that it was just perfect having him there.

Beating Jeina was also important to me. Though she was first year Under-17 whereas I was second year, there wasn't a lot between us. In our previous meetings, she won some and I won some. Before the Nationals – it may have been the Southern Counties – we were ahead when I broke away running downhill and she subsequently fell. Though Jeina picked herself up and chased, there was no chance of her getting back at me. At the finish people could see that Jeina had fallen and jumped to the conclusion that I was a fortunate winner.

That gave me the added motivation of wanting to show I could beat her fair and square.

During these years we had a group of girls at Bedford & County that was the best in the country. At Liverpool where I won the Under-17 individual, we also won the team title. That day, in fact, we won the team prizes at Under-13, Under-15 and Under-17. Thinking of our extraordinary success, there was no one reason for it. A lot of good things happened at the same time; a group of talented and committed athletes came together in a club where Alex and Rosemary Stanton provided excellent coaching and support and where an unusually high number of parents helped with the organisation simply by marshalling the training sessions or supporting at races.

Bedford & County was definitely a happy club, and the spirit was tangible. We were always having fun and finding the smallest reasons for having a laugh. During the races, we would have fifty or sixty of our club-mates shouting and roaring us on. Most clubs had nothing like our numbers and, of course, our success and our camaraderie set us up there to be shot at.

At the 1990 National Road Relays, Liz was running our second leg and I was the anchor. As Liz got ready to set off, there was time for me to nip to the toilet which was set up in a Portakabin near the changeover zone. While I was inside, someone locked the Portakabin from the outside in an attempt to prevent me from running. This person must have seen me go in and then tried to make sure I wouldn't get out in time to run my leg. Banging as hard as I could on the door, the fuss was enough for someone on the outside to come to my help and open the door. The anger had my adrenaline pumping and even though I was only just in time, the attempted sabotage just made me run all the harder. Such was the strength of our team, it was the only way we could have been beaten.

The following year – at the Southern Relays, if my memory is right – Liz had taken over in 2nd place and overtaken the girl in front of her when she took a wrong turn. Though she saw Liz go the wrong way, the girl never shouted and instead allowed her to keep going, and by the time Lizzie realised her mistake and returned to the right course, she had run 800 metres extra. That destroyed our chance and Liz was in tears as she came in. What upset her and us was the fact that nobody called out to get her back on track, but it just made us more determined to go on and win the National Relays, which we did.

As happens with young athletes, some drop out and new faces emerge. Kate Foster, Clare Wilson and Emily Williams all dropped out of the sport but Elinor Caborn, who had been at the club all the way through from Under-13s, improved every year until she was our third scorer at Under-17. Liz, of course, remained a pillar of our team and other girls came through. On that Under-17 team, Amanda Pack was our 4th scorer. Now, all these years later, I look around and only Liz, Elinor and Claire Peet, who was a year older than us, and myself from the original team are still running. There is a natural thinning-out in our sport. Attitudes, circumstances, body shapes: they all change, and people end up drifting out of athletics. That is why it is so important to get big numbers involved at junior level because then it is possible to have enough athletes still involved as seniors.

Things have changed and it is now harder to get young people involved in athletics. The National Cross-Country Championships that were one of the high points of my year would have 600 runners in a race. Nowadays it is more like 200. Working to bring those numbers back up is something that has to be done, and when my competitive running career is over, I would like to help out more and give something back to a sport that has given me so much fun and joy. Even our once supreme Bedford & County club is not the force of old. Alex and Rosemary, Mum and Dad, they are all still involved – but the club has lost its place at the top of junior athletics. Maybe there just aren't enough youngsters coming in, maybe today's runners don't want to work hard enough and make the commitments, maybe there are too many other things to do out there. Maybe the parents don't have the time to support as much any more, or maybe things just move in natural cycles. Part of the strength of Alex's contribution was his sense of balance: athletics was just one part of your life, and not in fact the most important part. Family and homework came first. But we never wanted to miss training and rarely did. He never pushed us to train, saying – wisely – that we had to have the desire there, if we didn't want to and enjoy putting the work in then there was no point.

Antwerp had given us a sense of what would be required to win in Boston the following year. That year, 1991–92, was my second A-level year and as I'd set myself the target of four A's, it was a big year for me academically. Towards the end of the year, around November or December, the training and the studying were intense. The mock A-level exams were coming up and the cross-country season would begin in earnest in January, leading into the World Championships in March. Something, though, wasn't right. My performance at the international cross-country race at Durham was substandard and my Monday night training sessions with Alex were not producing the kilometre times we had hoped for. Bud Baldaro, the national cross-country coach, suggested I see a physiologist friend of his called Andy Jones.

At the time, Andy was doing his Ph.D. in sports physiology in Eastbourne. Mum and Dad drove me down. It was our first meeting and the start of a relationship that has continued through the years. Every so often, I like to do some testing with Andy, if only to confirm indications from training sessions and make sure everything is on the right track – if it isn't, then we can then modify the training accordingly. That day Andy did a battery of tests but found nothing wrong with me. He suggested blood tests and, sure enough, when these results came back, it was clear the problem was anaemia. With so much running and studying, I was run down and totally lacking in iron. In a funny way it worked to my advantage, because as soon as the course of iron tablets started to kick in, the improvement in strength and energy was palpable. Each week after Christmas I was getting stronger and stronger. I won the British cross-country trials and then those National Junior Championships in Liverpool. Then, two weeks before Boston, I went to the English Schools, a title that had always eluded me.

'What I would like you to do,' said Alex, 'is imagine this is the World Cross-Country in Boston and set off hard and keep it going. Never mind how far ahead you are or whether you've got the race in control, keep running as hard as you can. Don't take your foot off the accelerator.' That's what we did. Setting off as fast as possible, getting an early lead and just trying to increase it all the way, I ran the race as hard as I could, imagining the Kenyans racing alongside me. At the end I was 68 seconds clear of the second-placed girl and really pleased that the work we had put into the training was starting to bear fruit.

'Why did you run so hard?' lots of people asked.

'Well, the World Cross-Country is not going to be easy, and we thought the best preparation for us was a really hard race today.'

The performance had obviously raised a few eyebrows. As well as the enquiries about why I'd raced so hard, a couple of journalists from *Athletics Weekly* asked some questions about Boston and how I thought that race would go. I have remembered that first exchange with journalists because it was an indication that things were changing in my life: it was a first sign to me that as you climbed up the ladder, more people were interested, and you became subject to a scrutiny that would increase greatly as the years passed. That first chat with the guys from *Athletics Weekly* was where it started.

The encouragement of being able to run so hard to win the Schools title put me in the right frame of mind for the trip to the United States. Things got even better during the final week's training. We were now doing 4 × 1km sessions, and in the last one before leaving for Boston I averaged 3.02 minutes per kilometre. That was easily my best session and it left me feeling very positive about Boston.

We travelled out as a team the weekend before the race. One thing that has stayed in my mind is the confusion over the trip to the course in Franklin Park two days before the race: with too many people for our small mini-bus it was decided the junior girls would have to wait until the following day. That night there was a heavy snowfall that covered Boston and I never got to see the course without snow, something that with hindsight was probably an advantage. The American guy who drove us to the course the next day was an athletics enthusiast.

'We had the US Championships here in 1984,' he said. 'Pat Porter accelerated at the top of Bear Cage Hill, a famous landmark on the course, and then surged on the downhill. From the top to the finish, there's only about 500 metres. They never caught him.' Then as we walked over the snow and round the course, I checked out this Bear Cage Hill and it was pretty much as the guy said.

Jeina Mitchell was a reserve on that team, and I was sharing a room with a very promising young girl called Sharon Murphy, who was just fifteen. The team all got on very well and that helped to shorten the week leading into the race. Expecting a glare from the snow, I bought some sunglasses and was trying them on in the lift when Brendan Foster, the former athlete who is now a commentator for the BBC, got in. Jeina and I were in awe of Brendan and it took all my courage to ask him if the BBC was showing the junior race. 'No,' he said, 'I don't think we are, and we definitely won't if you decide to wear those sunglasses.' In the end I decided not to wear them, reasoning that with the way my head bobbed around, they probably wouldn't stay on anyhow!

Liz McColgan was one of the big favourites for the senior race, the one the BBC was there to cover. I understood that, but was thinking of my grandparents and friends back home and how nice it would be if they could watch me run.

The junior race was the first of the day and before it, Liz McColgan took the time to drop by the warm-up area and wish us luck. That was such a thoughtful thing for her to do. Earlier on Peter, her husband, had been looking for spikes because Liz had only little track spikes, which weren't suitable for running in snow. I had spent ages wondering about the configuration of my spikes and considered different combinations before opting for 12mm spikes in the back and 15mm in the front – I felt I needed good traction both up and down the hills and on the twisty corners, and had tried them out to make sure they weren't too long for the hard icy sections. After explaining this, I gave Peter some spare 12- and 15-millimetre spikes and was really excited at the thought that Liz McColgan might use my spare spikes. But she never put them in and afterwards she complained she couldn't keep her footing in the conditions. Unfortunately she struggled to 41st, suffering also from a virus.

Pre-race nerves almost overwhelmed me the evening before the race. My anxiety was in part attributable to the fact that I was so well prepared. Others may have seen me as an underdog, but Alex and I knew that we were as strong as any rival in the race. I was ready and just wanted to get on with it, but as with anything that is important to you, there are always some nerves. What if I didn't do everything right? At the team meeting on that Friday evening there was a lot of motivational talk, which was probably good for others but it was the last thing I needed as it just increased the tension. Before the meeting Alex had given me a signed card from all the girls in the club at home and reading through the names and the messages, I was overcome with emotion and the desire to do really well.

Going into the team meeting, already feeling very nervous, I just burst into tears when they started talking about how big the race was and how this was the greatest challenge of our lives. It was all too much, I just wanted to get on with it. But it's funny – the next morning I felt totally in control. Race day was finally here. The determination and desire to do well was still there, but it was now a steely, controlled, unemotional feeling.

Alex had taken the Thursday and Friday off work so that he and Rosemary could be in Boston the day before the race. They brought Martin with them. Mum and Dad both worked on Friday and travelled out from London that evening. The race began at ten o'clock on Saturday morning so they had very little sleep, and as Dad had a slight chest infection, the freezing cold of Franklin Park that morning was the last thing he needed. With the biting wind chilling the air, temperatures were as low as minus 10, the coldest conditions in which I had ever competed. They gave us goose grease to smooth over our arms and legs as it would protect us from the cold wind.

But the conditions didn't bother me. What mattered was that my preparation had gone as well as it could have. I knew I was as ready as I could be, and I was excited about it. If anything, Alex's calmness and confidence were surreal. 'Listen, just go out there and don't worry about anything. I've a really good feeling about this race and we're going to be fine. I guarantee you that you will be fine.' Alex is never anything but positive before a race, but occasionally he is emphatically so. It's like a gut instinct he gets, and when it happens, we know things will click. This was one of those occasions and it had an enormous effect on me. It was like he knew, and he infused that same belief in me. It is still the same now: Alex is often the last person I like to see and speak with before going to the start line.

'But Alex is only telling you what you already know,' Gary says. 'Why do you need that reassurance?'

'I don't know, it just helps. It's like hearing it from someone else that you trust reinforces it several times over.'

The snow that had fallen earlier in the week still covered the ground but it was now hard and icy. Having spent time choosing my spikes, the conditions were not a particular problem and the race could not have gone better. Four of us broke away: my team-mate Jenny Clague, the defending champion Lydia Cheromei from Kenya, and the Chinese girl, Wang Junxia. Going up Bear Cage Hill for the last time, Jenny got dropped, as did Cheromei. That left Wang and I. We raced up the hill, side by side, each trying to find a weakness in the other. Going across the top, we were still together, and she seemed incredibly strong. Lots of people were scattered around the course but even with all the shouting, Dad's voice was easy to pick out. 'Come on, Paula!' As at all my races, I could hear him clearly over all the noise in Franklin Park.

As we began the downhill, Wang seemed to weaken a little. This was my moment – I thought of Pat Porter, whoever he was, and made my attack. Instinctively feeling that Wang was close to her limit, I accelerated hard down the descent and quickly got a little gap. Not daring to look back, I pressed hard and kept going. There was only 400 metres to the finish so no matter how painful, I knew I could keep it going. It was one of those good days when the buzz of breaking away and the possibility of winning obliterated every other sensation. Dad's voice still carried further, more vibrantly than all others: 'You've got a gap, keep it up!' At the line I had five seconds to spare over Wang, Cheromei was third and Jenny Clague an excellent 4th.

It is hard to explain this but when I crossed the line I didn't show any emotion or react in any kind of celebratory way. No punching of the air, no raised arms, just a calm smile. I walked through the chute, calmly pulled my briefs out of my bum and immediately wanted to get my clothes back on. Mum was waiting there, crying, but inside I felt serene. It was like I was so happy and pleased that I didn't need to do all the jumping around. That would all come later. On the victory rostrum, they gave us our medals but I was disappointed they didn't play the national anthem and I remember being very cold. Then we had to go to doping control, and as I waited in the queue to deliver my urine sample, Dad walked in. He had been out on the course and I hadn't been able to see him since the finish. I was really glad to see him and get a big hug, but really he had no right to be in the drug testing room. It is always restricted to the athletes being tested plus one accredited team doctor or official.

'Dad,' I said, 'how did you get in here?'

'I wanted to congratulate you.'

'That's great, but you could get me banned.'

'What!'

'How did you get in here anyway?'

'I just showed them my Whitbread ID card.'

That was Dad. He has always maintained that if you look like you belong, no one will stop you. He had got past armed US security with just his work ID. The girl who sat beside me was flabbergasted.

After my instinctively low-key response to victory, the magnitude of the victory began to sink in. There was the joy of Mum and Dad and Alex and Rosemary, and then there were the British journalists who wanted to speak to me. They were in Boston primarily to report on Liz McColgan in the senior race but because of her illness and the conditions she hadn't run well. So they changed tack, and decided they would write about the girl who won the World Junior title. Vera Duerdin was our team manager. She was a strict, schoolmistress type of character, a very good team manager, and also very protective of her girls. If the journalists were going to speak with me, they would do so in Vera's presence, and so they all came to my bedroom. What happened then was, for me, an eye-opener.

My room-mate Sharon Murphy, at 15 the youngest member of our team, had produced an outstanding run to finish 21st and was our 3rd scorer. We missed 3rd place and the bronze medal by one point, and Sharon blamed herself for not doing better. This was crazy – she had done brilliantly and all of the team had done their best. When the journalists arrived she was in the toilet, crying her eyes out, and Vera was then trying to find a way of discreetly consoling her away from the view of the journalists. It was the first time I had done a little press conference like this and all the time I was aware of Sharon's anguish. I just wanted to go and give her a big hug. She had run her heart out – her 21st place was a fantastic effort, but she was inconsolable. The entire scene offered an insight into sport that I would come to appreciate all the more over the following years: the line that divides the victorious from the heart-broken is a very thin one. One extra place from any of the team and she'd have been celebrating too.

After Boston, my focus for the rest of the year was twofold. First my A-levels, which were very important, and then in September, the World Junior Championships on the track in Seoul, South Korea. The academic target was an A in each of my four subjects, French, German, Maths and General Studies. In the mocks I had got an A in the first three and a C in General Studies. Through April and May there was a lot of revision, but most of the time I was able to manage my time and dovetail studies and athletics. Occasionally I would arrive at training totally wiped and Alex would take one look and say I was doing no training that night. Either he'd give me something really easy to keep me happy or I'd help out timing the others.

During study leave in late May and June I decamped to the back garden and revised in our trailer tent. I prefer quiet while working and this allowed an escape from the music Martin liked to play when he revised. It helped, of course, that 1992 was a good summer. Alex and I decided I wouldn't be able to race quite as much as usual during the build-up to my A-levels and he even suggested at one point that we stop training. That wasn't a possibility for me because running was my release, my reward for the hours of study, and I couldn't contemplate giving it up, even temporarily. There were some days when, exhausted from endless hours of study, my training was terrible, but it was still good for me to get out and run.

At the league races I did do I would take my books and find a quiet corner to do some revision between races. However, I also tried to structure my revision so that I had time to relax at the weekends. It was important for me to see my friends and to get out and compete.

The exams came and went and soon I was back in competition. Tired and lacking race fitness after the months of intensive study, expectations were not high. But I was also really glad to be free from school work. I took my place in the senior women's AAA Championships. This 3,000m race also doubled as an official trial for the Barcelona Olympics with the first two British finishers certain to get into the team. Lisa York won, the Australian Krishna Stanton was second and I almost caught Alison Wyeth for third place. 'Aren't you disappointed to have come so close to qualifying for the Olympics?' I was asked many times in the immediate aftermath. Not in the slightest. My time, 8.57, was 26 seconds faster than my previous best and Alex and I were just thrilled with the run. Exam pressure had been lifted off my shoulders, my competitive running life had just recommenced and, at the first try, there was a 26-second improvement in my personal best.

Being outsprinted by Alison was no disgrace; in fact it seemed a miracle to me that there had been so little in it at the end. Growing up in the sport, I had always looked up to Alison as one of the very best performers in our sport. She had won National titles and was coached by Bob and Sylvia Parker at Parkside Harrow Athletic Club, who had also coached the great distance runner Dave Bedford. I was 18 years of age and before the race, Alison had belonged to another world. We had raced before at league meetings and although she was always really friendly she was always comfortably ahead of me. As we sat around after the race, she was telling Mum about how hard it had been for her in the home straight: 'She kept snapping at my heels all the way to the line and I really had to sprint to get it.' That made me so pleased. There was also the fact that my 8.57 was the fastest 3,000m of the year by a junior and it would enable me to prepare for Seoul with a lot of confidence.

Later that summer my A-level results arrived and brought the four A's I had been hoping for. The results were a huge relief and it seemed to me that life could not be better. The year had begun with the World Cross-Country victory in Boston, then the exam results, and I still had the World Junior Track Championships in Seoul to come. One evening in the garden of our house at Oakley I remember admitting to Alex that I was scared about how well things had gone – I was afraid that it just couldn't last.

'Everything's gone so well it scares me, Alex,' I remember saying. 'I've worked hard for it, but so have a lot of people. Why should it all go well for me? I'm scared it won't continue.'

'I am too,' he said.

'What can we do about it?'

'Look, you can only do the best you can. You've got to try your hardest at everything you do, treat everyone fairly and hope you get treated fairly in return. What you mustn't do is worry about the future, you mustn't even worry whether people are being fair to you. As long as you're fair to everyone else, there's nothing more you can do.'

Alex is a bit like my grandma. She believes that we only get one life, you should make the most of it – no looking back. Always be true to yourself and treat other people fairly and as you would want to be treated. Enjoy and appreciate it when things go well because you've worked for it. What goes around comes around. Often life doesn't quite work out like that but if you believe it does, it is easier to make sense of it. Of course things still go wrong sometimes, but it's easier to get over these obstacles if you're prepared to learn from them, put the problem behind you and work hard to get back to the good times. It's a philosophy I've always believed in too.

5

And, of course, things didn't continue perfectly.

Held in Seoul, South Korea, the 1992 World Junior Track Championships were too far away for Alex to travel. It was the first time that he would not be with me for an important race but we spoke on the phone as often as possible. On time, I was the fastest runner in the field, but that guaranteed nothing and in my eyes it didn't make me favourite. From the World Junior Cross-Country Championships in Boston and the performance of Wang Junxia, it was obvious the Chinese women were becoming formidable in distance running. There was also the young Romanian, Gabriela Szabo, who was talented and had always beaten me on the track. Having the fastest time of the year for 3,000m simply meant there was a lot more pressure on me than there had been in Boston.

Malcolm Brown was our team manager. Malcolm's from Scotland and is a nice guy. 'How do you plan to run the race?' he asked beforehand. Alex and I had already discussed this and it was our intention to go out fast from the start and try to make it hard for the other girls. 'You can't do that,' Malcolm said, 'they'll eat you alive if you do that.' This was Malcolm's view and it may or may not have been right but, before the race, it wasn't what I needed to hear.

On the start line, a voice in the back of my mind repeated his words.

'*They'll eat you alive if you go out hard.*'

Another voice offered a different view.

'Remember what you agreed with Alex. Run how you feel. Hard from the start.'

'*They'll eat you alive if you do that.*'

'Stick to your plan.'

'*They'll eat you alive if you do that.*'

The conflicting views caused doubt, and when the starter sounded his gun, I hesitated, I didn't commit to getting to the front and found myself boxed in as the Chinese girls set the pace. It was quite fast. Uncertain about how to react and definitely unsure about whether or not to pick up the pace, I just sat there. For most of the race, I was boxed in and bumped as everyone jostled for better positions. At a decisive moment, the Chinese girls kicked, Szabo got between them, I went after the three of them but couldn't close the gap. Szabo won silver and I was left in 4th place, which is about the worst result you can get at a major championship. You get so close but are left with nothing to show for it.

It wouldn't be my last fourth place, but I was devastated. In one respect I shouldn't have been because my time, 8.51, was 6 seconds faster than I'd ever run over 3,000m. That evening I spoke with Alex and explained how frustrated I was because I just hadn't run *my* race. Alex later spoke with Malcolm and suggested that it wasn't helpful to put doubts in the runner's mind just before the race. It wasn't Malcolm's fault, he was only trying to help, and of course there is no certainty the result would have been different if I had run the race we had planned. However, I would have been a lot happier and that does matter. Eighteen years of age, inexperienced, I wasn't able to lock the door to my mind in the lead-up to the race and left ajar, doubts crept in. It is only through making mistakes that you properly learn what works for you: never again would I listen to anyone other than Alex and, in future years, Gary. I learned to believe and stick to my own plan. They are the ones closest to me, they know me and I trust them. Ask too many people or people who don't really know you, and though they mean well you just get confused.

Winning the World Junior Cross-Country title and doing well in my A-levels made 1992 a good year, but I was disappointed with that fourth place in Seoul. Still, I was just 18 and young minds are a little like young bones: they mend and move on quickly. The future seemed such rich and boundless terrain. Alongside running, there would be a university career because I had accepted a place in Modern European Studies at Loughborough University. Mum and Dad would not have been happy for me to concentrate exclusively on athletics at that point and I had no wish to. Going to university and getting a good degree was just as important to me as developing my athletic potential, even if I much preferred running to studying. It was important to get the qualifications I would need later in life.

After Seoul, I started at Loughborough. Eighteen, about to turn 19, it wasn't like I needed to rush things along. But when you're that age, you look forward to the future and at the same time you can't wait for it. So, first term at Loughborough, I was building up for the cross-country season, looking forward to my first Senior Cross-Country Championships which would be held at Amorebieta in Spain. Thanks to the refreshing motivation of new surroundings and people I was running really well before Christmas. However, adjusting to change can be problematic too and I also had a few hiccups that first year. The first mistake was my choice of accommodation at Loughborough.

My parents had driven me up and Mum cried when she left me. Loughborough was about an hour up the M1 from our home in Bedford and Mum was not clingy, the tears were not because of the separation, the reason was more practical. Mum took one look at the cramped little room that I had been allocated in the university halls and her heart sank. The room had a narrow, single bed, and a space about the same width as the bed in which there was a desk, a chair, a wardrobe and a little washbasin. Even I had to admit I felt a little trapped and claustrophobic in the room.

However, in the first flush of enthusiasm for university life, nothing was going to demoralise me. I was excited about meeting new friends and having fun. Also I set myself my target from the start: my ambition was to leave Loughborough with a first-class honours degree. Someone asked a lecturer what it took to achieve your full potential and he said you would have to work 40 hours each week. That meant you totalled the number of hours spent at lectures, subtracted it from forty and what was left was the amount of study hours you had to do each week. There was nothing complicated about my plan: 8 hours a day, five days a week. The difficulty for me was maintaining that commitment while fitting in two runs per day and making the most of a university social life. While my class-mates went for coffee when they had an hour between lectures, I tried to get the study done so that I had the time for training and seeing friends in the evening. I never really did work after 6 p.m., that was my time for the things I enjoyed doing. By organising myself like this I was able to get my study hours in and still fit in the things I loved. Then most of the weekend was left free for R and R, running and relaxation.

Having run well before Christmas, my form tailed off in the build-up to Amorebieta. It shouldn't have been a surprise; bugs spread easily in the halls and I came down with the flu in the New Year. Having to spend a week in bed did not improve relations between the room and me. Things worsened when I became slightly anaemic which, again, should not have surprised me because I was in catered halls and the cooked evening meal finished by 6.30. Six-thirty was impossible for me as my evening run took place before my evening meal and training usually began at 6.30. Most of the time after a hard training session I was having to make do with a packed lunch.

For weeks, I wasn't getting enough proper nutrients. The flu and the anaemia came and went, leaving me weak and flat and with not enough time to get fully back to form before the World Cross-Country Championships in March. In the race itself I felt flat all through and finished 18th. It was not exactly an auspicious start to my career in the senior race. 'I just didn't run well,' I said to the journalists afterwards. 'Look,' they said, 'eighteenth isn't that bad for a first-time senior.' But I was disappointed and I knew it could have been better.

By now my athletics career had progressed to a point where there was a need for someone to help on the management side, and someone else to try to get me into Grand Prix races. I got to know a guy called Geoff Wightman who worked for a management company called Park Associates that subsequently became the much bigger SFX. Geoff was based in nearby Nottingham, he had been an international marathon runner and he was interested in working with me. His company had a lot of footballers, most notably Gary Lineker. The idea was for Geoff to represent me commercially and the company would also provide advice on the financial and pension side of things. For our first meeting, Mum and Dad and I went along. I wanted their opinions on the people that might represent me. We all agreed pretty quickly on Geoff.

Then there was the choice of an agent who would negotiate on my behalf with race promoters. We arranged to meet the late Kim McDonald who came to our house in Oakley. Kim turned up in a Porsche to meet and then be scrutinised by a young athlete and her four mentors. The car, I must admit, impressed me. Kim didn't like it and didn't like driving it but he saw it as a status symbol and that's why he had bought it. That was typical Kim. Though I respected him and liked his bluntness, there were a couple of reservations. While he was there, Mum made a big bowl of chilli con carne for dinner and afterwards asked if anyone would like seconds. 'Yes,' I said, 'I'll have more.' This was during the rest period at the end of 1992, and no sooner had I volunteered for seconds than Kim's eyes darted disapprovingly towards me. He said, 'Look, you're not training, you've got to be careful about putting on weight.'

Stupid, I know, but I resented that. It wasn't like it was more dessert. Something, probably my natural stubbornness, made me want to say, 'If I put on weight, it's my problem; your problem is to sort out my races.' It was also an instinctive reaction against someone wanting to control me. When Kim went through his portfolio of athletes, it was obvious he had many of the world's best. He was saying I would be able to train with this athlete and that athlete and this also worried me, because he might just have seen me as a good training partner for some of his higher profile athletes.

That was unfair of me, because Kim wasn't like that. Over the years I got to know him and grew to like him a lot, both as a person and an agent. He treated people properly; if someone produced a good performance, he would acknowledge that performance regardless of whether it was one of his athletes or someone else. Similarly, if one of his athletes under-performed he would not make excuses. His premature death in 2001 was a huge shock and a massive loss to the sport and those who knew him. At the time we were talking about working together, I just didn't know him well enough.

After Kim we met Andy Norman, who was another successful agent at that time. Wilbert Greaves, Andy's driver, brought him to the Bedford & County clubhouse where we met. The usual committee of four awaited him: Mum, Dad, Alex and me, plus Dan Davies — a friend of Andy's and also the grandfather of one of my friends at the club. He had asked Andy to meet with us. It was actually funny because Andy is very sharp. In his mind, he had come to see what I was like and whether or not he wanted to work with me. Then he walked into a room at the club, saw the five of us, and soon into the discussion the penny dropped: 'Hey,' he said, 'are you here to interview me?' Dad said, 'Yes, that's right.' But it went well, even if he was never quite comfortable with the idea of being the one under scrutiny. 'First time in my life I've ever been fucking interviewed,' he said to Wilbert afterwards. Wilbert still laughs about that. Basically we believed that Andy was a strong character who would be able to get me into the best races and would treat me fairly. He would do this without trying to encroach on the coaching side and that, too, was important. He agreed to represent me. I think he was pleased that my goal was to be the best in the world and to win championships, not chase money on the Grand Prix circuit.

Andy was very straightforward. 'Tell me what races you want to get into.'

I told him.

Then he said, 'Okay, is there anything that would make your life easier?'

'Well, my car's a bit beaten up and I need it to get back from university to train with Alex. I'm saving to buy a new one.'

'Right, that's fine, we'll facilitate you an advance on your earnings to help you get a decent car. You've got to be able to get to and from training safely.'

He arranged for the advance, which I then paid back over the next year or so. In his direct, no-frills style, there was a lot to respect about Andy. If you were willing to work hard he was willing to help.

The big target for the 1993 track season was the World Championships in Stuttgart, but to get there I first had to qualify. What should have been a relatively straightforward matter turned into a nightmare. That year the 3,000m trial was part of the UK Championships at Crystal Palace, and even though it was unlikely that I could beat Yvonne Murray and Alison Wyeth in that race, 3rd place was well within my scope and would get me into the team for Stuttgart. Because of the extra stresses of studying and training at Loughborough, I was skipping my periods for a lot of the year. The

British Athletics doctors were worried about this affecting my bone density and decided to put me on the contraceptive pill to even out my oestrogen levels.

However, I didn't feel good while taking the medication and my body didn't accept it. On the morning of the race, something was amiss. 'Alex,' I said, 'I just don't feel right. I feel really dizzy and a bit sick.'

Then during my warm-up I suddenly got a breakthrough period. It was totally unexpected and threw me. So instead of concentrating on my race, there was a frantic search for someone to lend me something to get through this. Alison came to my rescue. Ian Stewart was on the other side of the crash barriers as the crisis played out: 'You and your bloody doctors, you and your bloody pill! If you'd only left me alone.' I'm sure he was really embarrassed and didn't know what was going on, but I was really frustrated and angry at the situation I had found myself in. I tried to calm myself down and the race began. Predictably, I ran terribly. Having led for most of the way, I was passed by Yvonne and Alison before finally being overtaken by Sonia McGeorge close to the finish. In my mind that was it, my chance of going to the World Championships had gone. I was distraught; how could I have felt and run so badly? Sonia was a good athlete but I shouldn't have let her beat me and in my anguish, the thought that overwhelmed everything was the sense of having blown it. Blown it, big time.

The tears flowed, I apologised to the people around me and didn't sleep a wink that night. Next morning Alex came round and followed on his bike when I went for a 10-mile run. It was not unusual for a long, punishing run to be the reaction to the previous day's disappointment because that has always been my refuge. Perhaps it is the endorphin rush that makes you glad to be alive, or maybe it's that after a tough run there is too much tiredness for the frustration to survive. After I got back, the phone rang. It was Andy. 'Do you know,' he said, 'I've been up all fucking night arguing for you to be on that team for Stuttgart. Anyway, you're in. They've picked you on the basis that you have the qualifying time and Sonia McGeorge doesn't, and the fact that you've got youth on your side. By the way, you're in the Oslo Grand Prix race and you'd better run well over there.'

I didn't know how to react to the situation. It was good news, but although I believed I was capable of running better than her, I wasn't sure it was fair on Sonia. She had finished in front of me in the trial and even if she didn't have the qualifying time for the 3,000m, should she not be given the opportunity to get it? This was May, the World Championships didn't take place until August, and it wasn't a question of Sonia not having the time to get the qualifying standard. It was also embarrassing for me because she worked with George Gandy, who was the coach at Loughborough. George and I got on fine but I had never considered leaving Alex to work with his group. I saw no reason not to continue working with Alex – I was happy and the set-up was working well. There was one occasion when George spoke to Alex after a session I'd done alone. 'Do you know she did such and such?' he said. 'Yeah, I speak to her all the time,' Alex replied, unfazed. 'She tells me everything she does. There are no secrets between us.'

Of course there were times when I trained with George's group and his track sessions were exceptionally good. Runners came from all around – Jon Brown from Sheffield, with others coming from Birmingham and sometimes even London. There could be up to forty guys and it was brilliant for me. I could get in among them and push myself harder and the improved quality helped me to get really sharp. However, Alex knew what I was like so I didn't do this every week as it would have been too much. Yet even though I had often trained with George's group, I was never one of them. I certainly felt very uneasy that I might have been given preferential treatment over one of his athletes, or over anyone for that matter.

It was a double-edged feeling: I was ashamed to have run so badly in the trial and embarrassed by the thought of not deserving my place on the team. Had it been the other way round, had I finished in front of Sonia and she been picked before me, I wouldn't have been happy. So how could she and George be happy?

I went to see my doctor and discussed whether there was any need for me to be on the pill. He reassured me that so long as I was getting a few periods a year, there was no risk to my bone density. We even had that checked and the results were very strong. I immediately stopped taking the pill and my body regained its equilibrium. That was the first thing sorted out. The next week there was a 1,500m at Loughborough and it gave me another chance to race against Sonia. Because of the controversy, this was one 1,500m I felt I had to win to justify my position. The race was pretty physical. With 350 metres to go there was some bumping behind me and I sensed there might be a fall. Not wanting to wait around for that, I sprinted hard with 300 metres to go and kept going all the way to the line. In my entire life, it still might be one of the fastest final 300 metres I've run: the image of a scalded cat comes to mind. Sonia was 2nd but had been decisively beaten.

Mark Sesay, a friend of mine at Loughborough, stood near the finish line. 'How did you sprint like that?' he asked. He didn't know how I felt about my selection for the worlds and the sense of having to justify myself. It worked out okay for everyone in the end: Sonia never made the 3,000m standard but qualified in the 1,500m and got to compete at Stuttgart.

Oslo was my first venture under Andy, and my first taste of the Grand Prix circuit. It was memorable. Everything about the experience remains vivid. The meeting fell on the same day as the English Schools Championships, which was unfortunate for Yvonne Murray, my room-mate in Oslo. An afternoon sleep was part of Yvonne's routine but every time she nodded off, Alex would call from England with news of how my Bedford team-mates were doing in the Schools. Having already left the room to allow Yvonne get on with her sleep, I wasn't aware Alex was calling. 'Tell her Lizzie has just won,' Alex told Yvonne. Poor Yvonne wasn't bothered whether Liz won or not, she just wanted to sleep.

Downstairs in the lobby, I struck up a conversation with the late Cliff Temple, who was then athletics writer for the *Sunday Times*. We spoke about what elite athletes did on the day of a race; how many went for a run in the morning and how almost everyone slept in the afternoon. All this stuff was new to me. 'You've just got to do what feels right for you and what is normal for you,' said Cliff. I felt he was speaking to me and helping me as a coach, which was another hat he wore, rather than as a journalist.

The race itself went really well. I finished 6th but ran an 8.44, which was 7 seconds faster than my previous best, the 8.51 from Seoul. This was hugely exciting for me and it showed that running in top-class races made you dig deeper. Well, that and Andy Norman. Andy stood in the infield during the race and every time I passed he muttered, 'Run fucking faster.' In all honesty, I was totally inspired and running as hard as I possibly could, but I ran a bit faster anyway. He had got me into the race, he had spent a night arguing my case for inclusion in the World Championships team, and he deserved some return.

Later in the evening I remember standing with Ian Stewart watching the Kenyan Yobes Ondieki become the first athlete to break 27 minutes for 10,000m. Fans were banging the sides of the stadium, making unbelievable noise, and it exhilarated me. This was my first night at a Grand Prix meeting and it was everything I dreamed about. On evenings like this our sport is as exciting as any in the world, and that night, as both a competitor and a spectator, I loved it.

Back at the hotel Andy walked past me and as he did, he slapped an envelope into my hand. 'Well done, girl,' he said. 'You ran well.' Not knowing what was in the envelope, I showed it to Yvonne. 'Open it,' she said. There was £500 inside. 'That's your prize money from the race,' she said. Brilliant, I thought. You get well paid for doing this. Full of the joys of the sporting life, I went for a run the next morning and joined up with a few of the lads. Dave Lewis was there, so was Paul Dugdale, along with a couple of others I didn't know. Still floating on the euphoria of the night before, I was keen to stretch out a bit, as was Paul, who must also have run a personal best the night before. Somewhere along the way we started winding it up, each of us going that bit faster until we ended up racing. This was supposed to be an easy recovery run.

Poor Dave Lewis was dropped. Dead from his 10,000m, he was in no condition and in no mood to run fast. In the end Paul and I were messing around and even sprinted laughing right up to the revolving doors of the hotel. Later, Ian Stewart told me how Dave returned to the room fuming: 'That bloody Radcliffe,' Dave was saying, 'doesn't have a clue how to run with other people, should never be let out of England; should never be taken anywhere.' Of course it was my fault. No one mentioned Paul and the fact it takes two to tango. The lads could have let me do my thing and just carried on at their own pace, but Paul was up for it and neither of us had any regrets. What they said didn't bother me because the whole experience was just one long high.

August 1993, the World Championships, Stuttgart: a room shared with Yvonne Murray.

'Who do you think are the main threats in the final?' I asked.

'It's got to be Sonia O'Sullivan,' she said, 'then after Sonia, Yelena Romanova.'

'What do you think about the Chinese?'

'Nah,' she said. 'Don't think they'll be strong enough.'

'But you saw the way they kicked in yesterday's heats?'

'Heats are not the same as a final.'

'But their times?'

'The times they did in China? Don't believe them. They're out of China now, I don't think they'll be doing anything like that here.'

'Yvonne, I've raced against these girls. In the World Junior Cross and last September in Seoul, and they are strong. They're going to do something.'

I thought the Chinese would be good but didn't really expect them to be as unbelievably strong as they were. Coach Ma Junren's team of women would be the story of Stuttgart. My memories of those championships are still clear, probably because at 19 years of age, I was a dry sponge ready to soak up every drop of experience. We lodged in an old Army barracks that had been converted into pleasant living quarters for the athletes. Not far away the GB men's team had their lodgings. Linford Christie and Colin Jackson would sit out front and to get to the restaurant you had to walk past them. The banter was friendly but it was intimidating for me just to pass by because these were two of the giants of British athletics. The championships in Stuttgart were memorable because Linford, Colin and Sally Gunnell all won gold medals and both Colin and Sally broke the world record.

Sometimes, though, it is better to be young and inexperienced. Frank Dick was our team manager and gave us a motivational talk that, to me, was excellent. But afterwards most of the team were taking the piss, making jokes at Frank's expense, and it puzzled me. Apparently, his motivational talk didn't vary from championship to championship, and once you had heard the first, you'd heard them all. The other memory that has survived is of Kelly Holmes. In her 800m semi-final Kelly was eliminated. Diane Modahl went through from the other semi-final even though she had not run as fast as Kelly. Getting back to the athletes' quarters that night, Kelly was so frustrated she kicked a cup still half-full of coffee that someone had left on the floor. Next morning when we got up, her disappointment was splattered all over the wall. 'That woman,' I thought, 'she's going to survive and come through in this sport.' Because even then it was obvious to me that attitude was just as important as talent. Those who wouldn't take no for an answer and could fight back from the setbacks would eventually get the answer they sought. Eleven years would elapse before Kelly reached the pinnacle in Athens, but I'm sure the length of the journey made the arrival all the sweeter.

How innocent I was back then. I went to the Asics hospitality building in Stuttgart and someone showed me some spikes that had been specially made for Liz McColgan. I was the same size as her so they gave me a pair. 'Take them but don't wear them in the race because they're not fully tested yet.' They were incredibly light. 'Alex, I'm definitely wearing these, they've got to be way faster than what I've got.'

Our strategy in Stuttgart was simple: we would treat the heat like a final and look no further than that. In the same heat as Sonia O'Sullivan and one of the Chinese girls, I went for it with 800 metres to go, and even though they came past me in the straight, I qualified for the final. That made me really happy because that was the target. At 19 years of age, no one expected anything of me and the final was something to be enjoyed. It was during a free afternoon before the final that Yvonne and I had our talk about the Chinese.

By the time the race ended, Yvonne had seriously revised her opinion. The Chinese completely dominated. With 800 metres to go they were 1st, 2nd and 3rd, and then they accelerated. All three still full of running. Yvonne, Sonia O'Sullivan and Romanova were all caught in the wrong place at the wrong moment because as they tried to close the gap on the third-placed Chinese, the strongest of the three, Qu Junxia, was clear. To have had any hope they needed to be in among the Chinese, not chasing the 3rd in line. Sonia was the strongest of the rest of us but even she couldn't peg back Zhang Lirong, who eventually got 3rd. Qu Junxia won decisively, Zhang Linli was 2nd, then Lirong, with Sonia 4th, Alison Wyeth 5th, Romanova 6th, me 7th and Yvonne a little further back. Alison had run a smart, even race and I followed her through. I could barely believe it as I passed Yvonne and was over the moon with 7th. Hardly had the race ended than the mutterings began. How could the Chinese be that strong?

It all flew over my head because, as I said, I was well pleased with 7th. On the last lap or so I had come through strongly and passed some of those who had tried to go with the Chinese. By making it as hard as they had, the Chinese girls helped me to a higher finish than I expected and also to improve my personal best by 4 seconds, 8.40 from 8.44.

A few weeks after Stuttgart, Liz Yelling, myself and four other girl friends drove down to the south of France and had a good holiday. One night we were in a bar, having a few drinks and not paying much attention to the television high up in the corner. That changed when it showed pictures of athletes running; we could see they were Chinese. Someone said it was the Beijing Games. There was a girl turning into the straight, it seemed to be the home straight, but the time was only 29 minutes-something. It couldn't be the home straight; no woman could run 10,000m that fast. She had to have another lap to go. But she didn't. We could just about make out the time, 29.31, and I honestly didn't know if I was drunk. What they were showing was a highlights clip from the previous day, and even though the television pictures made clear what had taken place, I still went in search of a newspaper. There it was: Wang Junxia, 29.31; a new 10,000m world record. She hadn't beaten Ingrid Kristiansen's seven-year world record of 30.13, she had demolished it, and set a new mark 42 seconds faster.

At the time, the question of drugs hardly registered with me. It was something that might have been a problem with sprinters and throwers, but in my mind it wasn't a factor in distance running. Over the following years, that would turn out to be a naïve point of view.

One of the things you learn about life, and this is certainly true of the sporting life, is that you should make the most of every up because this can help you get through the down times.

One morning towards the end of January 1994, a call came from home that Granddad had died. This was Granddad Bill in Liverpool, and sadly he had been suffering from Alzheimer's for a while. At the time my running was going well and everything was geared towards the World Cross-Country Championships that would take place in Budapest six weeks later. Granddad's death hit me really hard because I loved him so much and missed him enormously, but I also felt the intense anguish and suffering that my grandma was going through. I couldn't bear to see her hurting so deeply and being able to do nothing to help. My mum called me that morning with the news. There was no way I felt like going to lectures. I grabbed my running gear, jumped into the car and drove to Bradgate Park where I did so much of my training. I ran hard up the steep hill that had so often been the route of training runs but, for once, the anchor in my life could not exercise its steadying influence.

At the top of the hill, near the tower of Old John, a ruined castle that many say is one of the highest points in Leicestershire, I sat on the stones and just thought about Granddad. The way he always wanted to tell jokes and make us laugh. How he loved to watch us race and how he laughed about that day Martin stopped in the 800m to take off his tracksuit top and then carried on to win.

Once I got a bout of chicken pox on my birthday and Dad dropped me at my grandparents' who were to take care of me for the day. For my birthday Mum and Dad had given me a Sindy doll that came with a horse and cart and Granddad said not to worry, he would put it together for me. Even though I was very young, the memory of his frustration and then disappointment at not being able to assemble this thing made a deep impression. He had this passion for life; it showed in his love for his grandchildren and in his loyalty to Liverpool football club, something he, Dad and Martin all shared.

I thought too about Grandma and how devastated she would be without him. The Alzheimer's had been tough on Grandma. He could no longer understand things that previously had been of great interest to him and when I won the Junior World Cross-Country in Boston, I don't think he was able to totally take it in. There were days he didn't even know Grandma or us. 'I don't know you,' he would say and to see how that affected Grandma was hard. I knew how very much he loved her, that's what made it so awful.

Alzheimer's is a terrible disease because on one level, he knew there was something wrong with him but didn't know what it was. That wore him down and made him angry. For a while Grandma covered it up and tried not to let us see that he was no longer himself, but when things got worse, she couldn't conceal it any longer.

There is one story she tells that is intensely sad but, in a strange way, it has made us smile too. Grandma needed to go shopping one morning and, not prepared to leave Granddad by himself, she took him to a day-care centre. She told them where she would be shopping, just in case anything went wrong. An hour or so later, one of the nurses was at the shopping area searching frantically for Grandma.

'Oh Mrs Radcliffe, you're going to have to come back to the centre and take Mr Radcliffe home. We can't cope.'

'Why, what's happened?'

Grandma went back to the centre and heard the full story. Believing he was back in the Army, Granddad had marshalled all the elderly folk in one of the rooms there and began marching them up and down. He wouldn't allow any interference from the staff. In no time he had caused chaos in the centre, and though everyone there was sympathetic, they thought it would be better if Granddad didn't come back. I have wondered whether it is right to recall this story but know that the Granddad we all loved would laugh like a drain if he had been told it.

Sitting on the grass that cold January morning and thinking about Granddad, I vowed I would win the senior cross-country title in Budapest. It would be for him, a little tribute to how he had lived his life, and most of all to how much I loved him. After making that pact, all I wanted to do was get back to the house and get on the road to Liverpool to be with Grandma. Back in Loughborough my house-mate Justin Pugsley and Ian Grime, a good friend, were getting worried because they didn't know where I was. Mum was on the phone, checking I was all right. The lads were concerned about my driving to Liverpool, Ian even offered to drive me there, but my head was clear now and I just wanted to get to Grandma and comfort her as much as I could.

After Granddad's funeral, there were just five or six weeks before Budapest and the World Cross-Country. Because of the promise to win this title for Granddad, the race became a huge ambition. But a week or so later my foot began to hurt and after running it would stiffen. Perhaps it was because I had never had a serious injury in my life, but because it seemed to loosen up after ten minutes or so running, I never thought it necessary to stop training. By flexing it and otherwise warming it up, it was possible for me to still run and just forget about the pain. I carried on racing and won the National Cross-Country Championships, although I remember having difficulty walking the next morning.

Two weeks before Budapest, the foot broke down completely. The pain became so bad that it was no longer possible to run through it. Doctors diagnosed ligaments and handed me a pair of crutches. The powers that be in British athletics asked me to go to Hungary anyway, believing it would help team spirit. Sometimes, with the best of intentions, you agree to do the most stupid things. This was one of those times. In my hobbling and pretty demoralised state, what could I do for team spirit? Depress everybody? I desperately wanted to compete in Budapest and instead I spent my time moping around on crutches, trying to keep the tears from my eyes while supposedly cheering on everyone else.

It didn't help that Catherina McKiernan, whom I had beaten earlier in the year, ran well to finish 2nd and in doing so convinced me that I could have gone very close.

After returning and realising my foot was no better, it was time for a re-examination. They decided to put the foot in plaster and as it was ligaments, it would need to stay immobilised for three weeks. With the foot in plaster, I had to ride my bike to get around to lectures and that was all I could do to keep in some kind of shape. The plaster came off after three weeks but when I tried running the foot felt exactly the same. No improvement. Obviously it needed more rest and that's how it was all spring, waiting for this ligament injury to sort itself out.

There were times when the pain eased enough to allow me to run on grass but it always felt like I was running on one and a half legs. With the Commonwealth Games and the European Championships later that summer, I was desperate for the injury to clear. By now my training consisted of twice-daily sessions in the swimming pool and on the Nordic ski-machine, but the foot stubbornly refused to get better. Spring became summer and I was still struggling.

What was so frustrating was the sense that no one really knew what was wrong. They said it was damaged ligaments but ligaments heal in weeks, and months were passing without any sign of a recovery. Getting an unsatisfactory answer from one doctor, I would try another and between specialists and physiotherapists, I saw about twelve in all. One of the physios said he didn't think I would ever run again. That deeply upset me and afterwards I spoke to Dad.

'This can't be,' I said. 'I have to be able to run again. I can't cope if I can't run.'

'Don't be silly, Paula, millions of people go through their lives and don't run a step and it doesn't affect their lives. They go on.'

'They are not me. This has to get better, I can't carry on with my life and not be able to continue running.'

'You would get over it. There are other things you could do with your life.'

'And I'll do those too, but I want to be able to run.'

As well as loving the act of running, of feeling the wind in my face and the ground moving beneath my feet, I also wanted the chance to see how good I could be at this sport.

One moment I remember vividly from that difficult time was going to the cinema to see the film *Schindler's List*. That film hit me so hard and really put things into perspective. Sometimes we get all caught up in things that, although at the time are extremely important for us, in the big scheme of things really aren't so important. That film reminded me of all the very harrowing and traumatic times that people have fought and lived through; I really had so much in my life to be grateful for, what I was going through was not that big a deal. I felt very sad, but also both grateful and ashamed.

In July there was another round of X-rays, and finally a bone scan. It was discovered that, in fact, the problem was a stress fracture. With Dad, I went to see Simon Costain at his Harley Street surgery in London. After doing some analysis, he showed how the source of the problem was a collapsed arch. 'The actual stress fracture,' said Simon, 'won't get better until you get the arch corrected. And that won't happen without some arch support.' He made rigid orthotic supports for my arch that would be inserted into whatever shoes I wore.

Such was the acute nature of the problem that if I wanted to go to the loo in the middle of the night, I either had to tiptoe or slip on a pair of arch-supported shoes. They reckoned the arch had collapsed around January or early February, maybe when I had slightly increased my training mileage, and that as the bones rubbed against each other, they caused a fracture in my navicular, one of the big bones in the foot. It is, apparently, an injury that often occurs in ballerinas, but not often in runners.

It wasn't difficult for me to trace its origin: one morning, doing my hill repetitions, there had been a sudden dart of pain in the foot that stopped me for a few steps. That was probably the arch falling and as it then settled, I resumed running, but the problem was really only beginning. After the proper diagnosis and the making of the supports, there was a further six weeks' rest and it was 1 October before I started back running. An injury that should have taken six to eight weeks to heal had lasted nine months.

My first run back was in Düsseldorf, Germany where I was beginning a year abroad that was an obligatory part of the Modern European Studies course at Loughborough University. Having resumed running on 1 October 1994 it was well into November before things got back to normal. For a while there was stiffness and pain in the foot and for every run, there was a corresponding session in the swimming pool. Early that summer I had contacted Roger Black, as I knew he had also had a bad foot problem and I needed advice on what to try next. He had told me about the German doctor, Hans-Wilhelm Müller-Wohlfahrt, whom he believed was excellent. Dr Müller-Wohlfahrt couldn't see me until the middle of November and by that time I was living and working in Düsseldorf. From the first time I met him I could tell he was a strong, caring character.

'Your joint has healed,' he said, 'but there's a lot of fluid around it, which is the body's response to inflammation.' He then stuck a long needle into my foot and I waited for it to come out of the other side. Instead he pulled the plunger back towards himself and drew off enough fluid to saturate three cotton wool balls. Once he did that, the foot felt a lot better. 'We'll have to do that two or three more times because it will continue to build up again for a little while. But don't worry, I know someone in Düsseldorf who will work with you and you won't have to make the journey to Munich.' He then gave me a strength programme, rubber bands and other things that would help me to stretch and improve the strength in my foot. He also set me up in a football rehabilitation centre in Düsseldorf where I would do a daily two-hour session. 'After two weeks of this, I want you to come back and we'll see how things are.'

The daily sessions in the rehab centre meant juggling things round at my new job in Düsseldorf. The reason that I was spending six months in Germany was to improve my fluency in the language as part of my degree. However, because I wanted to spend the French half of the year at the French altitude training centre in the Pyrenees, I had to find my own job in Germany and use this to finance the stay in France. Whitbread, the company Dad worked for, owned a chain of steakhouses, Churrasco and Maredo, in Germany and I was able to get a job in the marketing department of the Düsseldorf offices. The job was full-time and I was committed to it, but I was also prepared to do whatever was necessary to get my foot back to 100 per cent. My boss was helpful, and for those two weeks allowed me to start at just before eight rather than nine in the morning, stay an hour longer in the evening and take off the extra two and a bit hours in the middle of the day to do the rehab programme. It was a tough schedule because to fit in my morning run, I had to be up at 6 a.m., and it was late when I got home and later still when I began my evening run.

Those runs were mostly in the dark and one day one of the German guys at the football centre laughed and wondered what caused all the scratches on my face. 'When I was running by the Rhine this morning,' I said, 'it was dark, I didn't see the branches that were hanging down in my path.'

That foot injury taught me a lot. For so much of the time, there was a lot of frustration, anger and helplessness. I had been getting physiotherapy on what we thought was damaged ligaments and weeks were lost trying to find answers without knowing where to look. The medical system for athletes in Britain was very different then from what it is now. The advent of lottery funding has enabled UK Athletics to set up a much better and more efficient structure. Back then it was much more difficult to see the specialist relevant to the injury you had. Everything took much more time than it does now. Although there were some good physiotherapists, if there wasn't one nearby then you often had to just look in the Yellow Pages. Or go by word of mouth – usually a better bet, as then at least the physio would be one used to dealing with athletes.

I learned too about my own response to injury, and how easy it is to do the wrong thing. Trying to run through the injury was a big mistake, made worse by the fact that I have a naturally high pain threshold. People see this as my being brave or tough but I genuinely don't feel it as much as someone with a lower threshold would. If a physio tells me to try a run and that a little bit of awareness of the injury was fine but when it gets to pain, I must stop, I find it very difficult. For me it's very hard to work out where awareness crosses the line into pain. It doesn't take any great courage to block out pain, but often something that I can still run reasonably with is actually making a niggle or an injury worse. Now I try to err on the side of caution, give the bigger niggles one or two days' rest and try to return to running when I feel nothing or am totally sure it is only an awareness.

A lot of the time it is a question of learning to listen to your body. Over the years I have become better at this although it is still a question of balance. The life of a distance runner training hard is full of small tightnesses and niggles. You can't stop for them all. Sometimes you feel a slight discomfort that will soon go away. Other times the tightness is an early warning of something that, if untreated, will become a real problem. Because of the intensity at which I train, injury is a constant possibility and that thought remains uppermost in my mind: could the tiny sniffle develop into bronchitis, what's causing the stiffness in my left hamstring? There are times in training when you feel invincible, but the threat of injury or illness is always lurking. It simply goes with the territory and I am sure it is the same for most athletes. For all our physical fitness, we are fragile creatures. It is a very fine line between peak fitness and going over the edge.

Warning signs do precede many injuries and the key is being able to read them. It is just one of the reasons why I have worked so closely with Gerard Hartmann over the years. As well as being an excellent physical therapist with a genuine gift in his hands, Gerard is also an expert at picking up on the little things before they become big things. He will find a soreness in my knee that even I am not aware of and he will tell me to ease back for a few days and allow more time for rest and recovery.

Nineteen ninety-four was a tough year of prolonged injury but it was also a valuable experience. Not being able to compete reminded me of how much I loved to race and after completing Dr Müller-Wohlfahrt's rehab programme and being passed 100 per cent fit by him, my enthusiasm for training and the build-up to the World Cross-Country, which in 1995 would be held on home ground in Durham, was at an all-time high. The lessons from '94 would never be forgotten. So good did I become at listening to my body that for much of 1995, I could tell the weather from the much put-upon joint in my left foot. If it became stiff, that was an indication that the humidity level had changed and rain was on the way.

One evening we were racing at Crystal Palace, it was a fine evening without a hint of rain but my foot had become stiff.

'Girls,' I said, 'it's going to rain.'

'No, no, it's not.'

'I am telling you it is.'

'How can you say that?'

'I just know because my foot has stiffened up.'

By the end of the evening it was raining cats and dogs. The girls were freaked. That joint has improved over the years and it now needs just regular manipulation, flexing and warming up to keep it totally loose. But it isn't nearly as sensitive as it once was and can no longer tell the weather.

If there is a postscript to the year that was lost to injury, it occurred right at the end of 1994, shortly before Christmas. My back was stiff and in need of treatment. I went to a chiropractor in Bedford who in his general assessment before beginning said he thought the problem could be helped by some manipulation of the left foot that had been the cause of so much heartache. At that point I was back running, the injury was fully cleared and the foot was not a part of my body that I wanted anyone messing with.

'I've been through hell with that foot and I'd rather you didn't touch it,' I said.

'Okay, we'll just work on your back,' he replied and got on with doing that. Then out of the blue he suddenly grabbed my foot and manipulated it in some way. I totally snapped, burst into tears, quickly got my stuff together, paid for the session and left.

Though it might seem irrational, he had touched a raw nerve. Even now, ten years on, it is hard for me to relax that foot and allow someone to treat it. I think it's because it took so long to get it right that I'm deeply scared of being back in that situation again. At that time all the suppressed emotions came rushing to the surface. Leaving his surgery, I was an emotional wreck. Driving round to Liz's house, I turned up at her door with tears streaming down my face. Afterwards I tried to work out what had caused such an extreme reaction.

For nine months I suppressed all negative thoughts about the injury and forced myself to be positive: 'I will get through this, there will be a time when I will get back running.' When eventually we got the injury properly diagnosed and treated, I felt unbelievable joy at being able to run again. But the fear that had been suppressed was still there, a dark force lurking that I was no longer aware of.

When that chiropractor betrayed my trust in him, it was like he let loose the demons that I had kept under lock and key. By catching my foot, he just scared the hell out of me. For the previous two months I had been consistently holding my breath about that foot, almost wanting to wrap it in cotton wool all the time. Would it stay sound? It had to. Would it allow me to have a normal career? It had to. Then a chiropractor that I hardly knew went and cracked it like it was any old joint when I wasn't expecting it.

'Seeing you at the door, I thought you had been attacked in the street,' said Liz.

'No, I just didn't realise how much I was still scared and protecting that foot.'

I couldn't believe I had reacted in such an extreme way, but maybe it was good that the emotions were finally released.

6

I remember the night more clearly than Gary. It was after one of our Tuesday evening runs in Loughborough and, as was customary, we all met up afterwards for a drink in a small pub in the centre of town. A lot of the guys were there – Mark Scruton, Justin Pugsley, Ian Grime, Mark Sesay; lads who had become friends during that first term at Loughborough. But alongside me that evening was this tall, good-looking 1,500m runner from Northern Ireland, Gary Lough. With so much noise, we could barely hear our own voices and Gary had to lean towards me and almost speak into my ear. Whatever he said has long vanished but not the memory of his voice and the tingles as he spoke to me.

The next day, I rang my best friend Liz from the payphone in halls for a chat.

'Have you met anyone?' she asked after we'd been talking for a bit.

'Well, not really . . .'

'What do you mean not really? You have?'

'Well, there's one guy that I quite like. He was in the pub tonight. He is good-looking and he's got a really sexy accent.'

A lot of things would happen, and years would pass, before Gary and I became a permanent item. It was an uneven, occasionally bumpy ride, but even through the off points, we remained very close friends and his friendship still meant a lot to me. What makes our relationship so strong now is that for such a long time before we finally committed to each other, we were close friends. What attracted me then and still does today is that we are soul-mates. Maybe this sounds a bit corny, but it's how it is. We are very different people but he accepts me for who I am and doesn't want to change me. Neither do I want to change him. We understand what makes each other tick. We sometimes get mad at each other, we argue about things, but we don't lose respect for the other person's individuality.

Many years ago something clicked between us. It's just that it took him a little bit longer than me to recognise it.

My life at Loughborough University began in October 1992, just a few weeks after my 4th place at the World Junior Championships in Seoul. Everyone in athletics thought, 'Ah, Paula Radcliffe, it's only natural she'd end up at Loughborough.' It was actually a matter of chance, attributable to the fact that on an academic level, Loughborough offered exactly the course I was looking for: the combination of both French and German languages and economics. From our earliest family holidays abroad I loved listening to and trying to speak different languages. Being able to speak another language fluently was something that appealed to me. I especially loved French – it is a beautiful language, and I really liked the way of life there too. At school I had a French exchange partner, Isabelle Melou: I spent some great times with her and her family and our families have remained in touch. Now Gary and I spend a lot of time at Font-Romeu in the Pyrenees, where the French have their high-performance training centre – it really feels like a home from home, especially with all our friends there.

When we moved from Cheshire to Bedford, we moved into a

different educational system and instead of starting secondary school, as I would have in Cheshire, I went into the middle year in middle school. Mum visited the school before they broke up for summer holidays and realised that the class I would join the following September had been doing French for two years. 'What does she need to do to catch up?' Mum asked. They gave her some text books and as Mum was qualified to teach French up to the age of 11, she knew she could help me during the summer. Towards the end of my first year in middle school, Mum asked the French teacher if I had managed to catch up with the rest of the class.

'Catch up?' said the teacher. She had totally forgotten that I had never done French before joining her class. Mum was a good teacher.

Even though languages were my first love, I didn't want to do an exclusively language-based degree. What would it lead to? Teaching? Translation? Interpreting? They weren't what I wanted to do. Loughborough was one of the few universities that allowed you to combine languages with economics and, from my point of view, that was perfect, as it opened up the world of international business, where fluency in French and German and an understanding of economics could work hand-in-hand. English and Maths were also subjects that I would have liked to have taken further and my teachers at Sharnbrook Upper School gave me a lot of encouragement but, again, I couldn't see where they would lead in terms of what I wanted to do with my life. There is a very pragmatic and logical side to my character.

Athletics was not the determining factor in my choice of university. In fact I tried not to let it influence my choice at all. I knew that wherever I went, running was going to be a central part of my life – choosing the right course and a university where I would be happy were most important. Loughborough's reputation for sport and its excellent facilities were a bonus that came with the right academic course and a friendly campus.

First term in the autumn of 1992 coincided with my end-of-season break, and that meant there was more time for socialising. Of course, the athletics club was the first thing to be sussed out and because our sport exists in such a small world, there was no difficulty catching up with old friends and making new ones. There was Mark Sesay and Matthew Hibberd, guys I already knew as we had been competing together and on the same junior teams for a while. They introduced me to a few of the other lads who ran at the university. Mark Scruton became a good friend and was someone who helped me a lot through all my time at university. A 3.38 1,500m runner, Mark took me under his wing, showed me the best runs around the campus and surrounding area and introduced me to more people.

It was an exciting time in my life because although I was well used to travelling and being away from home through my athletics, I was ready for the independence of living away. For the first year I had chosen to live in halls, as it seemed a better option for settling in, but as I explained earlier, that didn't really work out for me. As well as being a small and cramped room, it was located in a dormitory that was home to a lot of first-year students whose idea of fun was often an indoor cricket match right outside my door at 3 a.m. I enjoyed having fun as much as the next person, but also needed my sleep in order to keep my training level up. However, my biggest problem were the fixed mealtimes which just didn't work with my training lifestyle.

It wasn't that bad, though – I did have a lot of fun and met some good friends there. Friends like Alison Rayner, who was also on my course, and one of my future housemates, Justin Pugsley. First week of the term was freshers' week and there was a get-to-know-each-other social evening in our hall. Music was blaring and I was quite happily mingling quietly when suddenly out of nowhere this tall, gangly bloke with a massive sombrero was dancing crazily and pulling me out in front of everyone. 'Come on!' he said. 'Everyone, this is Paula Radcliffe, she's a world champion runner!' I was so embarrassed and wished the floor would just open up and swallow me. On first impressions I thought Justin was totally crazy and silently cursed him for making me stand out in front of everyone, but we became really good friends. He always manages to make me laugh and is always there for me.

Justin is an extremely naturally talented runner, the kind of guy who might not have run for six months but who can then go out for a hard run and stay with or even drop everyone – infuriating! Over the years I did a lot of running with him and one of his favourite things was what he called 'the fresher's burn-off': this was supposed to be an introductory run for new students – Justin turned up in his racing flats and ran as hard as he could! Justin won the National Cross-Country and made the World Cross-Country team but, deep down, his heart wasn't in it.

Drama is more his passion and he is very good at acting. He now teaches at one of the Oxford cathedral schools and he is still a good friend. Back in those days at Loughborough, even when he was just messing around, he could really run. On one of our first evenings down at the club, when the session was a six-and-a-half-mile loop, he told me of the rule that you had to stop at traffic lights, make sure the road was clear and then cross. We got to the first set of lights, with him just behind me. I stopped and he shot straight past me. 'You don't actually stop!' he shouted back. 'You lose twenty seconds doing that.' That was Justin.

Mark Scruton also became a close friend and I am godmother to his daughter, Emily. On one of our first runs together he took me on a tough, hilly run. One of the hills was very steep and had a bench near the top. As I struggled up the hill, he surged to the top and then sat on the bench waiting for me! That drove me mad and I vowed to do it back to him one day – it took me three years and a trip to altitude to manage it. Mark is a great friend. Later on in my time at Loughborough, when I preparing for the Atlanta Olympics and my final exams, I used to have to get up at 6 a.m. to do my hill repetitions in the park as I had lectures all day and it would be dark when they finished. Mark would come with me. We would warm up in the dark and just as dawn was breaking, we would begin the session. He didn't need to be up at that hour and wouldn't have been apart from the fact that he wanted to help me. It was Mark who introduced me to Gary.

Gary had been on a running scholarship in Iowa, in the States, where he had met the British distance runner Jon Brown, and trained with him quite a bit. Jon spoke to him about his coach George Gandy, head of athletics at Loughborough. Shortly before Gary was due to go back to Iowa State University and begin his second year, he contacted George and asked if he would be prepared to take him on. George agreed and Gary decided, almost overnight, that he was moving to Loughborough. It was too late for him to switch courses, so he had to wait a year before continuing his Sports Science degree at Loughborough. This is how we came to meet in the pub that night, though neither of us knew then that it would lead to so much.

Such was my zest for life at university that I was busy taking everything in. Once settled in a routine, there were lectures and study each day, training sessions and plenty of socialising to fit in. Plus once I decided halls weren't for me there was the search for a new place to stay. Most of my Loughborough friends were male – maybe because I already had so many close girl friends at Bedford and also because at Loughborough I trained and hung out with the guys all the time. They accepted me and didn't judge the way I trained. When training, I like to run at the pace that suits me. If someone wants to go faster, that doesn't bother me, I'll hang on as long as I can but I don't expect them to wait for me. Equally, if someone wants to go slower: sorry, but I'm not waiting. It doesn't matter if it's one of the guys or a girl friend, there is no way I will alter my training to facilitate someone else. At Loughborough I ended up running and hanging around with the guys and there was maybe a little bit of jealousy from a few of the girls because they were a good-looking group of lads. They adopted me, almost as their sister, and looked out for me — someone would always walk me home from the pub or make sure to keep me company on long runs in mid-winter.

Not every guy was so chivalrous, though. One evening most people were doing the six-and-a-half-mile loop when I decided to do the nine-and-a-half-mile run for the first time. We came to the point where the two loops separated. 'See that fellow up there,' one of the lads said, 'he's on your route. Just shout and he'll hang on.' Pete Davies ran for Leicester and although he wasn't at the university, he came to Loughborough to train. I shouted to him, but he pretended not to hear and carried on. Though running hard, I couldn't quickly close the gap. He went around a corner and by the time I got round the same corner he was out of sight. Then, of course, I got lost. Afterwards Pete was unrepentant.

'Did you not hear me shouting?'

'Yeah, but I wasn't waiting for you.'

'Why not?'

'No way was I waiting so a girl could beat me!'

I recognised the mentality. He wouldn't wait because he knew if he did, there was a possibility I would drop him on the way in. Who wants to be beaten by a girl? The 100m gap was his advantage and he wasn't giving it up.

Another time when Liz was up staying with me, she ended up stranded in no-man's-land on the Tuesday night run. She was too fast for the girls' group and not quite able to stay in touch with the guys — Mark and I ended up out looking for her all over Loughborough.

Before going to university there had been a few boyfriends but no one that could have been described as serious. I didn't see myself as very attractive, Liz claimed men were intimidated by me and, anyway, there wasn't much time for looking. Running, study, friends and family were four balls that had to be juggled at the same time and it felt like a full-time job to keep them all airborne. If a boyfriend came along and tried or threatened to upset the balance, I would have quickly made my choice. At Loughborough, my life was still hectic, but maybe I was more prepared to make the time. Or maybe I just sensed that Gary was just the right guy for me.

From seeing each other around, we became friends. We hung around with the same people. Mark Scruton told me Gary liked me, but nothing happened. With so much going on in my life, finding a boyfriend wasn't high on the list of priorities. No sooner had my training begun in Loughborough than the cross-country season started and I was building up towards the World Cross-Country in Spain. I was settling into university life, enjoying my course and new friends and also running well and preparing for my races seriously. Not that there wasn't an attraction between us – there definitely was – but after our little conversation in the pub early on, nothing developed until the night before we broke up for Christmas.

A gang of us ended up in a nightclub. Gary and I chatted for quite a bit and towards the end of the night he kissed me. The next day we were all going home and with the cross-country season now in full swing, we left it at that.

GARY LOUGH:

'That time in the nightclub, I was talking to Mark Scruton about Paula. There were two rooms in the nightclub, we were sitting on the edge of a stage and I was telling him she intrigued me. I couldn't put my finger on why. She had come to the college with a bit of a name for what she had done in athletics but she was totally without ego. I'd seen her in the Olympic trials much earlier in the year when she ran like a demented chicken but only just missed out on going to Barcelona. For a junior to do that, I thought, was something. Everyone knew she could have gone to any university in Britain. She was shy back then, very quietly spoken, and I couldn't make out how someone could be as successful as she was but never act like they were successful. Was I reacting as an athletics fan or as a guy who thought this could lead to something? I don't know. Later that night we were sitting around in one of these alcoves, talking for a while, and I kissed her. The next day was her birthday. I wrote

her a note, which I think she's still got, and left it on the windscreen of her car. It was written on the back of my bank statement. If I was trying to impress her I would not have left a message on the back of my bank statement.'

When first-year exams ended, my time freed up a little. By now I had moved out of halls and rented a small house that didn't have any heating. That didn't seem much of a problem in summer, and it gave me a base in Loughborough and allowed me to spend time there during the summer holidays. One evening that summer a group of us went to watch an athletics meeting at the track in Loughborough. There was Mark Scruton, Matt Hibberd and his girlfriend Claire Peet, who was a friend of mine from Bedford. Called the Reebok Challenge, this was an important meeting as pacemakers were organised in many of the races and athletes had the chance to run fast times. Gary was in the 1,500m and as it was his last race before the World Student Games in Buffalo, New York, it was important. Somehow he misunderstood the starting time and turned up late. We had to quickly tell him when the race was and he had to hurriedly put on his spikes and rush off to the start. He was stressed and ran badly. That evening he was upset about the way he had run. I tried to console him, we got talking and we just kind of ended up together. My feeling was, 'Yes, this could work now'. We had both been busy doing our own thing but now we had more time to spend with each other.

That summer I fell in love with Gary. This was, I decided, a relationship that was worth the effort. He went to the World Student Games in Buffalo where he got a bronze medal, I went to the IAAF World Championships in Stuttgart and we continued to meet up when we could and to speak on the phone. By now I would have said we were boyfriend/girlfriend.

At the beginning of my second year Justin Pugsley and a long-jumper called Gareth moved into the house I had rented towards the end of the previous academic year. It was a modest abode and freezing in the winter but it gave me my freedom and a happy base. I got on very well with Justin and Gareth also, even if they did always leave the washing-up to me! Mark Sesay and Ian Grime were just around the corner in another house, Mark Scruton was a hundred yards down the road and Gary was about a mile away.

As a little community within the student population at Loughborough, we had a lot of fun. There were the usual student nights out. One particular night after a Loughborough match Matt Hibberd was staying over and we were in the house when Justin came back from the union with Ian Grime and another guy. It was late and Justin put on the stereo full blast.

'Justin,' I said, 'you've got to turn that down. It's going to wake the neighbours.'

He pushed me away, knocking me over, and turned the volume up even more. I enjoy having a drink and a laugh as much as anyone, but somehow I always know what I'm doing and I never lose my consideration for other people. Unfortunately that usually makes me the boring sensible person looking out for everyone else. Our house was a small terraced house but it had three floors; my bedroom was on the second floor, Justin and Gareth were in the attic, and with the music blaring, I knew the neighbours would be complaining any minute. Justin and Ian then decided they were going to have a race around the block in their boxer shorts. As soon as they went outside the back door, I locked it and turned the music down.

They didn't believe I would hold out for long, so when they got back and found the door locked, they dropped their shorts and thought it would be really funny when I opened. Except that I didn't open the door. Woken by the commotion, one of the neighbours looked out of a window and saw the guys there with their pants around their ankles. The lads then decided they would run around to the front door. Matt and I watched from a window, laughing. However, as we saw them take off around the corner, Matt noticed a police car turn down our road. Joke over, I had the door open quick as lightning and the lads were safely back inside.

My relationship with Gary continued through my second year at Loughborough. Things had developed during the previous summer holidays. Though I was mostly staying at home in Bedford, I went up to see him for his birthday and we found other reasons to get together. After sharing some nice times during the summer break I was keen to develop our relationship, but wasn't sure whether he felt the same. He isn't the best at telling people how he feels about things and working it out wasn't easy. On the other hand, there were no doubts about our friendship. We got on well, were comfortable in each other's company, and after a first year at university when I didn't feel there was time for a relationship, I now wanted to put some time into this. Lots of evenings, maybe four or five times a week, I would walk round to Gary's house and we would spend an hour or two chatting together. With a seven o'clock morning run, it never went on too late, but they were evenings I enjoyed. Gary's housemate was rarely around, while Justin and Gareth were pretty much always at our house, so it was better for me to go round to his place.

That Christmas, 1993, we went to the Athletics Club Christmas dinner as a couple. His memory of this night is not that sharp, but he got drunk and spent the evening talking to anyone and everyone. It is what he does when he has a few drinks; his natural shyness disappears and he bobs around the room, having fun with everyone. Being young, naïve and a little insecure, I was upset because it felt like he was ignoring me and didn't have any time for me. Nowadays, I know that's Gary: wanting to have a word with this person and that person and then ending up in conversations that go on and on. Justin, Mark Scruton and some of the other lads could see that I was upset and were annoyed with Gary because they were always looking out for me. They knew how I felt about Gary and thought he should treat me better. However, he hadn't really meant to leave me on my own.

GARY:

'I was so immature back then. Not so much playing to the crowd as trying to be the "cool" guy but actually being the opposite. There's lots of stuff I did back then that if she'd been different, if she hadn't been the person she is, she would have thought, "What the hell is he about? Forget him, move on. He's not worth bothering about." Thank God she didn't.'

After the disaster of the Athletics dinner, Gary and I went home for Christmas and sort of went our separate ways. There was a real coolness between us: I was angry with him for the way he had deserted me at the dinner and wanted to let him know. But it wasn't a total end to all communication because that Christmas he had a hernia operation and I phoned to make sure he was okay. Then he came to watch me run at the Mallusk cross-country race in Northern Ireland over the holiday period. At first we recommenced our relationship purely as friends but over the spring term, we drifted back to where we were. I still liked him and he liked me.

But it was far from the perfect relationship. Gary wasn't as committed to it as I was and that became clear at the end of my second year at Loughborough. As part of my course, as I have mentioned, I was set to spend a year in Germany and France, improving my fluency in both languages. I had the job in Düsseldorf through one of Dad's business contacts, and Ian Stewart from UK Athletics said he would be able get me something at Font-Romeu. The year 'away' came in my third year, and although it would mean Gary and I would not be able to see that much of each other, at that stage that wasn't going to stand in the way of what I wanted to do. My feeling was that if we were prepared to make the effort, it shouldn't be a problem.

Before leaving for Germany, Mark Scruton came to Bedford to say goodbye. Gary was meant to come but didn't show. Mark and I went canoeing, messed around and had a good time. But it upset me that Gary wasn't bothered enough to come down. It turned out he had tonsillitis and was in bed, but he didn't pick up the phone and it seemed he just wasn't interested. Mark could see that it hurt me and made me angry, but my attitude was, 'Okay, that's the end of it, it's just not worth it, forget him.'

GARY:
'One night, around this time, I had a few drinks and ended up with someone else. Then I couldn't face seeing Paula and couldn't even face ringing her, even though she was going away. I did get tonsillitis but that was an excuse. I just wanted to disappear, not have to face this.'

I went off to Germany and moved into a little flat in Düsseldorf while working in the marketing department of the steakhouse chain. I was unhappy about the way things had ended with Gary, and down after missing the entire athletics season through that mis-diagnosed injury. But I was also excited about spending the year away and was determined to have a good time. I settled in and made new friends there and my parents, Grandma and Alex came to visit at different times. After about two weeks in Germany, the phone rang in the middle of the night. Three o'clock in the morning – my first thought was something terrible must have happened at home. It was Mark. He had been out late and was wide awake.

'Paula, it's about Gary. He got this new girlfriend. I just think you should know.'

A little bit drunk, Mark didn't think about how this would affect me. On my own in a strange country, this wasn't the best news: my supposed boyfriend, with whom I had not officially broken up, had a new girlfriend. After the conversation with Mark, I looked at the clock and thought: 'Only three hours to go before work, no point in going back to sleep.' Perhaps this was because the news from Mark made it unlikely there would be any sleep. Angry, I wrote a letter to Gary expressing my disappointment. He says he still has it somewhere. What really got to him about the letter was its reasonableness — he wouldn't have felt so bad if I had really let fly. The next night, again at three in the morning, the phone rang once more. It was Mark, calling to say how sorry he was about the previous night. He had since thought about it and realised that what he said had probably upset me and he was concerned to see if I was all right.

Mark was a friend to both Gary and me, and his conscience had forced him to tell me Gary was seeing another girl. He would have known for a while, and would have wondered whether to tell me or not, only deciding that he should when his inhibitions had been lowered by alcohol. Not long after that, Mark called a third time, but this time at a respectable hour. Gary was in the house with him and he wanted us to talk. We did speak and although it was a civil conversation, it was one that formally ended a relationship that had already died. 'Let's forget it and move on,' I said. 'We can still remain friends, but let's leave it at that.' He agreed, and even though it wasn't really what I wanted, there wasn't much pain. It wasn't like I had much choice; he was already going out with someone else and, anyway, I had a lot of other things in my life to be getting on with. But during my time in Germany and later in France, we did always continue to speak on the telephone and we actually began writing to each other regularly. The friendship that had always been the basis of our relationship remained intact.

What was typical of Gary was that he didn't tell me he had previously been in a five-year relationship and had tried to keep things going while he was away at Iowa State University. From that experience he didn't think long-distance relationships could work, and didn't want to try to keep it going while I was on my year away. So, with his new girlfriend, he and I went back to being friends. There was only one difficult moment. In the short interval between my time in Düsseldorf and then at Font-Romeu in the Pyrenees, I went back to England and while there had to do some filming for a television programme. We decided to do it in Bradgate Park just outside

Loughborough, where I had done so much training, and as we were due to begin early in the morning, I called Gary and asked if he would mind putting me up the night before. 'Fine,' he said, 'not a problem.'

His girlfriend at the time was a student based at a London college. She happened to be with Gary in Loughborough the night I went up. In Gary's mind, there was no issue: there was a spare room in the house, I was his friend, and of course I could stay. So I came up the night before and the three of us had dinner. Gary and I hadn't seen each other for months and it's possible that in catching up with each other's lives, she began to feel a bit left out. It would have been accidental, and I had no idea that she was in any way upset, but she just got up and left the house.

Without knowing what had happened and expecting she would soon return, I went off to bed oblivious to the fact that she didn't in fact come back and had stormed off in a bad mood. Next morning Gary and I went for a run. He didn't mention his girlfriend hadn't come back. After the run, I had a shower and left for my rendezvous with the TV crew. That evening at the athletics club, all the guys were there and we were chatting when one of them quietly told me Gary's girlfriend was very upset about the fact that I had stayed the night at his house.

'Why? Nothing happened,' I said. 'I was asleep in the spare room. Did she not come back?'

'No, she didn't, and she's convinced something went on between you and Gary.'

I have often wondered if she saw something that wasn't apparent to Gary or me: chemistry between us that had been there so long we didn't notice it any more. But that's the only time there was ever any awkwardness during our days of friendship. And we were just friends that night. I didn't resent the fact he had a girlfriend, and while I might still have fancied him, my moral standards and our friendship were too important for me to have thought about saying or doing anything that would cause problems. I was actually hurt that she would think I would do that. From what Gary later said, it appeared his girlfriend felt threatened by my presence and sensed there was something going on between us all the time. There wasn't. It was ironic that she felt this because Gary was actually my boyfriend, or was supposed to be, at the time she started seeing him.

After the year spent in Germany and later in France, I returned to begin my final year at Loughborough. It was a big year because my final exams would take place two months before the 1996 Olympics in Atlanta, Georgia. The aim was still a first-class honours degree and I was also determined to make the Great Britain team for Atlanta — so, after the ending of my relationship with Gary, having so much on my plate was no bad thing. I still had feelings for him but was determined to let time take care of things. Friendship was better than nothing. Gary was very good about it because he knew I would have liked more, but he never made it awkward for us to continue as friends. For me, there might have been a slight ache, but it was never painful. By remaining friends, I may have made it harder to get over the loss of our relationship, but I didn't want to lose such a good friend as well.

Such was my closeness to Gary that on the day my final results were due, he was the person I asked to collect mine for me. I was training for Atlanta in Font-Romeu at the time. He got the results in the early afternoon when he knew I would be having my nap and, typical of Gary, he decided not to call until he knew I would be up. Instead he called home but only got the answering machine and left a message for Mum and Dad with my results. Martin got home before my parents; he picked up the message and rang me immediately to offer his congratulations.

'Well done,' he said, 'that's brilliant, just brilliant!'

'What's brilliant?' I asked.

'Your results, Gary rang with your results, left a message. Well done, well done!'

'He hasn't rung me yet. How did I do?'

'First-class honours! You got a first.'

'Gary didn't call because he knew I'd be asleep.'

'Oh, no! Look, Paula, don't tell him I called. Act surprised when you speak to him. Pretend you don't know a thing.'

After getting my results I did a brilliant hill session and Alex, Rosemary and I celebrated together in Font-Romeu.

Later that year I bought a house in Loughborough. It was always the plan to try full-time athletics after my finals and see how far I could get. I needed a base where I would be happy and where training would be good. Loughborough had good training facilities, it was not too far from Alex, and was a town I had grown to like. And there were many people there who were now good friends – not least Gary. It so happened that at this time he was looking for a place to stay. 'Why don't you ask Gary to be your lodger?' Mark suggested. It suited him and in September 1996 he moved in.

Yes, I had spent a lot of time carrying a candle for him, running after him, hoping we might get back together, but in the early part of 1996, I had truly given up on it. This is why I felt able to share a house with him. Proof of this was my readiness to get involved in other relationships.

After Atlanta, I entered into another serious relationship and was very happy juggling that and my training for a while. Curtis was also an athlete, we'd known each other for a while and as well as being attracted to each other we got on well. That year, after spending Christmas Day at home with my family, I went to Liverpool and spent the New Year with him. At the time he was finishing his medical training at Sheffield and there were lots of trips to and from there. He was a good guy and I cared a lot about him, and at one point I was probably falling in love with him, but at the same time there was a nagging doubt in the back of my mind. We were both pretty determined about our careers. He also had his medical career and we were both in need of a lot of support. The truth is we probably both needed someone to support us.

I didn't see myself as a little homemaker, putting my career on the back-burner to be able to provide the kind of back-up that a young doctor and top-class athlete needed. Neither did he see himself in a position to compromise what he was doing to make things easier for me to get where I wanted to go.

I don't think my friendship with Gary or the fact that he was my lodger affected the relationship with Curtis. I once asked Curtis if it bothered him. 'Should it?' he asked. I replied that there was no reason for it to be a problem, even though Gary had since split up with his girlfriend. Gary and I were just friends, he had nothing to worry about. It was the truth, and he was happy with that. People wondered if my new relationship made Gary think he was losing me. Maybe it did, but that didn't bother me: I had genuinely moved on and would not have wasted time and effort on going to those lengths to try to make Gary jealous. Nor would I have used someone in that way. As far as I was concerned that was in the past – Gary and I had given it a shot, it had not worked out, and after allowing for a certain amount of time for emotional healing, I had moved on. We still liked each other and it pleased me that we were able to remain friends. Generally this was a good time for me as, with my final examinations completed, I was now free to devote myself full-time to athletics.

Being full-time brought new things to consider. A winter training camp became a possibility and Gary told me about Albuquerque in New Mexico. He had gone there with Loughborough's athletics coach George Gandy and a group from the university. They had liked it there. In my first winter as a fully professional athlete Albuquerque became home for four and a half weeks soon after the turn of the year. Alex and Rosemary Stanton came with me, and so did Gary.

He was in the throes of rehabilitation following knee surgery. After finishing 9th in the final of the 1,500m at the 1995 World Championships, injury caused him to miss the Atlanta Olympics and required an operation towards the end of 1996. Albuquerque offered him the chance to get back into shape, and although he had to spend a lot of time cross-training on the Nordic ski machine, we would run together in the mornings.

We arrived back in England two weeks before the World Cross-Country Championships in Turin, and I felt in good shape. Though I was beaten, it was easily my best performance in this event so far, and it convinced me that one day I would win it. I was actually leading with about 50 metres to go and thought I was going to win. It was there I learned never to think you have a race won until you've crossed that line.

That evening I sensed my relationship with Curtis was destined not to last. We had been going out since the previous October and after getting the silver medal in Turin it was natural for me to call with the good news. He was very pleased for me but in his voice I could pick up on the frustration he felt about an injury he was struggling with at the time. Half-jokingly, he said, 'Just what I need, you phoning me telling me you've done well when I can't even train properly.' He didn't mean it the way it sounded but, not surprisingly in the circumstances, there was a lack of real excitement in his voice. That kind of upset me.

Of course, when I later phoned Gary he was so pleased for me and understood how much it meant to me. He too had suffered enormously through injury but his joy at my performance was unqualified. I thought it just wasn't right – my boyfriend should be just as happy for me, if not more so, than my friends.

GARY:

'After breaking up at Loughborough in December 1996, I was getting prepared to go home to my parents in Northern Ireland for the holidays. Coming in from what was probably my last training session before going home, I got a phone call to say that Tony McKnight had died. Tony had coached me for six years, from when I was 15, and we had remained good friends. Occasionally we would meet up during the year and we would almost always meet on Boxing Day because there was a race near where I lived that he would

come to. *Two days before the fateful phone call, he had written to say he would see me at the race. Now he would not be there. He suffered from angina and had died suddenly. It was snowing outside and I just sat there, devastated. Then I found a note downstairs from Paula. It said 'Gone to see the doctor'. That was her light-hearted way of referring to her boyfriend. Typical, I thought, the one person that I would have turned to in this moment was off with someone else. I felt unbelievably alone. And I realised that you don't appreciate what you have until you are without it. I had been complacent, even blasé about someone who was really important to me. I was so busy searching for what I thought I wanted that I couldn't see that what I really wanted was right there in front of me. That evening, the evening I learned about Tony's passing, things started to change in my mind.'*

7

After the nightmare of being unable to finish the marathon at the Athens Olympics in 2004, a few people suggested I had given up too easily – that I had stopped simply because I was out of the medals. On top of the enormous pain of losing out on my biggest dream, this hurt me so much. Only I can ever know how I really felt in that race. I knew that I had been in trouble since about 6 miles, and by the time I got to 22 miles I just was running on empty – I could not push my body any further. Imagine a car with no petrol: no matter how good the engine or how hard you press the accelerator, it cannot keep running.

In the end, though it really hurts for people to think me a quitter, what really matters is that I know I'm not. Giving up easily is not my way, and it never has been. At times in my running career the problem has been the reverse. In training and racing I push myself hard; pain is a friend to welcome and push through to get the results I want. You keep going using any number of techniques to override the voices that tell you to slow down, visualising the aim and blocking the negative thoughts and pain. In races this is good; in training it needs to be tempered. Sometimes it's good to push hard in training, other times you need to heed the voice telling you your body needs a break. This is where I sometimes need Alex or Gary to tell me it's the right thing to back off. Sometimes I just know and I'll say, 'No, that's enough for today' or maybe, 'I'm taking a rest day.' Other times the other voice dominates: 'You're getting lazy', or 'You'll never get where you want to be if you back off just because you're a bit tired.' A couple of times I've had a little cold but still gone for a punishing training run and the next morning I've woken up with bronchitis. Why was I so stupid? I've felt leaden-legged and lacking in energy but didn't back off. Then, two days later, I've contracted a virus. Been there, paid the price — but most importantly, for the most part I've learned from the experiences. Eventually the illness is gone, strength returns and part of me forgets what it was that brought it on. I'm feeling good again and the sense of invincibility returns. That's why I have to remind myself and listen to people around me. I know with my asthma that I have to be very careful that colds don't develop into bronchitis. I take my pulse every morning — any more than 5 or 6 beats up and I pull back on the training or take a day or two off. I do sometimes need the reassurance of Alex or Gary, though, because the nature of the top athlete is to ask the guilty question, 'Am I just being lazy?' — especially if you are feeling a bit down and your confidence is low. On the other hand, if I backed off every time I felt tired, I'd never have achieved all that I have. What I need is to get the right balance. Sounds simple, but unfortunately it isn't always so. Like the blue line on the marathon road — it's a very thin line.

What I've never been able to do is accept second best or walk away from a challenge. I recall the 1995 World Cross-Country Championships at Durham. Because 1994 was virtually wiped out by injury and these championships were being held in England, they were hugely important for me. After winning the World Junior Cross-Country title in 1992, the senior version was the next logical target and I believed that winning it was well within my capabilities. There were another two reasons for wanting to do well in Durham:

the promise I had made for my granddad, and the fact it was on home soil. My aim had been to win the title six weeks after his death in early 1994 and dedicate the victory to his memory. Injury had denied me that opportunity. A year later it was in Durham, and I went there with a lot of passion, hope and belief. I had really missed racing the previous year and was loving being back, my form was steadily improving, the home crowd would give me lots of support and it was a course I knew well.

Athletes play mind games to ensure they take a positive mindset into a race. You block out the negatives and concentrate on the positives. In this case, I ignored the fact that injury had kept me out of action for nine months of the previous year. Forgot too that while in Germany in the months immediately before the race I had a 9-to-5.30 job and training was crammed in before and after work with the only rest being seven or eight hours of sleep each night. These thoughts weren't entering into the equation. Instead, three weeks at home in Bedford before the race, training well twice a day, resting properly, getting regular massages, eating Mum's food and all doubt was obliterated. I went to Durham to run the race of my life and do my best to win the world title. The crowd was fantastic and it really propelled me right from the start – maybe just pushing me on a little faster than I had the fitness to sustain. I really forced out everything up the final hill figuring I could definitely keep going as it was all downhill to the finish. At that point, with just 800 metres to go, I was in 3rd place. Yet in pushing to stay with the leaders and then forcing myself when my whole body screamed 'Slow down, slow down', I had taken too much out, and pushed too far.

Right there, at the top of the hill, the world began to swirl, stars appeared and then disappeared. Running downhill felt like running uphill, people went past me and I could do absolutely nothing about it. My body cried for me to stop and the overwhelming feeling was of utter helplessness. That finishing straight went on forever – 3rd place at the top of the hill became 19th place less than 3 minutes later. I had tunnel vision down the straight and lost control of bodily functions. I had used my last reserves; there was nothing I could do. But the finish line was near and I fought to make it. As I finished I collapsed, but I seemed to recover reasonably well afterwards – at least until I got back to the halls of residence at Durham University, where we were staying.

We had an hour or so to get ready for the post-race meeting, which would be followed by a banquet. We went to our different rooms, agreeing to meet downstairs before heading out. Some time later there was a loud banging on my door and the commotion woke me.

'Paula,' said a voice, 'are you not ready?'

I found that I was lying on the bathroom floor, still in my running gear. After getting to the room, I had gone to take a shower but must have lost consciousness somewhere along the line. Luckily I didn't hit my head on anything on the way down. The race had depleted my blood sugar to the point where I was hypoglycaemic. It wasn't the first time this had happened and, once I realised what was going on, it didn't alarm me. I knew I would have a bad migraine for the rest of the evening, but that would be it.

'Sorry,' I said, getting off the floor, 'almost ready. I'll be with you in ten minutes.'

This chronic depletion of my blood sugar had not happened for a while, though, and the annoying part was that I thought I was growing out of it. Not long afterwards it happened again – and this time it coincided with my first visit to Font-Romeu and my first experience of altitude training.

The three months spent in Düsseldorf had taken care of the German part of my academic year away from Loughborough. That left another five months to be spent in France. I chose Font-Romeu in the Pyrenees because Alex and I really wanted to try out altitude training and see whether it worked for me. In preparation for the 1968

Mexico Olympics the French had established a high-altitude performance training centre 1,800 metres above sea level near the Spanish border. Alongside the 'Lycée', or secondary school for the area, there is a fully equipped training centre, accommodation, a running track, excellent trails and good medical and physiotherapy facilities for those wishing to prepare at altitude. Ian Stewart, at the time part of the British Athletics Federation, had suggested it would be a good place for me to try. He used to go and train there with David Bedford. I turned up thinking Ian had spoken to the people there about my stay, and was under the impression that I could help in some way to ensure I would be practising and improving my French as well as my running. I'd misunderstood; they knew nothing of my arrival and hadn't heard of Ian. Luckily they had an available room and they let me help out in the office doing some jobs that needed fluency in English. They also allowed me to attend French classes that would have been the equivalent of a French person sitting in on an English A-level class.

The class was two or three days each week and it helped me to progress in the language. Most people at the training centre spoke French, so I was doing that anyway, but it was also interesting to sit in on the classes without the pressure of exams at the end of it. For me, though, the most valuable part of Font-Romeu was the opportunity to see world-class athletes go about their business. At that time the Moroccan distance runner Khalid Skah was there, along with Vincent Rousseau − a 2 hour 7 minute marathon runner − as was the Romanian Gabriela Szabo, who was quickly establishing herself as one of the stars on the women's circuit. There were other good Moroccans and Europeans there and also many of France's best athletes. What struck me was the intensity of their preparation: they trained hard in the morning and then rested in the afternoon in order to be able to run better in the evening. They were pushing themselves but were also very committed to the recovery process. It was a full-time job in every sense. Within a few days, it was obvious to me that to get where I wanted, this was what I needed to do.

I quickly fell in love with the town and the beauty of the area. I also soon learned that training at altitude was much harder, and also much more effective.

That fact dawned on me early one morning on a training run with the British runner Paul Evans. The first forty minutes were uphill and hard; after that it levelled out, and my plan was to run for an hour and a half. Paul was going a bit further. I had left without having eaten a proper breakfast, something I often did at home. However, things began to go wrong for me at the top of the climb. My vision blurred and then parts of it disappeared, symptoms that I'd encountered before. 'Sorry Paul, you're going to have to go on alone, I've got to head back.' Even that was a tricky process as my vision became so impaired I almost collided with a guy coming the other way. He was wearing a fluorescent pink vest.

It would have been very scary except that the sensations were familiar to me and experience had taught me what needed to be done. Back at the centre, I went straight to the vending machine, got myself a couple of bars of chocolate and quickly devoured them. My blood sugar was too low and my body needed energy, fast. Upstairs I collapsed on the bed and went out like a light. I woke an hour or so later with a bad migraine and ready for a big lunch, but was otherwise okay. The run was at the end of a hard week and at altitude you need more energy for the same level of activity. Running with Paul I had quickly used all the carbohydrate energy reserves I had left, and this is when the hypoglycaemia occurred. After that I never ran more than an hour at altitude before breakfast. Running before breakfast can sometimes help, though, as it teaches the body to burn fat stores and cope when energy is low.

I was fourteen when the black-outs started happening, and the first couple of times it was worrying. One evening after a training run in

Bedford, I passed out walking up the stairs at the clubhouse. Mum took me to Dr Brookes, our local GP, who was also involved in sports medicine and he quickly picked up on the low blood sugar and suggested taking energy tablets during training. Before running, I would put energy tablets under my watchstrap and take one every twenty minutes during a training run. At races Mum or Alex kept a pack handy and as soon at it ended, Mum would have a sugary drink and a Mars bar waiting for me. The doctor seemed to think my body was having difficulty regulating the glucose levels during exercise, but believed I would grow out of it. Running hard would set it off, especially if it was very cold weather and I had to wait a little while before eating a meal after training. Dad has a lot to answer for here. He loves his Sunday visits to the DIY store, often stopping on our way home from training. He would always say I'm only going in for five minutes but it was always longer. Often I'd feel the blurry vision thing coming on and have to hassle him to hurry up!

At around the same time as the blood sugar problem was discovered, I was also found to be exercise-induced asthmatic. This became a problem after we moved from Cheshire to Bedford where the proliferation of oilseed rape in Bedfordshire brought my asthma problems to the surface. It caused a tightness of breath and wheezing. Dr Brookes put me on a preventative (Flixotide) inhaler morning and night, and I also use a blue reliever (Ventolin) inhaler as and when necessary, as this has an immediate anti-inflammatory effect.

My doctor was very reassuring about the black-outs and the asthma. 'Neither need be a problem,' he said. 'For the asthma, you just need to monitor and control it. You will be able to run as fast as you would if you'd never had this condition.' What was good about the way he explained it all was the fact that he didn't make me feel there was something wrong with me, or that my asthma would be a disadvantage to my running. So in my mind, it never has been. That is one of the reasons I'm glad to be a patron for Asthma UK. It's important that youngsters diagnosed with asthma learn that it is something that you can control, and not let it control you by stopping you doing what you want to do. Asthma does not stop you from doing sports, in fact sport can help, by making the lungs stronger.

Along the way I discovered the things that trigger my asthma. In my case it was increased pollution in the air and exercising in severe cold – especially cold, foggy weather that stops the pollution escaping upwards. And, of course, pollen and allergens were also triggers. During pollen season I also use a nasal spray. Since then I have been able to control the asthma and have not let it affect what I want to do. I carry around a peak-flow monitor so that I can keep an eye on my levels and change the preventative dose accordingly. Through being careful, I don't often get attacks. There is no way of eliminating the danger completely, as was proven on the occasion of one of my worst attacks. It happened in a cinema in Loughborough, and as my asthma is usually exercise-induced I didn't have my inhaler with me. There was a group of us and when the attack came, it was a little frightening. What an asthma attack does is give you the sense of not being able to breathe out, so you inhale frantically and it is easy to be panicked by the experience. What you have to do is calm yourself and consciously try to exhale. You try to relax and slowly take yourself through the crisis. Being fit helps because you're more aware of your body and your lungs are stronger.

That evening in the cinema I was able to calm myself down, enough for me to be able to get home. Proof that it wasn't so bad is that I can't remember if someone ran to my house for the inhaler or if I was well enough to get there on my own. I have always thought I'm lucky in that mine is a mild form of asthma, because if it were very serious it surely wouldn't be possible to calm my breathing down a little during an attack. Usually an attack is brought on by hard exercise but once I decrease the exercise, the attack can quickly be brought under control. I also have to be careful always to warm up before starting running properly, especially in trigger situations. Probably the reason why the attack in the cinema scared me was because there was no hint of it coming; it wasn't the climatic conditions, nor was it exercise-induced.

During an attack, my lungs drop 12–20 per cent of their normal capacity. Due to my training my lungs are strong and have a big capacity. If you were only walking around, you would hardly notice that drop. Without using the inhaler, I could still get in enough air to survive, but not to perform at the peak of my ability. So without the inhaler, I would not be able to compete on an equal basis with my fellow athletes.

Looking back through a sporting career, it is natural to remember the big races and the bad injuries, the fourth place that you so desperately wanted to be a medal, the big victory that justified every second of every training session. What also mean a great deal to me are simply the good times that I've had along the way. In the mid-1990s the Fifth Avenue Mile in New York was one of the fun dates on the calendar. I find New York a great city – it is so vibrant and has such a lot of energy. The race was an amazing experience. With crowds lining both sides of the route, there was a tremendous atmosphere and it felt like the people were right on top of you. It was a race that suited me and I always ran well there. It was the city, though, that I loved as much as anything. The first year that I did it, 1995, Gary and I went out about a week before the race and just went sightseeing around New York. We did the Statue of Liberty, Ellis Island, Broadway, ran all the time in Central Park and visited the Bronx and Brooklyn. Such a mix of cultures and peoples, and I remember thinking what a lively and interesting city it is.

Being a runner, of course, I love running in Central Park. It is great: a proper park in the centre of one of the world's biggest and greatest cities, and no matter what time of day it is always busy. There are designated areas for runners and joggers, a lot of people go around the reservoir and there's another trail that runs the whole way around the park. Obviously it is in a big city and for safety reasons I had promised my parents I wouldn't run there after dark – nor would I really have wanted to. The loop around the perimeter of the park is about seven miles long. It was Sunday morning, quite early, when we first went for a run. 'There's got to be something going on here today,' we thought. There were so many people about, joggers, roller-bladers, walkers, cyclists. The place was jammed with people in search of some form of exercise. 'Is there an event on here today?' we asked. 'Just a normal Sunday morning,' came the reply. Part of the reason why the atmosphere is so good is that they close the park to traffic at the weekends.

Though I hadn't intended running through the park at night, I did leave it a bit late one afternoon when I ran without Gary. Towards the end of my 45-minute run darkness was falling. It was September and I had come off the reservoir path where you have lots of other runners and had about a mile or so to go through the park before I got back to the hotel. This is where the New York Marathon approaches the finish but, in darkness, that part can be unnerving until you get out on to the bright lights and hustle and bustle of West 59th Street. Our hotel was between Fifth Avenue and Broadway, close to where I would exit. Running through the trees my mind was working overtime and the silence was broken by the jangle of rattling keys. Someone was behind me and I was getting the impression that they were trying to close on me.

If you recall the opening scene in the Steven Spielberg movie *E.T.* you will remember the jangle of the keys that hung from the belt of one of the men chasing E.T. What made the scene scary was the noise of the keys and how it increased in volume as the men got closer to the frightened little alien. I know how E.T. felt, but at least running fast was something that came naturally to me. I began to pick up the pace, but however fast I went, the person behind me also seemed to accelerate, and all the time there was the sense that he or she was getting closer. At this speed, it had to be a man. I went even faster, the keys got even closer, and suddenly I burst out into the lit-up area at the southern end of the park. Waiting at the lights to cross the road a man came up to me.

'Gee, lady,' the guy with the keys said, 'you sure were runnin' fast. I was going all out to try and keep up with you.'

Probably because I was scared to death and the adrenaline was pumping I thought but didn't admit to the fears that had been going through my mind.

'I like to finish with a sprint,' was all I could manage.

He was actually just another runner in Central Park, a guy who saw a woman in front of him and set himself the challenge of catching up. Over the years there have been lots of awkward or just plain funny moments like this while out running. When we were teenagers in Bedford, a group of lads on the street once joined in with us and started messing around. It wasn't like they were going to assault us or anything, but we were in the middle of a training run and weren't in the mood for jokes. So our strategy was to keep our heads down and not react, wait for them to get out of breath and stop. But Vicki Russell, one of our group, decided she wasn't putting up with this any more and she just decked one of the guys. No arguing, no explaining, just one punch and he dropped right off. Michelle Matthews was just in front, heard the punch and started yelling and panicking. She was convinced we were being attacked. There was an attack, but we weren't the victims.

Another time in Bedford there was a flasher on the embankment where we liked to train because it was a wide footpath and well lit. Apparently he had walked up to people and exposed himself. We were told he was likely to do the same to us. We were young and it didn't really scare us – we were runners, we thought, we could just run away. Another problem runners face can be dogs: I remember once one of the older girls explicitly describing what they would do with the dog lead if the owner failed to control it once more! It's always the same excuse – 'They only want to play!' We were mostly slightly-built girls in our early teens but together you wouldn't have called us timid.

And we knew how to have a laugh. Another time we were training on the embankment when swans attacked and chased Alex Stanton. We stopped and watched and thought it was hilarious to see poor Alex run up and down the embankment pursued by swans.

In my early career there were of course some disappointments, but they were easy to get over. No one expected you to conquer the world in your early twenties, and even though I might have been disappointed and keen to do better, I always learned from the experiences and used the frustration to make me stronger. I was devastated to finish 19th in that cross-country in Durham – the disappointment was terrible – but at least there was a rational explanation for why I fell apart over the last 800 metres. And at that time, if one battle was lost, the war still went on. No sooner was Durham over and done with than I was focusing on the World Track Championships. They were to be held later in the year in Gothenburg in Sweden. Before that I had my long stint in Font-Romeu and began a love affair with the place that would endure.

It wasn't just the beauty and motivation of Font-Romeu, the harder training at altitude also worked well for me. After returning from that first experience in the early spring of 1995, Mum noticed that when racing I was rolling my eyes back in my head, something that I had never previously done. 'Why have you started doing that?' Until she mentioned it and I looked at pictures and videos, I hadn't a clue it was happening. In the middle of a hard race, you would see my eyes roll back in their sockets, to a point where all you can see are the whites. Thinking about it I realised that because running at high altitude was so much tougher, it was a little device that enabled me to switch off from the pain and push myself harder. A pain-management technique, I suppose. Apparently we all have a comfort zone that we find by rolling our eyes back; babies often do it before falling asleep. It's like I had found a way to escape the pain to my comfort zone and still be able to maintain the effort.

What appealed to me about training at altitude was mainly the fact that I could escape a lot of distractions, train very effectively and in very beautiful and inspiring surroundings. It was far harder than training at sea level but you could get your body used to being pushed that bit more, and get much more from the training. I got stronger and stronger from working at altitude and my mind got tougher too. Everyone who runs seriously suffers pain, in training and in races. Some regard that pain as their enemy, some look upon it as their friend. To me it was a friend. I thrive on hard training and love the buzz and feeling I get when running as fast as I can.

At Font-Romeu I also love just being able to run through the forests and up the mountains and take in all the natural beauty. Sometimes I don't see another person, and I like it that way. It's just me and my thoughts and the clean fresh air. There are people who believe the clever thing to do is to live at altitude and train at sea level – that way you enjoy the physiological benefits of being at high altitude without stressing your body too much. I have never seen it like that, and enjoy training at altitude simply for the reasons above. Anyway, for me the blood physiology doesn't change much and my benefits come from the fact that the training is harder and thus more effective. My haematocrit (red cell count) and volume of red blood cells don't really change that much at altitude. My usual haematocrit is 39–42 no matter how long I spend at altitude, and my red blood cell count never goes above 4,250,000. Given that altitude training doesn't really make much difference to my blood, people ask why spend so much time there. The reason is that I don't go to altitude to try to change my blood physiology – I go because they are usually beautiful, remote places where I can get away from things and focus on what I want to do. What I get out of extensive training at altitude is a tougher mentality: if you can survive hard sessions high up in the mountains, endlessly repeated, there are enormous psychological benefits. It prepares you for the brutal moments in races when you want to slow down but you have to keep going. The other great benefit of training at altitude is physical.

Given it is so much harder, 100 miles a week at altitude is the equivalent of a good few more at sea level but without the extra stress on your body and joints. You can achieve the equivalent physiological benefits in terms of fitness and mental toughness while running fewer miles and thus less pounding than you could at sea level. It's a very natural way of making my training more effective and my body more efficient. This more severe training builds up my strength and to me the effects last far longer than the general three-week benefit accredited to altitude training. With all its facilities, beauty and the absence of distractions, Font-Romeu is just perfect and apart from the athletic advantages, I have a lot of friends there and love the place. Finally, as any asthmatic knows, dust mites don't survive higher than 1,500 metres and for me, that is another important plus.

So much was new to me in 1995. I'd had very little experience of the Grand Prix circuit in 1993, missed all of '94 through injury, so '95 was my first full season on the circuit. It worked like this: Andy Norman and I would have one, maybe two meetings through the year. I would tell him the races that were part of my season's programme and he would do his best to get me into those events. He was very good at this and soon would come back to me with everything arranged. But my working relationship with Andy ended sooner than expected after the athletics writer Cliff Temple took his own life in early 1995. It was a shocking tragedy and one that ended Andy's involvement with the British Athletics Federation.

In my short time on the senior circuit, I had got to know Cliff, who seemed a really nice and sensitive guy. We had first met at Oslo in 1993 at what was my first Grand Prix event, and then I had seen him again shortly before his death. He was at Durham for the International Cross-Country race in late 1994, which was an important event because the World Cross would be held on the same course three months later. I won at Durham and spoke to Cliff afterwards. 'I'll see you in Belfast for the Mallusk race,' he said before we went our different ways. Mallusk, in County Antrim, was the following week but Cliff didn't show up and the other journalists were really surprised at his absence. Then we heard he was dead.

It must have been a dreadful time for Cliff's family and it also turned out very badly for Andy. Before his death, Cliff had been writing articles in the *Sunday Times* that portrayed Andy in a bad light, and Andy was putting pressure on Cliff to stop. It was perhaps understandable that some people might think that the pressure was, in part, to blame for Cliff's state of mind. There was a British Athletics Federation inquiry into Cliff's suicide and it concluded that Andy had behaved improperly in trying to get Cliff to stop writing stories that were damaging to him. That ended Andy's relationship with the BAF and although he continued to work with some top athletes, he no longer represented athletes like me on behalf of the Federation.

I liked Andy, but recognised that with his back to the wall, he could use some strong-arm tactics and I understood how he could react to the stories in the way that he did. However, I'm equally sure he would never have intended things to turn out the way that they did. It was clear that there were a lot of other things going on in Cliff's life and that he was feeling very down. There is no doubt Andy was pressuring him, but it is impossible to know how much that pressure contributed to Cliff's death. I don't agree with what Andy did, but I'm sure he never imagined it would end like that. I also got the impression he probably felt a bit guilty himself too, and in that sense, I felt sympathy for him. He is likeable in so many ways: tough, straight-talking and with a genuine passion to do the best for athletics as a sport. In the beginning he also enjoyed taking the piss out of me – probably to test out if I could stand up for myself.

'Are Mum and Dad coming to pick you up or are you allowed to drive home on your own tonight?' he would ask. He liked to tease and try to make me look vulnerable and almost helpless, but he knew really that wasn't me. I might have appeared a little that way but I've always known exactly what I wanted and been well able to stand up for and look out for myself. With Andy, if you stood up to him and held your ground, he respected you for that. Let him walk all over you and he would do just that. I felt he appreciated what I was doing and what I was trying to achieve, and in his own way he helped me to get on with doing that. He always treated me as an adult and respected me as an athlete.

After Andy went, I needed someone to get me into Grand Prix races. At the same time Geoff Wightman of Park Associates, who were already taking care of the commercial side of things, was keen to get into athlete representation. I agreed to work with him and let him deal with the meet promoters to arrange my races. Geoff had a couple of other athletes but I was the main one racing on the circuit. He didn't travel to races with me but he arranged the races and the fees which were either wired back to my account in England or had to be picked up on the night. This was sometimes awkward because Andy had always done it, and now there were some nights when after running a tough 3,000m or 5,000m, I would have to sit in a queue with all the other managers until one or two in the morning to pick up my money for that evening's race. Occasionally Gary's agent, a really nice man called Ray Flynn, would offer to collect it for me. Another couple of times the agent Kim McDonald did it for me. 'Look, Paula,' he would say, 'you shouldn't be here, go and have some dinner, I'll sort this out.'

That summer of 1995, everything was geared towards the 5,000m in Gothenburg. Twelve weeks at Font-Romeu had increased my strength but it wasn't a smooth, trouble-free run to the World Championships. What we really want is never easy or everyone would achieve it. The difficulty I had was in adjusting to training at altitude, accepting that it was harder and that it put quite a bit of extra stress on my body. Also that I had to be careful because of my asthma. Early that summer I got bronchitis, a constant danger for someone with asthma, and it was bad enough to stop me from running for a while. It was worrying enough for Alex to fly out and spend a week with me in Font-Romeu, just to make sure I made a proper recovery. I was already on strong antibiotics when he arrived and by the end of the week, I was back running. Later that summer Alex came out again, this time with Rosemary, and they stayed in the campsite for part of their holidays. That's how committed they are and have always been to my career.

Having missed 1994 through injury, a year and a half had passed since I had run on the track and I really didn't know what sort of shape I was in. When I came down to sea level though, my first training run felt like I was flying along – it was so easy. My comeback race on the track was a 1,500m at Dijon in France and in winning I ran a personal best. That reassured me that things were okay. After that I did a 5,000m in Hengelo, my first ever race at that distance – during my year out, the championship distance for women moved from 3,000m to 5,000m. That meant upping the training and I didn't feel it would be a problem but no matter how much you prepare, there is nothing that can completely replicate an actual race. I was excited to see how I could do over a 5,000m race.

Jos Hermens, agent for so many of the world's top athletes, had taken over as promoter of Hengelo and he was hoping that Derartu Tulu would break the world record for 5,000m that evening. That didn't concern me and it wasn't going to affect my approach to the race. I led for a bit, Tulu then took over and I was happy to follow in her slipstream. Jos wasn't so happy and he stood by the edge of the track exhorting me to do more of the pace-setting. I did go to the front for a while but in the back of my mind, I was trying to win the race, nothing else – and when Tulu passed me with about 500 metres to go, I still had a little bit left. With 200 to go I sensed her tiring a little, got back up to her shoulder and then managed to out-kick her in the home straight. She was an Olympic champion and I was pretty pleased about that win. After a year out through injury you don't know if you will come back as strong as you were before; the 1,500m had been encouraging, but this 5,000m was even more so. I had run just outside 15 minutes.

After another three weeks' training at Font-Romeu I was ready for the last couple of preparatory runs before Gothenburg. Back home in England, I ran a 4.06 1,500m at Gateshead, which was another big personal best, and was then second to Sonia O'Sullivan over 5,000m at Crystal Palace. That, too, really pleased me, as the 14.49 time was another personal best and it suggested that for the World Championships I would be in the shape of my life. Perhaps in trying to convince myself that the year's injury had not lessened me as an athlete, I was ready a little too soon for Gothenburg. Whether or not this was the case, it would be a question that would surface a few times over the years: in trying to be the best that I could be, had I maybe tried to keep adding in training rather than backing off a little and maintaining freshness?

Gothenburg didn't go badly – at 21 years of age and after a year out through injury, it was no failure to finish 5th. But there were some reservations and a touch of disappointment. Even though my final position was two places better than my finishing place in Stuttgart two years earlier, I wasn't as pleased with my performance as had been the case in Stuttgart. Before a packed crowd and with a terrific atmosphere in the Ullevi Stadium, the race had a strange beginning as Gabriela Szabo, who had become a world junior champion on the track the year before, started out as if she were running 800m, not 5,000. She covered the first 200 metres in 30 seconds and had by then established a clear lead. Of course she couldn't sustain that pace and eventually things settled down. Sonia and Fernanda Ribeiro were the two favourites in the race and it was always going to be difficult for me to beat either.

Through the last 800 metres, Sonia, Ribeiro and the Moroccan girl

Zahra Ouaziz got about 30 metres ahead of Szabo and me, who were well ahead of the next little group. Sonia went clear with 200 to go, Ribeiro was 2nd, Ouaziz 3rd and even though I tried very hard in a long sprint with Szabo for 4th, she got there by a couple of metres.

It bothered me a little that Ouaziz could come out of nowhere and win a medal. I had never heard of her, never seen her run, and from what we knew, she had never really run outside of Morocco.

When you follow the sport really closely, you read all the magazines, talk to people about who ran here and who ran there and you think you know who's out there. Then sometimes at a major championship someone that you have never really seen or heard of before can turn up and win a medal. It can be frustrating but it's also one of the things that makes our sport so interesting. Two years before, Chinese athletes had completely dominated the women's 3,000m in Stuttgart and yet not one of them was a contender in Gothenburg. After her bronze medal in Gothenburg, Ouaziz didn't run well for two years but returned to form in 1998 and then ran very well in '99.

The 1995 season finished with some races on the European Grand Prix circuit and then my first visit to New York for the Fifth Avenue Mile. Back in those days, I was still very much learning about fitting in training with racing at such a high level. It had been normal for me to do a tough track session on Tuesday and race well at the weekend. However, I quickly found out that I couldn't do that and be fresh enough to race well at Grand Prix level on the Friday evening. By trial and error, Alex and I realised it wasn't necessary to do the hard track session while racing pretty much every week in the circuit races. Racing at a high level with just easy runs in between was enough to sustain my fitness, and often we were both surprised by how long I could maintain this. It was about getting to know my own body and, little by little, learning what worked for me.

As was our custom, Alex and I sat down at the end of the season and tried to summarise where we now stood. Had we made progress? The answer was an emphatic yes. Injury had killed the previous season, so to get back running was the first achievement and there was actually a lot of encouragement in the way I had performed. There were new personal bests in all of my distances and fifth place in the World Championship 5,000m final – and even if that didn't fully satisfy me, it was two places better than Stuttgart in 1993. Proof that things had progressed lay in the fact that while 7th at Stuttgart was a source of satisfaction, 5th in Gothenburg felt mildly disappointing.

But the 1995 season was also my first experience of altitude training and once I learned to train more efficiently in this environment, the benefits would surely increase. What we were always agreed on was that as long as I was making progress – improving my times, running better in championship races – then we were on the right path and justified in going forward as we were doing. We both felt we had a good base to build on and were capable of improving and performing steadily better in the years to come. We were looking forward to doing just that. Certainly I had reason to justify my decision to try to concentrate fully on my running when I graduated in 1996.

8

Given the way modern sport is presented on television and in the newspapers, and also the way in which elite athletes can look so in control when everything clicks and comes together, it is easy to forget the humanity of those who perform. The commentator might say, 'Paula Radcliffe, churning out mile after mile, she's making this look easy.' Without meaning to, he makes it sound automatic, machine-like, in calling it 'easy'. The reality is very different. In my experience, getting your preparation 100 per cent right is extremely difficult and when you do, it tends also to require a little bit of luck as well as the knowledge of your body and how it reacts to different things. You think you've done everything right, worked harder than you've ever worked in your life, and at the eleventh hour your body reminds you of its fragility. And sometimes not even that – you can come across a small hiccup that at any other time would be no problem but can take you out of action for a couple of days at exactly the wrong moment. If I count the number of times I have gone through the build-up to a major race without a setback and compare it to the occasions when there were one or two illnesses or small injury problems, I know which column would have the more entries.

However, as an athlete you accept these risks and just try to do as much as possible to minimise them.

Part of trying to get the most out of yourself means trying to push the envelope as far as you can without going over the line. It is the scenario of the five balls that I explained at the beginning: you take the risks and try to throw that 'career' or 'achievement' ball as high as you can in the hope that you'll get it through the top hoops. Sometimes you throw a little bit too high and miss; other times the wind might blow unexpectedly and through no fault of your own it will still fall. What is important is that you don't damage or drop the 'health' or 'integrity' balls – if you hang on to these then you just have to wait for the career ball to bounce back and gradually work back to and beyond the heights you'd already achieved.

It is true that the mileage involved in the preparation for a 10,000m or a marathon necessarily involves a high injury risk. It is also true that I have achieved the success that I have because I have been able to push my body and mind through training sessions that are intense and punishing. However, this encapsulates more risks and I have also had to change and adapt things at different times to try to minimise these risks. This point applies to all who compete: sport is not an exact science, and no matter how formidable people may look on their good days, they are still human beings operating in an environment more challenging and more likely to end in failure than the vast majority of comparable situations in real life. It is that fact that has to be remembered: however important sport is to me, it isn't life and death. Ultimately it helps to keep it all in perspective and remind myself that it is just sport – my hobby!

This point has been clear to me for a long time. For example, when preparing for my final-year exams at Loughborough in 1996, it was possible for me to control most of the factors that would determine my final result. The target was a first-class honours degree, the means to getting that was devoting 8 or 9 hours to lectures and study every day through my final year. It was a tough grind, not especially enjoyable, but it was perfectly possible to do that amount of study. It meant getting up very early for my early morning run, skipping coffee breaks with my class-mates, devouring lunch in double-quick time and making sure that almost all of the study was done before my evening run. There were also gym sessions to be squeezed in. The diary from 1996 makes me laugh now – how was it possible to fit so much into so few hours?

But I did it and, contrasted with the parallel challenge of preparing for an Olympic Games, the study was actually straightforward: you put in the hours; you got the result. If only it was as logical and straightforward in sport, with rewards following predictably from the amount of effort put in . . . Alas, it can't be, but that is part of the thrill too. In every class of pretty much every university, there are people who get first-class honours degrees. In each event at the Olympics, there can only be one gold medal. That is what is so special about it. You get to compete for that medal by being in the top 3 in your country and even then, you have to achieve a qualifying standard. Athletes come from over 200 countries and in each event, there is only one gold medal. In pursuit of such a goal, you realise how vulnerable you are. No matter how well you prepare, regardless of how lucky you have been with injury, you have to be perfect on that one day and many things remain outside your control. For example, there may be one or two – or even three or four – athletes who are more talented than you and as well-prepared. You may wake up on the morning of the race feeling ill or even just inexplicably listless and months of preparation are destroyed by one off day.

When the results of my finals came out and I got my first, the feeling was one of relief as well as satisfaction. It was the target, it had been achieved, and the long hours of study had been rewarded. However, it didn't give me quite the same buzz that crossing the finish line in first place can do. Maybe it is the difference between satisfaction and exhilaration. The long hours of study were endured;

the long runs and the track sessions in training were enjoyed. It wasn't that I didn't enjoy my course – there was real satisfaction in learning to speak French and German, but after my results there was no desire to pursue further structured education. I am very glad to have and to use my languages, I love being in a foreign country and being able to understand and interact, being able to appreciate and take in the amazing differences between cultures. It was important to go through university and get my degree, but once it was over, it was over.

What I wanted was to finish university and devote myself totally to running for a while, to immerse myself in the uncertainty of the sport's world and give myself every chance to get as far as I am capable of doing. I had my degree and if, God forbid, anything should happen that meant I couldn't continue as an athlete, the future security to get a 'proper job' was there. However, now I felt I had worked hard enough to give myself a few years to enjoy doing just what I wanted to do, so the decision was straightforward. Not being able to run is something that I never want to have to face, and I hope I never have to.

What was it that allowed me to be talked into cycling into college on a February morning early in 1996? My form had been good, I'd won the International Cross-Country race at Durham, won again at Mallusk and at the beginning of this Olympic year, I was fit, healthy and in winning form. That morning the temperatures were sub-zero and the overnight snow was already hardening on the roads. Underneath the snow, you suspected there was ice. 'I'm going in the car,' I said to my then housemate Phil Tulba. Phil was an 800m and 1,500m runner and we generally biked in together. He didn't think the conditions were that bad.

'Oh, come on,' he said. 'We'll be fine.'

Like a fool, I agreed. We were going through the college when we hit black ice and my bike just skidded from under me. Sitting up on the ground, I tried to take in what had happened but couldn't see a thing. Phil was shouting at me. 'Put your hand over your eye.' What was the point? I couldn't see a thing anyway. 'Just put your hand over your eye.' I did and gradually the vision returned to what was now the good eye.

'What happened?' I said.

'You've cut your head wide open,' he replied.

A car full of students stopped and the driver ordered all of his mates out.

'We'll get you in the car and take you to the medical centre.'

'But I'm going to get blood all over your car,' I said.

Phil took care of my bike, this guy drove me to the medical centre on the campus and after prising my headgear away from the gash the campus doctor stitched me up. To me it was just a minor head wound, enough to merit one day's rest and the next day it was back to training. Quite a big bruise formed under the wound and every time my foot hit the pavement, the bruise was jolted and hurt. But it was only a bruise and that weekend I raced in Portugal. The girls couldn't stop laughing. With this big black and blue lump and assorted cuts on my face, it looked like I'd been in a fight with Mike Tyson. 'No one's going to mess with you today,' they said. The race went okay, I finished third, but the year had begun as it was destined to continue: one little problem followed by another.

Liz Yelling and I went to a cross-country race at Diekirch in Luxembourg where the course was snow-covered. At one point you climbed a steep hill with wooden steps built into it. After descending, we circled a football pitch and then headed off up the hill again. Running on snow has always appealed to me; my World Junior Cross-Country title came on a snow-covered course and I invariably run well on snow. In this race, everything was going fine until one time on the steps. The long spikes that I used to help keep my footing on the snow got stuck in one of the steps and, as I continued running I twisted my back awkwardly.

At the time there didn't appear to be a problem – I carried on and finished second in the race. After a few weeks' training, however, the area below my left knee began to feel sore. The physio at Loughborough treated it but couldn't tell what was causing the discomfort. The World Cross-Country Championships, to be held in South Africa, were less than a month away and while still trying to get the problem cleared I continued to train.

A journalist came to interview me about the forthcoming race and we went for lunch. From the bowl of chicken soup that I ordered came severe food poisoning. I was unable to hold anything down and even had to spend one night back in the medical centre, though I discharged myself early to get to a physio appointment. In a week I had lost three kilos in weight and with that quite a bit of strength. As well as that, the lack of proper nutrients getting through wasn't helping my sore leg. But you can't stop time or wind the clock back, you have to get on and make the best of things. Heading down to Stellenbosch in South Africa for the World Cross-Country Championships, I weighed just 49 kilos, which was extremely light for me. My left leg felt terrible and I was petrified that I wasn't going to be able to run as well as I wanted to. At the back of my mind I was a little worried about it being a stress fracture, especially as it was Olympic year and I was worried about anything that would mean a long time out, but the physios seemed confident that it wasn't.

South Africa was a disaster for me. These were the old days before UK Athletics moved into the modern era and began to make sure elite teams had the committed expert support they needed. For that trip, the physiotherapist assigned to the team refused from the start to do massage. Right before a competition the majority of athletes just need massage while a few may need physiotherapy. But she said she didn't do massage because she was a physiotherapist. On the Thursday before the race, there was a sign on her door that said 'Gone Sightseeing'. Luckily there were some South African physios available as part of an IAAF set-up for teams that didn't have physios with them, so I walked over to see one of them. He did some acupuncture and other things to try to sort out my leg. 'There is something pulling on it,' he said, 'but you won't do any further damage by running the race.' The disrupted preparation meant I wasn't in condition to do much damage to my rivals either. All through the race, the leg hurt, especially on the steep downhill ramps. I couldn't run powerfully and I finished 18th.

Four years had passed since my win in the Junior World Cross-Country in Boston, and it seemed I was as far away as ever from winning the senior title. At Amorebieta in Spain, I was 18th; the stress fracture prevented me from running in Budapest the following year, then 19th at Durham and now 18th in Stellenbosch. It was a moderate record and yet in my own mind, I wasn't making good progress towards my goal of winning the Senior World Cross-Country title.

When Alex and I spoke about it, we could always identify the reasons behind the poor performance and generally it related to my preparation being interrupted by some mishap or injury. It was probably true too that, as a full-time student, I didn't have the time for rest and recuperation that many of my rivals enjoyed. Even with all the disappointing results, I never stopped believing that I was good enough to one day win that title and honour the pledge made to myself after Granddad died.

The athletics road is forever twisting – whenever you think you have made it on to open road, there is another, previously unforeseen twist to negotiate. After Stellenbosch, the Loughborough coach George Gandy was taking a group of athletes to Krugersdorp for three weeks' altitude training. With the Atlanta Olympics four months away, Krugersdorp was a logical starting point for the build-up to that, and as we were already in South Africa and the three weeks embraced the Easter holidays from university, Alex and I decided to go along too. Alison Wyeth was there and after the World Cross was also struggling with a lower leg injury. As soon as we both arrived in Krugersdorp, we checked out where we could get a bone scan and were pleasantly surprised to discover it could be done for 200 rand, which translated into the most inexpensive bone scan I have ever had.

The verdict was that Alison's injury wasn't too bad – she could continue to train but on soft grass rather than the track or roads. In my case, the news wasn't good. The left hamstring was so tight that it had pulled away a little bit off the bone, causing a stress fracture and requiring three weeks off; that is, three weeks where I was not to run but could cross-train. It actually worked out okay: there was an excellent leisure centre near where we were based, with a swimming pool and gym. Aqua running session in the morning, exercise bike in the afternoon, study as much as I could in between. I had taken my laptop and used most of my spare time in Krugersdorp to do all the final dissertations that were due in when I got back. Overall, considering the circumstances, it was a reasonably productive three weeks.

If you had asked me at that time what was the number one priority, the Atlanta Olympics or my final exams, the answer would not have been straightforward. Both were extremely important to me and I wanted to do as well as possible in both. At the beginning of each year I often write down my goals and put it somewhere safe. Nineteen ninety-six had first-class honours, make the Olympics and improve on my personal bests. The aim was to give 100 per cent commitment to both sides of my life. The Olympics excited me far more than my finals but in the back of my mind, there was the thought that these exams were a one-off experience in my life. There would be no second chance, no opportunity to re-sit. Even if the Olympics in Atlanta were hugely important, there would be another Olympics, even two or three more. As well as that, at the time we were in Krugersdorp my university exams were six weeks away while the Olympics were still four months distant. So once my work in the pool and on the bike was done, it was easy for me to devote the rest of the time to study.

With my mum Pat in Cheshire, 1974.

With Dad, and Martin.

Holiday snaps from Austria and France, with Mum and Martin.

One of my first cross-country races in Cheshire. I'm in the red shorts, looking anxiously at the starter.

With Dad, Martin and cousins Joanne and Sian before one of Dad's marathons.

An early cross-country race for Bedford & County Athletics Club, which I joined soon after we moved from Cheshire.

The only picture I have of Dad and me running together, taken in about 1987 during a half-marathon Dad ran in Windsor.

Bedford & County's first national team title, at Bexley in Kent in February 1987. I came fourth, a huge improvement on my race the previous year.

My first English Schools International, in Irvine, Scotland, 1988. With me are my Bedford team-mate, Clare Wilson (left), and Joanne Keenan from Northumberland.

Competing in Irvine. I missed the first part of my French exchange to take part and travelled out alone straight afterwards to join everyone.

I came third in this Under-15 race in the National Cross-Country Championships of 1989.

On the victory rostrum with some of the England Intermediate girls' team after a Schools International race in Barry, Wales, in 1989. With me are (left to right) Gillian Stacey, Charlotte Mayock and Ruth Ellway.

With my friends Mark Sesay (left) and Matthew Hibberd at the European Junior Championships, 1991.

There is also a good illustration here of how hit-and-miss injuries and their diagnosis can be, particularly in the early years of my career. After the bone scan in Krugersdorp, Alison Wyeth's situation seemed much better than mine. She didn't have a stress fracture and was able to continue running. I wasn't. Yet, when Alison returned from South Africa, she was still in pain. I had begun jogging and was definitely making progress. Though the pain never went away, Alison soldiered on but couldn't run her best. When she came home from the Atlanta Games in August, they did another X-ray and discovered she had been suffering from two stress fractures, one in each leg. Basically, the injury destroyed her whole year.

Further investigation on my return from South Africa showed the source of the problem to be that moment at Diekirch in Luxembourg when I wrenched my back on those wooden steps. As a result of the back being out of alignment the hamstring was under so much strain it had eventually pulled partly away from the bone where it attached below the knee. It is what happens when you continue running over 100 miles a week with a particular muscle under too much tension. I went to see an osteopath, Terry Moule, who was based in Harpenden in Hertfordshire and was very good. 'It's been wrong for so long now that it's naturally going to keep going back out of line, so you'll need to come down regularly so that we can get it corrected once and for all.' If that's what was needed, so be it. With just four weeks to my finals, there were times when I was getting up at 5.45 and on the road from Loughborough to Harpenden by six. Terry would treat me a little before 7.30 and there were a couple of mornings when I had to be back in Loughborough for a nine o'clock lecture.

He also gave me an exercise programme that took another half an hour out of the day, but it was worthwhile. The more Terry treated me, the better I felt when running. It was not what you would call ideal preparation for the Olympics and it was natural that in the two weeks before my finals and during the exams themselves, study took precedence over athletics. Once the exams were done I went straight out to Font-Romeu, at last in a position to concentrate totally on my training. Four weeks of solid training in the Pyrenees definitely improved my condition and I felt I was heading out to the BOA pre-Olympic holding camp in as good a shape as I could have hoped for, given the disruptions of the year.

The Great Britain team went to Tallahassee in Florida for two weeks' acclimatisation before going on to Atlanta. Tallahassee was much hotter and far more humid than we would actually find in Atlanta. Although that made it difficult to train properly in Tallahassee, we were pleasantly surprised and well adjusted to the conditions when we got to Atlanta. So hot was it in Tallahassee that our morning run began around 6.30 and would finish by 8. Even at that hour, it was warm, and I can remember one run causing a little tension between us as Jon Brown, preparing for the 10,000m, was annoyed because I was running too fast. He was easing down his training and was running an hour and a half one morning while I was running for just an hour.

My attitude was then and always has been that I run at the pace that suits me. A couple of us ran together, Jon included. Later he went back to bed complaining I had pushed it too fast. No one made him run with us, at any time he could have slowed and run his own pace!

Obviously I had planned to do track sessions in Tallahassee but such was the heat, people were concerned about the consequences. To walk from an air-conditioned room out into the afternoon sun was like going from a normal room straight into a sauna. The session we had planned was 800-metre reps and as this was more than anyone had attempted in Tallahassee so far, I remember a lot of the coaches watching it. It was almost like – we'll see if she can handle it first!

Maybe they wanted to see if I was going to keel over before they would commit to doing their own track sessions. Alex laughed. It was tough but not impossible. The times were slower than they would normally be but they weren't bad, and there was no sense of it being dangerous. What the intense heat did was force you to go that bit slower but that would be the same for every athlete. Often we face difficult conditions in races – my attitude is always that it is the same for everyone, so get on with the race.

Another lesson was learned on another run in Tallahassee. Alex and I had found a cycle path marked out every 100 metres, which was ideal for doing our 5×1km reps. We went there one morning and I set off on the first kilometre with Alex walking up and down watching. After doing one kilometre I would take my recovery and then do the next rep back to the starting point. At one point I had noticed a small branch or twig lying across the path.

Each time I skipped over it, hardly noticing it. Then after the fourth, this guy on a bike shouted, 'Be careful of that snake!' What snake? The twig was in fact a snake and suddenly I was scared. And then it dawned on me: the sheer irrationality of my fear. For four reps this snake had lain across the path and because I didn't realise it was a snake, there wasn't the slightest problem. Knowing about it didn't change the reality; a snake was a snake whether or not you knew it was a snake. It would be as little threat on the fifth rep as on all the others. I told myself to grow up and get on with it. Thankfully there was only one more rep to go!

From the Atlanta Olympics of 1996 there are two pictures that remain vivid.

In the first I am standing around in the tunnel with the other competitors for our heat of the 5,000m. There is a commotion going on in front of us that is turning into a problem. We are there with the volunteers who are carrying the boxes containing our kit, but there is this hold-up and instead of moving forward, we're being told to wait. Everyone is on edge, unprepared for the delay. Word begins to filter back that it is a problem with the Reebok kit being worn by Sonia O'Sullivan, one of the favourites for the 5,000m.

The Irish team has done a deal with Asics, another kit manufacturer, and according to IOC rules Sonia should be wearing Asics, not Reebok. No one can believe she could be prevented from going on the track, but this is what is happening. Someone has the Asics gear she must wear and she is told that unless she changes into it, she will not be allowed to compete. It is an awful situation for Sonia because not only is she being forced to do something against her will, she isn't wearing anything underneath her kit and is being made to change while standing in a tunnel with all of her rivals. Sonia is the 5,000m world champion. She shouldn't be in this situation. You think of the years of preparation for an Olympic Games only for the crucial minutes before your first race to be spent in a nasty argument about what kit you're going to wear.

In the other picture, I am warming up before the final of the 5,000m. The Olympic Stadium is packed to the rafters and the excitement creates an atmosphere that is extraordinary. Immediately before the race, I do strides down the back straight to prepare. Calmly, I think about how the race will be run and focus on my plan, but something is happening to cause a buzz in the stadium and I can't resist the temptation to sneak a glance from the corner of my eye to see what it is.

Not that far away, the men's long jump is in progress and Carl Lewis is trying for the gold medal. It has nothing to do with me, at this moment it should be completely irrelevant, and yet I take another look over towards the long jump area to see if Lewis is on the runway. Perhaps it's because I'm a novice in my first Olympics that I can't switch off the external distractions. Maybe it is because the excitement is simply too great for me to ignore. The greater truth is that we're human beings, not machines; we have emotions, curiosities and weaknesses, and they are part of the package as much as the strengths. Underneath the professional athlete I am a sports fan too.

*

My aim at Atlanta was to do better than the 5th place at the World Championships in Gothenburg a year before. It hadn't been a perfect year but the last six weeks had gone well, and my feeling was that I should be in the scramble for the bronze medal. If things went very well, maybe the silver or gold. Sonia O'Sullivan and Gabriela Szabo were two of the big favourites. But the formbook counted for nothing in Atlanta as the race played out on the weird side of surprising. How could anyone predict Sonia and Szabo running as poorly as they did, with Szabo not even making it through to the final?

China's Wang Junxia and the Kenyan Pauline Konga broke away and though we weren't running fast, it felt fast. Wang had been brilliant when winning the 10,000m at the 1993 World Championships in Stuttgart and had also set an incredible 10,000m world record that year. Not a lot had been seen from her since then. Before the race you would have said that if she was in good shape and on form, she would be hard to beat. Pauline Konga wasn't someone I really knew much about before the race. There was Sonia, Szabo and probably Wang; after that I expected to be right up there with the likes of Italy's Roberta Brunet, Kenya's Rose Cheruiyot and the top Japanese runner. Early in the race Wang and Konga broke 30 or 40 metres clear and after that, the race became one long pursuit and I spent much of it leading the chasing group.

Though the two leaders were near enough to catch, I wasn't strong enough to close the gap. At times I would fall back and allow someone else to pick up the chase but the gap never closed. Now a look back at the video shows that technically I was all over the place, trying very hard but not having the energy to go as fast as I needed to. Maybe the conditions were tougher than I'd thought, maybe I had a slight off day. With three laps to go, Wang and Konga were about 50 metres in front, and I was leading four others – Brunet, Cheruiyot, Romanova and the Japanese Michiko Shimizu. Eight hundred metres from the finish, Wang accelerated away from Konga and I upped the pace of the pursuit.

Only Brunet stayed with me and, for a moment or two, it seemed we had the bronze medal between us. At the bell Wang was still increasing her lead over Konga who was in turn clear of Brunet and me. With 350 to go, Brunet went past me, getting a 7-metre lead. I had used up a lot of energy and that gave Shimizu the chance to close on me. She got to me and sprinted past. I tried to get back to her but there was nothing left and I ran in as hard as I could for 5th place, exactly the same position as I had finished in Gothenburg a year before.

The race was won in 14.59, not an exceptional time, and I should have run faster than I did. The conditions had taken their toll. Back at the Village that night, tiredness and disappointment were the dominant emotions. My first Olympics, and I was there or thereabouts, but not good enough for a medal. Why couldn't I have run faster, run a personal best at least? I had tried my best on the night but in my disappointment that didn't count for much. Given the year I had had, maybe I should have been happier with 5th position, but I felt that I should have been able to run a bit faster and that would have placed me higher. Still it wasn't a disaster either, and I had learned a great deal from the experience. Hopefully next year, with more time to devote to my training and preparation, I could finally get into the medals.

Truthfully, I hadn't expected a medal this time, I had *hoped* for one. There is a difference, and at the end of the day I had given all that I could on the night.

Generally, though, I thoroughly enjoyed my first Olympic experience, and explored the village and Atlanta itself. However, I also continued training as I still had targets and objectives in mind once I got back to racing in Europe afterwards. I remember going for one run with 800m runners Curtis Robb and Craig Winrow. It probably demonstrates the competitive vein that runs through me. Such training runs often start out easy but this one took a more competitive turn along the way. It was Curtis who started the ball rolling.

'Yeah, yeah,' he said, 'all we have to do is sit on you, hang on to you and then at the end we'll just outsprint you.'

'Don't wind her up,' Craig said, 'for God's sake, don't wind her up.'

So I started to pick up the pace. It was good-natured teasing about the fact that I wasn't the fastest finisher around, but I knew I was stronger than them over a hilly 6-mile run. Okay, they were guys and would be tough to drop, but it definitely wasn't going to be as comfortable as they imagined. The speed got faster, and Curtis kept needling me. 'I'm just going to sit here until the moment comes and then I'm gone.' This made me go faster. Poor Craig wasn't ready for this kind of run after his race and was dropped after a couple of miles; still Curtis kept at me, trying to see how far I was prepared to push it. On this big hill near the finish, the pace got even hotter and finally Curtis couldn't hold on. I was so determined especially after he'd wound me up so much. Maybe then it should have been a sign to me that my greater successes would lie over longer distances.

From 1991, when I competed in the junior version at Antwerp in Belgium, the World Cross-Country Championships have always been my first major target of the season, and as so many of my early experiences in the sport were over cross-country, it is a race that has always been important to me. Through my four years at university there was a pattern where my form was good in the early season races; I would often win Durham, would win or do well at Mallusk soon after Christmas and other races through February. Everything would seem on course for a good performance in the World Championships, which took place in March. Yet by the time March came round, my form might have taken a dip but also the other athletes would often come out in much better shape than they had been in the early races. To me, my results in Amorebieta (1993), Durham (1995) and Stellenbosch (1996) were disappointing. To get where I wanted to be, I reasoned that I had to go away to train, focus and prepare well and come back in better shape in March, when it really mattered.

In 1997, having finished university and dedicated myself full-time to athletics, I was able to do this. This allowed me to get on to the same start line as my rivals, who were almost all full-time professionals. One of the bigger privileges conferred by being full-time was the opportunity to leave England in January for a place at high altitude where the sun shone and the conditions were conducive to good training.

In January that year, 1997, Alex, Rosemary, Gary and I left for Albuquerque in New Mexico. We really enjoyed our four and a half weeks there, the training went well and when we returned, I was really looking forward to the World Cross-Country Championships being held in Turin two weeks later.

Everyone thought I looked in great shape, commenting on how strong my legs looked. Most of that was because they were tanned from the Albuquerque sun, but the extra time to do more running, leg weights and take more rest had definitely made me stronger. On the morning of the Turin race, everything seemed right for a big performance. Alex is always a reassuring and calming influence on race days. It is why I like him to be around. While he would never say anything to put doubt in my mind, there are times when he simply oozes belief that it is going to be a good day. It's his gut feelings and when he gets these he is invariably right. That morning he kept saying, 'I have a good feeling about today, I know it is going to go well.'

Alex was definite about how I should run the race. 'Stay in the lead group, at the back, and when little gaps appear, close them but without taking too much out of yourself. Don't make any move until the last third of the race and then you can do what you want. If you're feeling good enough on the last part of the last lap, make your move. Not before. But, please, do me a favour, for the first two-thirds just stay at the back of the lead group, always in control but never at the front.'

The advice was intelligent. We both knew that in this event the start is ferocious and often people get carried away in the early part of the race and do too much. Our experience told us the race was not won until the closing stages, and even if you are someone who is unlikely to win in a sprint finish, there is still no need to be up there making the pace over the first couple of laps. It's not like the track – there's always a fast pace in cross-country and if you can preserve your strength, then you'll be the one in the strong position. Sonia O'Sullivan and Catherina McKiernan were both running in Turin and they were up near the pace for much of the race.

Then the Kenyans and the Ethiopians went to the front, surging and then easing slightly before surging again. People started dropping off the lead group: Sonia first, then Catherina a little later. I kept closing the gaps and going out on the last lap there were the Ethiopians Derartu Tulu and Gete Wami, the Kenyan Sally Barsosio, the Spaniard Julia Vaquero and myself. After what had seemed a lifetime of trying to get into this position, I knew I was in there with a good chance. Vaquero was at the front for a bit and I kept the pace up as we had to make some dent in the African challenge before the finish. It was Barsosio who cracked first and lost a little ground, Vaquero struggled too and then, getting towards the finish, Wami attacked. Still feeling strong, I waited until about 250 or 300 metres from the finish and then made my effort. Going past Wami, I went hard and didn't dare look beyond.

Turning into the finishing straight, all I could hear was the roar from the crowd and it felt like I was away. Wami, I sensed, was beaten and I just didn't know where Tulu was or how much she had left. Then the noise from the grandstand erupted and unable to hear a thing, it felt like I was winning and only had to keep going all the way to the line. The tape was now 80 metres away and the race was mine. 'Don't look back. This is it,' I thought, 'I've got this at last.' Then 30 or 40 metres from the line Tulu came past me and though I tried to respond, there wasn't enough time or energy left. She won by about 5 metres, officially 2 seconds. The gold medal had been almost mine and then was suddenly snatched away.

My emotions were mixed. Before Turin, 18th place was my best performance in the senior cross-country race and to jump from there to 2nd was a big leap. That should have pleased me and on one level I was happy, but the satisfaction was lessened by the mistake of thinking that I had won the race before crossing the line. However, it wasn't like I had slowed down or taken my foot off the accelerator. If I had been aware Tulu was coming, I still would not have been able to go any faster. It was simply that for a split-second there I believed I had the race won, and after that, coming second seemed a bit disappointing. But the disappointment proved short-lived and I left Turin very pleased with the run.

For the first time in my life as a senior athlete I had won a medal at a major championships. Equally important was the fact that second place justified my belief that one day I would win the cross-country title. You can believe something like that all you like, but if you are finishing 18th and 19th as I was, then people are going to wonder if you are kidding yourself. From Turin I went away with the confidence of an athlete who knew she would come back and win this title.

That there were no lingering regrets about the loss of the gold medal is proven by the banter between Dad and me after the race. Before the start, Dad set up his camera on a tripod at the point of the course he thought would be a good place to encourage me and also get good photographs. Just as he was setting up, a pigeon overhead took aim. In a performance of impressive marksmanship he hit the target – directly on top of Dad's head. Being the calm, matter-of-fact man he is, Dad just wiped the muck from his hair, cleaned himself off and resumed his station by the tripod. His persistence must have irritated the pigeon who upped the ante by dropping a second load and again hit the bull's-eye.

'If only you'd moved after the first, as the pigeon wanted you to, maybe I would have won,' I jokingly told him.

The logic of this made perfect sense to me. Twice had resulted in silver, once might have meant gold!

For me, Turin was a turning point. A step onwards and upwards that I intended to continue.

After returning from Italy I went to New Orleans to compete in a 10km road race called the Crescent City Classic. Among the opposition was Lynn Jennings, the outstanding US runner who had been three times world cross-country champion (1990, 1991 and 1992). Lynn wasn't quite the force she had been but was still very strong and it meant something for me to beat her. The time, 31.47, was respectable and that pleased me as well. That was my first senior race on the road and the outcome confirmed what we had long known: competing on the road would suit me and especially when racing over longer distances; half-marathons and marathons.

The physiological testing that I had been doing with Andy Jones since 1991 showed clearly what my strengths were, and that they would be seen to best advantage over long distances. Even though we knew this, there was no inclination to desert the track for the road and no plan to move up to the marathon just yet. I had yet to win a title on the track and didn't want to prioritise the marathon until that was achieved. Equally, in 1997 I didn't yet feel ready to make the change of focus that would be required. That summer's World Championships in Athens gave me the chance to get an elusive track medal. I went there in good shape, feeling optimistic about my chances of doing something in the 5,000m.

During the competition the British team stayed at the Hotel Grand Bretagne in Constitution Square, in the heart of the city. Across the road were the Houses of Parliament but the nearby National Gardens were of more interest to us athletes. Although not ideal, this little park allowed us to escape the Athenian traffic and by sticking close to the park's perimeter, we found a circuit that was about a mile long. Unfortunately there were many twists, turns and some steep downhill parts. As well as that there were wild cats all over the park and the place stank of cats' piss. There were a lot of runners using the park and a couple of days before my race I had to twist awkwardly to avoid an oncoming athlete. At first I thought nothing of it but later discovered I had strained a stomach muscle, giving me pains like a severe stitch. For the days leading up to my heat, I was getting a lot of treatment from Neil Black, one of the physiotherapists with the British team. Though I was worried, Neil assured me that it would not bother me during the race and, thankfully, he was right.

Getting through my heat comfortably gave me a lot of confidence going into the final, but there was still the usual danger of ending up with two or three faster girls alongside me with a couple of laps remaining. I decided that the pace had to be fast but I didn't need to be at the front the whole way. In my heat I had accelerated in the latter part of the race and felt very strong. So I waited until about halfway before going to the front and pushing the pace, trying to eliminate as many of my rivals as I could. With the big screens inside the stadium, it takes just one glance for you to know precisely what is happening behind you. Quite a number lost their places and with two laps to go, the American Libbie Johnson-Hickman and the Chinese Liu Jianying dropped off the lead group, but four remained directly behind me: Gabriela Szabo, Fernanda Ribeiro, Roberta Brunet and Lydia Cheromei. Of the four, Cheromei was the only one I was confident of out-sprinting. It wasn't that the others were that much faster than me, but after leading for over six laps I was going to be vulnerable whenever they kicked.

From 800m to the bell, I upped the pace but to no avail. There comes a point towards the end of a race where it becomes so much harder to shake off those in your slipstream. By then they can sense the finish and know they have a chance of winning or taking some kind of medal, and that gives them renewed energy. Whatever the tiredness, it is drowned by the rush of adrenaline. At the bell they were still there – Ribeiro, Szabo, Cheromei and Brunet. Hardly had the bell stopped chiming when Ribeiro accelerated past me, Szabo moved easily on to Ribeiro's shoulder and I was now boxed in on the inside in third place. To make matters worse Cheromei then came on my outside shoulder and even though I was capable of accelerating a little, I couldn't get out. The situation became totally impossible when Brunet, surging from the back, then went past Cheromei and lay three wide on the track, outside of Ribeiro and Szabo. At that moment there was 300 metres to go and Szabo decided to go for it. She stretched a few yards clear, Ribeiro pursued and as soon as the race quickened, Cheromei cut in front of me suddenly, making me chop my stride and go around her before beginning my final sprint effort again. It was far from ideal.

Having moved out and gone past Cheromei with a little over 200 metres to go, I set off after Brunet and Ribeiro because even then my feeling was that Szabo would not be caught. But it was a fruitless chase, Brunet was strong and got up to deprive Ribeiro of the silver medal. Three seconds later I finished 4th. All that I felt afterwards was frustration and anger. There were no 'ifs and buts'; no point in saying fourth in Athens was better than fifth in Atlanta. In a five-year period I had run four major championships on the track; my placings were 7th (Stuttgart), 5th (Gothenburg), 5th (Atlanta) and now 4th in Athens. Sitting down with Alex after the race, I cried.

'What do I have to do to get a medal in these championships? 7th, 5th, 5th, 4th; why must I always miss out? I haven't run badly in these championships, I just haven't been quite good enough each time.'

'You're right,' Alex said. 'We have to do something because at the minute you are just not quite strong enough. We've got to find a way to build from where we are right now. We've got to make you stronger.'

I had thought Turin was a turning point, and in terms of the cross-country it probably still was. But on the track I still was some distance from where I wanted to be. At times the sporting life is a series of stepping stones and reassessments: you need to keep persevering, trying new things and building on each level that you reach. The awful disappointment of that 4th place in Athens was another real turning point. It marked the moment when I knew fourth or fifth place was no longer acceptable to me. It wasn't the same as the disappointment after fifth in Atlanta – there it had been an immediate reaction but in my heart, when I thought about the build-up to the race and how much I had given of myself in the race, I believed 5th place in the Olympics wasn't too bad.

Athens in 1997 was very different. It forced me to consider the possibility that unless I worked to change some things I might spend my career in front-running performances at major championships that would always end with 4th or 5th. That prospect frustrated me. It wasn't what I wanted. I wanted to be among the medals and believed if I worked harder I could do just that.

In the media and among some of those around me there was a growing sense that it would be hard for me to win major track titles. I run better off a strong pace, but increasingly I was realising that if I didn't make that pace it was unlikely that anyone else would. I was racing alone without the team back-up that the Kenyans and Ethiopians often have, so if I was going to make the races suit me it was down to me. Most people dismiss me as an athlete who doesn't have a sprint. In my opinion that is not true, but it is correct to say that in a World Championship or Olympic final, there will often be two or three athletes quicker than me on the last lap. To make the race suit me and increase my chances of a medal, I had to get myself to a strong enough position – mainly physically, but also mentally – where I could run exactly my race and dominate the pace. I was prepared to accept that and work hard towards being in a position to execute that.

Alex and I completely believed that in time I was capable of getting there. I have always said that if I ever reached a point in my career where I was no longer enjoying my training and racing, or if it became clear that I couldn't cut it as a professional athlete, then I would move on with my life and find a new career. I would never stop running but it would become my hobby, something to be fitted in around my career. This was nowhere near that stage, I was simply disappointed with the result and willing to work harder to improve future results.

There was also my growing awareness of drug abuse in our sport and how it affected the clean as well as the doped athlete. The question had existed from my first senior World Championships experience in Stuttgart, when the Chinese had pretty much dominated the women's distance events. I hadn't been really aware of the issue at that time; my overriding thoughts were excitement and elation at what was for me then a very creditable 7th place, aged just 19. However, afterwards I became increasingly aware of the whispers and suspicions not just about the Chinese runners but also other athletes. Sometimes people who weren't seen on the circuit much turned up, ran fast and generated suspicion. Sometimes huge margins of improvement also sent the rumours flying. There was often no proof of wrong-doing and in many cases the suspicions were probably unfounded, but it was creating a changed environment. Not many believed the playing field was level.

In my mind I felt the situation was wrong. In a day and age when science is so developed in so many fields how could it not be possible to catch the cheats and prove the innocence of those who were clean? The difficulty and extreme unfairness for the clean athlete was the doubt that seeped into your mind about what others might be doing: 'If they are on EPO, what chance have I got?' All it took was for you to start believing this was true and in your mind you are beaten before even starting the race. Later in my career I too would have to face the unfounded rumours and accusations after reaching levels I was still dreaming of and aiming for in 1997. It hurt me deeply and I was frustrated at the inability of the drug testing system to improve its credibility, test for the substances being abused, and give the athletes the chance to prove that their performances were and are clean.

I made the very definite decision not to entertain doubts about those against whom I raced unless there was proof. Regardless of what I heard or what was written in newspapers, they were all innocent in my mind until they were proven otherwise. There was no alternative to this approach because if I believed a rival was using drugs, I gave her an important advantage. One that would make her even harder to beat. Instead, my approach would be to train harder and make myself stronger.

Alex saw my disappointment in Athens and typically questioned his own role.

'Do you want to go another year?' he asked. 'Should we keep going?'

'Of course we should. Why shouldn't we?'

'Well, if you want to try someone else, you should do that.'

'Look, I desperately want to run well and improve what I'm doing. We both do. I'm disappointed, but I believe we're still progressing and have a lot more to come. You do too.'

'But you might improve even more working with someone else . . .'

'I don't believe that and don't want to. Who else would have me?!'

Alex is a very humble man, who never fully appreciates his own talent and strengths.

9

From that first evening in the Loughborough pub when he whispered in my ear, my relationship with Gary Lough has always been special, but not always what you would call straightforward. Boy meets girl, brief courtship, fall in love, get married: we travelled a very different road. Gary jokes that he likes to take life's scenic route, and he is not wrong. We took a long time getting to where we both wanted to be, but that is not a lament, because along the way we came to understand better what we truly wanted. Others may look from the outside and think 'weird'. Okay, sometimes it was a little unconventional, it had more than its share of uncertainty and, for me, a period when my feelings for Gary were not reciprocated. However, there was never a time when we weren't the best of friends, and I feel all of the testing times ultimately made us stronger.

Let me summarise. We met in the autumn of 1992, in that Loughborough pub. It was my first year at university and even though I had a lot of things going on in my life at the time and having a boyfriend wasn't a priority, I was very attracted to him. Just before breaking up for Christmas holidays that year, we got together, more romantically this time. That evening when he kissed me, I knew that the attraction was still strong. Nothing much happened until the summer of 1993, when we both had more time and a relationship became more important to both of us. Through my second year we were an item but it wasn't an all-consuming relationship and some people may have wondered how interested he really was. At times I certainly did.

Then my third year at university meant spending the academic year abroad. As I've described, Gary wasn't really interested in a long-distance relationship and didn't particularly voice his concerns. But anyway, it wouldn't have stopped me going even if he had – pretty much nothing stands in my way once I decide to do something! So I went off to the continent, licked my emotional wounds and got on with my life. Lots of people have similar experiences and if there was one thing a little different about ours, it was that we remained good friends through and after the separation. He had his new girlfriends, I had the odd boyfriend, but we stayed in pretty close contact at all times: our friendship was something that was always extremely important to both of us. And it was an understanding, warm, supportive and unconditional friendship.

For example, we went together to New York for the Fifth Avenue Mile in the autumn of both 1995 and 1996, when I won. After the 1996 race Gary and I went for a week's break in Florida. To us it was natural. We were best friends, extremely comfortable in each other's company, we enjoyed hanging out together and shared lots of interests, but it was a totally platonic relationship. It was around this time that I bought my first house in Loughborough – almost on the spur of the moment as I knew the minute I saw it that I would be happy there – and it just seemed logical that Gary should be my lodger. There was no thought in my mind that our relationship might go back to where it once was. That didn't seem a possibility and, to be honest, I was happy where we were and didn't really envisage the situation changing.

When I realised that Curtis and I weren't quite meant for each other and we broke up in the spring of 1997, there was still no hint of what was to happen between me and Gary. My focus was on that summer's World Championships in Athens and it was just good to have Gary as a friend and offering the support he always gave me. With the benefit of hindsight, however, maybe something did change with the ending of my relationship. For it happened that neither Gary nor I was now in a relationship, and that created a situation that had not existed for some time. That summer I spent a lot of time away training in Font-Romeu and Barcelona while Gary was back at the house in Loughborough. We spoke on the phone all the time but only actually saw each other when I was back home in England between training trips.

It was around that time that other friends started mentioning things to me. One of the lads at Loughborough told me how he had been with Gary one night when they both had a little bit to drink and Gary opened up and said he regretted the way things turned out between us. At the time I didn't give this much credence: people say things when they have had a bit to drink. There had been plenty of opportunities for Gary to make his feelings known and as we were now both unattached, what was there to stop him? No, I thought, I don't really believe there's anything in this.

Certainly, because I had spent a long time chasing him early on, there was a definite feeling that if anything were to develop between us, this time it had to come from him. Otherwise there was a danger that at some point in the future I would look back and worry if his feelings were as strong as mine. At the time, our friendship was enough for me. He loved me, I knew that, but I believed he loved me only as a friend. It's hard to distinguish those feelings. I knew he cared for me. If I were ever upset or hurt in any way, he would be so protective and so supportive. Kind of like a best friend or a big brother, but it wasn't like a romantic 'in love' feeling at that time.

A few nights before my departure for Athens and the World Championships, Gary and I had our evening meal together at the house in Loughborough. He might have had a couple of glasses of red wine. That's how I remember it, because he began speaking in riddles and I asked him what he was trying to say. But Gary doesn't easily open up, so I pushed him and pushed him to say exactly what was on his mind. Without much success. Then later that night, as we were upstairs getting ready for bed, we almost bumped into each other on the landing. Instead of walking on, we stopped, and looked at each other momentarily. Suddenly I sensed the strength of his feelings, and mine, and I hugged him. It just felt really comfortable and right, like we fitted together perfectly. Something, I knew, had changed for ever.

GARY:

'When Paula and I were close friends, we were an unusual pair. We lived the life of being romantically involved even though we weren't. We did the things that a couple would do but we did them purely as good friends. My family thought we were together, but I kept saying, "No, we're not, we're just very good friends." Paula's family would say, "Are you together?" "No, we're not." The situation was changing, though. Little things. I would be in the room when Curtis telephoned and would overhear the conversation. Things were a bit strained between them and she was hinting that she didn't think they had a future. And I thought this is so sad, here I am and she has no idea how I feel. I wanted to tell her but couldn't bring myself to do it.*

'People look at me and they think I am cocky. I was never cocky. But I do put on an act, put up barriers, something to hide behind because I have always been terrified of rejection. It was beyond me to work out that the worst that could happen was she would say she wasn't interested. You'd feel terrible for weeks, months, whatever, but eventually you'd move on. I mean I could have ruined my whole life by holding back, waiting for Paula to put herself on the line for me. See, I felt that wasn't a big deal for her because I was never going to reject her.*

'So that evening, when we got talking, I made up this cock-and-bull story about a friend who had this girl with whom he was really good friends. My *friend wanted to take the relationship further but didn't know how to go about it. So what should he do? Because I wasn't prepared to take the risk of putting my cards on the table, that was as far as I was able to go. She asked me to explain it better and I remember thinking, "Oh shit, she actually believes I'm talking about someone else." I can't remember where the conversation went from there, except that it was uncomfortable for me.*

'Then later that night, something happened. I can remember the second part much better than the first. In my convoluted way, did I reveal exactly how I felt? Why did things change that night? I wonder if Paula remembers the precise details. What I remember is that it was around bedtime. She was in her bedroom at the back of the house, my bedroom was at the front. There was another small bedroom, like a box room, which we used as an office. I don't know what was going on but I was in that room and can remember walking out. As I did we met on the landing, we stopped, she gave me a hug and it was like, I don't know, it was different. Then we just went to the other bedroom, her bedroom, and from then on we stayed there.

'How did I feel the next morning? I was quite relaxed about it. It wasn't like we were relative strangers. We spoke about it. There was definitely no sense of, "Oh my God, what have we done? Are we spoiling a beautiful friendship?" There was no fear, no wondering whether the other person had any doubts. It felt a lot more natural than that.'

Friends of mine were protective and reluctant to encourage me to get back with Gary. Liz, I remember, thought it was great that Gary and I stayed friends after our original break-up, and she also thought it was nice that we were relaxed enough about the situation to become housemates. Did she approve of us getting back together again? I'm not sure – I think she would just have been concerned that I was happy. At the time she didn't know, and had she known, she would probably have asked, 'Are you sure you're not going to get hurt again?' Gary and I didn't feel the need to rush out and tell people immediately. I suppose it was partly because a lot of people were maybe going to say, 'Oh yes, we always knew you two weren't just the friends you claimed to be,' and partly because we didn't see the need to shout about it. We were happy and that was what mattered most. Neither Gary nor I said a word but I went off to the World Championships in Greece feeling on very good terms with life.

I understood that my friends might have been concerned had they known, but there were absolutely no doubts in my mind. The previous experience had been painful but that wasn't going to stop me. There are people – and Gary is a bit like this – who choose not to let others get too close, or to put themselves in certain situations, because they are afraid of getting hurt. I have never been like that. Being hurt once is no reason to lock your heart away. Hurt heals, and if you never take chances you might never find who or what you're looking for. It's a little bit like my attitude to racing: I give all I can and lay everything on the line; if sometimes it doesn't pay off and ends in severe disappointment that's no reason to be afraid to come back again and again and keep trying. If something is important to you there is no limit to how hard you will try to achieve it. Yes, I had been hurt in the past, but it wasn't an experience I regretted. There were never regrets; there were good times and there were sad times, but through them all we maintained our friendship.

Earlier, when we had first split up, people asked if I regretted that my feelings about Gary were so obvious. The answer is that I didn't – your heart is not really that fragile, and if you don't put it out there you'll never get the rewards. At least I made my feelings clear, and if the relationship didn't work out, it wouldn't be because of a lack of effort or willingness to try on my part. What would have happened if it hadn't worked out the second time? In my view it would have been easier for me to get over it, knowing I had done everything possible to make it happen. The alternative would have been for me to pretend that I didn't care, that it didn't matter a damn, that there was no upset after the break-up. For me, that simply wasn't true, and anyway, I've never been any good at hiding my emotions!

People gradually became aware that our relationship had changed. Certainly that was the case with my parents. Their attitude with my brother Martin and me has always been that we are individuals, that we should make our own choices and decisions. They have always supported us and been there with advice when we've needed it, but it's always been up to us to determine our directions in life. The sports we took up, the friends we hung out with, the universities we chose; it was up to us. They hoped we made the right decisions but thought the decisions should be ours. They might have been curious about the nature of my relationship with Gary at different times, but they wouldn't have dreamed of interfering.

Not long afterwards, however, we did hit another bumpy patch. This was getting towards the end of 1997 and Gary's injury was refusing to get any better. Desperate to get it right, he tried to get an appointment with an Irish physical therapist, Gerard Hartmann, who worked with Kim McDonald's athletes in London during the summers. Gerard had been a successful triathlete and then qualified as a physical therapist. At the time he was based in America but was on the cusp of returning to his native Limerick. He worked with many of the world's best athletes and Peter McColgan had suggested to Gary that he should see him. Gary had one treatment session in London during the summer and saw some immediate improvement. They agreed Gary would go to Limerick for two weeks in November, and I went along too. It was my end-of-season break and I went along to support Gary. Given Gerard's reputation, I was also keen to meet him.

We stayed in the lodge at Gerard's parents' house in Limerick. At the time Gerard was setting up a clinic in the centre of the city but hadn't yet developed the residential apartments over the clinic that, in time, would become a frequent home to me. Gerard's approach with athletes is very hands-on. He uses very deep and penetrative tissue work and massage to stimulate quicker recovery of the injured area. He is about the best there is in this branch of medicine but for

Gerard to produce results, his patient must be able to withstand a reasonable level of pain. This was not Gary's strong suit, and the sessions with Gerard drained him to such an extent that all he wanted to do afterwards was hide away and sleep. He really withdrew into himself and though I had come to support him and keep him company, he barely spoke to me at all through the first week.

GARY:

'That time at Gerard's I just felt drained all the time. The thing about the injury was it had been going on for so long and it was really getting to me. Half of me was convinced I would be fine, that these two weeks with Gerard would put me on the road to complete recovery. The other half was less optimistic: this was my last shot, if this didn't work I was screwed. I had been built up and shot down so many times that I was all over the place mentally.

'Then there was Gerard's treatment. It was really intense and I had never been through anything like that in my life. I didn't know what was happening to me but it sure as hell wasn't much fun. It was necessary; I accepted that. I hadn't been able to run for weeks and before that, every time I'd run there had been pain. Gerard did some things to the knee, really deep friction, that almost killed me. Then he did more things. "Go now and run," he said. I gave him that you-must-be-fucking-joking look. "I can't, I know I can't," I said. "Try." I tried. I could run without pain. I knew then he was able to help me.

'But the treatment never got easier and I didn't get any better at dealing with it. Paula was in the wrong place at the wrong time. Unable to cope with the pain, I started to act like a psycho. She would ask, "Are you okay?" and that was the one question I didn't need to be asked. All I wanted to do was curl up and sleep. I look back on how I was for those two weeks and I think of all the times I have watched her on Gerard's table, getting therapy far tougher than the stuff I couldn't deal with. I just don't know, I have never known how she copes with the amount of treatment that she does. I know I couldn't.

'That first time she was meant to stay with me in Limerick for two weeks. But my moods were too much. Even for her. She left early.'

There was no point in my being around if it wasn't possible for me to help Gary, and I wasn't having much fun. I had also been wanting for a while to spend some time with my grandma in Liverpool. A little over a week after arriving in Limerick, I changed my flight and headed home. Just before getting on a bus to Shannon Airport, I spoke to Gary. 'Look, there's not much point in us carrying on with this relationship if you can't treat me with respect and can barely speak to me whenever things get difficult for you. It's not going to work. I'm going to stay with my grandma and when I come back, we've got to sort something out, because this isn't working.'

I don't know if Gary and Gerard discussed the situation, but I suspect they did. Ger appreciates how his treatment can affect people differently. Given time, Gary would have seen that he was out of order. Whatever – when Gary came back from Limerick he made a big effort to apologise and make things better. I still wanted to take a step back and re-evaluate the relationship: I needed to be sure that every time things got tough he wasn't going to shut me out. So for a while we went back to being just close friends and housemates. Pretty soon I knew that he was totally serious about us and back to what to me is the real Gary and, of course, we got back to where we were again. And have been together ever since.

Two years later, we got engaged. Given how long we had known each other and how much time we had spent in each other's company, the engagement wasn't going to shock anyone. We had talked about things and knew we wanted to get married and spend the rest of our lives together. As for the engagement, it was a question of time. If Gary had his way, it would have been the scenic route again. He is old-fashioned in some respects and he had this notion that before he could propose to me, he would have to have a secure career and a means of supporting me. At the time he was still hoping to return to his athletic career but struggling to regain his fitness after the serious injury. His old-world view of the man's responsibilities was complicated by the fact that I owned the house and had the greater earning power at the time. He wasn't going to do anything until our circumstances changed. As for me, the tradition that decreed the man must propose, earn, provide, was totally irrelevant. What mattered to me was happiness and love. That was the only security I needed.

The day before his 29th birthday we were down in Bedford staying with my parents. His birthday, 6 July, is also Mum's birthday, and I was out shopping with Mum trying to think of something to buy him. We were in a jeweller's and there was a man's ring that I liked.

'That's a nice ring, isn't it?' I said to Mum.

'Yeah,' she said, 'you could get him a ring.'

'No, he has a ring already. He got it when his grandmother died.'

We left the shop and as we were walking around town I thought about the custom of the man always proposing to the woman and it dawned on me how sexist that was: the woman waiting for the man to make the move. There was no reason why a woman should not propose to her man if she wanted to. And I wanted to. But wanting to do something is not the same as being able to do it, and I was hopelessly torn. Should I? Shouldn't I? Would Gary be pleased or not? As I was flying out to Rome for a race the following day, there wasn't a lot of time. What the hell! Back I went to the shop, bought the ring and had them wrap it up nicely. Mum knew that I'd bought the ring but had no idea why.

In the evening we had a barbecue birthday meal in the back garden for Mum and Gary. That night in bed, I gave him his present and asked him to unwrap it.

'But I've got a ring,' he said.

'Yes, but maybe you could wear this one on that finger.'

That was as close to a formal proposal as I was able to get. The penny didn't drop immediately with my ever so romantic husband-to-be. Eventually, he saw what I was saying.

'But, this is not right,' he said. 'You have to have a ring as well. We can't be engaged and you not have a ring.'

As I was flying out to Rome the next day, we got up early and went in search of my ring. It meant a lot to me to get engaged. Gary wouldn't have known that but it made me happier, more secure, and it didn't bother me in the slightest that I had been the one to take the initiative. If it had been left to him, it might have taken a long time. As far as I was concerned, getting married means being together and sharing everything. I didn't care about who asked who or who contributes what, so long as we were both happy and committed to each other. After we bought my ring, Gary did the traditional bit, going down on one knee and asking me if I would marry him. Given what had taken place the previous night, the chances of rejection were slim. We then told my parents and Dad joked with Gary that he had not been asked for his permission. Seriously, they were both very pleased for us.

I went to Rome on cloud nine and ran a personal best – actually I ran PBs in nearly every race until the end of the season. Having that ring on my finger definitely didn't slow me down. I remember Gary, all excited, phoning his brother saying, 'I've got a big surprise to tell you,' and his brother just said, 'What, you finally got engaged?' Like I said, it came as no surprise to anyone.

GARY:

'We were definitely going to get engaged, but I was doing it in my own time. We talked about it and I would have suggested it was something we should do, but I would have put it in a really twisted, cryptic way, nothing direct. I was thinking further down the line. Then she gave me this ring and I said I had a ring already. She said well you could wear it on the other finger. "Then it would be more like an engagement ring." Doh! That's how it happened. She asked me. Some people might have seen that as a sign of weakness in a woman, I saw it as totally the opposite. It just showed her strength.

'Being male, this made me ask some obvious questions. "What can I offer

you? How can I provide for you?" Paula was thinking in the twenty-first century, I was still back in the nineteenth. I was saying, "What can I do to support us?" and she was saying, "Bollocks to all that, I know what I want and I am not afraid to go after it." Then for the next five minutes, I agonised over whether I was about to lose my identity as an athlete. Had Gary Lough, one-time 1,500m runner, just become Paula Radcliffe's fiancé? It didn't take long for me to get over that. What was the big deal? If that was how it was going to be, that was how it was going to be. Imagine the stupidity of doing something you really want to do, but kicking and screaming about your loss of identity on the way? That stuff just wasn't important.'

The wedding had to take place at a time of the year that fitted into the athletics calendar, especially as we planned to marry in 2000, the year of the Sydney Olympics. We had been living together for three years before the engagement, we had known each other and been best friends for the best part of eight years and neither of us wanted a long engagement. So after getting engaged in July 1999, we got married in April 2000, the ceremony arranged to coincide with the break immediately after the World Cross-Country Championships and before the training started in earnest for that year's Olympic Games. We decided to get married in Oakley, the village just outside Bedford where I had grown up and where my parents still live. After looking at different options in the area, we decided to have the reception in a marquee erected in their back garden.

Both our extended families are quite big and there were a lot of people we wanted to invite, so in the end we felt the only way we could comfortably have everyone we wanted at our wedding was to have it in a marquee. Mum quite liked the idea as well. She is very good at organising and while Gary and I were away preparing for the World Cross-Country, she helped out with a lot of the arrangements. I was able to do quite a bit but Mum was brilliant at taking care of things and liaising with the caterers and she had great plans for how she would have the garden blooming for the big day.

One of her plans was to make these floating flowers that would have candles and other little things in them and float them on the pool, which was right outside the marquee. Mum, to her great credit, made these magnificent floating flowers and had the garden just perfect for the big day. The evening before, Liz stayed over with me. She was my chief bridesmaid; Gary's sister Catherine was the other. On the morning of my wedding Liz and I got up early and went for a run. We didn't go far but that wasn't the point: this was my last run as a single woman and it was also the perfect way to start off what was one of the happiest days of my life. We got back and were just showered when the heavens opened. It bucketed down all day, non-stop. Mum never put the floating flowers out and no one got to appreciate all her work in the garden. That was all I regretted. The French have a saying: 'A rainy marriage is a happy marriage.' There were a couple of little hiccups. At the hairdresser's, Gary called me.

'You're not supposed to speak with me until we see each other at the church. What do you want?'

'I lost my wallet last night.'

'You what?'

'We were out last night, a big group of my family and friends, and when I woke up this morning, I couldn't find my wallet.'

He cancelled his cards and twenty minutes later, his friend turned up with the wallet. 'You kept leaving your wallet on the bar and I thought it would be safer if I put it in my bag and kept it safe for you.' Then later, as Gary and his brother prepared to leave their hotel for the church, they found that the security barrier in the car-park was stuck and they couldn't get out. He quickly telephoned my dad to tell him to delay our departure to the church, so that our arrival could be after Gary's.

As I walked up the aisle, there were tears in his eyes and it reminded me of what the vicar had said to us before the wedding. People expect the bride to cry and be the more emotional on her wedding day, but in her experience, it is more often the groom.

Brides tend to have thought things through beforehand and been emotional in the preceding weeks, whereas it hits the groom on the day. After the ceremony we went through to sign the register and as we did, two butterflies descended and landed on the book. One was perched on top of the other, the way you often see butterflies, and as they sat there motionlessly together, I thought it a good and beautiful omen.

The weather didn't dampen the party mood and everyone, especially us, had a brilliant time. It was a great, great occasion that may actually have been helped by the rain. Because it was so wet, everyone had to stay in the marquee and because they did, the atmosphere was terrific. Totally lacking a dancer's natural rhythm, I tend to stay sitting when the disco music blares but on my wedding day, I was never off the floor. It was all so wonderfully relaxed. Later in the evening we had an entertainment group who were going to put on a cabaret.

By that time the Irish contingent had started their own impromptu cabaret, each one singing in turn. As it turned out, they were all amazing singers. The cabaret guys didn't try to intervene and just let the party flow. They do say no one knows how to party like the Irish!

The next day dawned bright and beautiful. Blue skies, glorious sunshine, an April morning perfect for a wedding. Mum and Dad had open house for everyone that was still around. We laughed about the change in the weather as we sat in our shirtsleeves in the garden, waiting for Dad to get the barbecue going. Mum too had her moment as she got the chance to float her flowers in the pool. The day after was, in fact, another great day. That evening Gary and I set off on our honeymoon and had an amazing time together.

10

Through the 1990s there was a pattern to my running career. If you were summarising the years from 1992 to 1998, the phrase that would have best encapsulated my career to that point would have been 'climbing the ladder rung by rung'. I was enjoying my running, fairly successful and near the top of my sport, but still felt that there was a lot more to come. I was happy and understood that there was no use rushing things; my speed and strength were growing stronger as my body matured and the training backlog built up. I was absorbed in the day-to-day challenge of enjoying my running, staying fit and preparing for the next big test; mostly I focus on each target at a time, race to race and then from season to season. I don't often allow myself the luxury of standing back and looking at the overall but still incomplete picture. At that stage, in our end-of-season assessments, slight disappointment over not being able to get among the medals in the big championships was lessened by the continual improvement in my times at all the distances. As long as I was improving and moving forward – and, most importantly, happy – there was no reason to question whether the journey was worthwhile. I knew that it was.

As the years passed, all my times continued to get faster and I bettered and improved the national record over 5,000m, but I was frustrated by the lack of tangible reward in terms of championship medals, especially on the track. I wanted to run fast, but more importantly I wanted to win races and titles. At the major championships from Stuttgart in 1993 to Athens in 1997 – three World Championships and the Atlanta Olympics – my results were 7th, 5th, 5th and 4th. Progression in the right direction, yes – but in another way, a case of so near and yet so far. I was well aware that people were highlighting my lack of finishing speed as a reason that I could never win big races. My record was better in cross-country as there was the silver medal from Turin in 1997. Still, that was a title I had hoped to win, maybe even expected to win early in my senior career.

In three of the four finals on the track, I had made the pace for the group that I was with only to be passed in the closing stages by those who had benefited from my front running for most of the race. Fans felt sorry for me because they thought it unfair the eternal front-runner should have nothing to show for her efforts. However, what was important to me was that I ran as well as I could: I could ask no more of myself. It was frustrating to miss out so narrowly, though, and I badly wanted to be winning races and medals more often. It was kind of people to praise my 'guts' or my 'courage', or my 'spirit', but I don't run for praise or admiration, I run to be the best that I can be. Most of the time I led the races because it suited me to have a fast pace. If by hanging back I could have improved my chances of winning, that is what I would have done. In any race you do whatever optimises your chances of winning. That is what sometimes frustrates me when I watch a race where the competitors are all jogging round looking at each other. Not everyone in that race can believe they are going to win in a last-lap burn-up, so why don't they have the courage to run the race that suits them?

Inside me there was also an iron will-to-win and a desire to show people I was a winner, not just some plucky English girl who tried hard but couldn't get there. I believed that each year I was getting stronger and better and with perseverance and patience I could get to where I wanted to be. Until those results and titles came I could do nothing about the perception of the gallant front-runner, and anyhow it never really hurt or upset me. I suppose I was more confused at how people could see any more courage and spirit in me than in other athletes. In my mind I was the same as any other athlete out there trying to be the best. At the beginning of 1998, we looked ahead and saw the opportunity presented by the European Championships in Budapest and the Commonwealth Games in Kuala Lumpur. In both there was a track title I could win, and we saw this as another step up the ladder to where we wanted to go. The competition at the Europeans and the Commonwealth Games may have been slightly easier than at a world level, but I knew it would still be difficult – all three medallists ahead of me in 1997, for example, were European. On the women's distance side there isn't the huge difference between the African runners and the rest of the world that sometimes exists on the men's. We Europeans have always been able to compete right up there with the rest of the world, and I certainly saw no reason that I couldn't. Europe's women distance runners are strong and I grew up seeing that there was no reason not to be able to compete with anyone else. That has never changed – I believe that races are races, we are all in there in the mix if we work hard enough at it and continental differences are not an excuse.

The year began promisingly.

Again Alex, Rosemary, Gary and I headed off to Albuquerque together. Gary was essentially still doing his own training programme but again we did a lot of our steady running together and this helped the overall quality of my training. Being together also made our time there more enjoyable. I had increased the training volume slightly and the times were better than the year before, when the work we did had been the key to the silver medal in Turin. The 1998 World

Cross-Country Championships were to be held in Marrakech in Morocco, and for the first time there would be two senior events: an 8-kilometre race on the Saturday and a 4-kilometre race the following day. The 8k race was the principal one and my plan was to make a decision on the shorter race only after running in the previous day's longer event. That created a problem for the GB team, which was explained to me on the eve of the race by the endurance performance director, Norman Brook. 'The difficulty,' he said, 'is that we have to submit our team for Sunday before Saturday's race. If we put you in and you decide not to run, then the girl who has come here on standby will not get to race.'

It was impossible for me to commit 100 per cent to Sunday because the 8k race was what I had prepared for and I wanted to focus fully on that with no other thoughts in my mind. Although I felt that I would be able to regain my strength and run well again on the Sunday, I didn't want anyone to lose out if my body was unable to recover. I thought about the girl who was next in line in the 4k. 'How would I feel,' I thought, 'if I were in her position?' If I was declared to run and then didn't, she would be very disappointed, and understandably so. The place would have been wasted. 'Look,' I said to Norman, 'I am just going to go for the 8k, pull me out of the 4k, that's the best thing.'

The Marrakech race came down to a battle between me and Sonia O'Sullivan. The pace had been decent. By the last lap I was trying to wind it up and was making it tough for the other runners. Most of them dropped back but Sonia was very strong. Turning into the finishing straight, there were still about 350 metres to go and I was poised to launch my last, long sprint effort. However, instead of allowing us to exit the race loop on to the finishing straight, the race steward directed us around another lap. The finishing straight was still blocked off. I knew there wasn't another lap and, momentarily disorientated, I wondered what to do. Obviously I had judged the pace according to the distance and running another 2km lap was not a possibility. I considered pushing through the officials and cones to get on to the straight, but I saw Sonia veer around the marshal and stay on the course, as if she meant to run another lap. Instinctively I followed her and gave chase, thinking, 'Okay, I'm racing all-out until I'm level with the finish gantry, and then I'm stopping. Hopefully by then the officials will have realised their mistake.' Afterwards Sonia explained that she knew there was a gap through some ornamental trees close to the finish gantry where she could get through on to the finishing straight. When she did this I followed her and some quick-thinking supporters tore out some trees to make the way easier for the other runners. My fleeting hesitation had allowed Sonia to get the jump on me and I couldn't ever get back to her. Maybe I wouldn't have beaten her anyway, but it would have been easier to accept defeat if the finish hadn't been so confused. A second consecutive silver medal was good, but I was disappointed as I had gone there to win. However, Sonia had run very well and the next day also went out and won the 4k race. The thought of how I would have placed in the 4k did strike me, but I had made my decision and there were no regrets. Generally I was happy with the result; I had run as well as I could and was ultimately beaten by a better athlete on the day. My quest for the World Cross-Country title continued . . .

It was going to be a long year: the European Championships would not take place until August and the Commonwealth Games weren't until September. As it was my intention to move to the 10,000m at the European Championships, we decided to compete in the European Track Challenge race over that distance in Lisbon two weeks after the World Cross. This was to be my first-ever 10k on the track, and although everything suggested the move to the longer distance would suit me and that I would run well, the real test would be in the race, and there is always some uncertainty and apprehension when attempting something for the first time. Although I was excited and looking forward to it, I was extremely worried about the after-effects of the stomach and intestinal infection that most of the team had managed to contract in Morocco. We had all had a course of antibiotics but my stomach was still giving me some trouble.

Beforehand my uppermost concern was whether it would be possible to run the 10,000m without needing a toilet along the way. Alex was his usual calming influence. 'This is just a little trial for you, no pressure, just go out and enjoy it. The aim here is to learn, so you run entirely how you feel.' Of course, he knew that I wanted to break Liz McColgan's British record of 30.57 and we had worked out the kilometre splits needed to achieve that. However, his last words to me are always that I am the athlete out there, I'm the only one that has all the facts about what is happening and how I feel, so I make the final decisions about how to race. From the beginning I set off at a pace to run around 30.50 and being used to 5,000m racing it felt very comfortable.

Running in her home country, Fernanda Ribeiro, the Olympic 10,000m champion, wanted to do well and for much of the race she also contributed to the pacemaking, not an equal share but far more than she would have had it been a championship race. We maintained the pace and as the race went on I forgot about the time targets and concentrated on trying to win the race. I knew I was comfortably going to get a championship qualifying time and was well on the way to setting a new British record, so I focused on winning.

Into the last couple of kilometres, Ribeiro stopped coming through to do her turns at the front and instead positioned herself directly behind me. Through the last kilometre my stomach began to churn but I blocked it from my mind. Into the last lap we were still locked together but in the sprint Ribeiro got past me and won the race. My disappointment at being beaten, albeit by the reigning Olympic champion, was lessened by the achievement of setting a new British record of 30.48. To run my first 10,000m on the track and beat Liz's record by 9 seconds was encouraging and ended all debate about what race I would run at the European Championships in Budapest in the summer. I had qualified for the Europeans and had no need to run another 10,000m before Budapest. Feeling good after Lisbon I went to Balmoral a week later and set a new world best for 5 miles on the road. It snowed the weekend of the race, conditions I always relish, and I loved the race. I had my first two world bests (8km and 5 miles). That road racing suited me was becoming more and more obvious.

After Balmoral I went out to Boulder in Colorado where Gary was training with George Gandy's Loughborough group. It was more relaxation for me as I would be taking my end-of-season break, and it was really just an opportunity for Gary and me to be together. After Colorado we went back to England and then I was soon off to Font-Romeu to prepare for the Europeans. Gary would join me later, as he had taken on a teaching job while trying to get back to where he had been athletically. That 10,000m had become a very important goal, as I was beginning to sense that my time was coming and that this summer I could make my mark at the championships. We worked harder than ever in Font-Romeu, again improved our training times on the previous year, and by the time we left the Pyrenees I was feeling confident.

Before the championships I decided to run a 3,000m at Sheffield and then a 5,000m at Stockholm. They were race tests to sharpen my competitive edge and racing form, and even though I beat Sonia O'Sullivan to win in Sheffield, the performance worried me. For whatever reason I didn't feel quite right, my legs were heavy and every effort took more out of me than it should. Alex said not to worry; it was probably nothing more than that I needed a little longer to freshen up after the severity of the training in Font-Romeu. However, a few days later when I travelled to Stockholm I had my answer – I was suffering from a head cold. It should have put me off racing in Stockholm, but I was already there, looking forward to it and felt I needed the 5,000m race in my build-up to Budapest. It was only a head cold, I reasoned, not a chest infection.

Zahra Ouaziz won the race by a long way, running 14.40, and though my 14.51 for 2nd place was okay, the spark was missing and I felt flat. It was the following morning that brought the really bad news: I felt rotten, totally flat and without energy. The cold cleared up and I began to feel a bit better, but I still felt more tired than usual and my training runs between then and the European Championships all felt a little harder than they should have done. It is times such as this that are the bane of all athletes. You work hard for months to be at a peak of fitness and form for one important week, but it doesn't always come right and those times can be very confusing and frustrating. I tried to convince myself that I would feel better as I eased up for the championships, but at the back of my mind I was worried.

Budapest seems to have nothing but unhappy memories for me. However, I am determined to one day go back there and beat the demons. Four years earlier the World Cross-Country Championships were held there but injury prevented me from competing. That was the time I ludicrously agreed to go anyway: hobbling around on crutches, I was supposed to be good for team spirit. Four years on, I was feeling flat and listless in the days leading up to the 10,000m final. Gary, who was travelling out to Budapest to support me, was involved in a serious car accident when someone pulled out in front of him while on his way to the airport. He didn't want to tell me at first as he didn't want me worrying, but I rang him while he was getting checked out in the hospital and he had no alternative. He had suffered some concussion and bruising but insisted, in telephone calls before the race, that there were no serious injuries and that he would see me the next day.

The 10,000m final at the European Championships is a race I shall not easily forget. The thing about an injury or feeling below par for some other reason is that however much you try to think positively and convince yourself it will be okay, deep down your body senses something is wrong. Often the injury or the bug only affects you at the moment of maximum effort, so by backing off a little in training it can seem okay, but sometimes even though you think you're all right your body shows signs that it is not. Once in Budapest, the worry and doubt got pushed away to the back of my mind, but they must still have been there. Alex said afterwards that I just didn't seem quite myself in the warm-up area, I was distracted and more nervous than normal. During the warm-up my legs felt leaden and lifeless but I tried to tell myself it was just pre-race anxiety. It can be true as I rarely feel great in warm-up, even for some of my best races. I told myself, 'Don't worry about it, once the race begins, you will snap into life.'

I dispelled the negative thoughts and remained committed to my race plan. That meant setting a fast pace, making it as hard as possible for the other girls and burning off as many of them as I could.

From the start, though, everything felt harder than it should have. I went to the front as planned and led, trying to make the pace as punishing as possible, but it wasn't there. No energy, no strength, and I wasn't running fast enough. I wasn't stretching those behind me and I could sense the presence of too many runners. I was running 73- and 74-second laps but needed to be at a 71- or 72-second pace. I knew I needed to be running faster but simply wasn't able to. At different points I would try to surge, but the lap times kept reminding me the pace was not changing. However hard I tried, nothing changed. I began to feel panic and frustration as well as weakness and exhaustion.

Ribeiro, Sonia O'Sullivan, Lydia Simon, Olivera Jevtic and Julia Vaquero were in a line behind me and apart from Vaquero, they were all comfortable. The race wasn't fast enough. I tried to force myself: faster, harder. I pushed on, momentarily shutting the pursuers out of my mind, trying to force every last ounce of energy out of myself. Yet they were all still there. This is the worst feeling in sport, like a dream I've had where I am running through quicksand, desperate to get out but the harder I run, the deeper my legs sink in until I am clawing hopelessly with my arms. As we went into the last kilometre, then 800 metres, 600, 400 to go, I could feel those behind me getting ready to move. Sensing their energy while knowing I had absolutely nothing left, no counter to their strength – that is the dread, the horrible helplessness of a leader out there with nothing left in reserve. Through all of this, my mind was alert and conscious of what needed to be done, but physically my body could not respond.

As they went past, I tried desperately to find something else, arms flailing, shoulders rising, head bobbing frantically as I disappeared into the quicksand. I didn't stop fighting but my muscles were powerless. I watched them go: first Ribeiro, then O'Sullivan, after that Simon and Jevtic; 1st, 2nd, 3rd, 4th. The fourth girl passes me and as she does it is confirmation of how terribly the race has unfolded. Simon and Jevtic are not athletes that would ordinarily beat me. Afterwards I thought back to what it felt like as they overtook me and it was like someone punching me in the stomach. Emotionally you know you cannot respond and the exhaustion increases. All I could do was hold on and get to the finish before collapsing.

The exhaustion that had accompanied me all through then assumed complete control once the race ended. This was a different collapse to the normal exhaustion at the end of a hard race. My body felt totally empty and drained. The paramedics understood it wasn't normal post-race tiredness and they took me away on a stretcher. There were so many questions in my mind. What had happened to me? Why such overwhelming exhaustion? The race hadn't even been fast – the time, 31.30, was nowhere near my best. It should have felt easy. After being checked out and regaining enough strength to get off the stretcher, I saw Alex and Gary. I felt I had let them down too. All I wanted was a hug but when I tried that Gary was in agony due to the injuries from his car accident.

The next day wasn't any better. Still feeling miserable about the race and not exactly a bundle of energy, I tried my usual response:

going out for an easy run and trying to make myself feel better. But I still felt awful; there was nothing there, not one scintilla of strength. The easy conclusion was that my problem was purely physical, but my mind was in worry mode. What if it was psychological? Had the pressure and ambition I put myself under to do well become too much and left me unable to cope? Did the nerves get to me? Needing to speak with someone who understood these questions, I went to Alma Thomas, who was psychologist to the GB team in Budapest. I knew Alma from previous GB teams but had always considered myself mentally strong and in no need of her expertise. Where once there weren't even questions, I was now full of doubt.

'Honestly, Alma,' I said, 'I don't know what happened to me in that race. Did I just bottle it? Why couldn't I push myself harder? Can I just not do it any more? I train routinely at a certain pace and yesterday in the race I couldn't run at that pace. How can that be? Could it be that my mind won't let me go through that pain barrier? I should easily have been able to run much faster than I ran. I have to find out what's wrong with me.'

Alma dealt admirably with the situation. 'Well,' she said, 'the first thing you must do is calm down so we can get some answers here. Knowing you, I don't think it's psychological and before you go tearing yourself apart over this, you must go back home and get some blood tests done. If the results of those say that physically, you are a hundred per cent healthy, then it might be time to look at the mental side.'

We talked for a short time, and Alma asked lots of questions, but the bottom line remained the same: she felt the most likely explanation was physical.

The blood tests showed the existence of a virus that had attacked and depleted my red cells, lowering my haemoglobin to a level that fully explained why there had been so little energy. That, the doctors believed, was a secondary effect of the virus and my system showed all the signs of having had a debilitating battle with the bug. 'You've got to take it easy,' they said. It's possible that after the hard training and then racing with a bug my immune system was temporarily compromised and needed rest to recover fully. However, the Commonwealth Games were just four weeks away and I now had to make a decision about whether I was in condition to go and compete. The only way to know if it was possible to run in Kuala Lumpur was to race again, and a week after Budapest, I raced over a mile in Glasgow.

Kelly Holmes, who had missed the European Championships through illness, used the Glasgow race for the same purpose as me. She won in 4.28, I ran 4.31 but while she felt fine afterwards, I still felt uncommonly weak. Very much in the back of my mind was the thought that injury had ruled me out of the Commonwealth Games at Victoria in British Columbia four years before and I didn't want to miss them again. Besides, there was a chance that I might still be able to win in KL even if I was less than 100 per cent. We agonised for days on end; the tiredness I felt after the Glasgow run was countered by the fact that it hadn't been a disastrously bad run. But, in the end, the decision was made for us.

While we were locked on the horns of this dilemma I hardly had the energy to walk up the stairs and had to force myself out the door to train. And the doctors' advice was that my body needed rest. I might get away with racing at a slower pace than usual but my body would be further set back by forcing it, and I'd need a lot of time off afterwards to recover. I was still young, with a long career ahead of me. I didn't want to risk damaging my body's immune system long-term. So I made the sensible decision and pulled out of the team. The next day Gary and I went and booked ourselves a last-minute holiday on the island of Antigua in the West Indies. Missing the Commonwealth Games hurt, but we both needed a holiday and time to relax. And I didn't really want to be home watching the Games on television.

*

The two-week break at the Mango Bay Hotel in Antigua was badly needed. We spent the first week on the beach and by the pool. My tiredness persisted – I was sleeping more than when training hard! Feeling a little better in the second week, we hired bikes and went on a few trips around the island. Towards the end came the news of Hurricane Georges which was expected to pass close to the island a day or two later. We had become friendly with a couple called Stephen and Nicola. At the time of the hurricane talk, Gary and Stephen were looking at the likely route of Georges as it was shown in the local newspaper. Joking around with a pen, they tempted fate and changed the path of Hurricane Georges, diverting it to come directly over Antigua. That evening we heard the hurricane's actual course had changed and was now expected to hit our island.

Nature has its own way of dealing with things. Earlier that day we were snorkelling and the sea was choppier than normal. As well as the usual fish we had seen earlier in the week, the bigger ones were now coming in to seek the shelter of the coastline. 'Look at that one,' I motioned to Gary, pointing to the biggest one that was just a few yards away. 'That's a barracuda and they can be vicious. They have been known to kill small children so you'd better get away from there.' He was gone and I didn't need any further persuasion myself.

If it was interesting to watch how the fish reacted to the imminence of the storm, it was fascinating to observe the humans. Many pretended to be not in the least worried. Georges was a serious hurricane that caused loss of life and extensive damage in Antigua. Beneath the superficial bravura we witnessed among our fellow holidaymakers, there was genuine fear. Boarding up the hotel, the staff advised us that we would all have to stay in our rooms when the hurricane struck but when it was delayed they opened up the bar and people were free to have a drink. Some people just wanted to party and drink to forget what was about to happen. They got drunk and enjoyed a great night. Others went quiet and couldn't stop thinking about it. Still others just carried on as if everything was normal. Needless to say, Gary's reaction and mine were very different.

My mood was quiet but apprehensive. The hurricane worried me a little but also made me curious: what would it be like? The eye of the storm was headed directly for us, would the hotel withstand it? This thought struck me as did the fact that I still had so much in my life left to experience and to achieve. Gary, however, was in the bar, drinking, laughing and generally partying a bit. He wasn't as bad as the guys who were getting hammered but neither was he quietly reflecting on the meaning of life. After a while they gave us a packed lunch and told us to go to our rooms with firm instructions to lock our doors and make sure the door to the outside stayed closed at all times. We knew the storm was coming but it was boring at first because nothing happened. There was a fair amount of rain and the wind picked up. It was only six o'clock in the evening and it had the makings of a long night. Soon after the wind increased, the power went in the hotel, and around this time, Gary fell asleep. With a lighted candle, I sat up and listened to Hurricane Georges' arrival. I could hear coconuts and debris flying around outside banging against things, hitting the walls and boarded-up patio windows of our room hard, sometimes so hard that the glass would bend inwards threatening to shatter. By now the wind was raging at speeds of over 100mph and there was a sense of the devastation being caused outside.

In the middle of the night, the eye of the storm passed over the island and there was suddenly a weird temporary respite when the wind dropped and everything fell quiet. Then it began again, the howling and lashing of the wind and rain, this time from the opposite direction but with the same ferocity. As the storm passed over and then turned back on itself, Gary got out of bed, went to the door and opened it. He was trying to look at the eye of the storm, but was a little late! Maybe he was disorientated, maybe still a little drunk, but this was the one thing they told us not to do. 'Shut the door, shut that door!' I shouted at him.

We were lucky because if he had opened that door half an hour before, when the wind was blowing in the opposite direction, we would never have got it closed again. Gary, who had been asleep, hadn't heard the door being torn from a closet where they kept cleaning materials near our room. Part of that door went flying in the air and crashed against our bathroom window. I heard all this and then watched in horror as Gary got up and opened the door.

Next morning there was the calm and the carnage after the storm. Roofs had been torn off houses, some houses demolished, the roads were littered with debris, trees were down everywhere, and the beach where we swam had disappeared. The hotel across the road from us was totally wrecked. They hadn't boarded it up as well as ours and someone said the owners believed it was cheaper to rebuild it after a hurricane than to build a hurricane-proof hotel in the first place.

The airport at Antigua had suffered damage and incoming aircraft could not land. We were put on an air shuttle to Barbados and flown home to London from there. Because of Hurricane Georges, we spent an extra two days in Antigua and had the unexpected bonus of a lovely day in Barbados.

There is one part of the Antiguan experience that has stayed with me, a little epiphany that has come back at different times over the last six years to remind me that however important it is to win a race or a title, there are things that matter more.

A couple of days before the arrival of Hurricane Georges, I was by the pool when Gary came along with a newspaper.

'I've got a paper with the results of the women's 5,000m in Kuala Lumpur, do you want to hear?'

'I suppose so.'

'Only if you want to know?'

'Okay, tell me.'

'The Australian Kate Anderson won, Andrea Whitcombe got the silver. Now do you want to hear the winning time?'

'Okay.'

'Fifteen fifty-two.'

'What!'

'Yeah, fifteen fifty-two.'

Even though I had accepted not being at the Commonwealth Games, it really got to me that a prestigious championship final could have been won in such a slow time. Part of me felt that even below par, if only I had gone there, I could still have been in the fight for the gold medal. Even with a virus I thought I could have won the race. The news from KL put my mind in turmoil yet again – had I thrown away the chance of a Commonwealth title? Then I thought again about the five balls. What was important was that I had to keep that fragile health ball safe and intact. It had been a hard decision not to go, but I would have felt worse if I'd gone and maybe done serious damage to my health. This way I was disappointed but I knew I'd be healthy and strong again quickly and hopefully for a good many years to come. I had made my decision and there was no looking back. As it was I was starting to feel strong again, and six weeks after the decision to pull out I would be back training again.

However, this rationality didn't help the anger and frustration at the way things had panned out. I had to get away and think this through on my own. I went off walking and after a while found a cliff that looked out over the ocean and sat down there. From the cliff you could see far out to sea, the swells, the white horses and the gathering dark clouds foretold the hurricane that would arrive the following day.

I could also see my world in clearer outline because it was a mirror reflection of the turmoil out at sea. I tried to be rational and to accept that missing Kuala Lumpur had been the right decision: what if I had gone and completely wrecked my health in the process? But it still seemed unfair that so much hard work could be put into preparing for a race that you can not even contest.

Then as the thought of life's unfairness settled and offered some sort of dark comfort, I looked again at the ocean and the skies and could see a change for the worse. Slowly, this hurricane was coming Antigua's way. It made me think of the devastation that it would cause, the suffering it would inflict on people, those who would lose their homes, the few who would lose their lives. In an instant, nature had put things in perspective. In my small world I miss a race and think of it as a great injustice. What should people who lose their homes or their loved ones think?

It dawned on me that reasonable people would look at my situation and think it is not such a big deal. Not compared to the havoc caused by a hurricane. With that perspective, the anger subsided and I began to think positively. 'I am,' I thought, 'going to get healthy again. I will come back, and as a stronger person. This setback will not keep me down. In fact I am going to learn from it. I am not going to brood any more over what is lost, but concentrate on the future and what it offers. There is a hurricane approaching, it will prove bad things happen, but no matter what damage it inflicts, people will face it, cope with it and move on. You learn what you can from the experience so that you can use it to prepare better for the next time and then you put it behind you and carry on.'

Things were pretty much sorted in my head when Gary's voice disturbed the peace.

'Please,' he said, 'just come back to the hotel, this hurricane is coming.'

'Okay,' I said, 'I'm ready now.'

It is part of my nature to want to put things right. When Mum and Dad argued over Mum's map-reading on road journeys in Europe, I was the little girl in the back seat pleading with them to stop. They called me the little peacemaker. I don't like making mistakes and having to accept that my body is human like anyone else and can break down sometimes. When things go wrong in my running career, the instinctive reaction is to want to question why I wasn't stronger, to try to undo the mistake, relive the moment, rewind the clock, start over. Yet this isn't possible, and it is sometimes the hardest part of sport to accept; once the opportunity is missed, it is gone forever. There will be other races but the one you have lost cannot be re-run. I try to learn from the situation and accept that it has happened. The great thing about sport is that there is always another target, I can always get out there and run again, and by being able to do this I'm happy again.

Endless self-questioning and going over what happened depletes your energy and drains your morale. This is why I believe that it is important to face what happens and learn what you can from it, but then to put it behind you and move on with life. In this situation, nothing helps me as much as getting back into running and feeling good, then back to competition and winning.

The second week in the Caribbean improved my health and gave me enough strength to begin to want to run again. After the virus the return had to be gradual and sensible. Unless the recovery was complete, any resumption of training ran the risk of setting me back again. We had gone to Antigua on 2 September and my first run was twenty-three days later. The break helped me enormously but even so, the easy runs that got me back into the swing of things were followed by sore throats that came with a warning: don't do too much and push the body too hard just yet. Instead of what would have been the routine two runs each day, I ran just once a day and mixed that with some light cross-training and sessions in the gym. I kept a very close eye on my resting and exercise pulses and was extra conscious of how my body was feeling.

For some time I had wanted to get an apartment in Font-Romeu and have a base out there. I loved the area and knew I would be going back there year after year. That summer an apartment had become available exactly where I wanted it. In the same block as the Riff family and Vincent Rousseau, already good friends, and a stone's throw away from the training centre, the apartment backed right out

On the way to my first World Junior Cross-Country title in Boston, 1992. I was just about to break away from Wang Junxia to go on and win the race.

Me and the team: my coaches Alex and Rosemary Stanton, and Mum, in Stuttgart at my first senior World Championships, 1993.

Competing in Stuttgart, with Sonia O'Sullivan. I came seventh, and thought that was pretty good for a first final at this level. I loved the experience.

With Gary in New York, overlooking Central Park during our first visit in 1995. I love the city's energy and always enjoyed the Fifth Avenue Mile and 10k race.

Getting my degree was very important to me. It also meant I would always have a career to fall back on if the athletics didn't work out. With me in this graduation picture from 1996 are my parents and grandma.

I was born during a blizzard, love the snow and usually run well on it, and my World Best in 1998 for the 5-mile road race at Balmoral Castle was no exception.

Training in Font-Romeu, in the French Pyrenees, in 2000. The high-altitude training camp has become a home from home, with the excellent facilities and beautiful scenery making it a great place to prepare.

Gary and I got married on
15 April 2000. My bridesmaids
were Liz Yelling (left) and
Catherine Allen, Gary's sister.

PA

Olympic disappointment: exhausted after finishing fourth in the 10,000m final in Sydney, September 2000. It was one place better than Atlanta, but still a blow to be out of the medals.

Victory at last! Winning the senior World Cross-Country title in Ostend in March 2001, ahead of Gete Wami. Having come second twice it was brilliant to finally win gold. Surprise and elation show on my face.

With Hayley Tullett, protesting at Olga Yegorova's participation in the 5000m World Championships in Edmonton, August 2001.

That picture – Gary and me during our famous track-side domestic in Edmonton.

And a photograph I'm happier to look at — a portrait from a fashion spread I did in
Los Angeles after running in Chicago in October 2002.

on to great running trails. It was perfect and Gary and I agreed straight away to go for it. It turned out that the current owners, M. and Mme Nouvel, worked at the centre and they have since become friends too. They didn't want to move until October which suited us fine. As soon as we saw it we fell in love with the superb view, which looks out right across the valley to the Spanish Pyrenees. Six years later we still find it just as beautiful. So a few weeks after returning from Antigua, Gary and I drove down to Font-Romeu to exchange on and set up the flat. It was a good time to go as the weather in England was turning wet and wintry while Font-Romeu was cold but dry and sunny. Training continued but I was still building up and a lot of energy was also focused on assembling furniture and painting and decorating.

If the Budapest experience forced me to listen ever more attentively to my body, it also forced me to question the efficiency of my nutrition. Previously my feeling had been that I ate well (I've always loved my food!) and had a good distance athlete's diet that was high in carbohydrates. For normal members of society it would be a huge amount but normal people are not running 100-plus miles a week at a high level of intensity and don't burn calories or break down muscle at anything like the rate of an elite distance runner. I had tended to underestimate the speed at which it was necessary to refuel after hard training. Neither did I understand the importance of getting some protein in immediately as well. The failure of my immune system to cope with the volume of training and fighting off the illness in the months before the European Championships encouraged me to look into this area, and it was the reason I began working with Brian Welsby, an expert on nutrition.

Brian taught me about the dip the immune system takes immediately after hard exercise and how important it was to bolster it quickly with protein and amino acids as well as the carbohydrates I was used to. We also adapted my diet slightly to include more alkaline foods, thus neutralising the acid build-ups of hard training, and to include more protein to help rebuild the muscle fibres constantly being broken down during the more intense sessions. From past experience, I already knew the importance of picking up on the early signs of trouble. From the moment my career began, Alex taught me to take my pulse first thing every morning. If it's elevated, that is often an indication of tiredness or that the body is fighting something. During this critical time it was important that I listen more than ever to these signs and if in doubt err on the side of caution and miss the run or take an extra day off.

Helped by the furnishing needs of our new flat and the motivation of the beautiful surroundings, we got the balance right in Font-Romeu that autumn. Feeling a little stronger every day, I decided to prepare for the European Cross-Country Championships in Ferrara, Italy, two weeks before Christmas. It was a championship that I had not yet competed in and a title that I wanted to win. Also, very importantly to me, it was the chance to end the year on a positive and happy note. First I had to qualify for the team and I won the trial in Margate the weekend after returning from Font-Romeu. Although I had been feeling good in training nothing quite replicates a race and after the awful experience of the 10,000m in Budapest, it was good to blow away the racing cobwebs and feel strong again. I was looking forward to Ferrara.

Although I was the favourite, the race in Ferrara was certainly no formality. The Portuguese Fernanda Ribeiro was there, as was the Yugoslav Olivera Jevtic and the Finn Annemari Sandell. The first two had finished in front of me in Budapest and Sandell was also a former World Junior Cross-Country champion. The course itself was excellent except for the steeplechase hurdles that had to be jumped along the way. I have the utmost admiration for steeplechasers – when my legs become really tired, I cannot imagine being able to safely clear high barriers. These barriers were pretty high and were the one thing that worried me on the course inspection. Luckily I wasn't the only one and course organisers agreed to lower them slightly.

'Don't be worried,' Alex said to me before the race. 'I have been out on the course and saw Ribeiro as she looked at those barriers and I can tell you she is far more worried than you.' That did help me, as I thought Ribeiro must really dislike them if she is not even bothering to hide it. Anyhow I'd practised the lower height and was a lot happier by then. My plan in the race was to run controlled and sensibly through the first two kilometres and then gradually increase the pace all the way to the finish. A little after halfway, Ribeiro, Jevtic and Annemari Sandell were the only three still with me. Ribeiro was the danger because I was confident that I could finish faster than Jevtic and Sandell. People always think of me as having no sprint finish but that is not true. Against excellent finishers like Derartu Tulu, Sonia O'Sullivan, Gabriela Szabo and Gete Wami, I might struggle, but at different times they have all been the best in the world. There are many others that I feel confident of beating in a sprint finish. Neither Sandell nor Jevtic frightened me.

Surging on the hills, increasing the pace on the flat sections, I got rid of Ribeiro with about a kilometre to go. The other two were still with me but knowing that Ribeiro was dropped boosted my spirits and almost without deliberately trying, I raced clear of Sandell and Jevtic through the last 500 metres. Though it wasn't the biggest victory of my career, it was nonetheless a European Cross-Country title and my first senior title outside the UK. That was important to me, and ensured I went into 1999 on a positive note.

11

There is a natural rhythm to my life that has become well-established over the twelve years of my senior running career. January comes and generally brings with it the cold, wet weather and dark evenings, so at that time I cross the Atlantic for the drier climate and the high altitude of Albuquerque in New Mexico. Although it can be very cold there it is always dry and sunny. We might spend six or eight weeks there, training in the thinner, cleaner air and doing the training that will be the bedrock of my preparation for the new season. The return to England is usually timed to give me a couple of weeks back home before the World Cross-Country Championships, the first major test of the year. Nowadays there is also often a spring marathon. After the spring target I take my end-of-season break before beginning my preparations for the summer campaign on the track. Most of the training through the summer is done in Font-Romeu in the Pyrenees and is centred on the major target that summer, the European or World Championships or Olympic Games. I always start with the main target and then work backwards from that in choosing and planning the other races that will fit in well to get me to the championship or major target in the best possible shape.

The Olympic Games, the World Championships, the Commonwealth Games and the European Championships are generally held in August, and even though there may be some racing after these, the season winds down in September and October. Once I've competed in my last event, I take a rest of three or four weeks before the cycle of training and racing begins again. When things have gone well I might want to carry on but I take the break and enjoy the first couple of weeks of lie-ins and doing what I like; then the itch begins and I want to get back running again because I miss it so much. By taking the full three weeks, however, it means that when I do start back I'm really fresh and looking forward to it. Over the years there have been a few disappointing occasions when I have left major championships with far less than I had hoped for, but after spending a little time analysing the reasons, the desire to get back to what I love doing takes over and my life moves on. Running remains the passion it always has been since long before it became my profession. There is nothing, but nothing, I would rather do for a living. All through my career I have been fortunate in that there has been gradual improvement each year and there is the potential for further progress. I know I'm really lucky to be able to have a career doing something that I would be doing anyway. I also know that as long as I still enjoy what I'm doing, I intend to keep doing what I love.

The disappointments are part of life; so long as I learn from them and get stronger the experience hasn't been wasted. In a way all the rough times just make you appreciate the good ones even more, although it is hard to see this when you're in the middle of a tough time! I am stubborn; a few setbacks don't stop me doing what I enjoy and striving for what I want and believe I can achieve. If anything they make me even more determined. And I don't like to give up.

Picture the scene. It is late December 1998, and we are all in Font-Romeu, having a white Christmas in the Pyrenees: Gary and I, my parents, Gary's parents Sally and Dale, his brother Kenneth and his sister Catherine. We encouraged our families to come to France with the promise of some very good skiing. Font-Romeu has both downhill and cross-country skiing but is best known for excellent cross-country. Unfortunately, there was little snow when we first arrived and very little skiing. Luckily the snow arrived the day before Christmas Eve. It was perfect and the days were bright with blue skies and constant sunshine. The weather gods were on our side.

Cross-country skiing was great because it was fun for everyone and also a great workout. I can't do downhill skiing because of the injury risk but with cross-country skiing this is a lot less.

The scene that has stayed in my mind is of Gary and I on a cross-country ski loop, at a point where there was a steep downhill followed by a sharp left turn. With my limited experience, I struggled when turning left in full flow, but had no difficulty going right. So down I went, determined that this time I would negotiate the left turn successfully. However, I couldn't get the hang of it and kept ending up on my backside. Gary tried hard to keep the smirk off his face. 'Okay, I am going back up there and I am going to do it without falling,' I said. He waited at the bottom. Down I came, more determined than ever, but again I failed. Gary began to move on, presuming I would follow.

'I am not leaving until I do this.'

'Don't be ridiculous,' he said. 'There will be other hills with left turns.'

'I am going back up. You can go on if you wish.'

I went back up to the top of the hill and again fell at the bottom trying to take the turn. By now Gary was laughing and I was getting madder.

'Don't think I am leaving here until I get this done.'

'Whatever,' he said and waited for me to try again.

And, for the third time, I fell. It wasn't going to beat me and I trudged back to the top again. By now my parents had come upon this ludicrous scene and Gary, who could hardly speak for laughing, took great pleasure in giving them a commentary. 'We've been here for twenty minutes and she won't move from this bloody bend until she's got round it. She's tried and she's tried and she's not going to do it.'

Eventually, I did get round that bend and, in a way, the stubbornness, the bloody-mindedness epitomises what I am about. If I can't do something that I want to do, I will practise and practise until I can. If someone tells me I can't do something and I think I can, I will do everything I can to prove them wrong. Another point which illustrates this comes from my first summer in Font-Romeu. There is a great trail loop on a plateau called La Calme, to get to it you need to get up La Calme mountain via a ski slope. 'Most people walk up this,' Vincent Rousseau, the Belgian 2h07 marathon runner told me, 'I run up it but a girl couldn't do that!' The next time I was there I had a session to do on the plateau, it was raining and I would be wet and cold by the time I walked to the top. I remembered Vincent's challenge and decided I would run up. It was tough and I wasn't fast but I did it without stopping. Now we always jog up as a warm-up and I never think to walk up again. Of course I went straight back and told Vincent it was totally possible.

Each year when the athletics season ended, I would assess where things could be improved. With greater commitment, harder and smarter training, better rest and recovery, Alex, Gary and I knew that I would get stronger and faster. That's how I saw it. No matter what happened during the year, my inner resolve would not be diminished. As it was with that silly left turn on the cross-country ski trail, I would get there, eventually.

That Christmas was wonderful. Gary and I went for a long run early on Christmas morning and the two families had breakfast together after we returned. Around midday we put the turkey in the oven and everyone went skiing for about three hours before coming back for dinner. There was a lovely atmosphere with so many people out on the trails and the snow-covered mountains and countryside were so beautiful. It was the perfect way to spend Christmas Day. That both of our families were there made it that much better. After the skiing, we were ravenous and more than ready for our Christmas dinner.

It was the evening of the 10,000m final at the 1999 World Championships in Seville; the temperature was around 30 degrees and before warming up I had to work out how much I wanted to do. It was a case of doing just enough to be stretched out and ready to go without expending too much energy in the heat and being exhausted before the race even began. We warmed up in direct sunlight and the heat was intense. The bins containing drinks were packed with ice and I scooped some up in my peaked cap before putting it on top of my head. One way to keep cool.

There were shaded areas inside the stadium, and it felt good to stretch and do strides away from the sunlight. Because there had been no heats, thirty-one runners spread across the start line and even though I was expected to run well, not many would have been confident of my winning a medal. By now I knew I was beginning to gain a reputation as the gallant front runner who couldn't shake off pursuers, and would lose out to faster finishers near the end of the race. The field was pretty strong – Gete Wami, Fernanda Ribeiro, Tegla Loroupe, Berhane Adere and Merima Denboba – but I felt strong and knew this time I was ready and in an event I was more suited to.

Since 1993 I had run in five major championship races and my best result was fourth in the World 5,000m in Athens in 1997. However, all of the results had been constantly improving and Alex and I were confident that we were building in the right direction. Although sometimes I may have been disappointed at missing out on medals, for the most part I had been able to walk off the track and say, 'I did my best. At this moment, that's as good as I am' – that is apart from the European Championships in 1998. However, this year was totally different; I knew I was healthy, I felt strong and I was determined to go out there and show what I could do over 10,000m. Such confidence was born from the training I had done and the success of my races as I built towards Seville.

The quality of my training and general preparation had improved thanks to Gary. Early in the 1999 season he decided to retire from competing as his body could no longer cope with the intense training necessary to be an elite 1,500m runner without breaking down. Trying to make it back had been very stressful for him and, although sad once he made the decision, he actually became a lot more relaxed. He still continued to run with me and began helping me in the quality sessions as well; this really helped to improve the quality of my workouts. I had also begun taking an afternoon sleep on a regular basis. Up until then I would rest between the morning and afternoon training sessions by sitting or lying down and reading my book. Not tired enough to sleep, I thought it was enough just to stay off my feet. Now I found that although to begin with I felt sluggish and disorientated when I first woke up, I was able to get a lot more from the afternoon runs this way and generally recover better.

I made the change in Albuquerque in February 1999. Away from home, in a place where there are no distractions and the sole reason for being there is to concentrate on training and recovering, it is easier to control your routine. I slept every afternoon for those five weeks of altitude training, and the benefits quickly showed. After a two-hour afternoon sleep, I would feel mentally refreshed and physically stronger. Nowadays it is a mainstay of my hard training blocks and without it I really feel the difference.

That year we returned from Albuquerque on 12 March, just over two weeks before the World Cross-Country Championships which were to be held in Belfast that year. We had barely a chance to unpack and repack before heading off to Tirrenia, Italy with the rest of the Great Britain team for a pre-championship camp. Tirrenia, a small coastal town between Pisa and Livorno, was a good place for the team to prepare together. However, I remember it not just for the excellent training facilities and great team spirit but also for a run that became much longer than intended. We were staying quite close to a NATO Army base and for the first few runs, Gary and I ran about halfway round the outer perimeter of the base before doubling back on ourselves. It was an hour's run.

One morning we had a longer run to do and so I suggested we continue on and do a complete loop of the base; it would be a more interesting run than going out and back and I was pretty certain we'd be able to make a big loop around the base and back to where we were staying. Gary was unsure because his sense of direction isn't the best and he was worried we might get lost. All was fine until we'd gone about three quarters of the way around and the footpath began to degrade into a very bumpy grassy bank alongside the river. 'Come on,' I said, 'I know the training camp is pretty much straight ahead. If we keep going we are sure to get back.'

'Are you sure? This doesn't look like a proper path.'

'It'll be fine, a bit of cross-country, that's all.'

On we went and were doing fine until the bank ended. We could see our camp less than half a mile ahead but were faced with the river on our left, the high Army base fence on our right and a 10-metre-wide drainage channel ahead of us! By now we had been out over 45 minutes and I had a massage booked when I got back. There was no way I was turning back. I could see a concrete pipe running across the channel above the water. No problem, I thought, we can hold onto the fence and walk across the pipe then we'll be nearly back. I persuaded Gary to do this and we were soon running along the grass bank on the other side. Unfortunately after about 100m we came to a port area and soldiers stopped us at gunpoint. Inadvertently we had breached the security perimeter and were actually inside the Army base. We were surrounded and they demanded that we hand over our passports and any cameras we might have in our possession. Cameras? Passports? Unfortunately Italian is not one of my languages so we tried to explain in English that we were athletes on a long run from the training camp and hoped we could be understood. Luckily one of them began to speak English, explaining that we had infiltrated the NATO base. He wanted to know how we had managed it. This was shortly before the air strikes in Bosnia and they were naturally concerned about security at the base. We explained that we had simply walked across the drainage pipe and hadn't realised we were inside the NATO compound. They wanted proof of who we were but in our T-shirts, shorts and running shoes, we couldn't provide any. Eventually we persuaded them to contact UK Athletics officials back at the camp and after speaking to them, they were happy we were indeed who we said we were.

'Right,' they said, 'you've got to go back the way you came.'

'But where we're staying is just three or four minutes over there.'

'Can't go that way, you've got to go back the way you came, we need to see how you got in.'

'We've already been running for nearly an hour, another hour's run is the last thing we need.'

'Doesn't matter. You've got to go back the way you came.'

They even followed us in a car as we renegotiated the concrete pipe balance and ran back up the bank and saw for themselves that it hadn't been that difficult to infiltrate their base. Almost 2 hours had passed by the time we got back to the training centre and I'd missed my massage! This wasn't exactly what I needed just ten days before the cross-country championships. Me and my sense of adventure!

Second in Turin two years before, second in Marrakech the previous year, I went to Belfast with some good training behind me thinking this would be my year. Yet something was missing on the day of the race. I was very fit, my times in training had been excellent but the zip wasn't there. Instead my legs felt heavy and lifeless. That small percentage difference, though it didn't stop me from being competitive, meant that I couldn't run as strong as I wanted too. Gete

Wami was by far the strongest in the race and won by 12 seconds. Her Ethiopian team-mate Merima Denboba then rubbed salt into the wound by just pipping me on the line for the silver medal. The course was very muddy which wasn't ideal for someone whose legs felt heavy. I was so frustrated because I felt the run did not reflect all the work we had done in training.

That is one of the tougher defeats to take: when you know, for whatever reason, although you give all that you can in the race, you haven't quite been able to produce what you're capable of. The two previous years I had finished a close second and now, in the best shape ever for the World Cross-Country, I was a disappointed 3rd. We tried to work out what had gone wrong, retracing our journey over the previous three weeks. After returning to England from Tirrenia I remembered feeling very good on one hard run, but my heart rate was a little higher than it should have been. Maybe that was all it took to take a little too much out of the tank just a week before the World Cross and be unable to quite recover in time. That taught me a lesson about how important it is to rein yourself back and trust that enough work has been done.

When the disappointment of Belfast subsided, I realised two things: there was nothing wrong with my shape, and that I wanted to make amends through my performance at the IAAF World Track Championships in Seville later in the year. Nonetheless, I always want to run well in every race and two weeks after the World Cross-Country, I raced in the 10,000m challenge in Barakaldo near Bilbao in northern Spain. I knew my track form was good and felt I could get close to Ingrid Kristiansen's 30.13 European record. It was really windy, but it was the sort of race you could take risks in and I thought I would just go for it and see how close I could get. I set off fast and ran 15.10 for the first 5,000m, not too far off course. Then the wind seemed to get stronger; the sand from the long jump pit was blowing in our faces down the straight! Maybe Ingrid's record at the time was beyond my reach anyway, but in those conditions it definitely was, I paid for my exuberance through the second 5,000m and slowed quite a bit before winning in 30.40. The time was still a UK and Commonwealth record and 8 seconds faster than my previous best. It also set me up with the world's fastest performance of the year going into the championships. Even better, under ideal conditions I knew I could go faster. Soon afterwards I went to Balmoral for a 5-mile road race and ran 24.47 to improve my 5-mile world best, and end my winter campaign on high note. It is a nice feeling to produce a time that is faster than anyone has ever gone before and the run was proof that I was making progress. It augured well for the rest of the year.

My bad experience in Budapest had definitely sharpened my appetite for Seville. After Budapest, Seville would be my second championship race at 10,000m and my shot to show what I could really do over 10,000m when healthy. Even though I knew it was a virus that had destroyed my performance, not everyone else did and there would have been many who wondered if I was good enough. After Balmoral we travelled down to Font-Romeu and began the training programme that would take us to the World Championships in August. That summer we scheduled a lot of races in the build-up to Seville and they achieved precisely what we hoped they would.

After starting with two solid if unspectacular runs, the first over two miles at Loughborough and then a 5,000m at Hengelo in Holland, my sharpness improved and I began to run extremely well. Each race, whether over 3,000m or 5,000m, brought a new personal best and greater confidence. Running for the GB team at the European Cup meeting in Paris I won the 5,000m in 14.48, the year's fastest time for the distance at that point. The Paris win was doubly satisfying because the GB women's team was close to being relegated from the top division and it was imperative that we win the 5,000m, the last race before the relays. I always want to win the race but as women's captain I also felt a particular responsibility to the team.

Irina Mikitenko, the German athlete, was the main danger. She had beaten me earlier in the season at Hengelo and had a very good finish, making her a worry if she was still close in the final stages. So I set off fast and felt good. I remember the beating drums in the Stade de France helping me maintain the rhythm. I got maximum points and the team avoided relegation. Afterwards came Oslo, Rome, Crystal Palace and Zürich and at each venue a new PB. Nothing nourishes an athlete's confidence as much as a good performance and in those weeks before the World Championships at Seville, I almost came to expect that every run would be better than the last. Zürich was especially pleasing as I captured Zola Budd's UK record over 3,000m. I already owned the 5,000m and 10,000m records but this one was a tough one and 3,000m was short for me. I remembered Yvonne Murray's anguish in Oslo 1993 as she just missed beating Zola's time. She was a great 3,000m runner yet never able to beat it, now it was mine and meant I went into the GB team's holding camp at Monte Gordo in Portugal in the best of form.

For any athlete there is a delicate balance between being in peak fitness and staying healthy. Arriving in Monte Gordo my back felt a little tight after Zürich. I went for treatment from one of the GB physios and they tried manipulating my back, unfortunately this strained my sacral ligaments in my lower back. At first it wasn't too bad but after a couple of days I could hardly lift my left hamstring to stride out. Luckily, Gerard Hartmann arrived on that day and was able to treat me. He realised how serious the situation was, so close to the championships, but convinced me that I would be okay and succeeded in reassuring me that I would still be able to race to the best of my ability. Nevertheless it was close; I had to have a couple of days' complete rest and intensive treatment, but four days before the scheduled heats of the 10,000m I was able to do my final track session and though it was later than we would have liked, it went extremely well. The following day we left Monte Gordo for Seville; the work was done, all that remained was for me to deliver the performance.

The day we arrived in Seville was one of the hottest I can remember. It was still 40 degrees for our evening run and we felt like we were running in a giant oven. Although it had been chosen to prepare us for these conditions, Monte Gordo had been nothing like this. The shock of the conditions in Seville, however, was countered by the good news that there would be no heats, just a straight final. That importantly gave me a couple more days for my ligaments to recover and to acclimatise.

It was nine o'clock on a Thursday evening when thirty-one of us set off in pursuit of the World Championship title. Maybe few outside of my immediate circle expected much, but Gary, Alex, Gerard and I believed this time it would be different. I had spent the morning reading through the results of past championships and knew I was capable of being right up there if I ran my race the way it suited me. We warmed up outside the track and though it was after eight in the evening, the temperature was just over 30 degrees. As bad as that was, it was nothing like the searing heat we had experienced on our first evening in Seville six days before.

In such temperatures you are in danger of dehydrating and overheating even in the warm-up. I was so conscious of drinking as much as possible, I must have consumed almost 8 litres of fluid replacement drink throughout the day. During the warm-up, I tried to counter the effects of the temperature by staying in the shade, doing stretching and minimal running and keeping my cap full of ice. It did its job well, melting on the top of my head and slowly cooling my neck. Luckily the call room was cool and when we came into the stadium the sun had gone down low.

My plan was to go out fast but controlled, to make it hard for the other girls from the start and then gradually increase the tempo throughout the race. If the plan worked, then I would run the second half faster than the first, and remain strong through the critical closing kilometres. The conditions were tough but not impossible, there was more shade in the stadium than I had

MY STORY SO FAR   203

anticipated and, in any case, I have always felt relatively comfortable running in the heat.

I led pretty much from the start, getting into my stride with a comfortable 3.11 first kilometre. After that my kilometre times dropped to 3.05, 3.04, 3.02 and 3.03, and reaching halfway in 15.25 I was still comfortable. At that point only Gete Wami, Tegla Loroupe and Fernanda Ribeiro were still in touch. One kilometre later Ribeiro dropped out and that was a big boost. Not only did it remove the Olympic champion and someone whose finishing speed would have been a threat, but it also left just three of us clear. Barring something unforeseen, I would get a medal and that thought lifted my spirits no end. Of course I then turned my attention to Wami and Loroupe and although Loroupe wasn't likely to beat me in a sprint finish, Wami was. To win the gold medal, my best shot was to try to get rid of her.

Loroupe finally did some of the pace-making through the sixth kilometre covered in under three minutes (2.59). It was then that Ribeiro dropped out and through the 7th, 8th and 9th kilometres, I kept the pace close to 3-minute kilometres. Loroupe came to the front again with five laps to go but this time tried to slow the pace down so I moved back into the lead, increasing the pace, but still unable to shake off the Ethiopian. The last kilometre (2.54) was easily the fastest of the race but Wami still had something in reserve and stayed comfortably in my slipstream.

One thing is characteristic of the Ethiopian girls: they run with such grace and appear effortless; they always look comfortable. I know, however, that this is just an illusion; the ease is more apparent than real. They are hurting too, it's just that it doesn't show. They can go from looking so comfortable to beaten in a couple of strides. It can be frustrating because you never know how close you are to breaking them, but it's important to remember how close you *can* be. Unfortunately on this evening in Seville, I couldn't get close enough and Gete Wami was comfortably sitting on my shoulder. She waited for the final lap and down the back straight accelerated past me. Instinctively reacting to her surge, I stayed reasonably close to her for about 150m. She increased her speed again and was away. I was well clear of Loroupe and gave everything to the pursuit, but I couldn't get back to Wami. She ran the last 400m in 64 seconds against my 67; the 3 seconds being the difference at the finish line. Sixty-seven seconds off a fast pace was a highly respectable last-lap time. Wami, myself and Loroupe were all inside the championship record, and in conditions that were far from ideal, I had run a personal best by 13 seconds.

In the finishing straight, my legs were totally gone and as the lactic acid and exhaustion caught up with me I felt like I was swimming rather than running, my arms flailing desperately through the air trying to pull my legs and body over the line. Yet it was pleasurable exhaustion because after giving everything, there was something to show for the effort. At last, a medal from a major championships: a silver medal. Wami went off on her victory lap, I was too exhausted to join her, and besides I had come second not won. I was more than happy to celebrate my joy with the crowd of British supporters at the end of the straight.

Reflecting on it afterwards, the performance assuaged the slight disappointment of not winning. My split times were 15.25 for the first 5,000m, 15.02 for the second half. More than the tactics and the time, my second place showed that I was capable of getting among the medals and gave me confidence that in time I could build to victory. I could compete successfully at major championships and this proved it. On the day, Wami was in great shape and deserved to win, but I had done everything possible to win. It was one of those days when the performance reflected the hard work and the thought that Gary, Alex and Gerard had put into my preparation.

Though the race was run in 30 degrees, the heat hadn't felt an issue. Our times were a creditable effort for 10,000m in any conditions. After walking off the track, I went to doping control and the doctor was amazed I was able to provide a sample almost straight away. Having drunk so much liquid through the day, I was able to go once the race ended. Perhaps there was even too much fluid in my system for the race in that I had carried a little extra weight for the first part but that had been my insurance policy against dehydration. Looking back at pictures of before and after the race, my legs do actually look bigger beforehand.

I also felt my performance showed that a runner from Britain could compete with the African runners in hot temperatures. The presumption has always been that they cope far better than we do on burning hot days. My belief is that everyone finds it tough to race in extremely warm conditions. It is not going to be comfortable but nevertheless it is the same for everyone and we can all still run well.

The race in Seville drained me and I needed a week to recover and for my legs to feel normal again. Though that was just a few years ago, I wasn't as knowledgeable about recuperation as I am now. I did not know that even with the week's rest, the recovery would be less than 100 per cent. Yet after a good run, all you want to do is get back out there and try to set new personal bests. Two weeks after Seville I raced a 1,500m in Glasgow. I finished 3rd in a reasonable time, but the most eventful part of the evening came after the race as I signed autographs for kids at the track. As they pressed forward with their pens and pieces of paper, an advertising hoarding toppled over and fell on my foot.

So while everyone else went off to a pleasant post-race reception, I went to the Glasgow Infirmary with a bar of chocolate. The facilities in the Accident and Emergency ward are excellent but this was Saturday night and more than a few people were in the queue before me. Many of them had been drinking heavily and with their pronounced Glaswegian accents, I couldn't understand a word. Eventually the X-ray of my bruised foot was taken and examined. Thankfully, nothing was broken. We left the hospital four hours after we had arrived.

Before the season's end I raced again in Berlin, then in Munich and finally in the Great North Run at Newcastle. It was my first experience of the enormously successful Great North race and the amazing atmosphere there but it was a race too many and I finished an average 3rd. In those last three races there was nothing wrong with my effort and determination, it was simply that Seville had taken something out of me that could only be replaced with proper rest.

It was easy then to take a long break because 1999 had been such a good year. As well as improving my times over 3,000m, 5,000m and 10,000m, there was the silver medal from the World Championships. From being the runner who was always outside the medals, I could now hold my head up and say, 'Well, I can compete with the world's best distance track runners.' I was also extremely happy in my personal life with that lucky engagement ring on my finger.

Bring on 2000; I was looking forward to it.

12

The new Millennium began with an eye-opening warning for me. My preparation for the World Cross-Country in Vilamoura could hardly have been better and I knew I was in better shape than I'd ever been before. Yet on a dry and very fast course, the quicker African athletes were too sharp for me. It was clear that in Olympic year the stakes were to be raised and everyone had come out in better shape. I didn't run badly, maybe felt a little heavy-legged due to it being the wrong time of the month, yet I was unable to stay with the Ethiopians as they flew over the final couple of man-made hills to victory, and was also passed by Kenyans Lydia Cheremei and Susan Chepkemei. I collapsed over the line a devastated 5th in the short race and had to be carried away, yet still came back the following day to finish 4th in the 4k-race. I was disappointed but left Vilamoura knowing I had to build yet further on my training if I was going to achieve what I wanted to in Sydney.

Unfortunately sometimes the best laid plans just cannot be fitted into place. After a wonderfully relaxing honeymoon in the Maldives, I returned to training refreshed and extremely motivated for the season ahead. I had my week's check-up and was back to full training when I twisted my knee awkwardly one night. I had been kneeling on the floor writing thank-you cards for our wedding presents; as I stood up I heard my knee pop. Worried, I flexed it a bit but it seemed okay. However, the next day it became sore towards the end of my run. It refused to clear up and would swell after each time that I ran. After fulfilling an obligation in the US for Adidas I returned, worried, to Gerard's Limerick clinic. After intense treatment for a week the problem had still not turned the corner. I could cross train without pain but as soon as I ran, the pain and swelling under the right kneecap would return. I remember on the final trial run, when I had to stop in pain yet again, Gerard had followed me on his bike and I cried as we walked back to his clinic. It was the end of May and my Olympic dream seemed in tatters.

Yet, Gerard and I were far from beaten. First of all we had to find out what was happening inside the knee. Ger arranged for me to get a scan and see an orthopaedic surgeon. He sent me to see Dai Rees, a surgeon based in Oswestry on the Welsh border. He scheduled me in for surgery the following week. In the meantime I was cross training with a vengeance. At the beginning of June, Dai operated arthroscopically and found a blister on the articular surface on the underside of my kneecap. When I'd twisted it awkwardly I had caused the blister which, through running on it, had burst leaving a roughened area and small pieces of debris floating around. This was causing the pain and without the operation would not have healed. Dai did what is called a shaving, to smooth and clean up the surface so that it wouldn't cause further problems. I left Oswestry the next morning and flew to Limerick the next day. Gerard and I worked on the knee as much as possible to get the operative swelling down and the full range of movement back. After five days I was walking for two hours and back running after a week. We had to build back really gradually and pack the knee in ice after exercise, but we were going in the right direction. At the time Kelly Holmes was also in Limerick struggling with an injury. We would cross train hard each day down in the gym, her on the bike and me on the Nordic ski-machine; neither of us was giving up on Sydney without a fight. Less than three months later, Ger and I sat in the stands elated as we watched Kelly win her bronze medal.

I stayed in Limerick almost five weeks until I was back into normal training, then finally escaped to Font-Romeu. I was still icing the knee but able to train normally and was working as hard as I could to build up my endurance strength and speed. Before I was really ready I had thrown myself back into racing, hoping to bring things on quickly. For my first race we drove down to Barcelona for a 1,500m. It was a severe shock to the system and I struggled to a slow 4.11. Yet it had blown the cobwebs away and most importantly the knee was fine. Ten days later I was able to run an encouraging 14.44 over 5,000m at Crystal Palace and flew out to the Gold Coast feeling that things were definitely moving in the right direction.

Realistically, though, I had missed a lot of background work necessary for endurance events. We were always playing catch-up, although my fitness continued to improve out in Australia. I had done all that I could to build a strong stamina base in the time I had available and my speed was actually better than ever as an encouraging 4.01 1,500m time trial I ran with Gary ten days before the Olympics showed. That boosted my confidence and proved my sharpness had returned. Maybe I lacked the ideal depth of preparation you would hope for to see you through a 10,000m heat and final at the Olympic Games, but relative to my injury-disrupted year, I was confident that I was in as good a shape as I could be. I was going to Sydney to give it my best shot and didn't allow myself to think of where I might have been without the injury.

Sonia O'Sullivan was alongside me as I walked through the tunnel to the track for the Olympic 10,000m final in Sydney. In the days between the heat and the final, Sonia figured I would lead from the start, make the race as hard as I could and get rid of my rivals before the finish. That was the plan. Twelve months before I had used much the same strategy at the World Championships in Seville and it had worked to beat all but the Ethiopian Gete Wami. I was now a year stronger and more experienced. This time I was capable of going faster than I had in Seville through the first half of the race, and still being able to run a faster second half. However, as we walked through to the track, Sonia later told me how she had revised her opinion on which race tactics I would use. 'Paula isn't going to lead from the start in this wind,' she thought. 'She'd be mad to try to do all the work in these conditions.'

The wind was blowing strongly. It was going to be very tough, especially for the leading runner. However, I knew I was in good shape, I figured that there would be more shelter inside the stadium and I still believed that a fast pace was my best option. When you have decided what way you are going to run, the last thing you need is to introduce doubt. It wasn't possible to be certain what effect the wind would have on the race, or on the unsheltered runner heading the field. Was it going to make that much difference? In the moments before battle you go with what your instincts tell you to do.

I can handle the mental challenges and as the race started I was as determined and positive as I would have been on a calm evening, perfect for running. Straight into the lead, I set a strong pace and concentrated on keeping it tough. It had to be fast enough to take the sting out of the finishes of the Ethiopians Derartu Tulu and Gete Wami. In Seville I went through the first 5,000m in 15.25, this time the time at the halfway point was 15.06. Significantly faster and at that stage I felt okay, now the plan was to try and wind the pace up a little. Unfortunately around the 6th kilometre I began to tire; with each lap, pushing the pace into the wind began to take its toll.

GARY:
'After Seville I really believed Paula was capable of winning in Sydney. What she had to do was make it hard for the others. That's how she had to run it and how we decided she should run it. But the weather wasn't conducive to

trying to lead the race from the beginning. Even after a few laps I was glancing over at a medal ceremony going on in the middle of the track and the three flags were being blown all over the place. I didn't doubt her but one thought kept going through my mind: it's too windy to run the race from the front. We could have looked at the conditions, changed our tactics but that would have been a compromise; we would have been going for a medal, not for the gold medal. Paula never runs for anything less than first place.'

Having run well through the first 5,000m, I knew the key to gold was to increase the pace even more through the second half of the race. Knowing what to do and being able to do it are, however, different things and though I tried as hard as I could, I couldn't go any faster. If I had been able to gain a slight gap, the slight slowing down through the second half might not have been that important. But by slowing I gave Tulu, Wami, Fernanda Ribeiro and Tegla Loroupe, who were right behind me, the respite and encouragement they needed. At the same time as they were gaining encouragement, I was losing a little. I knew I was tiring and I also knew they were all still with me and that I needed to make it tougher for them. I dug deep within myself, confident that I could still beat Loroupe in a sprint. I knew that the three others were very dangerous and was desperate to find some way of weakening them. Though I tried so hard to keep negative thoughts at bay, the thought of them all still lined up behind me going into the last lap filled me with dread.

My mind could make me try harder but unfortunately it could not make my tired body run any faster. Was it the effort of leading for so long into the wind or was it the background strength I was lacking thanks to the training time missed due to the knee injury and surgery I had three months earlier? Most likely it was a combination of the two, but through the second half of the race, the message coming from my limbs was, 'Sorry, this is the best I can do.' Lap after lap we raced in a line of five, me at the front, the others content to wait for the last lap. So determined was I to shake them off that I fought and fought and blocked out the desperate growing fear that I wasn't going to be able to do it. With two laps to go, Ribeiro came past me and once at the front slowed down the pace. A glimpse of hope, I thought, she's tired and she wants it slower, don't let her, get back in front and fight for your medal.

That hope galvanised me for one last effort and I moved up on the outside to retake the lead. The crowd in the Olympic Stadium responded with a spontaneous roar of approval that showed their incredible and moving support for me. They willed me forward; gratefully I accepted the support and gave it everything I had left. The increase in speed was too much for Loroupe and she fell 10 or 15 yards behind. We were now approaching the bell and the other three were still positioned right behind me. The two Ethiopians Tulu and Wami went past first, so fast and with such ease that it was impossible for me to hold on to them.

Then Ribeiro overtook me. Drawing on every last ounce of energy and resolve, I tried desperately to go after her. For a few strides I thought 'maybe' but she was a fraction stronger. I knew that I had nothing left; it's a horrible feeling – treading water as you desperately try to get everything moving in the right direction and focus on the back of the runner you are trying to stay with. At that stage I wasn't thinking of the medals disappearing before my eyes, all my thoughts were desperately concentrating on getting across that line as fast as I could, holding that gap and not letting anyone else close on me. As I collapsed totally exhausted across the line, the overwhelming disappointment of another 4th place hit me full on. I lay dejected on the track, in part due to the sheer exhaustion of pushing all I could from my body, but now I also had the added psychological fatigue of missing out on my dream. I had given absolutely all that I could and had nothing to show for it. Fourth, who remembers 4th? I had hoped and believed for so much more than that. Tulu and Wami took the gold and silver, Ribeiro the bronze. It was no shock that the Ethiopians were so strong but Ribeiro had surprised me a little. She hadn't raced much before Sydney; I didn't know what kind of shape she would be in. I knew as defending Olympic champion she would always be tough to beat but felt that in a fast-run race, she might struggle. Instead she ran a huge personal best to finish 3rd.

My time was a personal best, a new British record, 1 second faster than Seville and in the windy conditions it was possibly worth more. But I barely even thought of the time. Disappointment, sheer exhaustion and frustration were the dominant emotions afterwards. After running okay through the opening 5,000m, I hadn't been able to execute the race plan in the second half of the race. My mind knew what needed to be done but my body wasn't strong enough to do it. In the mixed zone afterwards, the television and newspaper journalists were sympathetic and congratulated me on what they considered a good run. I kept saying it was hard to take any satisfaction from the race because 4th place left you with nothing. 'I came here to win a medal and I haven't got a medal.' It was hard for the media guys to understand that I expected more from myself. What was frustrating me was not being able to run the race I had planned, having given all that I could I had come drastically short of where I wanted to be.

They were saying how well I had done, 4th place in an Olympic final was not to be scoffed at and all I wanted to say was, 'It just isn't good enough, I want to be better.' They told me it was a gutsy performance but that didn't help. I didn't want to be a hero, I wanted to have been able to run faster and win a medal. Fourth was the worst place to finish, I'd given so much and was left with nothing to show for it but my exhaustion.

I called Gary on his mobile phone. He was still in the stand where he had watched the race. He was utterly dejected. He sounded like he was in shock at how the race had turned out and made no effort to hide his frustration. He couldn't understand and kept asking why I had not run faster through the second 5km. Being physically exhausted and mentally wiped out, it felt like he was accusing me of not trying hard enough, when all I needed was some consolation and comfort, but Gary isn't strong on tact and diplomacy. When I'm thinking rationally I accept this and respect his honesty. Right then I wasn't thinking rationally!

GARY:

'When she called me, I was sitting in the stadium, still shell-shocked. I'd built the whole thing up to be a very big deal. The Olympics gives you one chance every four years. I was torn. On one level I was frustrated she wasn't able to run the race we had planned. On another level that was my wife who'd been out there who had given everything, ended up absolutely hammered and got nothing in return. So when we spoke immediately afterwards it was tough because I was mad with her for not being able to run the race as we planned and I was desperately disappointed for her. But if I said to her, "You did really well, you were great!" she would have thought, "That's not what you really think. Don't patronise me." If I had come out with all that bullshit, she would know I was telling her something I didn't believe. That would have made her feel a lot worse. I don't fill her head with crap and it is not what she expects from me.

'The next day I sat watching the closing ceremony on television and they were looking back on the Games. I sat there and cried. It was such an anti-climax, the whole experience had come and gone and it was such a disappointment. My disappointment was solely for her. I knew, just knew, how much it meant to her . . .'

Gary understands what I want to achieve and his honesty reinforces my self-belief, if he tells me I'm running well or in shape I know it is true; he doesn't do confidence bolstering for the sake of it, it's just the way he is. In some ways he can be an even tougher taskmaster than I am on myself; at other times he can be the calm voice of reason. In the aftermath of the Olympics, I understood that his main emotion had been disappointment for me, but he just didn't know how to handle this. He spends so much time supporting me and helping me put in the hard work that he desperately wants to see it all pay off. He felt so frustrated standing watching and being unable to help or do anything. He had been right alongside me through all the tough training, towards the end of 1999, and we had also decided that he would leave his job and take over my management and race organisation. It made sense, he would be good at it, and it would mean we could travel together and spend the time we wanted to with each other. He could be with me all the time and I couldn't get an agent who would understand or know what I wanted any better than him. It works well and yet I am also always conscious and respectful of the sacrifice he has made. He put his own career aside to support me. Having also had to end his own athletics career prematurely due to the injury, I would have understood if he needed to get away from the athletics world for a while to get over the disappointment, yet here he was putting himself back into a world that had hurt him in order to be with and support me. It is why it took him longer than me to move on from the disappointment of Sydney. It is in the nature of the athlete, certainly in my nature, to look at and analyse the result, learn from it, then put it behind me and move onto the next target. It's the same whether the result is good or bad, as soon as the focus moves to the next target that is where my energy is focused towards. There is no changing the past, it is gone. Sport is about giving all that you can on the day, then accepting the result and concentrating on doing your best in the next event.

After Sydney it was a little harder to put it quickly behind me and move on because the public sympathy for my fourth-place finish was so enormous and so moving. On our return from Australia, the letters were already waiting. Countless people we had never met wrote to say how moved they had been by my effort to win a medal. I really appreciated so many people taking the time not only to think of me and to empathise but to actually take the time to put pen to paper and write to tell me how they felt. At the same time I struggled to understand why people would identify so much with me. What had I done that was any different from any other athlete who had gone to the Olympics? As far as I could see, everyone had done what I had: worked hard towards a goal and then gone to the championships and given all that they could in order to try and realise that goal. So why was I seen as being any braver or more deserving than others?

Part of it, I know, is the sympathy for the frontrunner overtaken on the last lap. Another reason is that I show my emotions. It's the way I've always been; I can't hide the truth of my emotions, it shows in my eyes and my manner. People can see straight away in my face what is going on in my heart. Utterly exhausted at the end of the race in Sydney, I collapsed after crossing the finish line and for a couple of minutes just lay there, my deepest emotions laid bare for the world to see. So people saw how totally drained I was, also the dejection, the utter desolation of giving everything you have and coming up short. I didn't want or ask for sympathy but it came anyway, in truckloads, and how could I not appreciate it, even if I didn't understand it?

Kids sent me medals they had made for me because they thought it unfair that I hadn't got one. I was so moved by the trouble people took to write and the heartfelt sympathy they offered, I resolved to write and thank every single one of them, though it took me until Christmas to do it. There was a lot of support out there. In one respect it cheered me but, ultimately, it was not what I wanted. I didn't want the tag of plucky loser who gives her all but never quite gets there. Everyone in an Olympic final gives 100 per cent; you shouldn't be singled out for that. The letters and my decision to reply to each one meant it took a little longer to move on from Sydney. Mentally, I was revisiting the disappointment every time I read or responded to a sympathetic letter.

It bothered me that people were seeing me as a loser, a fighter who tried hard but wasn't good enough to win. On the flip side, there was so much warmth in people's reaction, you couldn't help but be inspired by it. To sit down and write a letter of support to a person you have never met nor spoken to implies a great deal of thought and compassion. I wanted to personally thank everyone who wrote and also wanted them to know Sydney had opened my eyes further to what needed to be done. I accepted that I hadn't won a medal because I hadn't been good enough. I needed to go away and work harder, get stronger to be able to maintain the pace and run with the strength in my body to match that in my mind. I knew it was possible, there were things we could add in training. I would not stop until I got there. I would become stronger; I would run faster; I would not be disappointed, or disappointing, the next time.

It took me about a week to make my way out of the depression of that fourth place. I liken the major disappointments of my sporting career to falling from a horse or bike. Recovery comes quickest to those prepared to climb straight back on the horse or bike at the first opportunity. Plus running makes me feel better in all ways. To put Sydney behind me, I needed to get out and race again. Gary and I decided I would run a 5-mile in Loughrea, in the west of Ireland, and after that do the Great North Run in Newcastle.

First we had a week's holiday on Hamilton Island. I was still running but enjoying exploring the island and not doing such structured training as usual. As soon as the plans were made, the future became important and it became easier to put Sydney behind me.

Although I was frustrated by my performance in Sydney, I was by no means ashamed of it. Who, at the end of their lives, would look back and say, 'Well, I came 4th in an Olympic final and it wasn't any good.' Not many, and certainly not me. I simply felt that I was capable of doing better if I worked harder. Due to the injury I had had to curtail my pre-Olympics training with fewer preparatory races, I felt fit and very fresh and wanted to continue competing in the weeks after the Games to help me move on. I ran the 5-mile race in Loughrea and beat Sonia O'Sullivan quite convincingly. After that I ran 67.07 to win the Great North Run, and in doing so beat Liz McColgan's British record.

I was hugely encouraged. My time in the Great North Run was two minutes quicker than the previous year and suggested that Sydney had, in fact, come round just that little bit too soon after my recovery from surgery. The Great North Run win helped greatly to heal the wounds and tempted me to keep going for another three weeks so I could compete in the World Half-Marathon Championships at Vera Cruz. I was obviously in shape to do well there and it was an opportunity to win my first senior world title. Gary and I went out to Font-Romeu for a couple of weeks to prepare and then we headed to Mexico. I wasn't sure what to expect of my first World Half-Marathon Championships but I knew that I loved racing on the road and that this was a good first step towards a possible future at the marathon.

The race was run in oppressive heat and humidity. In fact my feet burned and swelled so badly that I was unable to wear shoes for 24 hours after the race. Nevertheless, it was one of those good days when the conditions were almost irrelevant. Sure, the winning time was going to be slower than it would have been in cooler, less humid weather but it wasn't important – winning was. I ran cautiously for two of the first three laps but on the final lap I broke away quickly and went on to win decisively. It was my third consecutive victory and my first world title as a senior athlete. A positive ending to the year 2000; I was showing that already Sydney had made me a stronger athlete.

GARY:

'*On the night of the 10,000m final in Sydney we walked from the Olympic Stadium back to the Athletes' Village. Although Paula was contracted to Adidas at the time, a friend of mine who worked for Nike invited us to this party at a Nike hospitality centre. I waited outside the Village while she got changed. When she came out she had two McDonald's burgers for me. We tried to hitch a lift to the party but nobody would stop for us so after a tough race she also had a long walk. At the party everyone told Paula how brave she had been, how great she was and she just didn't want to hear it. You know what, I didn't want to go out that night. I would have preferred to hide in my room. But she was prepared to face it; she wasn't going to hide away like a bitter and twisted athlete who didn't get a medal, like I would have been.*

'We went for a short holiday on Hamilton Island and after a couple of days we went for an easy run. She told me she was thinking of doing the Great North Run. I couldn't understand it. How could she think about racing again so soon after the greatest disappointment of her career, of her life at that point? I asked her, "How can you talk about this?" And she said, "Either you let it get to you, bring you down and make you bitter, or you move on and I'm moving on. Simple." I'm saying, "It's not that simple, this was a devastating experience." I really was uncomprehending. She said, "There's no going back, they're not going to light the Olympic flame in Sydney again and give us another shot. They're not going to change the result. It's over. Deal with it." And this didn't diminish or demean the hurt she felt, the huge burden of disappointment; it just meant she was picking herself up and getting on with things. Because if she didn't do that, it would have torn her apart and she would have screwed herself up. Mentally, she was too strong to let that happen.'

It was March 2001. We were in the tent of the warm-up area at the World Cross-Country Championships in Ostend. There was Gerard Hartmann, my coach Alex Stanton, Gary and I. Gerard is by nature an upbeat and positive person but on this afternoon, he couldn't keep the grin from his face and the expectation from his voice.

'Paula,' he said, 'you're in fantastic shape. Today is going to be the day.'

'Gerard,' I said, 'stop it. You're making me more nervous.' I felt good and was confident but preferred to keep that quiet until the racing was done!

'But no one's going to beat you, I have a very good feeling about today.'

'I have the same feeling,' said Alex cautiously, 'but let's get through the race first.'

'Yeah, but . . .'

'Gerard, just stop it,' I said. 'Keep your good feeling to yourself.'

It was true. That winter's training in Albuquerque had gone extremely well. Despite ten days off with severe bronchitis to begin with, my times were better than they had been on any of the four previous visits and after returning to England, a visit to the exercise physiologist, Andy Jones, in Manchester confirmed what had been obvious in training. By doing various tests on the treadmill, Andy calculated that my VO2 Max was 80, which is extremely high for a woman. My previous best had been 77, before that it was 75 and before that 73. Andy said in his research he had not come across a VO2 Max of 80 in a woman, which was the equivalent of 90 in a man. I am not sure if he was trying to bolster my confidence before the big race or if he was telling me the truth; all I knew was that I felt good and was looking forward to the race. After the tests were completed, he said: 'Paula, you are in brilliant shape, go to Ostend and fulfil your destiny.'

I didn't expect it to be easy. I had tried on six occasions to win the senior cross-country championships, missing out each time. My best efforts were second in Turin (1997) and Marrakech (1998). Our expectations were high in Belfast in 1999 but I was only third. Twelve months later we believed I had a chance at Vilamoura in Portugal and was a disappointed fifth in the long race and fourth in the short one. It was no surprise that Alex and I were reluctant to buy into Gerard's boundless optimism; we knew just how tough a race that brought the world's top distance runners from 1,500m to marathon together was to win. You could be in outstanding shape, but we knew you still needed that little bit of luck for it all to come together on the day.

It had rained a lot in Ostend and the course was very muddy and even waterlogged in places. I was worried at first because the muddy conditions in Belfast two years before hadn't suited me. However, there is a world of difference between the drier, sticky mud that we had then and the wetter, boggy mud in Ostend. The stickiness in Belfast had disrupted my rhythm, not so the wet mud of Belgium. Plus I was now a stronger athlete. Still, the conditions were tough and with a strong headwind in the finishing straight, it would have been suicidal to do too much too early. For two of the four laps, I sat in the pack, taking as much shelter as possible as I watched the race unfold. I felt totally calm and in control throughout, perhaps because I was in such good shape. Moving past those who were getting dropped, I kept the leaders within my sights. On the last lap I made my move as the speed increased and the number of leaders was whittled down.

With about a kilometre to go, it was down to Wami and me. Spectators were shouting, 'The two of you are away.' I sensed they were pleased for me because a silver medal was now the least I would get but I was after the gold. Wami was tucked in behind me and I am sure many of those on the course presumed she would beat me in the sprint. 'No way,' I thought, 'I am not coming away with 2nd place again. This one I will win.' Shielded in 2nd place, Wami did not realise the strength of the wind, nor did she know how strong I felt. My best chance of winning was to feign tiredness, slowing just enough to encourage her to take the lead well before the line and expose her to the wind.

With 200m to go she took the bait and passed me, sooner than she would normally do. Going into the wind she found it hard to sustain the acceleration that had taken her past me. It took a couple of seconds for me to change gear and find the speed to get back to her. As I did, I could feel and hear the support for me. For a number of years cross-country fans had watched me being overtaken in finishing straights. Now I had reversed the role. I could feel the groundswell of support almost propel me forward. I dared not look across at Wami as I drew alongside and past her, I only wanted to get across that line. Still, I sensed the shock on her face as she realised I was coming back. Once I inched ahead and established a small gap, she slowed and accepted defeat, something I was not aware of until afterwards. After my experience in Turin four years before, when I believed I would win only to be overtaken in the last 50 metres, I did not allow myself to think I had won until I was through the tape. Only then did the surprise and elation hit me.

Watching the video later I was struck by the disbelief showing in my face. Even though I had expected to run really well, my overriding emotion when I won was that of shock. Finally, I had done it, finally, and what was even better, I had won in a sprint finish. I thought of Granddad and how delighted he would have been. For nine years I had believed that I could do it, persevered through the setbacks and now the World Cross title was mine. It was perfect, too, that I won in 2001 because the following year I wanted to run the London Marathon and even though the plan was to run the cross-country beforehand, the focus would be different. Ironically I had returned the contract committing me to race in London on the way out to Belgium; it was almost as if I knew subconsciously that this was to be my year. Ostend was my last chance to commit myself exclusively to the championship.

Success was not likely to go to my head. Before the medal ceremony and doping control they gave us a bucket of cold water and a sponge to wash ourselves down. It was freezing cold. In the process I lost a ring that Mum and Dad bought for me at the very beginning of my running career. I had it for fifteen years, always wore it in races and regarded it as a lucky ring. I liked the familiarity of those three colours of gold on my finger when I went out on the track, the sense that it had been with me from the start. I didn't realise it was gone until after the ceremony. It must have slipped off because my fingers were so cold. We searched and searched but the buckets were empty and the ring was gone. Still, a gold medal for a gold ring; it was a trade I could live with.

Afterwards, for my warm-down I jogged along the sea front in

Ostend and met many fans going to and from their hotels. 'Well done Paula,' they shouted. 'Well deserved.' I was pretty emotional and extremely satisfied; it had been a long hard road. Alex cried afterwards. Gary's mum was so nervous towards the end of the race she turned away and when she looked up, the race was over. My mum was crying and Gary's poor mum didn't know if that was good news or bad. For a few never-ending moments, she didn't dare ask. We celebrated that evening but it was low-key because I wanted to go out the following day and win the short race.

Though the longer race had been my primary target, I felt I had nothing to lose and wanted to win both if I could. The second race came down to another battle with Wami. The course had been pumped a little drier overnight, making the conditions sticky and I didn't feel as comfortable. I was tired from the previous day and Wami's defeat had made her more determined. She ran a cleverer race and maybe wanted it just that little bit more. At 50 metres to go she made her finishing spurt, and though I tried to get back to her, this time I couldn't. It was close at the end, just one second, but she was a deserving winner. I was disappointed to have lost the race, but in my heart the 8k was the one I wanted more than anything, and the disappointment was short-lived. Often after the elation of victory there is a period of anti-climax, almost as if the desire to win has built the victory up to be more than it is. This time, however, there was none of that. I felt almost surreally calm and serene. I didn't need to jump around or shout about it, but the feeling of achievement, of satisfaction and of pleasure would stay with me for ever and add to me as an athlete.

13

I remember feeling so frustrated and angry at the end of the 10,000m final at the 2001 World Championships in Edmonton. It was five months after the win in Ostend and though I was a stronger more confident athlete I had taken a gamble, run a totally different race to normal and it hadn't paid off. Again I had finished outside the medals at a major championship. Fourth behind Derartu Tulu and two other Ethiopians, Berhane Adere and Gete Wami, I had failed to win by less than two seconds and was just eight hundredths of a second behind the bronze medallist, Wami. It was the same gut-wrenching result as Sydney twelve months earlier, only this time I knew I'd made mistakes, I felt I hadn't given every last ounce of energy. I just wanted to get back out there and do it again.

It is probably most remembered, however, for an altercation between Gary and me seconds after the race ended. I had just crossed the line and, glancing at the giant screen in the stadium, I saw they had mistakenly listed me as 3rd. I knew Wami had just pipped me, but for a split second there was at least the consolation of a medal, and this was an unnecessarily cruel error.

'Why did they do that?' I asked Gary, who had somehow got himself down by the side of the track.

He thought I said, 'Why did I do that?' referring to how I had run my race.

'Yeah, why the fuck did you do that? You should have gone earlier. Why didn't you stick to the race plan that we talked about before?' he yelled at me in frustration.

Gary's point was valid and I was confused and angry with myself already for not having done so. But his timing was wrong, very wrong. In a minute or two I was going to have to walk through the media zone, doing television, radio and newspaper interviews. I needed to be emotionally in one piece to get through that.

'Leave it for now. We'll talk about it later, just leave me alone,' I said, pushing him away as I walked past.

GARY:

'I barged my way past these security people, got down there and saw her cross the line fourth. I didn't see her name go up on the screen as third and when she said, "Why did they do that?" I had no idea what she was talking about and thought she said "Why did I do that?" "Yeah," I said, "why the fuck did you do that?" referring to the way she had run the race. She said she wasn't dealing with that now; she had interviews to do. I felt she was blanking me and never thought about the fact that there were television cameras on us. As she walked away I tried to stop her and she just kind of pushed me away. She then went up through this blue tunnel towards the television booths and I stupidly followed her. The BBC actually had footage of me inside this bloody thing which, thankfully, they never showed. While Paula was in the mixed zone with the journalists, I stayed in the background. That gave me a chance to calm down. When she finished her interviews, I apologised. I mean she was devastated by the race and to top it all there was all this bullshit from me.'

After winning the World Cross-Country title earlier in the year, I had gone to Edmonton feeling very positive. My last race, a 5,000m in

London, had gone reasonably well. At Crystal Palace I ran 14.44, won the race by about 10 seconds but wasn't pleased with the way I hadn't been able to keep my pace going over the closing laps. We put it down to the fact that I had just come from altitude training at Font-Romeu and still needed time to recover from the intensive training there. I fell into the trap of trying to prove to myself I was in shape through a series of high-quality training sessions in the days between then and Edmonton. Ten days before the race I was doing the best speed sessions I had ever done, but perhaps when I should have been backing off, I was still seeking final reassurance that I shouldn't have needed and losing a little of the freshness necessary to produce my best. Conversely, these sessions showed that my basic speed was now far better than ever before. Since the winter 1999–2000 I had been working with Max Jones on specific weight training and now was starting to see definite benefits. My confidence in my finish was at an all time high, for the first time I really believed that I could finish as fast, or faster than the Ethiopians. At the same time, I had learned the hard way in Sydney that it would be extremely difficult to run away from a world class field. To win, I knew I had to try something different. The really upsetting thing about Edmonton was that it actually came very close to coming off, but it left me with nothing but frustration.

The plan in Edmonton was not to lead from the beginning but to inject real pace into the race at different points to try and break up the rhythm and to make things as tough as possible for the others. But plans don't always work out, particularly if you don't feel good. As the race unfolded, I was positioned in the pack and was biding my time before going to the front. It was obvious that to really stretch the others, I would have to make my move around halfway but at that stage I wasn't feeling good. To go to the front and inject a fast surge you have to be ready and strong both physically and mentally. Hoping I would come through the bad patch and feel ready, I kept putting it off. 'Wait for a lap, you might feel better then.' But as the laps passed, there was no improvement. With four laps to go, there was no alternative and I went to the front with a definite sense that it was 'now or never'. It was too late, but I just didn't feel strong enough to go earlier. Perhaps there was that belief in the back of my mind that after the speed sessions I had been doing beforehand, I would still be able to outsprint the Ethiopians. As it was, I surged hard but there wasn't enough time left to hurt the others enough. It was close in the end, just one second dividing the first four finishers, but that only added to my frustration. Tactically I had got it wrong and I had blown a great opportunity. I wanted to start over again but of course I couldn't. The only outlets for my frustration were the races left in the season, and though I won in Gateshead and improved my 5,000m personal best massively in Berlin, neither was a championship medal and though important to me, could never quite make up for the disappointment in Canada.

Doing my warm-down afterwards, I apologised to Alex and Gerard for my performance. I felt I had let a lot of people down, myself first but also especially Gary, Alex and Gerard, as they had put so much work into helping me. It made me angry to think about it. By now Gary was very supportive and our little contretemps after the race wasn't an issue. It was just one of those blow-ups that happen between two strong-minded people with a lot of invested emotional interest. Couples argue all the time; we had certainly argued before and would again but the difference this time was that we were the focus of television cameras and photographers at a moment when our deepest emotions were raw and exposed. The television footage had been beamed into millions of homes, the pictures were everywhere and everything was totally out of proportion. Gary's mum called the next day about it.

GARY:

'My mother called and all she said was, "You are an arsehole". I had no idea what she was on about. She said, "I was meant to go to the bank this morning

but I can't now. Everyone is talking about it, I can't go out. What are Paula's mum and dad going to think?" That awful picture, the one of Paula pushing me away, was everywhere. The Times *newspaper ran an unbelievable story about the bust-up. It was so way out, it just made us laugh. A woman wrote afterwards about me using "a sawn-off water bottle" to bellow instructions at Paula. It was a bottle of Vittel, nothing like a megaphone. The funniest part, though, was where Paula and I were listed with all the celebrity couples who'd had a public falling-out. There was Liam Gallagher and Patsy Kensit, Madonna and Guy Ritchie, Paula and me: I kid you not. You just had to laugh at that.'*

Some of the overexaggerated and false reports were just so extreme they were hilarious and made me laugh. After the anger and frustration of the race that was a good thing. If there was one thing I found upsetting about all of that, it was the portrayal of Gary as rude, pushy and awkward. That's not him. He's just fiery. It's the way he is. I can be fiery, too. It's just that I am more aware of how things can be interpreted and maybe have a little more tact and concern for other people in expressing it. Dad once said I might look like butter wouldn't melt in my mouth but if you stand between me and what I want, you may discover the opposite.

The two weeks in Edmonton were certainly eventful. A few days before the 10,000m final, my GB team-mate Hayley Tullett and I held up a sign in the stands saying 'EPO CHEATS OUT'. This created serious controversy but I had thought about it a great deal beforehand and it was the product of serious frustration. The catalyst for the protest was the participation of the Russian athlete Olga Yegorova in a heat of the 5,000m which was about to begin near where we sat. However, the issue was much bigger than that. We were not specifically getting at her, we were making a protest at the frustrating inadequacy of drug testing in our sport. Yegorova, who had been around for a while, was an 8.45 runner for 3,000m who suddenly started producing times in the 8.20s. Athletes who improve a lot can be unfairly suspected of using performance enhancing drugs but Yegorova's progress was so startling the questions were inevitable.

Then, shortly before Edmonton, she tested positive for the blood-boosting substance EPO, metabolites of which were found in her urine, but the result was subsequently overturned because the French testing authorities did not adhere to IAAF protocol. Yegorova escaped on a technicality and was allowed to compete in the 5,000m at Edmonton, a title she would go on to win. To me and to many others it was an example of what was wrong with our sport and why clean athletes were so frustrated with the authorities. Such a small percentage of budgets are invested in anti-doping yet it is a vital issue. Without valid reliable tests for certain substances everyone knew that there was cheating going on and people getting away with it. It was seriously affecting the credibility of our sport and hurting the majority of athletes who were clean and working hard only to lose out to those taking short cuts or, worse still, be accused of cheating themselves. We routinely spend our time giving drug tests, yet the system wasn't capable of detecting the most effective and abused doping products. Finally when someone was caught they got away with it because protocol had not been followed. How could clean athletes sit back and do nothing? To have accepted Yegorova's presence without protest would have been akin to saying doping didn't matter. I have always believed that I should be true to my beliefs and opinions. To me, to sit back and do nothing would have been not to have the courage to stand up for what I believed in; it would have been almost condoning the situation, giving the impression that we athletes were happy with how things were when the simple truth was that we weren't.

As we held the sign up there were Russians nearby yelling at us; we worried about what other athletes would think of what we were doing. We knew we were taking a risk, putting ourselves up as targets for what we believed in. Yet I have always said that fear is no reason not to do what you believe is right. Someone had to do something and we held that sign up to get our opinion across. We felt that the IAAF weren't listening to us or doing enough to fight doping; we wanted the public to know that the majority of athletes were clean and not happy about the way our sport was being portrayed. We knew the media interest would get people's attention.

Athletics is an amazing sport. It has brought so much to me as a person. To see its credibility damaged, to think about parents not wanting their children to take up athletics because of the fear of them facing the spectre of drugs if they wanted to advance hurts me. Running is about who works hardest and then runs fastest. It is about getting to the finish first fairly. That has been my philosophy from the beginning. Every athlete must start from the same point, something that is not possible when some are doping. If you invest so much of yourself, you have a right to fair competition and a right to be able to prove your innocence. That is one of the bugbears of modern sport: how does the successful athlete prove he or she is clean? By passing the tests? Everyone knows the tests are not guaranteed to expose the cheats. We wanted to focus attention on the need for better, more accurate testing and greater use of blood profiling tests.

I got involved in athletics because I loved it and wanted to see how good I could be. If you used drugs how could you ever truly know this? I'm sure it is the same for so many others. Yet, as I grew through the sport I have heard so many whisperings and accusations, seen so much controversy. It was time, as an athlete, to also accept that we had a responsibility to our sport too; we had to do something and work with the authorities to do something about it.

Before the 1999 European Cup meeting in Paris, I read an article about the French 5,000m and cross-country runner, Blandine Bitzner-Ducret. She raced with a red hairband around her arm and in an interview explained it was her protest against the lack of adequate testing in athletics and a plea for blood tests. The day before we raced at the European Cup, I spoke to her about it.

'Blandine, I think what you're doing is right. Would you mind if I wore a something like this as well?'

'No,' she said. 'I don't mind at all. The more people that do it the better.'

I thought an armband would be restrictive and opted instead for a red ribbon on my running vest. Not having the time to get some proper red ribbon for the next day's 5,000m, I found a red card, cut a piece from it and pinned it to the vest. Blandine was pleased to see someone else making this show of support for drug-free sport. People ask me now would I mind if they wore a red ribbon and I tell them to go right ahead. What I don't do is preach to people and try to persuade them to make this stand. It has to come from the heart of each athlete. The red ribbon is now part of my racing uniform, it's my small statement for what I believe in.

I believe totally in testing, in competition and especially out of competition. It is my responsibility, as it is every athlete's, to keep the authorities informed of my whereabouts. You let them know where you intend to be three months in advance and keep them updated about any change to your schedule that would prevent you from being at the listed address. The updates are required three days in advance. If you are not at the registered address when the testers call it is recorded as a no show. Three of those are a case to answer. It's strict but unfortunately the way it has to be. I have been tested on my birthday at a restaurant in Belfast; the tester came into the loo with me and a sample was provided.

There is a British tester who regularly comes to our home in Loughborough. She is great, very courteous and always apologises for turning up when we're in the middle of something. 'There's no need,' I say, 'I'm glad you're doing this job.' Once she came just after I returned from a long run. It was a humid day, I had just been to the loo and there was no way I could produce immediately. She had to wait a long time, accompany me to the bathroom while I showered, and I was saying all the time, 'There's no need to apologise, testing benefits us all.' Other times she has had to come out at short notice after I had set a world best and needed to be tested that night. The testers do a great job in the fight against doping. Twice in my life, I have been cross and complained. Once was at a cross-country race near the beginning of my career. There were no female drug testers available so I had to be observed as I produced a sample by a male tester. Embarrassing and intimidating! Another time a tester showed up at our home when we weren't there and then phoned me to say I would get a warning. I had notified the IAAF I would be away and immediately phoned to confirm this. Unfortunately there had been a delay in forwarding the information but there had been no need for the tester's rudeness.

In 2002, after a year of considerable success, I had to face the whisperings and accusations about whether or not I was clean. Even when you know the truth, that kind of talk hurts. I had worked so hard for my results and yet what more could I do? I was being tested all the time and openly putting myself out to try to get the tests more developed. At that time I asked the IAAF to refrigerate my samples because I couldn't think of any other way to establish my innocence and my attitude to testing. In this way they can be tested in the future as more and more accurate tests become available. On the IAAF athletes commission we are talking about keeping blood profiles of elite athletes that could have double use as health screening for athletes and also as a basis to pick up on changes in blood parameters and evidence of doping.

One of those who publicly questioned me was Stéfan L'Hermitte, a sportswriter with *L'Equipe* magazine. He wrote that you couldn't trust my performances and insinuated that I doped. I am quite fluent in French but to be certain that I had fully understood the article, I asked two French friends to read it through. They both said the meaning was clear: the writer did not believe I was clean. I was so hurt and angry, I rang him at work and tackled him about his reasons for suggesting I doped, reasons he had not mentioned in his piece. He seemed to have been surprised by my phone call. All he could say was that he had the right to offer his opinion. 'Yes, you do,' I said, 'but in private or by saying it is your unproven opinion. Not by writing a piece that attempts to destroy someone's reputation and credibility without putting up one bit of evidence, not one iota of proof.'

He continued to say that as a journalist he was entitled to his view. I replied that he had no right to take away someone's reputation without having some basis for doing so. 'I've laid myself open to every test available and have samples frozen so tests can be conducted in the future. Do you, then, have a suggestion about what more I can do to satisfy your doubts?'

However, I can't allow such things to get to me and stop me doing what I enjoy doing and getting the pleasure from it. There comes a time when you have to switch off and concentrate solely on your training and preparation. What matters is what you know about yourself, what you think about yourself and what those closest to you think of you. Of course it affects me if someone accuses me. No matter how many times you tell yourself you don't care what a few idiots think, it still wounds and hurts. If I wrote an article accusing a journalist of plagiarism and did not offer any evidence to support the allegation, wouldn't that journalist be entitled to be upset?

It is the same with some chat boards. I read them and am hurt by the injustice and often outright hatred of some of the posters. It shouldn't, but of course it does still bother me. I want to discover their true identity, confront that person, reasonably discuss with them why they feel that way. Of course, that is irrational and the best thing to do is just not go there, not to read articles I know will hurt me. Being in the public eye and as such up for public dissection has certainly made me a tougher person.

There is a trade-off between the amount of time and energy you can devote to making the case for drug-free sport and the danger of it becoming a distraction and harming your career. Ultimately, during the short time I have available to make the most of my career, I want nothing to interfere with the quality of my training and recuperation because the *raison d'être* of the professional athlete is to be as good as he or she can be. But sometimes I get frustrated that I haven't pushed hard enough or devoted enough time to the anti-doping issue and once my career is over, it will become a priority. There are times I am angry with myself for not doing more because it is important, especially so for young people coming into the sport. Ours is a great sport. It has enriched me as a person and given me self-confidence. It pains me to think parents are now saying, 'But what happens if my son is offered performance-enhancing drugs?'

Officials at the Edmonton World Championships weren't pleased with our 'EPO CHEATS OUT' sign and wasted no time in having it removed. How unusual that in a country as free as Canada, a peaceful protest should have been so quickly suppressed. While sympathetic to my stance on drugs, the IAAF was not pleased that I had publicly highlighted a weakness in the testing system. They were also upset that I drew attention to the sport's greatest problem in the middle of its biggest and most prestigious event. They invited me to Monaco to discuss the subject with some of their doping officials.

I was told how difficult it was to come up with tests for certain products and saw how committed the anti-doping panel were to the fight against doping. Yes, I saw and I understand the difficulty of developing a test for something like human growth hormone, but we and the authorities need to do more. Another result of the Edmonton protest was the chance to interview and discuss the issue with IOC president Jacques Rogge. I honestly got the impression that he was very committed to trying to improve things. Without doubt there has been an improvement in the last two or three years and there is now a determination and a resolve to catch the cheats that wasn't always there. The establishment of the World Anti-Doping Agency (WADA) in 1999 was the key to taking the fight to those prepared to flout sport's doping laws and at the 2004 Athens Olympics we saw a new attitude and much more resolve from the International Olympic Committee. We are definitely going in the right direction but athletes and officials need to work together on this and there is no doubt that it will be a long hard fight. I definitely believe it is a battle that can be won.

14

And then there was 2002, an extraordinary year.

I ran just nine races but won the World Cross-Country Championships, the London Marathon, the Commonwealth Games 5,000m, the European Championships 10,000m and the Chicago Marathon. Along the way there were new UK and European records and, in my final race of the season, a world record. I was asked to present a Bafta television award the week after winning in London, to be a guest on the Oprah Winfrey show a week after winning in Chicago, Nike wanted me to give the keynote talk to 500 of their salespeople at a conference in Orlando and, most amazing of all, 605,000 British people voted me the BBC's Sports Personality of the Year. Each of those occasions was wonderful, but if I were to choose one experience among them that encapsulated the year and what it meant, I would bring you to the evening of 28 July, the first Sunday at the Manchester Commonwealth Games.

Everything about Manchester worked. The organisation was excellent, the atmosphere at the City of Manchester Stadium was inspiringly special, the Athletes' Village was great and even the weather was fine. I went to Manchester in search of my first title on the track and in the best form of my career. It was also my first time at the Commonwealth Games because injury and a virus had forced me to miss Victoria in 1994 and Kuala Lumpur four years later. In my one preparatory race for Manchester, I ran 8.22 for 3,000m at a Grand Prix meeting in Monaco, 4 seconds faster for the distance than I had ever run in my life and faster than even I had thought I could run. So fast that turning into the finishing straight in Monaco I saw 8.06 on the stadium clock and thought that couldn't be right. We couldn't have been going that quickly. We were. Gabriela Szabo won in 8.21, I was second and the Kenyan Edith Masai was third. Masai was also in the 5,000m final at Manchester, my event, and her presence meant there were no guarantees. It would be a very tough race to win the gold medal.

The fact that the Games were being held in Manchester made it extra special. We went there wondering if the city would rise to the challenge of hosting a major international sports event. There was talk that the Village might not be up to scratch and that Manchester would not understand what was involved. The fears were utterly without foundation. Our living quarters were Halls of Residence at the University of Manchester and they were great. The England team stayed in an old building overlooking a grass courtyard, a wonderful setting where we were able to gather outside on the grass to sit and chat; it created a lovely atmosphere. On the Friday evening, two days before the 5,000m final, Jo Pavey and I went to the warm-up track and then on to the stadium to check how long it would take us to get from one to the other. We also wanted to see where the last toilets were before you went through on to the track, but by the time we got to the stadium, Friday evening's events had begun and only competing athletes were allowed through the call procedure.

We spoke to two officials at the entrance.

'Any chance we could go through the tunnel, we just want to find out where things are for when we're competing?'

'Okay,' one of the stewards said, 'if anyone asks us, we'll just say we thought you two were competing tonight.'

It was a reminder of what home advantage means. Had it been in some far away country, Jo and I wouldn't have asked. Inside the stadium, the atmosphere was relaxed and friendly but also buoyant. Everyone was wishing us luck and telling us they hoped it went well. It was obvious that Manchester had taken this event and truly embraced it. Visitors were made welcome, competing athletes were made to feel special. I loved it.

The ambience in the Village enhanced the whole experience. As you mentally prepared for your event and other athletes faced their big moment, each wished the other well. The mood of the English team was very positive, probably because we were on home soil. This environment brings the best out in me. I thrive in it; being part of a group, wanting to do well for the team, supporting your team-mates, going for meals together, following each other's progress and, maybe most of all, just sharing the experience. As a young athlete with Bedford & County Athletic Club I preferred to travel with the rest of the girls on the team coach rather than with my parents. With them around me, I could tune into the race and enjoy the build-up.

My memories of the Sunday evening and the 5,000m final have not dimmed. Underneath the stand, before going out on the track for our last warm-up, officials checked the length of our spikes, made sure our kits were what they should be and that we were all wearing the right numbers. Many people thought this would be my night. That excited me but scared me as well. Masai was an excellent athlete and had beaten me more than once. She was just behind me when I ran that career-best 3,000m in Monaco and if I couldn't shake her off through this evening's race, she would have a good chance of winning. We were ushered out on to the track where the roar that greeted my appearance made my head spin. There was no mistaking the anticipation. 'Come On Paula's hurtled at me from every corner of the stadium. I was home.

That much was confirmed with the sight of Claire Peet, one of the volunteers carrying the baskets to collect the athletes' belongings. Claire and I had raced and trained together at Bedford since 1986. We are good friends.

'Oh my God, Claire! What are you doing here?'

Claire Peet was with me on the night we ran a mixed raced at the Copthall Stadium in north London. We were 15/16-year-olds in search of a qualifying time for the English Schools 3,000m. Knowing that the mixed race would give us a better chance of getting a faster time, Alex took us down there and for the first three or four laps we could hardly run because we were laughing. We hadn't raced against men before and some of them clearly didn't like girls being in among them. Some of them also smelled quite strongly! I ran 10 minutes, Claire ran 10.12 and we beat a number of them. As we always did, we shook hands with those nearest to us once the race ended. Claire, who is only about five foot two and has got this funky blonde hair, turned to shake hands with one of the men who had finished behind us. 'Are you taking the fucking piss?' he said. Clearly, he wasn't happy. Not in a million years would Claire have deliberately ridiculed him but how we laughed on the way home that evening.

Now everything seemed so normal, so familiar, with Claire right there, minutes before the start of the 5,000m final. In a funny way, it was wonderfully reassuring.

As I did my last few strides, the crowd roared even louder.

'This is mad,' I said to Claire, laughing nervously.

'They are so behind you,' she said. 'And by the way, good luck.'

Although pre-race plans are thought through carefully, they are nothing but a guide. Ideally you run to your plan but races don't often work out like that. You may be on a bad day, the pace may be slower than expected, the wind may pick up, an opponent may do the unexpected. Through a slow first lap in this final, there was a lot of bumping and barging and this forced my hand. The plan had been to hold back in the group for a little while and then accelerate, but that was ditched as I got to the front and out of trouble on the second lap. Running within myself but still at a decent pace I led the race through the first 3 kilometres before making my move and pushing it much harder.

Remarkably, there was a buzz of anticipation from the crowd at the very moment that I chose to make a prolonged surge. I remember thinking, 'They know what I am going to do. How can they sense that?' Their excitement was spurring me on yet faster; my acceleration was exciting them further. It was amazing. After pushing on, I glanced at the big screen and saw that I had drawn clear of everyone except Edith Masai. Keeping up the pressure, I could tell something was happening to Masai from a new explosion of noise around the stadium. I looked again at the screen but the cameras were on one of the other runners who had collapsed. Paramedics were lifting her on to a stretcher and I had to fight off the temptation to glance behind me to see what was happening to Masai. 'Looking back is a sign of weakness,' Dad had drummed into me since I was a little girl.

I pressed on, drawing from the unbelievable support of the crowd and enjoying the feeling of running well. Next time round I glanced up at the screen and saw the 50-metre gap back to Masai. At that point there were just three laps to go and the crowd was growing more frenzied with each passing moment. Whenever you get away in a race, the relief gives you an extra burst of energy. Now ahead of Masai, I wanted to turn the screw even more and make that gap bigger. There comes a point in a race where you can say, 'No way can I lose this one from here.' I was there, and the final laps were mine to enjoy.

At the bell I realised that an exceptional final 400m would bring me close to a world record. But it was going to be tough because I had to run in lane two to overtake lapped runners. The world record was 14.28, I was close to 14.30-pace but even if I couldn't break the record, I wanted to beat 14.30. I failed by a second but I didn't care, times were irrelevant that night. I finally had my track title and what better place to do it.

Claire was standing right by the line and gave me a big hug. Two more guys from Bedford hugged me, someone handed me a flag. The crowd was going wild. I searched the faces for Gary. I thought maybe he wasn't going to appear because of what happened in Edmonton. Maybe they weren't allowing him on the track. Then he was there and we hugged. I had wanted to see him before setting off on my victory lap. Down the back straight, Alex waited for me. We embraced. He was so pleased. This was as much their victory as mine.

The medal ceremony was very moving. My emotions were whirling, the wait was over; after years of trying, finally a track gold medal. Maybe the Commonwealths were not the Olympics but this was my best ever run over 5,000m and it had taken place in a stadium packed to the rafters with English people. We sang 'Land of Hope and Glory' as the English flag was raised. I marvelled at the outpouring of joy and the sea of St George's flags. And it was good to observe all this from the centre position on the victory rostrum. The atmosphere that evening in the City of Manchester Stadium is something that will always stay with me and give me goosebumps every time I think of it. I can only hope I get the chance to experience something similar again.

Mine must have been the last race of the evening because after the medal ceremony everyone was leaving the stadium. We found Mum and Dad, Grandma, my brother Martin and his wife Nicole, Gary's parents and his sister Catherine. But there was time only for hugs and the briefest of greetings. I had to go off to a shopping centre where the BBC had a studio and were doing a late-night show. Jonathan Edwards won the triple jump earlier in the evening and we were both guests on the show. It was well after midnight when we got back to the Village and hunger sent us in search of some food. The cafeteria we found was deserted, the food all but gone, but we enjoyed our cold chips and whatever else was left over.

I walked back through the Village. It was quiet; everyone was sleeping. Outside the building where we stayed there were big ice machines. I took out two plastic bags from my rucksack and filled them with ice cubes. Back in the halls I tipped the ice into the bath and turned on the cold water. It was 1.30 in the morning. I stepped into the ice-cold bath and lay immersed to the waist for 12 to 15 minutes. The first five minutes are always the worst, after that you get used to it. That night it was fine, I read my book and tried not to think about the stinging cold. The race was over. The race was won. And I was in my element.

I first ran in the senior World Cross-Country Championships in 1993 and for the following eight years, it was my big ambition to win the title. So much of my early experience as a runner had been in cross country; the freedom and unstructured nature of it always suited me. The breakthrough came in Ostend in 2001 and it meant a lot; it had been a long time coming. Having finally got the monkey off my back, I knew I could win again, so I looked forward to defending my title in Dublin the following year.

And now the time has come to do just that. I am sitting with Gary and Gerard in a car travelling from Limerick in the west of Ireland to Dublin on the east coast. I am in the front seat with packs of ice on my knee, and the telltale signs of disrupted sleep and anxiety showing under my eyes. It is Thursday, 21 March; two days before the World Cross-Country Championships which are being held at Leopardstown racecourse 10 miles from the centre of Dublin. It should be a pleasant journey, enlivened by anticipation of the race to come. It is anything but. For almost a month now my knee has been troublesome and though Gerard assures me running in the cross-country will not aggravate the problem, my enthusiasm for it is not what it should be.

The reason is the London Marathon, to be held three weeks later. We had decided almost a year before to run my first marathon in

London and for three months, we have thought about little else. Our winter training at altitude in Albuquerque was designed to prepare me for the marathon and though Leopardstown was always in the plan, it was the secondary target. The thought of missing London was one that hardly bore thinking about.

We had known for a number of years that road running suited me and that going up in distance would play to my greatest strengths, mental toughness and endurance. Every treadmill test I had done with exercise physiologist Andy Jones showed the marathon would be my ideal event. I had waited until I truly felt the desire to tackle 26.2 miles but it was always only a matter of time. Competing in the Great North Run over the half-marathon distance, and then in the World Half-Marathon Championship at Vera Cruz (2000) and then Bristol (2001) was in part a preparation for the move up to the marathon. At first, the half-marathon distance seemed so long. Afterwards I would say to myself, 'Imagine having to do another one of those without a break' and wonder if it was possible. The draw of wanting to find out what I could do was always there.

Winning that world half-marathon title in Vera Cruz gave me confidence. A year later the same championship was held in Bristol on the first Sunday in October and again it went extremely well. I felt in control throughout before winning convincingly in a time of 66.47, just a few seconds shy of the world best. By now I was seriously thinking about the marathon and believed I could be good at it. At the post-race banquet in Bristol that evening, a few of the journalists asked me how I felt about moving up to the marathon because, by now, it was known I would run London the following April. They wondered also how I felt about Naoko Takahashi's performance in Berlin the previous weekend. Takahashi ran 2.19.46, set a new world record and became the first woman to run a sub-2.20 marathon. The journalists felt Takahashi's performance raised the bar in the women's marathon and asked if I was worried about it.

How could I be scared without having run a marathon? Until I actually did a marathon there was no basis for comparison. I respected the distance; Takahashi's time impressed me but it didn't scare me. I was excited to see what I could run. Earlier that afternoon I had run 66.47 for the half-marathon and that was three minutes faster than Takahashi's time at halfway on her world record run in Berlin. My half-marathon time didn't prove anything except maybe that I had a right to believe one day I would run a good marathon.

So much thought had been put into when and where to begin my marathon career and now three weeks before the race, there is no certainty I will be on the starting line. The injury had crept up on me. A month before, we had left our training base in Albuquerque for a 10-kilometre road race in Puerto Rico. I was trying out different shoes to find the best ones in which to race the marathon. These particular ones were not right for my running style. The sole was narrow and because I land right on the outside edge of my foot, I was coming down on the outside of the shoe. After the race my legs were unusually tired. After a 2-hour 15 run a couple of days later, my knee was sore; the first definite sign of the problem to come.

Gerard wasn't with us in Albuquerque that year and Dana Paine, a very good American therapist, was giving me massage. Although the soreness in the knee was bothering me, it was not enough to stop me running. Or at least not until the last day in Albuquerque. I was due to do a 2-hour run before we flew home but had given up after 1 hour and 35 minutes because the knee became too painful. We were more than a little apprehensive as we took that flight home.

All I wanted to do was get to Limerick and let Gerard go to work, but that wasn't possible. We had agreed with the organisers of the London Marathon that I would spend the weekend doing press interviews at La Manga in Spain. A large number of journalists were committed to being there and it would have inconvenienced a lot of people if I had not turned up. It was a stressful time because instead of going to Limerick, I first spent three days in England followed by the weekend of media duties in La Manga. Not only was I compromising my chances of being fully fit for the World Cross-Country and London, I was speaking to journalists about a marathon I wasn't entirely certain I'd be able to run.

I did twenty-one interviews in two days and all I said about the injury was that it would not stop me from competing in London. I hoped and prayed that would be true . . .

I arrived into Limerick, via Dublin, on Sunday, 17 March, St Patrick's Day, just six days before the World Cross-Country Championships. My luggage was lost somewhere along the way but luckily there were spare running shoes of mine in Limerick and I always travel with my orthotic insoles in my hand luggage. Gerard looked at it, sent me out for a run then treated it afterwards. After running for 55 minutes, my knee was sore. From the Monday, Gerard gave me two daily sessions of intensive treatment and massage. These were physically draining but nothing compared to the alternative of not getting it right quickly. He also sat me down and spelled out the position.

'The problem in your knee need not stop you from running in the cross-country because you will not damage it any further there. But if the decision was being made right now, I would not let you run the marathon because in a race that long, the soreness in your knee could cause other, compensatory injuries and long-term damage. You're obviously in great shape and I don't want to see all that training go down the drain. So you've got to run the cross-country because, in all honesty, it might be the only race you run this spring.'

If it had been necessary to pull out of the cross-country to guarantee my fitness for the marathon, I would have done so. We had prepared so well in Albuquerque for London – increasing my long runs by 5 minutes each week, endlessly practising how I took my drinks. Gearing everything towards the marathon. The mood in the car as we travelled to Dublin for the cross-country was sombre when not downright bleak. Worried about the injury, I had slept fitfully and uneasily in the build up to the race. Sitting in the tent before doing my warm-up on Saturday afternoon, I was torn between wanting to win and worrying about my knee. 'Gerard,' I said, 'I can still feel it. It is not one hundred per cent.'

'You will feel it,' he said, 'it will hurt you in the race but I promise you will not make it any worse. You've just got to get through today.'

The knee did hurt me during the race, but not as badly as it had done in training, or maybe I just blocked it from my mind. After the stress and turmoil of the two weeks beforehand, maybe it was understandable that I felt flat, almost as if I was just going through the motions. My overall fitness was excellent, my competitive instincts very much intact and I won the title without ever feeling I was quite at my best. Deena Drossin, the American, led for much of the race but I was able to overtake her on the last lap and go on to win by 9 seconds. It was nothing like as exciting as Ostend, the year before. All I felt afterwards was sheer relief at having got away with it and anxious anticipation about getting on with the treatment that might get me to London.

I have looked at the pictures of my crossing the finish line that afternoon and then during the medal presentation. You can see the big bags under my eyes, the drained look on my face. There is joy but it is laced with anxiety and exhaustion. Coming up in the car on the previous Thursday, all I wanted to do was get the race over, get back to Limerick and begin the serious therapy that would sort out the injury. We left Dublin on Sunday morning; I was world cross-country champion for the second time, but the real race was about to commence.

The relationship between an athlete and her physical therapist is based on trust. This is why Gerard and I have worked so well down through the years; I trust his judgement completely. He assured me running at Leopardstown would not worsen my injury and he was right. His plan was then to work non-stop on the knee and do the kind of intensive and penetrative therapy that wasn't possible in the days before going to Dublin for fear of aggravating the injury further. 'We're going to really hit this now,' he said, 'we're going to friction it really hard and we will know in three or four days whether you'll be able to run London. Either it will improve or get worse in which case there's no chance of making that marathon start line.'

We had our first session that Sunday night and when Gerard says he is going to 'friction it really hard', he means just that. Gary stayed in the room at first but as the pain intensified and the tears streamed down my face, he had to leave. The pain was as bad as anything I had ever experienced when working with Gerard, but I welcomed it. This was my chance to be 100 per cent right for the marathon. If it didn't work, I would be able to say, 'We tried everything but it wasn't to be.' Gerard's gift is in his hands and in his instinct for pinpointing the source of the problem. Getting to that point, he breaks up scar tissue and stimulates quicker-than-normal healing. After three days of twice daily sessions with him, I was running without any discomfort and feeling positive about London.

It got better every day and by the time we left for England a week before the marathon, I was back to my old self and greatly looking forward to the race. We stayed at the Tower Hotel near Tower Bridge for the three days before the marathon and even though I was nervous, the relief of having come through an injury crisis gave me perspective. I was in the perfect frame of mind and really looking forward to it. For some obscure reason, on the night before the race I dreamed about Catherina McKiernan, the Irish distance-runner and former winner of the London Marathon. In the dream Catherina wanted me to come and see her house which she had just done up. Catherina and I got on well but hadn't been in touch, and I had no idea where the dream came from other than maybe it had some relevance to me being able to follow her and win the race. A psychologist would have had a field day. I got up at 4.55 that morning, ate a big bowl of porridge laced with banana and honey and then downed a mug of green tea. At that hour of the morning you are not eating, you are carbo-loading. I was immediately awake, anticipating what was to come and peeking out of the curtains to see what the weather was like.

Gary, Gerard, Alex and Karl Stith from Nike travelled with me on the bus to the start. Karl has become a very good friend and the mood was very relaxed. All my preparation, mental and physical, has been completed well before the day of the race and so we chatted and laughed normally. The mood was reminiscent of the days when I was with Bedford & County AC. In the loo shortly before the race one elite athlete told me I had better run well because she had put money on me to win. 'Thanks,' I thought jokingly, 'just what I need, a little more pressure.'

The nerves were kicking in and I had to go one last time to the toilet before the race. I just made it back to the start line in time to observe the minute's silence for the Queen Mother who had sadly passed away that year. One of the organisers said they would have to put the toilets nearer the start-line the following year. I agreed. The pace felt really slow through the first few miles and because my plan was to conserve energy until the halfway point, I stayed with the pack early on, deliberately holding myself back.

The crowd was amazing from the start. As we got to the Cutty Sark, about six miles into the race, they cheered so loud and so passionately, we instinctively and unwittingly increased our speed. At least I did. I went into the Cutty Sark in a group and came out of it alone in the lead. It wasn't my intention to attack at that point because we had only completed a quarter of the race. Alex's advice had been not to do anything rash, to wait until the second half of the race and to make a move only if I felt really strong. Everything he said made sense, I agreed with it and here I was, 6.5 miles into the race, throwing the script out of the window.

Even though I had surged and broken clear, the pace still didn't feel fast, certainly not too fast. Chugging along in third gear in the group, there was too much time to think. It was actually easier when I picked up the pace, something athletes will be familiar with. At 55mph the car doesn't feel right but at 70mph it is smooth and comfortable. With a good lead established, I could imagine what Brendan Foster was saying in the BBC's commentary box: 'You don't do this in the marathon, especially in your first marathon. I think Paula's gone too early.' But it just felt right: I was taking a risk but I knew my body and knew I could maintain it. That might sound arrogant but maybe you need a little arrogance to win. Whatever, I was having a great time and felt I had nothing to lose, after all it was my first one and a learning experience. It felt like a really hard long training run except that hundreds of thousands of people had come to the side of the road to cheer me and I was fresh, without the hard training still in my legs.

Once out in front I felt the gap widen between me and those chasing me. I was able to keep running at the pace that created the gap and it was logical, therefore, that the lead would increase. The finishing time was not an issue; all I was bothered about was winning and enjoying the race. I knew what the course record was, and the fastest time by a debutante, and believed they were both beatable but hadn't set out with that in mind. They were the only times I had checked. After a while, though, I began thinking about what sort of time I was heading for. At one point in the race Peter Elliott, who was on a BBC motorbike, shouted, 'Gary says you can break 2.20' to me. I was already running as hard as I could at that point just to see what I could do. My finishing time, 2.18.56, was just 9 seconds outside Catherine Ndereba's world record. Missing it didn't bother me. I had not been trying to get near it but now I knew that I could definitely beat it in the future.

The organisers of London insisted my time was the women's-only world record but although that meant something it didn't truly count for me. It may well have been easier for Ndereba to run the world record time in a race where she could feed off the faster pace set by men, but that didn't devalue her achievement. She had still run the

Off to the Tower – with some friendly Beefeaters before my first London Marathon, April 2002.

On my way to winning my first London Marathon: an amazing experience.

With Alex Stanton, my devoted and loyal coach, in London after the race.

Finally! A track title. Celebrating gold in the 5000m at the Commonwealth Games, Manchester, July 2002.

En route to gold in the European Championships 10,000m final at the Olympic Stadium, Munich, August 2002.

Smiling with my gold medal for the 10,000m in Munich. Exhausted, but over the moon.

Being congratulated by Kenya's Catherine Ndereba, who came second, after winning the Chicago Marathon and claiming my first marathon world record, October 2002.

With the BBC Sports Personality of the Year trophy, December 2002.

Looking a bit beaten up after colliding with a cyclist during training in Albuquerque, New Mexico, March 2003.

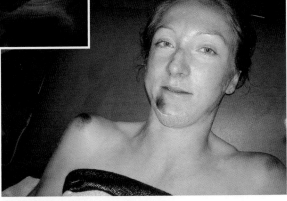

Waving to the crowd after improving my world record to win the London Marathon, April 2003, in a time of 2 hours, 15 minutes and 25 seconds.

With Gary at the World Sports Awards, Monaco, May 2003, where I was nominated for Sportswoman of the Year.

Meeting one of my heroes: with Muhammad Ali at Chicago airport later that year.

The women's Olympic marathon, Athens, August 2004. I started feeling awful at about 6 miles.

CAMERA PRESS

Roadside in Athens, at the 22-mile mark. I couldn't carry on any further, felt totally empty and this was the end of the road for me. By coincidence the two women who found me there, Melanie and Jane, were old Bedford team-mates.

REUTERS/CORBIS

After pulling out of the 10,000m in Athens, five days later. It was important to me to give myself every chance by starting the race. Unfortunately it was the end of my Athens dream.

GETTY IMAGES

Relaxing with Gary in Los Angeles, November 2002.

time. To avoid doubt I wanted to run faster than anyone. The advantage she enjoyed in the mixed race would be there for me in the future. Besides, I had run very conservatively through the first half of the London race but still got close to the world record. With the experience behind me, I would run faster in the marathons that followed. The record was definitely well within my capabilities, the only problem was the opportunity to bring everything together on the day and do so.

But the first experience was wonderful: the crowds at the Cutty Sark, the atmosphere coming across Tower Bridge, and the amazing buzz at the finish. The last 600 metres were what you imagine it must be like for Premiership footballers playing at Wembley. Unbelievable noise, passion, partisanship, and for the person in the lead, an incredible feeling. Years before I had watched Liz McColgan being outsprinted at the end of a marathon; it seemed she had not realised that her rival was closing on her. 'How could Liz not have heard her?' I thought at the time. Now I knew. I couldn't hear myself breathe at the finish, such was the noise.

It is not that often in life that something works as well as you had hoped. This was one of those exceptions. I was lucky and I was grateful. I was especially pleased for Gary and Gerard who had done so much to get me to the start-line, Gerard in particular. After crossing the line, Gary hugged me while Gerard told me to try to do a warm-down, but first there was a BBC interview. Although I felt fine, the effect of running a marathon became clear as soon as the warm-down started. My legs had stiffened in the few minutes since the end of the race and my jog was a shuffle. It was my body's way of saying, 'I've given everything I can today, now I need to rest!'

The year had begun with victory in the World Cross-Country Championships, followed three weeks later by the London Marathon. Three months after that it was Manchester and a memorable few days at the Commonwealth Games. In a normal season those three wins would have been more than enough but this was to be an exceptional campaign. A week after winning the 5,000m in Manchester, I flew to Munich to compete in the 10,000m at the European Championships. Winning creates its own momentum and I expected to run well in Munich. My form was excellent, my confidence was at an all-time high and speaking to Gary and Alex before the race, we agreed there was no reason why I shouldn't try to run it in under 30 minutes.

'People are going to expect me to go out hard and it's what I intend to do,' I said to Alex. I felt capable of breaking that barrier and also knew it would be the best tactic to win the race.

'You're in shape to run a personal best,' he replied. 'It's your best chance to win and I would like to see the person who is going to try and stay with you.'

'What if this comes too soon after Manchester and I'm tired?'

I didn't think it was true, but sometimes part of our pre-race banter is for me to voice any doubts so that Alex can shoot them down!

'You won't be. You've had eight days' recovery. You will be even stronger tonight.'

This is why I like talking to Alex before races. I air all my doubts and he banishes them. This is what he has always done. When we speak about tactics before a race, he offers an opinion on what he considers the best plan but understands that any pre-race strategy may have to be discarded. 'You're the one with the racing brain, go out and use it. That's how it's supposed to be and I'm right beside you all the way.' There wasn't much need for intelligence in Munich because the plan was to dominate the race from the front, taking control on the first lap and not relenting.

It was a foul evening and the teeming rain flooded the track in places. During the warm-up, the Yugoslav Olivera Jevtic asked me if I wanted any help with the pace-setting. It was nice of her to offer but no, I preferred to make my own pace and run my own race. And to be honest, I wouldn't have been comfortable with that kind of pre-race agreement at a major championships: Jevtic was my rival and had finished ahead of me in the 10,000m at the 1998 European Championships in Budapest.

I started positively, led from the beginning and went clear around halfway. The rain was even heavier at that point but from the screen in the stadium, I could see the ever-widening gap back to Sonia O'Sullivan who was in second place. Through the final laps, it was the 30-minute barrier that motivated me.

The stadium in Munich is very exposed and there were many empty seats on that wet evening. I could hear Gary's voice telling me the lap times were slipping. Apart from contending with the puddles on the track, I had to swing wide of lapped runners many times during the race, and on the last lap, I had to side-step a cameraman who had backed on to the track. I mention these little diversions because I missed breaking 30 minutes by just over a second. My time, 30.01.09, was a new European record and the second fastest in history. I had beaten Ingrid Kristiansen's 16-year-old European record of 30.13, which was really special because Ingrid had been my idol. She had done it all, on the track, on the road and in cross-country, and has always been very helpful with advice. To break her record was an honour and, typically, she was one of the first people to congratulate me. She wasn't in Munich but she emailed me to say how pleased she was that I had been the one to take her record.

Winning the 10,000m was the easy bit. As soon as it was over, we were faced with the decision whether or not to double up in the 5,000m. If there were no heats, it would give me more time to recover. I wanted to win another title but also knew that my body was still very tired and I had other targets in my mind to recover for. The problem was the uncertainty; three days before the heats were due to take place, it wasn't certain they would happen. We were told that if any athlete pulled out, there would be a straight final, but if all those who were entered competed, there would be heats. After the 10,000m I didn't want to run a heat as well as a final but the only way to eliminate the heat was to pull out.

There were complicating factors. Though they said it was my decision, it was clear to me that the GB team management wanted me to compete. We talked and talked, dillied and dallied, but I couldn't decide. In the end Gary lost his patience with me and shouted, 'Do you want to do this race or not?'

'I don't know,' I said, 'I don't know.'

He sat me down, and said calmly, 'Okay, can you watch the 5,000m and not regret pulling out?'

I looked at him. 'You know what, I can. I've got my title; I've had my race. I won't be gutted watching it.'

'Right,' he said. 'You've made the decision. You're not doing it.'

Part of the reluctance to double up in Munich stemmed from my decision to run the Chicago Marathon which would take place just nine weeks later. After the fun and excitement of winning in London, I couldn't wait to run another marathon. Chicago was the next feasible opportunity, a great race and a fast course and we decided to go for it. We didn't say it at the time but the aim was to break the world record there.

We got there but not without more injury drama. If the injury before London was an unfortunate result of hard training, this was plain exasperating. I decided to sharpen up in the Nike 10k, held in Richmond Park, which took place three weeks before Chicago. Two days before, I was rushing and slipped in the bathroom of my hotel, skidded into a wooden threshold between the bathroom and bedroom and bent back the second smallest toe in my foot. I iced it straight away and ran okay on it that night, but it was sore up my shin the next day. In the race two days later it didn't feel too uncomfortable and I won in 30.38 which was then a best-ever 10-kilometre time for me.

The next day, however, it was really sore and I wasn't happy trying to run on it. Straight away I was on a plane to Limerick to be treated by Gerard. He diagnosed my problem as tenosynovitis, a condition that occurs when the sheath surrounding the tendon becomes inflamed and swollen. As the tendon moves within the inflamed sheath, there is an audible creaking or crunching sensation called crepitus. Three weeks before the Chicago Marathon I had it and Gerard said there could be no running until it was completely gone.

For three days he gently massaged the area around the inflamed sheath and I soaked the leg in buckets of slush ice every hour and a half, keeping it immersed for 12 minutes. Every hour or so, Gary made the journey from Gerard's surgery to the Tesco's supermarket across the road and Dave Geraghty at the frozen fish counter filled his two buckets with crushed ice. The icy water got the inflammation down and stimulated the healing process. Between the bathing sessions, Gerard loosened the muscles around the tendon and we used ultrasound and other treatments. After three days of constant treatment and no running, I tried to work out on the Nordic ski-machine but felt it was too soon and stopped after 10 minutes. The next day I managed 50 minutes on the ski-machine, ran that evening and suffered no ill-effects. I was back on course to run my second marathon.

It would have broken my heart to miss the opportunity to end a fantastic year with another marathon victory and a world record. Besides that, London had given me a taste for the marathon and I wanted another shot. It is the challenge of running a 26-mile race that I find intriguing. It is like life itself. There are good moments and tough moments; you've got to enjoy the good parts and survive the bad ones. Along the way, you learn about yourself and how you respond to pressure and difficulty. You can't know for certain how you will be until you are faced with the questions. The hard part in London came at the 17-mile mark where I needed to stop and go to the toilet. In the difficult times you fight the feelings, try to calm and distract your body, while never letting the mental focus slip.

At the toughest moments in a marathon, you have to concentrate on staying in the present. Literally, to think about putting one foot in front of the other and to go from one mile to the next. To block other thoughts from my mind, I count from one to 100 and when I have done that slowly three times, I will have got through another mile. This helps to ward off negative thoughts, to keep me in the moment, and to be as in control as I can be when tiredness attacks. Any race that lasts 26 miles is a daunting challenge not only physically, but also mentally.

I wanted to test myself again in this arena and six months after London came Chicago.

Sunday, 13 October 2002; Room 1332, Chicago Hilton Hotel. It is 3.30 in the morning, the alarm has just gone off. But I am ready. Today I run the Chicago Marathon. Four hours from now, 7.30 a.m., it will begin. I get up at this time so my body has a chance to take and then digest breakfast and to be properly alert for what lies ahead. Gary rolls out of bed immediately after me, goes to the window and checks the weather. It is dark, but the streetlights illuminate the trees across the road in Grant Park. 'Windy,' he says, 'it's already windy.' For the past five days I have worried as my period is late. Not unusual in a stress situation but I wanted it out of the way before the race as it can make my legs feel heavy, just drop my performance a couple of per cent when today I want every half per cent I can get! I've tried everything: hot baths, deep relaxation, none of it worked; it wouldn't be rushed. Now, typically, it has arrived, at 3.30 on the morning of the race.

The effects on my body are so familiar. In the two or three days beforehand, my legs feel heavy and unresponsive. When it first arrives my legs begin to feel better but my stomach gets upset. I had tried once, early in my career, to control the timing but it didn't work. I suffered more from the medicine during the racing than from the problem it was meant to eliminate. So much for that idea! This morning I am not going to get stressed: my legs will feel stronger, yet my stomach may play up: it's a trade-off and I will make the best of it. And like the wind outside, it is beyond my control.

I put my porridge oats into the microwave and add banana and honey and I drink my cup of green tea. By the time the race starts I will have eaten an energy bar, some squares of dairy milk chocolate and consumed two energy drinks. I shower and dress into my race kit; briefs, cropped top, ankle socks, race number, the organisers' microchip is on my racing shoe, the red ribbon on my top, my skin-coloured compression socks ready to be put on when I put my racing shoes on. Gary has found me a lightweight Nike hat for the cold; he knows I won't wear anything too heavy but it is freezing cold outside. It is Smurf blue.

'I can't wear that, I'll look like an idiot.'

'It will keep you warm.'

'I'm not wearing it.'

Gerard comes into the room. It is 5.30. He does a last stretch with me before we leave for the start. He sees the hat.

'I can't wear that,' I say to Gerard.

'Who cares what you look like,' he says, 'if it keeps you warm. Anyway you can throw it away during the race.'

In races I wear nose strips that look ridiculous but I feel help me to breathe better due to my asthma. So why am I worried about appearances? I don't care about them. All that matters is that I give myself every chance to run well. So today I will be the runner wearing the Smurf-blue hat.

We walk from the hotel, across Michigan Avenue, into Grant Park where the race starts. Gary tells me I am drinking too much and predicts I will spend the race fighting the urge to wee. I ignore him, he always frets about this. He is worried about the effects of my period.

'Are you all right, is your stomach okay?'

'Look, I'm not going to think about it. It has come but in my mind, it doesn't exist.'

He stays with me and almost misses his ride on the organiser's truck. It will travel at the head of the race and give him a bird's eye view. 'Gary, get your fucking ass on that truck now,' shouts race director Carey Pinkowski. Carey has looked after us exceptionally well since our arrival in Chicago and I laugh at the way he asks Gary to take his place on the truck.

The run is about to start and the other elite women in the field are nowhere to be seen. It is my first time on such a mass mixed start and I panic for a moment. Then I see them, they are not that far away. The organisers have assigned two or three male minders to each of the elite women, to ensure other male runners don't hassle or get in the way of the leading women. Running alongside the minders, I don't find the wind too bad and concentrate on not going too fast too early. My other concern is that with so many runners around me, I might clip heels. At each corner I swing wide to stay clear of trouble.

To give me a chance at breaking the world record I aim to reach halfway in 69 minutes. I make it in 69.05. And I know I can go faster. Six miles from the end, I know the record is mine, as long as nothing goes seriously wrong, but I want to take it as fast as I can go. It is a curious experience, to be able to savour the achievement while it is still in the making. Between the 22nd and 23rd miles, my stomach begins to cramp badly; for the first time in the race I remember my period but blank the thoughts. It's bad, though. With the cameras following every step, it's impossible to do anything unseen. But I don't care; I will do what I have to do. I look for some discreet place to stop but before identifying it the need recedes and the cramps ease.

I race on head down into the wind, raising what sprint I have left in me, desperately trying to catch an Australian male athlete just ahead of me, using him to pull that extra second from myself. At the finish line, the clock stops at 2.17.17 point-something, a world record by almost a minute and a half. I am happy because I have won and got the world record. As well as that, 17 is my favourite number.

Well, it is Grandma's favourite number and I have adopted it. Grandma was born on 17 December, 1917; she got engaged on the 17th of the month and then married on the 17th of another month. Her two children were born on the 17th and I was born on 17 December, her birthday.

I ring her after the race. 'Have you seen the time, 2.17.17?'

'They're saying it's 2.17.18,' she replies. 'They've rounded it up to 18.'

'When I crossed the line, the clock said 2.17.17,' I say. 'And the wind, Grandma, the wind on the course was officially clocked at 17mph. It was our day.'

Later that week when I went on the Oprah Winfrey show she told me how she had watched the race and vowed to run for as long as it took the first woman to finish. She probably would have wished I'd run 2h07 but she was happy with 2h17 and so was I.

15

March 8, 2003 dawned a warm and pleasant Saturday morning in Albuquerque. Thirty-six days remained to my second London Marathon, imminent enough for me to start counting. On that morning I was doing my last 2-hour 15 run before the big race and was feeling good. Training had gone very well from the moment we arrived in the New Mexico city seven weeks before, and I was really looking forward to seeing what I could do in London. The very first tempo run around the academy, three laps of a 3.3-mile circuit, produced a faster time than anything I had recorded in 2002 or on any previous visit to Albuquerque. It was a portent of things to come because my times got progressively faster over the following six weeks. Two weeks earlier I had flown to Puerto Rico for a 10-kilometre road race and on a hot, windy day, won in a time of 30.21. That was 20 seconds faster than I'd run the previous year and it was a world best for 10 kilometres on the road. It augured well for London. I was running stronger than ever and with luck on my side I would lower my own world record for the marathon.

In my 2-hour 15 runs at altitude in Albuquerque I had been

covering just about 24 miles. That morning we were on the cycle path, Gary on a bike just in front of me. Twenty-three miles down, one to go and I was picking up the pace, finishing the run off fast as I want to be able to do in races. Ahead of us, there was a young girl on a bike, her mother lagging a little behind her; mother and daughter out for a Saturday morning stroll. There was nothing coming the other way, so Gary moved wide to overtake the cyclists. I followed, leaving a safe metre and a half between the young girl and me. As I went past, she turned her head to look back, searching for her mother; her front wheel turned sharply to the right and caught my trailing foot.

An unexpected trip leaves you little time to protect yourself, especially when you are dead tired and your reflexes are not as quick as they could otherwise be. Had it been at the beginning of the run, I might have been able to break the fall or even regain my balance. In the circumstances there was nothing I could do. Before I realised what was happening I was flying through the air, torpedoing towards the path, like an aircraft landing without wheels. I hit the ground hard with my face and shoulders, broke my sunglasses, dislocated my jaw and suffered multiple abrasions to my face, shoulders and knees. I don't know what happened to my hands. You would expect them to have broken the fall but they never reacted in time. Perhaps it was too sudden and my body just too weary to help itself.

My immediate reaction was to try to stand up, even to carry on and finish the run but everything hurt, especially my jaw. Gary looked at me and was clearly shocked at what he saw.

'Oh my God, your face is a complete mess.'

'I don't care about my face,' I cried. 'I don't run with my face.'

I was worried about my legs, especially my knees. The little girl was crying; her mum was trying to be helpful.

'Calm down,' she said to me, 'just try to breathe a little easier, stop panicking, try to calm yourself.'

'She's not panicking, she's been running hard for over two hours. That's how you breathe when you've been running hard,' Gary said.

'I'm a nurse, I can call someone.'

'We just need to get to our car,' said Gary. 'It's only a mile away. It's all right.'

It was an unfortunate situation. From the woman's point of view, I was just a jogger who had taken a fall, suffered a number of cuts and bruises, but was basically all right. All we could think about was the London Marathon and the weeks of preparation going up in smoke because of a stupid fall. We just wanted to get back to our apartment and assess the damage. I was able to jog the last mile back to the car, wanting to check out that everything still worked and also hopeful of jogging out some of the stiffness that I knew would be inevitable. Once in the car I couldn't stop crying and shivering. Gary kept asking me to stop crying. In a state of shock I couldn't control it. I was more scared of the damage and the consequences for what I had worked so hard in preparation for than I was of the pain. As the shock receded, the pain from my dislocated jaw became so bad it hurt too much to cry.

We first went to Gerard's apartment. He was on the phone, so we went to our own place. When he called round to us, I was lying on the floor holding one ice-pack to my jaw, another to my hip and Gary had yet another to my knee. My face was a mess. Gerard took one look and was speechless. 'Oh my God,' was all he could say when he found his voice. To make a bad situation worse, he was due to fly home the next day and though he offered to stay on, that would have messed up his arrangements and inconvenienced others that he worked with. I said no, you should carry on with your plans. He wanted me to go for a 10-minute run that evening just to check everything was okay.

Though I felt sore everywhere, there didn't seem to be a particular problem during the run. Gerard treated me the following morning before he went home. He worked especially on trying to put right my dislocated jaw. 'And if you're going to train,' he said, 'just try two gentle half-hour runs for a couple of days to keep things ticking over until your body recovers.' The next day I ran for 30 minutes and was in absolute agony. I was so drained. There was pain everywhere and I cried through every second of that run. All my instincts said, 'Stop, you're only making things worse' but another voice was louder and more insistent: 'The London Marathon is five weeks away. You can't let a stupid accident stop you now. You've only fallen over, get over it.' And that one prevailed over all the others. It won again that evening for another 30 minutes, but after a sleepless night of agony the sensible voice took over the next morning.

In hindsight, running twice on that Sunday was the craziest thing I've ever done. The following morning I went to see Dr John Berlin, an American chiropractor. 'No wonder you're getting headaches, no wonder you can't sleep; you've got serious whiplash in your neck and you've jammed your TMJ joint – that is the joint in your jaw. You can't run today, you must rest totally.' He tried to realign my jaw and adjusted my back which he got reasonably into line. We worked on it for the following three days after resting for a day. I went for another run on the Tuesday evening and felt better. It was night and day from the uncoordinated agony of Sunday, and when I upped the pace on Wednesday, it was clear that even if I wasn't at the pre-accident peak, I was travelling in the right direction. Ten days after the accident, I did my final 2-hour 15 run and it went off without incident. London and a new world record were still on the agenda.

GARY:

'I was calm, Paula couldn't believe how calm I was. Usually I would have freaked completely but I couldn't. Her face was just a mess. She said she didn't care, her face didn't matter, she didn't run with her face. And I was *standing there like a zombie, not understanding how it happened and definitely not understanding why it should happen. One minute I am cycling around this young girl on a bike, the next second I am looking back and Paula is on the ground, her face cut up, the girl standing beside her. Actually the girl is saying, "Mum, I'm sorry, I'm sorry." And the mum is saying, "It's okay, it was an accident, it's okay." I am thinking, "You don't fucking realise, you think we just get a doctor and everything is all right? She's just run twenty-three miles, she's got a marathon in five weeks." I don't know how she got to her feet and then how she got back to the car. It was just her instinct to keep going. In her head she was telling herself nothing was going to interfere with her marathon preparation. She couldn't sleep that night, every cut was sticking to the sheets. Next day I dropped Gerard at the airport, she went for a run and cried every step of the way. She had whiplash, she had a dislocated jaw, she had all sorts of stuff. But something inside her head was driving her. It was London, nothing was going to get in the way. How can anyone run for thirty minutes when the pain is so bad you cry the whole way? I couldn't do that. I don't understand how anyone could do that. And I am married to her.'*

My body healed in time for London and although I still bear the scars even now, I was 100 per cent when I got to the start line. Other issues became important closer to the race. At the time we agreed to do London again, race director Dave Bedford spoke to Gary about the possibility of my running with the men to increase the chances of setting a new world record. Understandably, each race director wants the record for his race and Dave wanted to give me every opportunity to do it in London. Gary and I spoke about it and my feeling was that in normal conditions, it wouldn't matter whether it was men's-only, women's-only or a mixed race. But if it was a windy day, it might be an advantage to have the option of taking shelter in the midst of the elite men. It didn't make a lot of sense to spend four months building up for a marathon and a world record attempt if everything could be undone by windy conditions. A marathon isn't like the shorter races; if conditions aren't conducive, you can't just come out again the next week and have another bash.

Dave came back to us and said running with the men wouldn't be possible because television wanted to focus on a women's-only race. Gary said fine. We presumed that was it. Next we heard an announcement that male pacemakers would run in the women's race. There was some criticism of the decision and it was suggested that I had asked for men be allowed to run in the women's race. People supposed that I was getting special treatment. This wasn't the case. This had the potential to become a distraction so Gary dealt with it and left me to concentrate on my preparation. He knew I was happy to run without pacemakers and if their inclusion was going to cause trouble, I would prefer they were not involved. We believed that in perfect conditions it wouldn't make any difference to how fast I could run.

There are always problems in the lead up to a marathon. On the Monday before the race, Gary and I flew into London from Limerick for a press conference and the race organisers kindly gave us a driver to take us home to Loughborough. We had a couple of days at home and drove back down to London on the Thursday, stopping for a sandwich on the way. That evening Gary was violently ill. At first we assumed he had contracted food poisoning from the sandwich as I seemed fine and we had eaten different sandwiches. On Friday he still felt terrible and couldn't hold anything down. He saw the doctor who told him that the driver who had driven us back earlier in the week had actually been sick since then and it was possibly a gastric bug or virus. To avoid worrying me further, he didn't tell me this but immediately got the race organisers to find him a room separate from mine, and when I called round to see him, he would only speak to me from the other side of the door. I thought he was overreacting a bit because food poisoning wasn't contagious and all the time he was petrified that I would catch the bug! He couldn't eat a thing and just wanted to sleep all the time.

I felt fine apart from my right hip which wasn't rotating properly and felt jammed. Gerard worked on it a lot in the two to three days before the race because it was causing the muscles in my backside and hamstring to tighten up a lot. On the day before the race, Gerard was doing another round of hip stretches. After one particular stretch, there was a loud pop. Something seemed to have fallen into place. I went for a short walk along the quayside near our hotel at Tower Bridge and my hip felt much freer. I was so relieved; talk about something coming right at the last moment. The problem had actually been caused by my fall in Albuquerque and although I could run with it, I wanted everything 100 per cent for the race and felt much happier about things now it was moving freely. Gerard was relieved too because although he couldn't find anything really wrong he was listening to me telling him that something wasn't right. That is one of Gerard's strengths; regardless of what X-rays say or what his own investigation tells him, he still listens to what you tell him.

The fun continued right up to the eleventh hour – or it would have if I had allowed it to.

On the night before the race, I wanted to be asleep by 8.30 or 9 p.m., giving me eight hours before I got up at 5 a.m. the next day. In the room opposite to mine, a group of marathoners had a slightly different pre-race schedule. Just about the time I was turning in, they began to party. Though they weren't intentionally trying to disturb anyone, the music was very loud and it made it impossible for me to get to sleep. I knocked on their door, called the room but they heard neither. 'You've got to come and sort this out,' I said to Gary. A few minutes later the music died and I was asleep.

It was one of the better sleeping nights; I went out like a light and slept solidly until the alarm sounded at 5 a.m. Gary came and sat with me while I ate my porridge because he knows that in the early morning before a big race, I don't like to be on my own. Gary, Gerard, Alex and Karl accompanied me on the bus to the start.

Gerard knew the two pacemakers and introduced me to the Kenyans Samson Loywapet and Christopher Kandie, who would run at 2.16 pace. We shook hands, said it was nice to meet each other but in the back of my mind, it wasn't certain we would run together. 'If we do, we do,' I thought, 'but this is not a big issue for me, I'll run my race as I feel.' It was a sunny morning and even at such an early hour, you could sense there were plenty of people and a tremendous atmosphere out on the course.

In contrast to the previous year, I felt a little sluggish through the first mile and was a little behind the two pacesetters.

'You need to go with them if you're going to run 2.16,' shouted someone from the crowd.

The voice was vaguely familiar. 'That's John Bicourt,' I thought, the agent who once worked with Kim McDonald. We were less than one mile into the race; I was feeling my way, trying to get a sense of my form on the day and was soon running well. That 'sluggish' first mile was a 5.10, which was close to world record pace and on the slightly downhill 3rd mile, I ran 4.57. That gave me a jolt, forcing me to pull back the reins because it was much too early to be running that fast. But then I was going too slow and I realised how silly it was to be paying so much attention to split times when it wasn't the way I liked to run. Far better for me to run as I felt, to find a pace that is fast and yet not too fast, comfortable but not too comfortable. The pace I had trained my body to run at.

I stayed with the two pacemakers but tried to run with them rather than behind them. One time they went ahead of me and I had to tuck in behind them for a bit, but that didn't last long. In the end they were rivals as much as accomplices, two more people I was racing. We went through halfway in 68.02, quicker than any woman had run a half-marathon in 2002 and close to a minute faster than my halfway time in Chicago. 'You went quicker through the second half of the race in Chicago and you can do the same now,' I told myself. Knowing the course from the previous year was a benefit,

I knew there were places through the 3rd quarter of the race where I could put in faster miles, especially from the 15th to 17th mile.

At the Isle of Dogs one of the Kenyans began to struggle and his bad moment came at a time when I wanted to push on. He was dropped and I saw it more as a rival being cut adrift than a pacemaker being lost. Then it got harder for me. I got stomach cramps but had to hold on. With the day warming up, I wanted to throw away my gloves but kept telling myself to run another mile before doing so. This was a mind game to break things down and take my mind off my stomach. It was not until after we went through 22 miles that the gloves were finally dispensed with. At that point we were at Tower Bridge, a part of the marathon course I enjoy because it meant there was less than half an hour to the finish. No matter how hard it would be or how exhausted I might feel, a half-an-hour run is one I can handle. It is the length of my easiest evening recovery run after a long morning run or very hard workout, and at that point I know that the hardest part is over.

Through all the tough bits in any race or training I usually play mind games with myself. These are little ploys to take my mind off the pain, to keep my focus in the here and now. Most often I simply count out a rhythm to myself. Up to 100 three times and, at marathon pace, I know I will have finished another mile. In London I also have my markers: there's Big Ben in the distance, before that a phone box on the Embankment just opposite the London Eye is exactly a mile to go. 'Get to that phone box, and it's easy from there!' About 2 miles from the finish, the truck carrying Gary had to leave the race route and take a pre-planned diversion to the finish. It slowed as it turned, the fumes filling the air, with some getting into my lungs. 'Damn,' I muttered but it brought me close enough to the truck for Gary to scream encouragement.

'Keep it going,' he said, 'just a bit faster and you can get under 2.16.'

'You come down here and try! I am going as hard as I can,' I wanted to say but hadn't the energy. Anyway, I knew what he was saying, that he was trying to spur me on. All through the time in Albuquerque he had repeatedly told me he really believed I could go under 2.16. I had just concentrated on running as fast as I could without setting specific barriers. That is always my philosophy. By setting barriers you also set potential limits in your mind, something I always try to avoid doing.

Running along the Embankment I glanced up at Big Ben in the distance and braced myself for the effort of narrowing the distance between me and this towering landmark. It was hard not to keep looking up but it was torture to do so because progress is slow at this point in the race. And Big Ben always seems so far away. I saw that phone box and passing it lifted my morale. Soon afterwards, I was alongside Big Ben and inside the final mile.

I had led throughout the race, accompanied by Samson and Christopher, and had not seen any of my women rivals. Along the way countless people shouted information. 'Paula, you've got a minute on Ndereba.' 'Paula, you're three minutes ahead.' Then, another voice: 'You're a minute and a half in front.' It was easy to understand the discrepancies. People watched the race on television and as it neared where they lived, they headed for the course but didn't realise that in the half hour they spent getting to the course, my lead had jumped from one and a half to three minutes. With so many different estimates of my advantage, I switched off and stopped listening. It didn't matter anyway, I was pushing myself on as hard as I could. I could only control how well I ran, not anyone else.

It was a joyful last mile. Passing the telephone booth, I checked the clock – if it took me 7 minutes to run the last mile, I would still break the world record. I knew there was no way it was going to take me anything like that and I wanted to beat the record by as much as possible. People always wonder why I don't save a little for the next day but that is something I could never do. Who can guarantee there will be another day? When you are in shape and you have the chance, you seize it. I wanted to take that record as far as I could, down to the last second. The last 800m were great because the density of the crowd and the volume of the noise rush you on to the finish line. I was also racing Christopher all the way to the finish too, and though he had to follow the blue men's finish line and I the green women's one, I remember being genuinely annoyed that he beat me and finished half a second ahead of me. The clock stopped at 2.15.25, almost 2 minutes faster than my Chicago record, my last mile covered in under 5 minutes. That confirmed my feeling that the windy conditions and the arrival of my period in Chicago had taken their toll on my performance. In my eyes, it was a fair reflection of the form I was in and how hard I had worked.

The organisers decided to do the presentation and press conference before sending us to drug control back at the hotel, which was a departure from the protocol of previous years. It didn't suit me because I had wanted to go to the loo during the final 10 miles of the race and needed to go immediately after it was over. You are assigned a minder who must remain with you at all times from the end of the race until the completion of the drug test. Luckily when they saw the condition I was in they allowed me to go, but obviously had to remain with me until the actual sample was collected. My bowel was cramping in agony; what I had blocked out during the race now took over with a vengeance. Between the press conference and presentation I was in and out of the portaloos. I was passing mostly blood; holding on when I needed to go had resulted in me sloughing off the lining of my colon.

As well as the spasms and pain, it also made me feel really sick, but I spoke to a doctor who reassured me and said not to worry, it wasn't uncommon and it would soon settle down and heal. In contrast to the year before when I wanted to eat immediately after the race, this time I didn't feel like food, nor did I feel much like talking. But the press conference had to be done. I was thrilled about winning and breaking the world record by so much but it was hard to express the euphoria I truly felt when I also felt so unwell. Gary even asked Mum if she had any make-up in her bag because I looked so pale and gaunt. Mum found it hilarious that he should have been concerned about appearances when I felt so miserable.

At doping control all I wanted to do was provide a sample and then find somewhere to lie down. Gerard came and flushed out my legs, Gary brought me some chicken soup but, still, the need to lie down was overwhelming. In stark contrast to the previous year when we had celebrated with champagne and chocolates, this time I was just curled up in agony. Here I was on top of the world but at the same time I just wanted to curl up and sleep. Having had the massage and sipped some soup, I got my wish, found a bed and sank into unconsciousness. Two hours later I woke up, a new woman. My appetite was back and my energy levels were okay. I was now ready to savour what I had achieved and worked so hard for, and enjoy the post-race banquet.

Poor Gary didn't eat a proper meal from the Thursday night before the marathon until we got home to Loughborough on Tuesday evening.

The reaction to the run was beyond anything we had previously experienced. There were so many interviews and so many requests for this and that. It was difficult for Gary. He had been very unwell for three days before the marathon but he had still ensured my preparation was not affected. When it was over, we still didn't have any time to ourselves. My husband had to share me with the nation after being ill and it was only natural that he resented that somewhat. We should have arranged to go away for a break together but because we had spent so much time away from home we thought we could have a break at home. It was a mistake. I might have had some time off training, but Gary was working harder than ever before.

'What was it like,' you might ask, '2003?'

'Difficult,' I would say. 'And stressful.'

'But that was the year you ran that unbelievable time in the London Marathon and beat the world record by almost two minutes?'

'Yes, and that was a great experience that will always be so special. Unfortunately the awful times I went through after that colour the year. I had one problem, then another; an injury that almost drove me insane, then a bilateral pneumothorax (two partially punctured lungs), and when I fought my way through all of that to where, against the odds, it seemed I might be able to compete at the World Championships in Paris, a minor injury killed those hopes.'

'You did recover though and went on to have a good end of season. You set a world best time for a 5-kilometre road race, you ran a fantastic fastest time ever in winning the Great North Run and you also won the World Half-Marathon Championship for the third time. Not exactly bad?'

'I had two major targets at the beginning of the season, the London Marathon and the World Track Championships in Paris. After London going so well, I really believed I could win my first world track title. My heart was set on being in Paris. My heart was broken by not being there.'

When things go wrong, you analyse to death. How did it happen? Why didn't it work? What mistakes were made? Could they have been avoided? Often it is better to just accept the way the cards are dealt; one day you get a good hand, the next day a bad one. I know that on the May day Gary and I left my parents' home at Oakley in Bedfordshire for the long car journey to Font-Romeu in south west France, we were in the best of spirits. We had the London Marathon behind us, the World Championships at the Stade de France in front of us and so much to be optimistic about.

On the way to our Pyrenean training centre, we would take in the World Sports Awards banquet in Monaco. Three weeks of almost total rest after the London run had given my body time to recover. The stiffness in the hip that bothered me before London had been bad when I first resumed training, but had now settled down and seemed fine. My belief was that in Paris I would be stronger and more difficult to beat than I had been previously.

We left Oakley at 5.45 on a Monday morning; our plan was to overnight along the way, spend another night in Monaco and then carry on to Font-Romeu. With the roads clear and Gary and I sharing the driving, we made good time. So much so we continued all the way to Monaco, deciding the long drive would be justified by my being able to train twice and rest properly during our day in the Principality on Tuesday. We arrived at our hotel in Monaco at 9.30 p.m., almost 16 hours after we had left that morning. Starving, we ordered room service and I knocked my right leg against the trolley that came with the food. Next morning I ran for an hour, then half an hour in the afternoon; we went to the awards ceremony that night and I ran for 45 minutes before we left for Font-Romeu the following morning.

Two days later my leg was stiff. The following day I did some hill repetitions and the next morning trouble reared its ugly head. Distressed, I rang Gerard.

'I can feel crepitus in my right shin,' I said. 'The same as I had before Chicago.'

'Can you remember doing anything that might have brought this on.'

'Not really.'

'Anything that would have put it under strain?'

'On Monday we drove for a long time and I did half of that driving. And that night in Monaco, I think I banged my shin on the food trolley in our room.'

'It could have been either. You need to rest and get it in ice as much as possible.'

Crepitus is the most demoralising injury because there is no easy cure. Fluid builds up between the muscle or tendon and the sheath around it, causing the creaking sensation because the muscle cannot slide properly in the sheath. Apart from constant rest and icing, there is little else that can be done. It plays with your mind too because there are times when you are convinced it has disappeared only for it to return after the slightest exercise. It can vanish overnight only to return during the day; it gives you hope, only to kick you in the stomach time after time.

At first Gerard didn't think there was much point in my flying back to Limerick because the treatment we would do at his surgery I could just as easily do in Font-Romeu. He wanted me to stop running, to stay off my feet for as long as I could and to ice as often as possible. At that stage I wasn't particularly worried as there was plenty of time. After two days, it felt better and Gerard agreed I could try a light run. I survived that and we agreed I could then go for a faster run. After the serious run it seemed okay but that evening it returned. One of the dreadful things about crepitus is the crackling, squeaking, crunching feeling it gives. Without even touching it you know it is there just by moving your foot up and down. You can feel the creakiness and sometimes even hear it.

Gary and I went down to Barcelona to do a photo-shoot for Nike. He drove and I iced my shin all the way. When we came back, it was still there. We ate in a restaurant at Font-Romeu that evening and my mood was reflected in a pessimism that was getting on towards despair. Even though I'd only missed less than a week then I had an ominous feeling.

'You know I have a really bad feeling about this.'

'You've got to stay positive,' he said. 'We've got plenty of time to get this right before Paris.'

'No, it's not getting better. I think I need to get back to see Gerard.'

I spoke with Gerard about my going to see him in Limerick, he suggested one more run to make sure the crepitus was still there.

After the run, it was a little sore but then it had disappeared in the afternoon. Gerard asked me to run again, to find out one way or another just what was going on. So I ran again that evening and the next morning the right shin was really sore and there was no option but to head to Limerick. For five days with Gerard, the only time I walked was to cross the road to fetch buckets of ice from Tesco's supermarket. Other than loosen out the muscles around it we did nothing other than rest and ice it, rest it some more, ice it some more. Still it refused to go away. I felt so helpless and cooped up, I have never watched so much daytime television in my life. I did all I could to stay calm and take my mind off this maddening injury but all the time I could see my hopes and plans for the summer slipping and all I could do was hope it would clear. What made it even harder was not being able to do any kind of cross training either; no weights, no gym work, no time on the Nordic ski-machine, no way of releasing the frustration caused by the injury and being cooped up so much to rest it better. I remember one day it had been gone in the morning, all I did was ice and go downstairs for treatment, then that evening out of nowhere it was back again. I hit rock bottom. I was alone in the apartment, doing all I could to shift the injury and nothing was working. I felt so desperate. I called Gary in an awful state – totally unfair because it only worried him further.

GARY:

'It was the lowest I have ever seen her. This injury is different to everything else. It comes, it goes. It builds you up, then brings you right down. She was staying in one of Gerard's apartments, over the clinic in Limerick. Train? She wasn't even allowed to walk more than absolutely necessary. I was back in England, talking to her on the phone all the time. It would be gone at lunchtime, back at tea-time; there at night, gone in the morning. I mean one day, and this is totally unlike her and she would never do it, but one day she told me she was ready to throw herself out the window. I was on one end of

the phone and she was telling me she was ready to do this. She was crying,
screaming down the phone. I mean this is the most rational person you could
find but she was totally irrational. The injury did that to her.'

The injury would seem to get better but if I tried it out by running
or even walking, it came back. After trying everything, Gerard
conceded he felt there was nothing more he could do and that I had
to look elsewhere. I had already seen Bruce Hamilton, the UK
Athletics doctor, and we had tried a strong course of anti-
inflammatory wraps and tablets without success. Finally I put in a call
to Dr Müller-Wohlfahrt, whom I had been to see nine years before
with a persistent foot injury that only got fully better after he got on
the case. We flew out there and he asked me to do a little run to
make sure the crepitus was evident. That request was not a problem.
I even still hoped maybe it wouldn't return after the run.

Dr Müller asked that I be X-rayed standing up. He talked about what
had caused the injury and concluded the long drive had probably
brought it on. 'But why isn't it going away, that's the bigger
question?' The answer was in the X-ray. 'See here,' he said, 'your
pelvis is slightly twisted and this right hip socket, it is jammed up and
it's causing a problem in the joint. As a result the flow of blood,
oxygen and nutrients, the fuel of recovery, is being restricted to your
right leg and because of this, your injury is not able to repair itself.'
Gary and Gerard were with me as Dr Müller spoke. 'No matter what
Gerard did, it was never going to get better because the body
couldn't function as it should. Not enough of a blood flow.'

It made sense but I was uncertain. Dr Müller then produced a
needle and first stuck it into my left shin. It bled. He put the needle
into my right shin. It didn't bleed. Gary, Gerard and I looked on,
feeling relief more than anything because this explained why so much
time had been spent achieving so little.

Dr Müller-Wohlfahrt sent me to see a chiropractor to manipulate the pelvis and hip and then lubricated the hip socket with heileronic acid, an oil-like substance. Instantly the hip, which had been stiff since the accident in Albuquerque, felt more mobile. I went back and forth to the chiropractor, getting some radiation treatment on the shin twice daily as well. The crepitus stayed away longer than it had before, I asked the doctor: 'Is there not some cross training that I could do?' and so on the Wednesday, two days after beginning treatment in Munich, I was allowed to train on the bike, once a day at first and then twice a day. By Wednesday the crepitus seemed to have gone, on Thursday the leg felt almost back to normal then bam! On Friday it was back. Dr Müller couldn't believe it.

'What I am thinking,' he said, 'is that this is a last gasp eruption of the problem. I have seen it happen before. Get back on the icing, cool it down, rest it, go back home, don't run until Monday and I promise you it will be okay then.'

Though Dr Müller-Wohlfahrt seemed confident and I wanted to believe what he was saying, I could see even he was a little shaken. It seemed even he couldn't eliminate that 1 per cent of doubt from his mind. One important thing about him is that he is almost totally homeopathic; he prefers what is natural and doesn't like synthetic, more potent but also more risky treatments. Yet now even he prescribed me a three-day course of high-powered anti-inflammatory tablets. I flew back to Limerick that Friday night, Gerard treated it on Saturday and Sunday and I tried to stay off my feet for the entire weekend. So scared of it coming back, I no longer dared to check it and even Gerard was on edge, asking me if it had returned and almost not wanting his question answered.

One conversation in his surgery has stayed with me.

'Is it okay?' he asked.

'I don't know,' I said, 'I've been afraid to check.'

'I don't want to check it either,' he said.

'If it is there I honestly don't know if I'll be able to handle it.'

On Monday Gerard suggested we take a walk to the riverbank in

Limerick. He then asked me to run, an easy run for just 25 minutes. He didn't have to tell me to take it easy for my fear was every bit as great as his. At the end of the run, there was no adverse reaction, no creakiness from my right shin. So many times in the past it seemed to have gone away only to return, I took nothing for granted. Walking quickly, I returned to the apartment to again ice the leg. I stayed with Gerard all that week, running once-a-day until Thursday and twice each day after that. By Friday I was running for an hour and doing an hour on the Nordic ski-machine and by Saturday I was confident that the crepitus had, at long last, been beaten.

That left just seven weeks to Paris and after the disruption of the previous six weeks it was not enough preparation time. Still I was determined to be on that start line. The bad luck, I hoped, was behind us. Sadly it wasn't. Five weeks before the World Championships, I did a 2-hour run in Font-Romeu, uneventful other than a severe coughing fit brought on by a kamikaze fly heading straight down my throat. That evening as I did my medicine ball exercise I felt a pain in my back and shoulders. When I bent over I could feel a rattling thump in my back. Michel Riff, a friend and osteopath/masseur, who lives next door in Font-Romeu, checked it out and suggested I see a doctor. That was a Sunday. The next morning I tried to run but felt terrible; my heart rate said I was running flat out when in fact I was running very slowly. More worrying, it felt like someone was sticking a knife between my shoulder blades. The doctor sent me to a village 20 minutes away for an X-ray and there, the radiologist handed me the X-rays and said, 'Take these back to your doctor and promise not to do any running before you have spoken to him'. That spooked me.

The X-rays showed I was suffering from a bilateral pneumothorax or, in layman's terms, two partially deflated lungs. There was no agreement on what had caused this; one doctor thought it might have been related to my asthma or to the coughing fit at the end of the long run, another believed it could have resulted from an acupuncture treatment. Either way the result was the same: rest until the body reabsorbed the air trapped between the deflated lungs and the ribs, and the lungs reattached to the cavity walls and were able to inflate fully again. After spending over five weeks overcoming the problem in my shin, this seemed to be the final nail in the coffin for Paris. We went down to Barcelona for a few days as at sea level there was less pressure on my lungs and the pain was less. The sensible thing might have been to give up on Paris then, but I couldn't let go of that dream. It felt strange to be almost on holiday in Barcelona just a few weeks from the championships but all I could do was hope that the next X-ray would show the lungs had reattached. Gary didn't want me to go to Paris because he couldn't see how I would be able to do myself justice and he wanted to concentrate on me getting healthy again. After all that had happened, I particularly wanted to be in Paris. After a week one lung was almost reattached, the other about a quarter left to go. I could run again but nothing maximal. Still wanting to compete in Paris, I chose not to tell the world what had happened so that my competitors wouldn't know how much training I had missed.

GARY:

'Gerard came out to Font-Romeu around this time and I said to him, "You know what, this is something she won't let go. No matter what I say, she is convinced she is going to Paris." There was this thing inside her, this drive that I hadn't seen before, she was like something possessed. Paris was all she could see.'

My lungs recovered just about in time and I continued to believe Paris was possible. Two weeks before the start of the championships, I was back in full training and more than hopeful of getting to the start. Then on the morning of 9 August, less than two weeks before the 10,000m final in Paris, I went for a tough session down by the Lac du Matermale near Font-Romeu. The training times that morning were not far from what they needed to be for Paris. That evening the mood again changed and the dream of going to the 2003 World Championships was virtually ended. It wasn't much of an injury, a slight strain to the outside of the leg above the ankle that needed three or four days' rest. It was time that we didn't have.

Gary and Ger watched closely as I tried to train two days later. 'You're favouring that leg,' they both said. 'You're trying to protect it and not running properly.' I returned home, still hopeful it would clear up but a couple of days later had to concede defeat as I was unable to run on it without pain. Reluctantly I withdrew from the World Championships and gave it a complete five days off. The injury soon healed and ironically on Saturday, 23 August, I went for five laps of the plateau at Font-Romeu where we so often train. It was the first time for many, many weeks that I felt strong and back to my old self. Perhaps it was release from the stress of trying to get fit for Paris that freed me to run so well. Though it was satisfying to feel I was back, close to my best, it was a bitter-sweet experience. That was the same day as the women's 10,000m final in Paris. To this day, though all the advice was against it, I still wish I'd gone to the line in Paris and taken a chance. I could have seriously injured the leg, but I'll also never know now if I could have got away with it!

Two weeks later I returned to competition in the Nike 10k at Richmond in south west London. It was such a relief to be able to race again and gratifying too to discover I was actually in pretty decent shape. My winning time was 30.50, which was 10 seconds slower than my time the previous year but on a route slightly tougher. The time wasn't an issue: I had spent the summer dealing with one problem after another; for four months I was denied the chance to race. I was just happy to be back racing.

The very next race proved I was getting into great shape. In winning the Flora Light 5km in Hyde Park I ran 14.51, a world best for 5km on the road at that time. A week later I went to the Great

North Run in Newcastle and ran 65.40 for the 13.1 miles. Because the Great North Run course finishes at a point slightly lower than the starting point, the time could not be officially recognised as a world best for the half-marathon. In my eyes the course for the Great North Run is a tough one and that 65.40 is a performance to be proud of. Berhane Adere, who had won the 10,000m title very impressively in Paris, finished almost 2 minutes behind me in the Great North.

After so much inactivity during the summer, every autumnal challenge appealed to me. Two weeks after the Great North Run, the World Half-Marathon Championships were held in Vilamoura in Portugal and I couldn't resist. It turned out more difficult than it should have been. After the Great North, I got a bout of food poisoning that necessitated a course of antibiotics. They got rid of the bug but also drained me of the strength I needed in the half-marathon championship. I had set off with an official world best in mind but with 4 miles to go, my energy levels felt dangerously low and without easing down, I feared I might not have got to the finish. This time I beat Adere by a minute and a half. The winning time was 67.35, decent if unspectacular.

They did blood tests before the race and afterwards the IAAF doctor said they knew from my sample there was no point in testing me for the blood-boosting drug EPO. My haemoglobin was unusually low, just 12.0, where I'm usually around 14–14.5. My B vitamins were also very low. Sensibly he hadn't told me before the race when it may well have affected my confidence. When told about my being on a course of antibiotics, the medics knew immediately what had happened. The antibiotics deplete the body of its stock of vitamin B which is water soluble. A couple of weeks rest and I was recovered.

I was able to end a difficult year on a good note when I won the European Cross-Country Championships held in Edinburgh at the end of the year. It was great to win this title again on home soil and with superb support and even better to lead the British womens' team to victory.

It would be nice to say the victories in the Great North Run, at the World Half-Marathon Championship and in Edinburgh completely wiped away the disappointment caused by missing the World Championships in Paris. But they didn't. A season that started off spectacularly well and ended very well will sadly be overshadowed for me by what happened in between.

16

Athens, 22 August 2004. It is the morning of the marathon, the long day before the longest race.

I wake at 9.30 because my bottles for the race must be with the organisers by ten o'clock. I have been in Athens for a week and the problem has not been waking but sleeping. I lie in bed at night waiting for sleep to come, remembering Dad's advice about imagining yourself on a beach. I try to relax but too often lose the battle. Night after night I have been getting up to go to the bathroom much more than normal. Is it because of the heat and the amount I'm drinking during the day? Is something not quite right with my tummy? Is it that I'm just awake anyway and so then need to go to the toilet? Why is it that every morning I get out of bed and don't feel properly rested?

Today, though, is not the day for questioning. It is the biggest day of my running life and I can get through it by eliminating all doubt from my mind, thinking of all my hard preparation and treating it like any other important race-day. To fend off unwelcome thoughts, I stay busy. I make sure the bottles are ready and then have breakfast. Later I chat to Gary on the phone, just trying to pass the time. I hang around the apartments chatting to the others: Liz Yelling and Tracey Morris, Jo Pavey, and in our apartment, Michael East, Lee McConnell and Hayley Tullett.

My breakfast is the same as always on race day: porridge, banana, honey. After eating, I ice the vastus medialis muscle above my left knee. It has been a major nightmare for the previous two weeks. Although you don't specifically use it to run, it is in constant use as a stabilising muscle on hills and uneven ground. My determination to run in the marathon has never wavered but there have been bleak moments when I have wondered if I am going to be able to make it. After icing my leg, I lie on the bed and read and try to relax. It kills a little time. Time is also spent going to the toilet. This is how it's been for the previous five or six days. My food is being passed rapidly and, looking back afterwards, my stomach has been feeling terrible for a while. On my last couple of evening training runs I had to stop at least three times in the 40 minutes. Right now that can't be a problem; it has to be just nerves. It will be fine in the race, I tell myself.

A little after one o'clock, 5 hours before the start of the race, I eat my last meal. Another big bowl of porridge, some banana, some biscuits, a yoghurt and a little chocolate: fuel for later in the day. After eating I relax again, force my mind to stop thinking about the race, take a shower and then go to the basement beneath our apartment for my pre-race ice-bath. The British Olympic Association has helped us by providing wheelie bins, an ice machine and a water supply in the basement. Athletes mix the ice and water depending on their appetite for discomfort. Some like it colder than others. I like it very cold and this afternoon I am thinking I will stay the usual 12 minutes. Ten, at the very least.

I climb into the iced water. It is very cold but rather than handle it as it usually does, my body begins to shake. First a little, then violently. 'Out,' says Gary, 'you've got to get out now. You shouldn't be shaking that much.' The other marathoners on the GB team, my friend Liz Yelling and Tracey Morris, say that, yeah, the water is really cold but they didn't shake and shiver like that. This should be a warning because I am normally the one who can stay longest in the ice, handle it the coldest. It *is* a warning, but, at this point, I can do nothing except ignore it.

There is another, more pressing concern. Since eating almost 2 hours before, the food has lodged in my stomach. My stomach feels bloated and awful, as if I've eaten too much. I feel dizzy and extremely nervous, as if I know something is not right. Rather than the excitement and confident anticipation that comes with the approach of a big race, I feel only nerves and dread. I can be honest with Gary.

'I don't feel very good,' I tell him. 'My stomach is in a knot, it could be a problem during the race.'

'Listen, calm down. You've eaten it now. You can't do anything about it. There are still over two hours to the race. There's no point in getting stressed.'

'But it doesn't feel good.'

'I know but just relax. You're getting yourself worked up; you've got to calm down.'

Subconsciously I know something is wrong. The food that I have eaten feels like it is too much for my digestive system. All the visits to the bathroom at our apartment have signalled a problem: is it the anti-inflammatories that I have been taking to keep the inflammation down in my leg and give me a chance of running? Have they upset my stomach? However, Gary is right: worrying about that doesn't help and will only make things worse. I try to sit calmly as we wait to leave. Gerard comes to join us and I hear Gary tell him that I am in a panic and they must calm me down. Gerard stretches me out and my legs feel okay. It is time to leave now.

We meet at 4 p.m. outside the British Olympic Association headquarters for our journey to Marathon. Alan Storey, the UK Athletics endurance coach, has spoken to the BOA about arranging a minibus to take us on the 40-minute journey so we will get there with the minimum of hassle. At the time this seemed a better option than the hour-plus bus journey provided by the organisers. First we need to get to the gate of the Village where the minibus should be waiting. We can walk, we suggest. No, the BOA will take us in cars, comes the answer. A girl turns up and says she will go and get the car keys. She returns 10 minutes later to take us to our transport. Gary and Alex, who cannot get into the Village, wait outside the main entrance from where the bus is meant to leave.

They bring a golf buggy to take us to the bus but it can fit only Liz, Tracey and me; Gerard and Alan Storey walk on afterwards. When we get there, the minibus is not there, and it is a different gate to the one at which Gary and Alex are waiting. The girl makes another phone call and eventually the driver pulls up in his bus. To pick up Gerard and Gary, we must travel for a mile down a dual-carriageway, turn back and come down the other side for a mile. I am naturally at my most tense before I arrive at the warm-up area but this is far more than normal. I am actually very worried that we may not make the start in time.

'It'll be fine,' Gary says. 'Just relax. You'll be there on time.' As we get nearer I am able to relax and focus on my thoughts for the race ahead. We arrive at the start only 5 minutes after the main bus from the Village but they won't allow ours access to the area. We argue, drive round in an effort to find a different route in, and argue with more officials before eventually getting there. It is after five o'clock, less than one hour before the start. We have just a few minutes before the first call. I start to relax and feel a little better. There are things to focus on now. I am there, so that is the biggest worry over.

Nike had developed an ice jacket to help keep me cool and ideally it needs to be worn for an hour before the start of the race. But now there is not enough time, and I can't really jog and stretch properly with it on. Anyway, although everyone says it is hot I don't feel it, I actually still feel pretty cool after that ice-bath. I want to jog just a little. Not too much but enough to make sure my leg is okay and also to help stimulate some bowel movement because my stomach still feels terrible. In the final countdown to a big race, Gary gets very nervous and wound up and today is no different. He wishes me good luck and then disappears, accepting there is nothing more he can do for me.

I don't do my last stretch with Gerard, I feel loose anyway and my legs actually feel the best part of me. Yet I still feel a little rushed and I notice my hands are shaking a lot as I tie my laces. I try to chat, to reassure myself that I feel fine. Gerard is there with Mark Buckingham, the other physio, Zara Hyde-Peters and the doctor, and they keep telling us to stay cool. Someone says the temperature is 39 degrees but that the road temperature is about 45. Actually the heat doesn't concern me; there are so many things on my mind but I do not feel the heat is one of them. In a sense, it doesn't even get a look in.

Just before the 20-minute call through to the start area I have my last visit to the toilet. This is perfectly normal for me; I am usually one of the last to go to the loo before the start. Yet this time something is wrong. I have been aware for the past few days of the frequency of the visits to the toilet and have a vague sense that what I am eating is not being absorbed properly but simply being passed through my system. Yet it has seemed secondary to everything else. For some reason I look now at what has been passed: it is white in appearance, virtually the same porridge I ate 4 and a half hours ago. It scares me.

'I'm really worried,' I say to Alex, 'I've just been to the loo and it was white!'

Alex finds Bruce Hamilton, the UK Athletics doctor.

'What do you mean it's white?' asks Bruce.

'It's coming out exactly like the porridge I had at lunch time.'

'Listen, do you feel all right?'

I do some strides. Actually I do feel okay; my leg is hardly stiff at all and my stomach feels a little better. 'It doesn't matter anyway, there's nothing I can do about it now,' I tell him. 'I'm here and I'm racing no matter what.'

'I'm sure it'll be okay,' he reassures me.

GARY:

'First time I saw her on the day of the race was around two o'clock in the afternoon. She had forced herself to eat her lunch and it made her feel totally bloated and sick. That's not like her, usually nerves make her hungry and she eats well before a race without having to force herself. By that stage, her body was just not able to do its job any more. She wanted to make herself sick but also knew she would need the fuel in her body during the race. I told her to calm down because if she stressed about the way her stomach was feeling, it would make the problem even worse. She did calm down and went then to the basement for her ice-bath. It was obvious something wasn't right when she started shaking in that bucket; a few days before she had been in the same ice bucket and was absolutely fine. In the last couple of days before the race, she talked about how her food was passing through her system very quickly and how her stomach didn't feel right. But at that point you can't dwell on stuff like that. On the day of the race, it came to a head. She knew stuff was passing through her system too quickly, it was not being absorbed. The anti-inflammatories had taken a heavy toll. I've seen pictures of her after Athens, she looked totally drained. Not drained from the mental torture she had to go through because she could have coped with that. She could have coped with the injury problems she had; I mean she can deal with stuff that nobody could deal with. But if there's no petrol in the tank, the car ain't going anywhere. By the time she stood on that start-line, the tank was more or less empty.'

How did we get to that point with so much not being right? The truth is that we did remarkably well to be in Marathon on that Sunday evening. Afterwards it would strike me that we ran our race in getting to the start-line. The last two weeks of the build-up had been torturous and, in the end, almost impossible. Had it been any race other than the Olympics, I probably would not have competed but I had trained and dreamed of this for such a long time. It comes around only once every four years and I wanted to be in there with, what I still felt was, a very strong chance of winning it. Unless my leg actually dropped off, there was no way I wasn't going to be on that start-line. The irony and the heartache was that, for much of 2004, I was running as well as or better than ever. It was just that when I most needed it, my body was unable to cope with the strain and stress it was placed under in trying to recover from that injury in time.

We went out to Albuquerque on 3 January, a week earlier than in previous years, but feeling good and looking forward to the year ahead. We were determined that I would reach Athens in the best shape of my life. In some respects, it was a straightforward year: the Olympics overwhelmed everything else in importance and made it easy for us to plan our season. I would run in a 10-kilometre road race at Puerto Rico in February, the World Cross-Country Championships in March, two or three preparatory races on the track in the summer, and then Athens. Having missed the previous summer campaign due to an injury I had a strong feeling that my bad luck was over and we had also planned for Gerard to spend more time with us than ever before to help support my body through the year.

Unfortunately problems did arise. The first three weeks it was just Gary and I out there and although I was training decently, a lot of the time my right hamstring was very tight and would take a long time to stretch out and warm up. Sometimes the hip would feel like a nerve was trapped and almost give way. However, once Gerard arrived out we worked on this every day and it seemed to settle down a bit, though still needing a lot of work. I did extra strengthening work on that leg as we felt maybe the muscles were not quite in the right balance. This seemed to help and training picked up well: I was able to beat my time on my tempo run from last year when I knew I'd been in great shape. Then problems hit again. About a week before we were due to leave for the race in Puerto Rico, I was doing a long training run and began to feel weird. My coordination went and I almost felt as if I would fall over. It is hard to describe: I didn't feel exhausted and my heart rate was still pretty low but there was queasiness and a sense of being spaced out, as if I was watching myself from above instead of feeling the normal sensations of running. I was dizzy and disorientated and there was also a lump in my throat that made me feel as if I either needed to swallow or be sick. I wanted to stop that run early but it was an out-and-back run and Gary couldn't see a lot wrong with me. 'You're running fine,' he said, 'can you really not keep going back to the car?' Of course I could do that, but, with hindsight, I was definitely coming down with something and was only able to keep running decently because of the shape I was in.

The next day was a rest day and after that a track session. It was a really cold, windy day, minus 10 degrees Celsius, and I couldn't run the session properly. I had that lump in my throat from the beginning but thought it was just a little indigestion. I would start the reps feeling okay but then become really tired halfway through and the times were dropping off badly. I stopped the session, knowing I didn't feel right and that it wouldn't do any good to force it. Gerard and Gary kept saying it was just the weather because I didn't look that ill but I knew I felt awful. I took a day and a half off, and when I wasn't running didn't feel too bad. Then I got back into some easy running before deciding if I should race. With hindsight it was a mistake, but at the time I wanted to race and kept thinking, I've another three to four days before the race; there can't be a lot wrong with me, I'll be all right by then. Knowing I wasn't 100 per cent, I thought I could still run well, I hoped to get away with it and almost did.

I started out the race feeling ok, then at about 3 km the lump was back in my throat and I felt as if I would be sick. By throttling back a little I could keep going. It was frustrating because my legs felt okay but I just couldn't raise the pace as I needed to do without feeling really sick and dizzy. I ended up second to the Kenyan Lorna Kiplagat who now runs for Holland. She ran 30.41, I ran 30.45 and while the journalists were surprised to see me beaten, it was a defeat I could accept as I knew there was something wrong with me. I could actually feel encouraged as I still ran fairly well while knowing I wasn't 100 per cent.

After we got back to Albuquerque, I went straight to the doctor who diagnosed viral gastritis. At that time a particularly bad virus was sweeping through New Mexico and a number of schools had actually closed. Gary and Gerard both had symptoms but because they weren't training hard hadn't noticed it so much. Apparently, as I tried to train, the acid reflux was rising in my throat causing the body to shut down to protect itself. It had burned the lining of my upper gastrointestinal tract and stomach. They put me on medication and within two or three days, I was feeling hugely better. With hindsight, I should have gone to see the doctor before Puerto Rico but because I could still run and didn't feel that ill most of the time, I thought it was just a small bug that my body could fight off on its own.

Apart from this setback, the training had gone generally well in Albuquerque and in early March we returned home in good spirits for the World Cross-Country Championships. Alex came up to oversee a track session and left confident that all was well. My last session was on the grass at Loughborough just a week before the championships in very strong winds. It went well but that evening on my run my right hamstring and tendon just above the knee felt very tight. This was the same leg that had been a problem when we were away but by having Gerard work on it daily, I was able to keep going. However, it had been worrying me when it was tightening up. I had begun to wonder if my body was starting to give up on me and there were times when training wasn't as enjoyable as it should be. Even though the problem manifested itself in the tightness around the hamstring and hip, I was also worried about a gland in my groin that seemed inflamed. I spoke to the doctors about it but they felt it was an effect of the virus and would gradually go down. That night I ran easily and the hamstring seemed to loosen off a little. The next morning, however, I got up and immediately knew something was wrong: the sartorius muscle above the knee was very sore and swollen. I went straight in to see the physio.

Mark Buckingham, a great physio with whom I have worked for a long time, loosened the tendon and the troublesome hamstring and told me to rest for two days. On the Wednesday, three days before the World Cross in Brussels, I tried a small run in the morning which was fine. There was no way I was going out to Brussels without knowing the leg was okay. We knew the course was hilly and would be muddy, so that evening I went for a run round the grass fields at Loughborough and tested the leg on one small hill. It was enough to tell me it would be impossible to compete in Brussels. Though I was very disappointed, I was able to put this setback into perspective: it was far better that something like this happened in March rather than in the weeks before Athens.

I had been in constant contact with Gerard through all this, and as Mark was going to Brussels with the team, I headed over to Limerick. On Sunday night, over dinner with Gerard and his girlfriend, Diane Bennis, we talked about what might be causing the tightness in my hamstring and hip. I mentioned the gland in my groin, how sometimes it was a lot more swollen than other times, how I had been told if it didn't settle it could be excised, and also how I was worried it was affecting the tracking of my leg. Diane, who is a GP, was concerned. She examined my leg. 'Gerard, I think Paula should get a scan to see if it could be a hernia.'

Next morning we went for a double scan and Diane's instincts were right. The leg was almost healed but I had a hernia. Concerned about the implications of having surgery and the possibility of it affecting preparations for Athens, I rang Dr Müller-Wohlfahrt in Munich.

'They've found a hernia. What should I do?'

'Don't mess around,' he replied. 'Get over here tomorrow. I can get you into surgery straightaway. We'll get you back fit with as little disruption as possible. Don't worry about it, you will be okay.'

I flew out to Munich on Tuesday and was operated on the next day. What I like about Dr Müller-Wohlfahrt is that he treats you as a professional athlete, understands your concerns and gets you back as quickly as possible. He is also very committed to anti-doping, working with the IOC and using all kinds of homeopathic treatments. He treats the body with respect and understanding. He also has amazing amounts of positive energy.

As it turned out, I had both a femoral and an inguinal hernia. A hernia is basically a tear in the abdominal wall, through which parts of the bowel and internal organs can protrude. The surgeon, Dr Meyer, put a titanium mesh over the damaged wall to allow body tissue to grow around the structure and seal the femoral hernia; he also loop stitched the inguinal hernia. It was done using keyhole surgery and normally the repaired structure is stronger than the original. The following Monday evening, five days after the surgery, I did a 20-minute jog. A week or so later I was back running twice a day and confident that I was almost back to normal training.

At the end of April we headed to Font-Romeu. With the hernia healed and the troublesome hamstring gone, I was really enjoying my training and soon running well. After six weeks in the Pyrenees, my sharpness and form had come back very quickly – almost too quickly – and as much to slow things down as anything else, we took a break to run two races. On 20 June, I ran a 5,000m at the European Cup in Bydgoszcz, Poland, followed a week later by a 10,000m at the

Grand Prix meeting in Gateshead. Both races went extremely well. The race at Bydgoszcz was my first track race for almost two years and having watched the Ethiopian Elvan Abeylegesse, who runs for Turkey, break the world record nine days earlier, I had it in my mind to try to better her time.

That ambition made me go that little bit too quick in the first half of the race and all alone I couldn't finish as strongly as I needed to. My winning time, 14.29.11, was 4 seconds outside of Abeylegesse's record but it was still the third-fastest time in history and it bettered my UK record by 2 seconds. The event was clouded by triple-jumper Ashia Hansen's terrible accident where she ruptured the tendons in her knee; we were all very subdued and hit by the unfair way in which her dreams had been ended. Hopefully she will be able to fight her way back. With such good form, the 10,000m at Gateshead was an opportunity for an outstanding time and I went there confident of being able to get under 30 minutes for the first time in my career. Alas, the weather was very windy and chilly; the temperature didn't bother me but the wind was strong. It actually dropped earlier in the programme and then picked up for my race.

The tough part of that run in Gateshead was that I felt great, better than I had been in Poland, but the conditions made my goal impossible. My 30.17 was the ninth-fastest time for the distance by a woman but it was worth far more than that. Initially I was hard on myself for not doing better because the crowd at Gateshead were magnificent and I wanted to run quicker for them as well as myself. But that feeling passed and I accepted the performance for what it was – a very good run.

Back at Font-Romeu, we had seven weeks to go before Athens and things could not have been better. Such was my form that it was a case of doing the work that needed to be done while not overdoing it. Then, a month before the Games I trod on a pine cone during a run causing my foot to slip backwards. Fearful that I might have tweaked something, I had Gerard check it; it seemed to be okay and

I carried on training. Then after an hour-and-a-half run, it became much sorer. We rested it for a day, treated it intensely. Saturday's warm-up for a track session told us it was still a problem: I couldn't jog in comfort, although perversely it was pain-free on faster strides.

So close to Athens, we couldn't take any chances. Again, I rang Dr Müller-Wohlfahrt in Munich and he agreed to see me immediately. We left Font-Romeu at 3.30 a.m., drove to Toulouse, got a flight from there and on Sunday afternoon, Dr Müller treated me. He and Gerard agreed it wasn't actually the calf muscle but the flexor hallicus longus (the big toe muscle running below the calf) and had probably been caused by the pine cone. I returned to Font-Romeu and trained on the Nordic ski-machine for two days to give the strain more recovery time. I was back into training well by the Thursday.

On Monday, 2 August, three weeks before the Olympic Marathon, I did my final 2-hour 15 run down at the lake near Font-Romeu. It was as good, if not better, than any of the long runs I had done that summer. I was in very good form. Just as importantly there was no reaction from the calf muscle, none during the run and none afterwards. Our scare had come and gone; like the ones we had before London and Chicago in 2002 and London again in 2003. It seemed like there was always something to test us and we had survived it. The next day we left for England where we would spend five days before going to the south of Spain to acclimatise for Athens.

We based ourselves on the edge of the Doñana National Park, near the town of Huelva, south of Seville. There were lots of trails, we had a nice place to stay and the temperatures were very close to Athens. We wanted to replicate the build-up for my previous marathons as much as possible. On Sunday, 8 August, two days after our arrival in Spain and exactly two weeks before the Olympic Marathon, we did our last long training session: a 2-hour tempo run in the evening to replicate the Athens marathon. As luck would have it, Gerard wasn't feeling well and didn't come. Gary and I went in the car to the cycle path from where I would set off.

Warming up, I felt a little tightness in the vastus medialis muscle in the quad of my left leg. Had Gerard been there I would have asked him to have a look but it didn't seem serious enough to drive back and get him to check it. If it became sore during the run, I would just stop. Through the first hour and a half I was aware of it but it wasn't painful. Instead, it would come and go. In the last half hour it gave me a little more trouble, but I could still run fine. As soon as the run was completed, everything changed for the worse. The leg seized up and we couldn't get back to Gerard quickly enough.

Gerard told me not to worry: the muscle causing the problem was not essential for running and there shouldn't be any panic. We first had something to eat and then Gerard set to work. As soon as he touched the area that was in spasm I was in agony. To loosen it, he had to be incredibly gentle with his massage and clever with his psychology: he didn't want me worrying about this.

GARY:

'She was warming up for this long run, she felt something not quite right in her quad but she never said anything to me. We have talked like a million times since and she said she was kind of scared to tell me. Why should she have been scared? Probably because I would have said, "Well, what the hell are you doing here? What are you doing this for? You're not going ahead with this run."That's where I go wrong. I would have said, "You're not doing this,"and there would have been a scene. "Yes I am." "Well then, go and do it by yourself. I'm not staying around."Maybe if she'd thought I would react more calmly she would have mentioned it.'

The next morning it felt a little bruised but otherwise seemed okay. I went for my run as normal but 5 minutes into the warm-up, it was obvious there was a problem. It felt as if I couldn't bend my leg properly and we immediately stopped so Gerard could look at it. On the massage table, I didn't have to be told it was serious. I could feel the same squeakiness in the area above my left knee that had been in my shin before the Chicago Marathon almost two years before and again in 2003. Crepitus had come back to haunt me.

Gerard said he couldn't go hard because the muscle itself didn't seem to be damaged; it was just aggravated and in an inflammatory cycle which we had to break. That meant a lot of ice. By evening it felt a lot better and the creaking or squeaky sensations had disappeared. The next morning, there was still no sign of the crepitus and because of how close we were to the race, I decided to give it another 24 hours before putting it to the test. That afternoon we went for a 20-minute or so walk on the seafront and returned for more treatment. When Gerard looked at it his face fell: 'It's back,' he said, and I could tell from his body language that he was shaken by the discovery.

So we turned again to Dr Müller-Wohlfahrt. It was now Tuesday, only twelve days before the Olympic Marathon. We had to get this sorted and quickly. Gerard and I went to Munich together.

GARY:
'This crepitus was something Paula had experienced before, even though it was now in a different place and it was actually different in nature. But the bottom line was she knew it was a tricky injury. It comes and goes, it plays with your mind. We had to make quick decisions. We had a crisis situation. It was eleven days to the biggest race of your life, what do you do? Do you sit back and hope it will just come right or do you do something proactive and try everything you can. You can't just give up. She was never going to give up.'

First off, Dr Müller said I needed an ultrasound scan so he would know what he was dealing with. That showed no damage to the muscle, just a lot of fluid between the muscle and the sheath, hence the crepitus. He treated the area that Wednesday with anti-inflammatory homeopathic injections. 'I can see you are really worried about this but you shouldn't panic. You can't do any serious damage in that muscle. Rest it tomorrow and you will be fine to run again on Friday.' Feeling much happier we travelled back to Seville that night; I rested the following day and when I ran on Friday the leg felt okay. But an hour later the crepitus was back. Gerard, who is normally so reassuring, was freaked by what was happening. Here we were, nine days before the Olympic Marathon, isolated in a place we didn't know, far from the medical back-up that we now needed and all the time the clock was ticking. Doing everything we possibly could, I spoke to my osteopath, Vaughan Cooper, who very kindly agreed to come out to Spain early and on to Athens with us. We wanted to be absolutely sure that nothing was coming from the back and slowing down the healing of the injury. I was very lucky to be surrounded by so many people willing to help so much in my hour of need.

We had come to this place to acclimatise to the heat we would encounter in Athens but couldn't run outside. After a phone call to the doctor I tried again to run on Saturday; again the leg was okay during the run but the awful creakiness was back soon afterwards. Gerard tried to be strong and to stay positive but I could see his anxiety. I was scared all our hard work was going down the drain.

Mum and I spoke on the phone. I was really upset. The injury and the uncertainty were making me stressed and, through the tears, I told Mum that I would fight it all the way. She said I had to be mindful of my long-term health.

'Mum,' I said, 'If it was a normal race, I would pull the plug on it. But I don't know how I could survive if I can't run in Athens. I really don't know how I could handle that and carry on.'

'Do you want me to come out and be with you?'

'Thanks, but there's nothing you could do, all we can do is hope it will clear up.'

That was my mistake – difficult to avoid in the circumstances but still a mistake. It was getting to me, I was very worried and the stress was draining my energy and disrupting my sleep. Maybe if Mum had come out she could have seen from the calm outside what was happening and helped me cope with the psychological wear and tear. As it was, we weren't there much longer.

Our acclimatisation camp in the south of Spain would have been fine in normal circumstances but with this injury we needed more medical help and back-up. I tried to get back to see Dr Müller but there were no flights. We considered joining up with the GB team in Cyprus but realised it would make more sense to go directly to Athens where we would have access to the full Olympic medical facilities we needed. Bruce Hamilton, physician with UK Athletics, agreed to leave Cyprus for Athens three days early so that he would be available to treat me there. In the meantime, the injury wasn't going to get significantly worse and I could run enough on it to maintain fitness although it was uncomfortable.

We left Spain for Athens early on Sunday, 15 August, one week before the marathon. I got up at 5.45 and went for a run. Normally at that hour of the morning I feel terrible but on this morning I was wide awake, energetic and driven by the almost manic desire to run in Athens. I realise now that some of that alertness was generated by stress. UK Athletics booked us into a hotel in Marathon, a 45-minute drive from the Athens airport and about 35 minutes from the Athletes Village. Bruce booked me an MRI scan for 8.30 p.m. that evening.

I was out running in Marathon when the arrangements were being finalised and we had a frantic rush to get accredited and into the Village in time for the scan. The scan was meant to last half an hour but lying there, it felt a lot longer than that and I couldn't help thinking the worst: 'If this was straightforward, I'd have been in and out of here in no time,' I said to myself. Once out of the scanner, I checked the time: I had been in there for an hour and a half.

'What did it show, what did it show?' I asked Gerard.

'We'll explain it when we get to the Lodge,' he replied. 'Bruce will be waiting there. I have asked Gary to be there as well. Some decisions may have to be made.'

The Lodge was basically a hospitality lodge and meeting place for the British team, about 10 minutes from the village. It was coming up to midnight and everything was quiet. Bruce was there when we arrived. He got out the scans and looked at them. I watched his face and the look of horror that came over it. They could see the problem in the vastus medialis where the crepitus was, but that wasn't the biggest problem. Underneath the muscle, between it and the femur bone, they found a haematoma. The scan showed some of it was dried and congealed but there was also some fluid there. They had no idea what had caused it. What they did know was that the haematoma was the underlying problem that led to the crepitus building up on the upper side of the muscle because of the pressure within the muscle sheath. Getting rid of the crepitus was a waste of time if the haematoma was still present; it would always keep coming back.

Bruce said he wasn't sure what to do. Liaising with Dr Müller-Wohlfahrt, he suggested a cortisone injection to clear the crepitus. Dr Müller felt that at this late stage it was the only option left – he only considered it as it was the last option, and because we were talking about the Olympics. I had always said I'd never have a cortisone injection because I didn't want to risk any long term problems, but this was a very low-risk area away from the tendons. Bruce was the doctor with responsibility for treating the injury. 'I can give you a cortisone injection into the side to help treat the crepitus, but for the haematoma, I'm not happy to go in there tonight. I'll have to look closer at the scans and discuss it. We'll decide tomorrow.' He did the first injection that night and put me on a heavier course of anti-inflammatories.

It was after one o'clock in the morning when we got back to Marathon and the next day I iced the leg for 15 minutes every hour. Around midday Bruce called and asked me to come to the Village sometime in the afternoon. He had booked an ultrasound scanner to help guide him and make sure he hit precisely the right spot with his needle. As well as Bruce and I, Gerard and Richard Budgett, the British Olympic Association doctor, were also there. A lady doctor took us into the centre.

'I am going to need you to guide me in here,' said Bruce.

'I am sorry,' she said. 'I can't let you do that medical procedure here.'

'Look,' replied Bruce, 'we're all doctors, we'll take responsibility for what we do.'

'I'm a doctor, but I can't let you do that here.'

We walked across a corridor, into a normal treatment room and Bruce basically did it blind. He was incredibly calm but it made things very difficult for him. You could see that when the lady doctor said he couldn't use the scanner he was taken aback but he adjusted immediately. Using the thinnest of needles, he went through the muscle, barely touched the coating around the bone – but enough for me to flinch. That told him he had gone a fraction too far. No harm was done and then a blood-stained fluid came seeping back into the syringe. He had found the right spot and he then injected a little diluted cortisone to break down and get rid of the dried blood that was left.

Afterwards Bruce told me I would have to rest for two days and continue with the high dose of anti-inflammatories, especially when I tried running again. I was bothered by the level of anti-inflammatories but both doctors reassured me that they were necessary to prevent the inflammation building back up.

On Wednesday morning, four days before the marathon, I ran for 40 minutes with Gerard watching, iced the leg straight afterwards and then we treated it. The fear that the crepitus would return and my Olympics be over was huge. When Gerard checked the leg it was one of the most stressful moments in my life. It was extremely difficult for Gerard too. I was almost shaking with fear, Gerard went to check the leg then stopped himself and walked away.

'I can't do it,' he said. 'I need to compose myself first.'

Once composed, he returned to the table and gently checked my leg.

'It's not there,' he said, moving it. 'It's not there.'

I burst into tears, overwhelmed by relief.

'Can we just try it again?'

'Okay.'

'No, it's not there. It's definitely gone.'

That evening I ran with Gary around the Village, so relieved that the crepitus had gone from my leg that I didn't pay much attention to the fact that I needed to use the toilet three times. 'It's just the anti-inflammatories,' I said to Gary. 'They make me go to the toilet all the time.' It didn't occur to me at the time that this would have serious repercussions. I was eating food normally yet it was passing straight through me. Nothing was being absorbed.

The stress levels decreased a little, but I still had the feeling we weren't out of the woods yet. On Thursday I wanted to try out the racing shoes I would use in Sunday's race.

'Don't do it,' said Gary and Gerard, 'you don't need to do it.'

'Why not?' I asked. 'My leg is okay.'

'You don't need to risk it.'

'But you don't wear new shoes in a race without first trying them out,' I said.

I had the feeling they knew something that I didn't. Why else would they want me in cushioned trainers all the time?

'What are you not telling me? I am talking about wearing racing shoes for twenty-five minutes. How can that be bad? Is there something still wrong with my leg?'

Something was wrong but I couldn't put my finger on it. After an ice-bath, I became momentarily dizzy when walking back to the apartment. It felt like everything was closing in on me and I was going to fall over and might have done so if I hadn't grabbed hold of something. Was I hypoglycaemic? Was it the anti-inflammatories? I asked Bruce if it was possible for me to come off the course. Worried about my leg, he wanted me to stay on them.

The leg was almost fine now, certainly it would hold out to do what I needed it to do. The problem, as I was about to learn, lay elsewhere.

17

As an athlete, even when a rational person might see grounds for doubting, the racer in me always believes. Especially after the previous races and all the hard work I had put in, I still believed that despite the difficulties, if the leg held out, I could still go in there and win the race. Otherwise there would have been no point in standing on that start-line. The wonderful thing about the people I surround myself with is that they totally believe in me and help to give me confidence and reassurance. On the day before the race, Gerard left a note on my pillow. He wrote that we had all been through a really tough and difficult time but the experience had reminded him of something once told to him by the great Kenyan distance runner Douglas Wakiihuri. Gerard and Douglas had worked together a lot and been good friends; Gerard actually helped coach him for a while. He remembered Douglas telling him that he believed the marathon was like a rose.

'A rose, Douglas? What do you mean?'

'In this way, Gerard: at the top of the rose you have a very beautiful flower. This is the race and it can be a very wonderful sight. Yet, along the way to the top, there are very many thorns. These are all of the difficulties that must be overcome. Have you noticed, the more thorns, the more beautiful the rose?'

Gerard went on to say that though we had been through hell in the previous four weeks, something told him it was going to be all right. He still felt I could do it. Douglas's likening of the marathon to the rose stayed with me.

At the beginning of the race I ran on the right-hand side of the road because that was where there was most shade and less of a camber. Through the first 10 kilometres, I felt okay. Not especially strong, but not weak either. If there was a slight worry it was the sense that I felt I was running faster than the split times actually showed. It was taking too much effort for the pace I was going. But my mind was sharp and saying all the right things. *It's a hot day, well over 30 degrees; just relax and you will begin to feel better. Keep going at this pace, when you get on to the hill you can pick it up, do a couple of surges to start with and then a long, sustained surge near the top.* Through most of the race, my mind did believe everything would still work out and I kept thinking, 'Just relax, you know you can close fast, just get to the downhill stretch and you can make it up'. In my previous marathons and many of the long training runs, I always go through bad patches, but by staying focused I am usually able to come through them and get back to feeling in control. Here, early on, I was trying to stay calm and prepare myself to cover any break that was made as well as get ready to make my move.

GARY:

'*I was going to be travelling in a bus from the start to the finish, so I bought myself this little portable television. At first I thought Paula was fine. It was a medium kind of pace and she was holding back. "That's okay," I thought. As the race got to the more difficult parts of the course, there were bits where I wondered, "Why hasn't she tried to test them there? Why hasn't she tried something?" Gerard was sat beside me and he was saying, "Yeah, she's going to do this, she's going to do that". "It's all right telling me what she's going to do, somebody needs to tell her." In my mind I suspected something wasn't right. I knew her; if it was the real Paula out there, if she was how she should be, she would have tested the others on the tougher parts of the course.'*

After 10 kilometres my stomach began to give me trouble and I needed to go to the toilet, a physical demand that my mind was well used to handling: *Don't get stressed, if you stay calm this will pass. You've had these problems in your last two marathons: they come and go. You will be able to get through it.* Except that this time it didn't go away. Prevented from doing what it wanted to do, my stomach began to cramp violently and the more I fought it, the worse it got. Liz Yelling had told me that in the Berlin Marathon she had had to go in her shorts while running. Though it was uncomfortable, she felt better after doing it. *If Liz can do that, so can I. I'm going to try this.* To hell with vanity. There was no way I was stopping in an Olympic Marathon.

I tried to empty my bowels as best I could while running and for a while it did feel better. But after a bit the cramp returned, got worse and I had to do it again. From the 12-kilometre mark, I was fighting this problem all the time. My stomach would cramp, I would feel awful until I could relieve myself a bit, then I would feel a little better for a while until it returned again and again. After about 18 kilometres, we got to the tougher part of the course and, once on the hills, the Japanese runners began surging. Suddenly my legs felt tired, really tired. I wasn't getting energy from them. At this stage, I must have known I needed energy because all I could think about was getting from drink station to drink station, not for the fluids but for the carbohydrate energy. In normal conditions, I drink about 100ml from each bottle; now I was drinking 200–250ml. After each bottle I would feel a little better for a short while.

At the very moment the Japanese girl, Mizuki Noguchi, made her break, I was having really bad stomach cramps. When the cramps eased, I started to work my way back. My mind stayed strong. *Don't panic here. Stay relaxed. You know you can run the closing 10 kilometres of a marathon faster than most people.* Near the crest of the hill, about 12 kilometres from the finish, I was closing on the Ethiopian Elfenesh Alemu who was in second place. I overtook her. Then Catherine Ndereba came alongside me; we ran together for a bit going up the hill before I pulled away from her. Coming down the hill, my legs felt really sore and almost numb. It was a really weird, empty feeling, not like I was in pain from running hard or specifically sore muscles, but rather that I couldn't seem to control my legs properly. Every movement hurt them and they were more and more unresponsive. The quadriceps muscles in both legs were especially tired and struggling and even though it was now downhill I still felt as though I was running uphill.

Early on in the race, I had intentionally run on the right side to get some shade but now this was involuntary. My brain kept sending the same message. *Hey, get back to the middle of the road.* Yet, my legs wouldn't respond. My body kept drifting to the right and I was powerless to prevent it. My legs didn't have anywhere near their normal strength or coordination. Getting to that part of the race where I usually feel strong and know that, no matter what, I will be able to finish, I was dying – killing myself to run at a pace that wasn't even fast, killing myself just to keep moving. Having fought back to second place, I was now slipping fast backwards again. Catherine overtook me, then Alemu.

GARY:

'*We got dropped off half a mile from the Panathinaiko Stadium. I had turned off my television and was walking towards the entrance, not knowing where exactly they were in the race and the UK Athletics coach, Alan Storey, said, "There's been a break". He didn't say who was in it but I presumed Paula was there. Near the entrance there was a room; some volunteers were watching the race on television. Paula and Catherine Ndereba were together. "That's okay,"*

I thought, "they've made the break." Then I saw Noguchi and Alemu on the
television and the word "leaders" flashed up on the screen. 'Shit,' I thought.
There was no way she would have let anyone go, just no way. Something was
wrong and I felt panic. God, even talking about it now, there was this feeling
of not knowing what was going on and not being able to do anything about
it. I left that room, walked into the stadium and stood in front of the big
screen. Paula was now going past Ndereba, catching up on Alemu and the
people in the stadium were saying, "Yay!" But I could tell it wasn't right, she
wasn't herself. I couldn't stand there and watch so I went back to the room
with the television. People came and went; they talked amongst themselves
about what was happening. I walked back out and watched again on the big
screen.'

By now, my mind accepted there was a huge crisis. *Okay, try to get to*
the next drinks station, another 4 kilometres and you're there. You'll get a
drink and a bit more energy. Going from drinks station to drinks station
had kept me going since 15 kilometres and around the 36-kilometre
point, I knew I was in big trouble. I could hardly pick my legs up at
all, they were like sore lead weights. I felt so empty, yet I was only
1 kilometre past my last bottle.

You're not going to be able to get anywhere near the next drinks station,
let alone to the finish. You can't do this, you have nothing left.

No I can't stop. No. Not now. It's only four-and-a-bit miles. This
is the Olympic Games, I can't stop. I have to keep going until I
absolutely collapse.

But you can't; physically you can't. Your legs are just too sore and dead,
too exhausted.

It got to the point where I couldn't put one foot in front of the
other. And I stopped. Though I had done it, I couldn't believe I had.
What have I done here?

There are different kinds of pain in a marathon: good pain and bad
pain. Going well, you can push yourself and though it is painful, you

can suffer that pain. It hurts but there is a satisfaction, almost a pleasure in the suffering, because it is a battle you are winning, mind over body and the body is responding. Things are working together in harmony. Then there is feeling bad pain and this is more of a numb, draining pain, where you feel so bad, your body doesn't respond, doesn't rise to the challenge; you can't even make yourself suffer and push through it. I was lifting my legs but, not totally in control, they hit the ground and I felt uncoordinated and wobbly. For a long time I had felt I was running up and down, instead of forwards. Now, I felt I physically could not run another step. By stopping I created another kind of hell. My mind couldn't believe what I had done. Maybe I could recover a little and get going again. I tried but could get nowhere. It wasn't even the stiff soreness you expect if you stop late in a long run; I just couldn't make my legs move. There was so much support for me all along the route, from the start of the race and now I had stopped.

Many voices tried to encourage me onwards, 'Come on, Paula, you can get there, keep going,' but it was no use. The tank was totally empty. Someone said, 'Can I take a picture?' Everything was swirling around me and I could make no sense of what was happening. I felt totally heartbroken, my stomach was still cramping badly and my body was killing me. People were being really nice but at that moment I couldn't handle sympathy. Other runners went past and seeing them go by was awful. *They're still in the Olympics, you're not. They're still running, you're not.* I then went to the other side of the road where there were less people and though in shock, I just wanted to get away from there. *There must be some sort of transport to get me back but where is it? There's a police van, why won't it stop? Why are they leaving me here?*

I sat on the kerb and cried my eyes out because I was so exhausted, so gutted, so angry and so helpless. Part of me hated myself and my body for being so weak and for giving up; part of me accepted this was the end of the road, I could go no further. None of me wanted to accept the situation I was in. I was still in a state of shock over what had happened. Even with all the problems, I had never ever envisaged it ending like this. It felt like I was in the middle of my worst nightmare and hopefully I would wake up and find out that's just what it was. I wanted to go back and start again. I wanted to curl up and sleep.

GARY:

'When she stopped there was this big sigh from the crowd inside the stadium. I felt totally helpless. My wife is sitting on the side of a road, totally distressed and I am trapped inside this stadium looking at her on a big screen. The protocol for an athlete who stops in a marathon? We hadn't a clue. It was something we would never, ever have considered. She looked awful, like I had never seen her before. I had to turn away. It's horrific to watch someone so close to you going through this . . . I couldn't bear to think about what was going on inside her head. Going from the big screen to the little room, I saw kids leaving the stadium with their parents. Some of them were crying because they wanted to see Paula. I can still see this guy talking to his boy: "It's not going well for her, we don't even know whether she's going to get here, we don't know if she's going to finish." The kids didn't want to leave, they were there to see Paula and they would have stayed till midnight. It was a morbid scene, the way people were leaving the stadium. I just wandered around, it was terrible. I just didn't know what to do.'

Then there were two English accents, voices that were faintly familiar. Jane Caine and Mel Hare were a little older than me but we had all been at Bedford & County Athletic Club together: Jane, a high-jumper; Mel, a sprinter. Though their faces were very familiar, I couldn't come up with their names.

'What are you doing here?'

'Paula, we're here supporting you.'

'Oh, I'm so sorry.'

'Are you okay?'

'I don't understand what happened to me, I just don't just understand.'

'Don't worry about that now. We'll find someone to take you back.'

'I just want to get out of here.'

'Do you want me to ring your Mum?'

'Yeah, but I don't know where we are.'

'Shall I ring Gary?'

'No, Gary might be mad with me for not being able to run better.' I wasn't even thinking rationally.

Jane and Mel had met Mum and Dad in Athens and they exchanged mobile telephone numbers in the hope of meeting up after the race. They rang Mum but inside the stadium, and concerned about what had happened to me, Mum couldn't hear her phone. So she missed a call from people who could have given her a precise update. The girls spoke to a volunteer who was nearby and asked why there wasn't a van to pick up those who had to stop. 'You get a van here now,' Mel said to the guy – and she was not a woman you wanted to argue with.

Then Bill Foster, a good friend from Loughborough, was there. How he had found me I don't know. He gave me a hug and I almost collapsed against him. Bill is a marathoner, had even run the Athens Marathon. I don't know why but it felt like he understood what I was going through; he would know what to do. I just kept repeating, 'I don't understand. What happened to me? I'm sorry, I'm sorry . . .' I was shaking all the time but didn't feel anything now, not cold, not hungry, just totally empty. He wanted me to get medical attention.

'There's a guy here,' he said, 'who's got a car and can get you to the medical staff at the stadium.'

'I can't do that,' I said, 'because I've been to the toilet in my shorts and it's somebody's car. I can't do that.'

'Come on, that doesn't matter,' Bill said, and I was going to go in the car. All the time I was crying and saying how I didn't understand what had happened. Then the medical van came along. They checked my pulse and my blood pressure because they imagined it was probably heatstroke. Pulse and blood pressure were both normal. They put me in the van, wrapped a blanket around me and took me back to the stadium. Sitting in the van, I couldn't cry any more because I had literally cried myself dry. What I felt then was sheer numbness, the feeling of being in total shock. I just wanted to disappear, to hide from everything. I couldn't cope with the fact that all the work, all the sacrifice, all the expectation had come to nothing. I couldn't cope with my own anger and emotions. I dreaded the looks on the faces of the people I cared about and felt I had let them down.

At the stadium Bruce Hamilton, the UK Athletics doctor, awaited my arrival. He took me into a room and I changed out of my wet and dirty kit. Then I lay on a table. I couldn't stop shaking. Mum and Dad came in, Mum was crying. It was good to see them, I needed the hugs. I felt that I could just go into a deep sleep, a coma almost, right there and then and I wouldn't have wanted to wake up for some time. Bruce examined me and said that my spleen was a bit swollen and my stomach pretty battered, but my vital signs okay. 'We need to get you back to the Village,' Bruce said, 'to get proper scans done on your stomach and get blood tests as well.'

Journalists were waiting outside, wondering if it was possible for me to talk. At that point I couldn't even be coherent with Gary or Alex, I didn't understand myself what was going on. So there was no way I could have spoken to anyone or made any sense at all. They got me out of there, into a van and then back to the Village. By the time I got to the medical centre, it was shutting down. They checked everything they could. The heat definitely hadn't affected me, I was totally hydrated. I had run over 22 miles of a marathon and my urine was still clear. What happened to me had nothing to do with dehydration or the heat. I had just felt totally empty out there, a feeling that I can hardly describe even now, after having had so much time to analyse.

GARY:

'She was lying on a physio's couch in the medical room when I saw her. She looked drained, broken-hearted. The worst thing that could have happened to her had happened and she looked like how you'd look in that circumstance. I put my arms around her, there was nothing I could say; she was inconsolable. All emotion had gone. She was numb now. I haven't had to deal with too many deaths but this felt like a death. It was like part of us had died, or at least a part of our lives had gone. For a few days afterwards I felt guilty about feeling the kind of grief that people feel when there's a death. There are people who are dealing with real deaths and real grief and ours was not that.'

Maybe it is true that I ran just to get to the start-line in Marathon but over the following days, even weeks, that wasn't much consolation. I had gone there to realise a dream after years of hard work and I had been unable even to finish – a horror I could not have remotely envisaged beforehand. In the aftermath, the same questions surfaced and re-surfaced: why didn't I realise my stomach was so bad and I was losing so much weight? Why did I let the stress get to me? Where did the injury come from? Could it have been avoided? On the day after the race I needed to get out of the Village. Gary and I went into the centre of Athens, found a Starbucks café and met with our friend Karl Stith. Later Mum, Dad, my brother and his wife came and joined us. It was good to see them all and helped me a lot. I felt like eating all the time, a reminder of how much I had taken from my body and of the refuelling it needed to do. Emotionally, I was still a wreck, fluctuating between feeling totally numb to not being able to stop crying, and back to questioning where it had all gone wrong.

We talked about whether or not to do a press conference. Gary's view was that I didn't need to do it until I was ready but I felt that people deserved to hear the reaction I could give at that stage to what had happened the previous day. The press has always been fair with me and I didn't want it to drag on. I was also conscious of all the people back home who deserved to know what was going on. At the same time, I had a strong feeling that after the race the focus should have been on the medallists – those who had run well and finished the race – rather than me. Yet, if I didn't speak to the press, the articles would be written anyway so I felt it was better to speak honestly. That Monday evening I went to the media centre and answered their questions as well as I could. Still emotionally very fragile, it was tough but they were mostly sympathetic. Before the race I had made the decision to keep quiet about the injury problems to avoid going to the start-line in a weakened position vis-à-vis my rivals. If it had worked as planned, no one would have needed to know afterwards. So now I had to explain the full story but also did not want it to sound as if I were making excuses.

Another reason I couldn't fully explain my performance was because the results from blood tests and the other tests weren't back. I knew that ultimately the leg injury had not been what prevented me finishing; I would actually have welcomed that pain rather than the emptiness I'd felt and would have been able to run through that better. So I was still unsure about what exactly had made me feel so bad. Had it just been depletion or was there something else wrong with me? It felt possible that I had broken down much of my body mass for fuel during the race because my legs felt so sore; that hadn't helped, but we were still in the process of trying to work everything out. At the same time, I was dealing with very raw hurt and emotions. I also had to make a decision about whether I ran in the 10,000m but it would take us a few days to know whether I wanted to put myself on the line again, and also to see whether my body would be able to recover enough even to consider it. At this point, I was struggling to walk properly, especially down stairs. In my mind, I felt I wanted to run if I could, simply because I had so much frustration in me, so much desire to get out and run well and I knew that I *had* been in good enough shape to do so and had worked so hard to get there. It came down to the fact that my next chance to run well at the Olympics was either in five days or four years. I didn't want to watch the race and wonder what I could have done; I wanted to be in there and find out, to give myself every chance that I could, and not be always wondering if I had made the right decision. The only way to ensure there would be no regrets was to run – but first I had to be able to. I ran/limped for just 15 minutes that day and the next few days were just easy running and ice-baths. My right ankle was also slightly strained but seemed to be improving. On the Wednesday night, 48 hours before the race, we went to the track. I needed to see if my legs could at least run at the race pace. I ran just two sets of 4 x 400m at faster than 30 min 10k pace. As I discussed with Alex and Gary, this didn't tell us much in terms of what I could do over 10,000m because it was too close to the race to do a testing session; but it didn't tell me it was impossible so I decided to race.

My stomach was far more settled before the 10,000m than it had been for the marathon. In fact, inside I felt normal but my body was tired. Warming up, I jogged the opposite way around the track and my ankle was very sore. I changed direction and it was a lot better. 'That's good,' I thought, 'you only have to race this way!' We got out into the stadium and the atmosphere was amazing; there was a huge amount of support for me and I was really touched and more fired up. Yet, as I did strides I had to acknowledge to myself that my legs were really tired. 'Please,' I thought, 'just get through this one race for me,' yet I knew it was a huge ask after the trauma of just five days ago. During the early part of the race, I didn't feel too bad. I stayed with the pace but knew the race hadn't really started yet. When the surges began the little gaps were created and I couldn't go with them, but to begin with I could maintain my pace and by staying mentally strong I could pull them back each time. By halfway I was feeling very tired but, worse than that, my quad began to tighten up and cramp.

I had promised Gary, Gerard, Alex, Bruce and all the medical people that I would not put anything at risk if I did not feel right. I was very conscious of this promise. This wasn't the marathon: this race wasn't about struggling on until I could literally go no further. If I could have staggered to the finish in the marathon I would have done, but this was different. This was about me trying to salvage something from the Olympics and running for me. I was not going to apologise for stopping when I was obviously not right out there. I was not going to run myself into the ground, risk doing serious damage to my body or health for the sake of finishing in a time and state that did me no justice. I had already done enough damage to my body. It had taken enough. If the quad hadn't spasmed, I probably would have soldiered on, but I was going nowhere in the race by that stage anyhow. Mum and Dad said afterwards they were shouting from their seats in the stadium, telling me to stop. Gary wanted me to finish because he was worried the media would crucify me if I didn't. In a way he was right, a lot of the press did do that.

'I don't care,' I said. 'This time I really don't care. I can push my body hard and maybe harder than a lot of people but only when my body is with me on it; you can't do it if your body will not allow you to do it. Your heart and body both have to be strong. It is my body, my race and my life. It is up to me to make the decisions. I have no regrets, I went out there to get an answer and I got it.'

The emotional impact of stopping in the 10,000m was nothing like what it had been in the marathon five days before. Unlike the marathon, I was prepared for the possibility of not being recovered enough to do as my heart and mind wanted, and when it happened, I accepted it. Of course it was still devastating. I remember walking off in a dejected daze and almost getting killed by a javelin! In the midst of it all, I was angry with myself for being so inconsiderate and messing up their competition as well. Afterwards I spoke to television, radio and then the newspapers. Everyone was sympathetic and made it that tiny bit easier for me to talk about it. It was still tough, especially as I suffered more dizzy spells afterwards. As soon as I could, Gary, Bruce, Zara and I headed back to the warm-up area where I was able meet up with my parents, who had actually flown right back out to Athens to be there for me when I'd decided to race again. It was good just to get a hug from them and also friends Alison and Steve. Understandably, after the state I'd been in after the marathon, everyone was very concerned, but I was more calm and rational this time around.

There was only one awkward moment when we saw someone we knew had been spreading rumours about us for some time. Leaks had been given to the press that I wasn't able to run in the Paris World Championships and Brussels World Cross-Country due to injury even before I had made those decisions, and we were pretty certain we knew who was responsible. Then, as I faced everything else that week in Athens, false rumours flew around and even went to press in Ireland about a split with Gerard Hartmann, a man who has always helped me so much and is such a good friend and constant support. From the journalists involved we knew who was responsible. Gary now saw him and wanted to confront him. Given my husband's fiery tendencies, I said, 'No, you just stand there and let me handle it, I'll be calmer than you.'

I surprised myself with how calm I was. I simply said that we knew he was responsible and asked him why he had done it. 'The competition and battle is out there on the track,' I said, 'and it should stay there. There is no need for backstabbing and malicious lies. You do that and you're the lowest of the low and I have no respect for you at all.'

He denied it and accused me of being over-emotional. Of course it was an extremely emotional time for me, but at that moment I was calm – but also angry – enough to confront him. I had a problem with him and I wanted him to know.

We flew back to Heathrow the following morning. My brother Martin came to collect us and of course there were some press people waiting. Looking back, it was actually funny, like a scene from the TV programme *Airport*. Even the same photographers! How did they know when I was coming back?

Some of the questions were frustrating and annoying though.

'Have you thought about the race at all since?' one of them said in reference to the marathon.

I was totally gobsmacked, so much so I just looked at him and couldn't even answer. Thirty seconds must have passed.

'I've thought about nothing else. I've just been over it and over it and over it.'

How could anyone think that I had not thought about it? I just couldn't understand how anyone could ask a question like that. Then the next: 'Will you be hoping Kelly wins? Would you be pleased for her?'

Again, I couldn't believe it. Of course I was rooting for Kelly to win and was and am so pleased for her and what she achieved. I have seen Kelly fight her way through many rough times. She thoroughly deserved everything and, whatever I was going through, I was extremely pleased for her. If anything, she is great inspiration, having persisted through the difficulties she has faced and won double Olympic Gold at 34 years of age.

Martin took us back to his house. Grandma was there and she was really worried about me, and I wanted to be as strong as I could be for her. She put things very simply.

'You love your running, don't you?'

'Yes, of course.'

'Then I know you'll carry on doing that, and doing it well. It's the way you are. You and I are the same, we adapt to things and move on. We don't stop doing what we want to do.'

Being with family was helping so much already. Here I wasn't Paula Radcliffe the athlete who had failed at the Olympics; I was just Paula and loved and treated the same as ever. My niece, Maya, was the centre of attention and I loved spending time with her. Without realising it, the healing process had begun. Then Gary and I spent a few days with Mum and Dad. It was good for us as we talked and cried a lot. Dad and I walked in the garden and I told him what was on my mind.

'I keep going over and over the same ground, just beating myself up about it. Did I cause the injury or make it worse? Should I not have realised it was there before it became a big problem? Did I put myself under too much strain? Why didn't I see that my stomach was a real problem? Yeah, I asked two or three times to be taken off the anti-inflammatory tablets, but why didn't I insist?'

'We feel the same,' Dad said.

'What do you mean?' I was surprised. What did they have to feel guilty about?

'We feel we should have done more. We should have realised the huge stress you two were under and taken some of that stress off you. We should have helped out even more. Gary feels like that as well. He said everybody around you feels that. We've all got lessons to learn here but you can't keep beating yourself up about this.'

What Dad said didn't make everything all right but it definitely helped. The trouble is I do think I should be able to handle everything thrown at me. I don't always admit to myself if I'm stressed or struggling so it probably wouldn't be obvious to others. Another lesson learned: accept you're human and admit it when you're finding things tough.

The recovery from Athens, both physical and psychological, was slow but sure. After a few tough but good productive days, Gary and I left the sanctuary of my parents' home and returned to Loughborough. Medical tests were done, the results gradually came back. My body was recovering from the stress of breaking itself down for fuel: I was regaining the weight and strength, and my stomach and bowels had thankfully suffered no lasting damage. We were getting on with our lives. At first I was afraid or unwilling to go outside the house. Almost ashamed, though I knew that wasn't right. I just wasn't yet emotionally ready to face people, although I knew most would be extremely kind and compassionate. The many letters and emails I received were really touching and though they often made me cry again, they also helped enormously. The Friday after getting back to Loughborough, we went to London, met with my friend and representative, Sian Masterton, and I pampered myself with a little shopping and getting my hair cut by my friends Lino and Richard at Daniel Galvin. During the Olympics, I had hacked away at it to keep the back of my neck cool. Something had to be done about it now. It was good to get out and face the world, and everyone I faced was kind. We even sat outside a restaurant that evening and people driving past were calling out to see if I was okay! After what I'd met in the press, it was far better than I'd expected.

For a while, I still had good days and depressed days. That night, after returning from London, I couldn't sleep. It was two o'clock in the morning and I was so tired, just going over things and blaming myself, doing what I had been doing on and off since the marathon ended. Gary woke at one point and he asked me what was wrong. I still felt so much anger and frustration.

'I hate myself,' I said. 'I let everything get to me.'

'You did but it was what any normal person would have done.'

At that point Gary was being rational and I was being totally irrational. I was so tired, so desperately tired, and yet as soon as I shut my eyes the same questions took over and sleep became impossible: Why hadn't I noticed things? Why hadn't I done this? Why did I do that? Over and over the same old ground, searching for answers that weren't there. I was angry and frustrated. I now understand the torture of insomnia – I was almost at the stage of hitting myself over the head to knock myself out!

'Look,' said Gary, 'please just take one of those tablets the doctor gave you in Athens and get some sleep for God's sake.' I did, and didn't wake until 12.30 the next day.

That day, after my 10-hour sleep, I felt really low. By nature I am an optimist, someone who finds it easy to look on the bright side, the woman who invariably says, 'It's not the end of the world; you have so much to be grateful for,' and moves on with enjoying life. Yet that day I was really depressed and didn't like it. I needed to do something about it. I was just walking around the house, unable to concentrate on anything or do anything. It was like being trapped. Nowhere to go. "I know,' I said to Gary, 'that I've promised I wouldn't, but I really feel like I need to go out and run.'

'Only do half an hour,' he said.

So I put my kit on and didn't even take my watch. I went out and headed into the woods at the back of Loughborough. Out in the woods, where I have trained so often in the past, I let my mind relax. Thoughts came and went and I found perspective; things made more sense. I felt happier and more in control. That is what running has always done for me: put things into perspective. If I could still run, I thought, there was no justification for being depressed. I was able to do what I loved doing. I thought of the people I cared about. They still loved me. The world was still out there and there were lots of people much worse off than me. I had no right to be depressed. All the time I was thinking more clearly than I had at any time since Athens. I was still the same person who had gone to the Olympics with such hopes. I had not lost the ability to run, nor the desire. There would be other races, other good times and I would be ready to seize them and appreciate them all the more after this. I promised myself that in four years I would be back at the Olympics. There was no way I was giving up on that dream yet. No way.

Thirty minutes became almost an hour before I finally got back to the house, far happier than I had left it. My legs were as sore as hell but this hadn't been about training or trying to run fast. This was about me, doing what I love doing, feeling invigorated, taking in the beauty of being alive and of my surroundings. I was more like my old self. It was a good feeling.

18

After several weeks at home, Gary and I really needed to get away. Everywhere we turned we saw reminders of the disaster and disappointment of Athens. Although most people we met were sympathetic and concerned, there were still the uncomfortable silences, an awareness that people felt awkward, didn't know what to say, and were worried that I might shatter at any moment. I have never liked to be pitied and this became an issue in the weeks after the Games. I really craved being able to go away somewhere with Gary and to just be myself. I wanted to blend in with everyone else and not be recognised. I needed to find myself, to become strong, and to learn to love life again. One thing I was really determined about: I was not going to let Athens make me bitter. It had happened, we all had to learn what we could from the experience, but sometimes life is unfair and things don't go our way. In sport especially, sometimes an athlete can put in all the hard work and commitment required without achieving the right result. I suppose that this is part of what makes it so interesting and thrilling to watch: the emotions and heartache exist because athletes have to invest and sacrifice so much, and yet still need that little bit of luck on the day.

We try so hard to do everything right, we put so much effort and emotion and passion into the competition. Sometimes we even try *too* hard, so when things don't go right we really hit the depths of despair. But I don't see the risk of failure as a reason not to carry on going after your dreams. In a way, it is like people who have been burned once in a relationship who decide never to trust anyone else again. By doing this they lose out not only on finding true love and happiness, but they also kill something inside them. I accepted that Athens could never be a good memory for me, but it wasn't going to be something that overshadowed or lessened the rest of my life. I was going to get healthy again and put Athens behind me. I wanted to carry on running for my own sake. I would have fun, and I would run faster than ever while I was at it.

I wanted to make sure that I had no long-term health problems, though, so I went through a barrage of tests and colonoscopies to make sure there was no serious damage or underlying issues I should be aware of. The medical team found I had picked up a nasty-sounding parasite called *Blastocystis hominis* and that I was also carrying a few pathogenic bacteria. This was probably because I had totally weakened my immune system and emptied my bowels of all the good bacteria that allow the gut to maintain a healthy balance. The bad bacteria had taken hold. But because my stomach and bowel were still so inflamed and sensitive, the experts decided to let me live with it for a while rather than put me on a very aggressive course of antibiotics to clear things up. Other than a few stomach problems on afternoon runs I wasn't really experiencing too much discomfort, so I agreed to allow my body to recover naturally before eradicating the parasite.

As well as the physical recovery, there was also a mental battle to fight. I wanted to be happy and relaxed again. For me, recovering and getting back to normal meant training with a racing goal in mind. I gave myself time to decide where I wanted to race first. Before Athens, at the very back of my mind, I thought that if I recovered well I could think about the New York Marathon, which takes place on the first weekend of November. It was a race I had always wanted to run and I felt it was possible for me, as it is known as a tough course and a fighter's race rather than a fast course and a record-breaker's race. Another option was the European Cross-Country in December but, to be honest, this didn't fire my emotions as much as the bigger challenge of the NY Marathon. I had already won the European Cross-Country title twice, while New York represented a challenge ever since I first visited and fell in love with the city in 1995, when I raced the Fifth Avenue Mile.

At this stage, though, I only flirted with the idea and mentioned it only to Gary, knowing that almost everyone else would think that I was mad and desperately in need of some serious time off! In fact, having time off was a long way from my mind. My injury had pretty much cleared up and I needed my running to help me rebuild and strengthen mentally. For me, holidays are to be enjoyed. You need to be in a good frame of mind to relax, unwind and appreciate a holiday – at this stage I would just have been depressed and terrible company. But I did take some time out to decide where to head next. I even had my first experience of a spa. My friend Allison Curbishley arranged a couple of days at the Seaham Hall and Serenity Spa to give us a chance to relax, catch up and pamper ourselves. This isn't something I get a chance to do very often and it was great to have a proper facial and relaxing massages rather than the painful sports massage that I'm used to. I also went for a run with Steve Cram, who was great about giving advice and just listening as well. As an ex-world record-breaking athlete himself, he totally understood where I was mentally and my need to get 'back on the bike' with a new challenge. However, I don't think even Crammie thought that I was considering making my comeback quite as soon as New York. Especially as my legs were so sore at that point that I could only just manage to drop him on our run!

One thing was crystal clear, though: we needed to get away

somewhere. The media pressure was becoming unbearable; photographers were waiting for me outside the house and on training routes and shoving lenses in my face to get their pictures. This was something that I had never previously experienced and I found it disturbing. Gary and I needed to get away somewhere so that we could properly come to terms with what had happened and heal in private. I had another MRI scan on my leg injury, which showed that my body was gradually absorbing the fluid left over from the haematoma and that, as long as I didn't stress the muscle too hard it would gradually return to normal. I was feeling no ill-effects other than a loss of nerve sensation to the area and occasional tightness that would ease with massage.

We decided to go to Flagstaff, Arizona and headed off on 23 September. It was a training place we had always wanted to try out and was perfect at this time of year. It also had the added benefit of being somewhere totally new, which meant that you couldn't compare fitness levels and training times from previous visits – something which I can be guilty of sometimes. I really liked Flagstaff, which is at about 2,100m altitude and nestles among Ponderosa pine forests. I love running in forests, because somehow they help you feel as if you are running faster and in a more relaxed way. There is also a lot more to look at, and because there were a lot of wide dirt roads there as well as forest, Gary could accompany me on a bike. He was going through rehab himself after having had knee surgery shortly after Athens to clear up problems he had been suffering from for some time. Flagstaff is a university town and the training facilities available there at the High Altitude Training Centre are excellent. Sean Anthony and others there looked after us really well.

GARY:

'Going to Flagstaff wasn't so much about escape as it was about turning the page. Life in the UK was crazy: too many reminders, thoughts and images of Athens, and this meant that moving on had to take place somewhere we could

be almost anonymous – but also somewhere new, where there were no
comparisons – so Flagstaff seemed an obvious choice.'

I was now even more determined to heal from the Athens experience
and put it behind me. I didn't want to become bitter and twisted
about how unfair life was and how things hadn't gone my way. Above
all, I didn't want it to taint the enjoyment of my running and affect
the way I lived my future life and career. Running has always been my
sanity, my escape, my release – but it has also brought me so much
joy. I still felt that I had an awful lot more to give. I wanted to carry
on enjoying my sport as I had always done. In Flagstaff we decided
that I would go through general training routines and be governed by
how I was feeling. If there were down days when I felt exhausted or
just didn't feel like running, then I wouldn't run. In fact, this
happened only once. I felt like I had caught the flu so spent the
morning in Baskin Robbins instead, eating ice cream. But it turned
out that they were doing a controlled forest-burning that day and that
had affected me. Surprisingly, after all the damage my legs had
sustained in Athens, they recovered well and my training went better
than anticipated. I knew I was fully back to normal when we had a
snowstorm a couple of days before we left Flagstaff. Although no one
else was out running, I didn't shirk at the prospect, and actually
enjoyed it. It was snowing so hard that the trail my footsteps left
quickly disappeared and Gary stayed safe and warm in the car,
insisting I was crazy.

We also took time out to visit the area. I found the Grand Canyon
an awe-inspiring sight, with the sheer size and scale of it just taking
my breath away. It also put everything into perspective for me. As I
sat on the edge of that huge chasm, formed and forged over so many
hundreds of thousands of years, I felt simultaneously really small but
also really inspired to forge my own life and dreams. It made me
realise that in the scheme of my whole life – of what I had already
achieved and what I was still determined to achieve – Athens was

only a small part. However important it was supposed to have been, it was now in the past and need not overshadow or alter the future. I was able to sit on the edge of the Grand Canyon and accept what had happened and let go. Athens would still really hurt for some time, but I was thinking about it less and looking forward to the future.

One of the things that did change after Athens was that I became tougher and less concerned about what others thought of me. I have always been the type of person who tries to please everyone and wants to be liked by everyone. To read and hear a mass of criticism, negative comment and opinion after Athens really hurt me, especially when they were ill-informed or based on the wrong assumptions. I tried to tell myself that it didn't matter, that I could block the comments out and not let them hurt me, but deep down they left their scars. When I was in Flagstaff I tried not to read any articles or comments but did succumb to the temptation to read a few online.

One day I remember clearly as a big turning-point. I read an article which really laid into me, accusing me of chasing money instead of medals, and using that argument to explain why I hadn't performed well in Athens. I was furious and went out for my run that afternoon really wound up. I had turned down countless offers for races and other endorsements in the build-up to the Olympics because I was determined to focus totally on being 100 per cent in Athens. In fact, one of the few times I did race during my preparation period had been the European Cup where, once again, I competed for my country while other athletes turned the event down to compete elsewhere for money or for better competition. In the end it was injury and illness and glycogen depletion which ruined Athens, certainly not over-racing for money or not being focused enough on my training.

This was one criticism too far in my opinion, and I was so upset that I even had to stop and walk at one point to calm myself down. I sat down among the trees by a really remote trail and cried my eyes out. It was getting dark and I really should have been heading back before the cougars and other wild animals came sniffing around, but I wanted to get it all out of my system. I thought about all the hard work and sacrifices and pain that peaked as I prepared to reach my major goals and how ignorant these journalists were, analysing the end results each time but understanding nothing about the build-up. I realised there and then that I was never going to be able to please everyone. There were always going to be people who disliked me or what I did or how I did it, and that I should stop wasting my time and energy worrying about it. I decided to concentrate on doing what is right for me, on doing what I want to do, and being someone that I am happy and proud to be. It was something that my friends and family had often told me to do. I myself had realised that it was something I needed to do, but I had never managed to do it. Yet now something finally clicked and instead of just saying, 'I won't let this get to me,' I really meant it. This was *my* life, and I was recognising that as long as I lived it in a way that I, and those I care about, could be proud of and happy with, then I wasn't going to worry about what others said or thought. I resumed my run with new resolve and calm. Maybe it was because of the advancing darkness and the thought of mountain lions, but I really felt like I had an extra spring in my step. I was running really fast, like a weight had just fallen off my shoulders, and I felt great.

GARY:
'After a few weeks in Flagstaff the "good days" were outnumbering the "bad days", but little things or reminders could still change the mood of the day. Life was relaxed and Paula was able to run free for the first time in a while. We didn't really do an awful lot and we didn't discuss the future, but I could tell that she had come out of limbo and things were starting to look clearer.'

A couple of days later, on 20 October, I did a long 23-mile run which was decent paced and felt strong. While I was running I thought about the New York Marathon, which was now only a few weeks away. After I finished the run I believed that I was in good enough shape to go there and win it. In my new state of mind I also no longer cared if some people would criticise me for going there or carp about my performance. That evening I asked Gary and my coach if they thought I was in good enough shape to run well there. They agreed that I was, but were both worried about whether I was mentally ready to put myself on the line again so soon, especially in a world-famous race which always has a big media presence. I told them that I wanted to run this race. I said that racing was what I enjoyed and loved doing. Ever since I was eleven my response to bad times and disappointments has always been to get out there and do something for me, something to enjoy and make me feel good about myself. I told them that I'd missed out on some races I'd have liked to do in order not to take risks and to get everything perfect for the Olympics – and that plan hadn't worked. Now I was going to run for me. I was going to run the races I wanted and have some fun. I had so many races left that I wanted to win and I just wanted to get on with it.

I had always had a good relationship with the New York Road Runners Club and the Marathon organisers, having met Mary Wittenberg and David Monti through the Mini 10km race in Central Park in 2001 and stayed in touch ever since. I had chatted to Mary a few times since Athens as she had rung me to check that I was OK and invited myself and Gary to attend the event as guests. Now I phoned her to say that rather than be a guest I would like to race. She was a bit shocked but pleased too, and we set the wheels in motion. Within twenty-four hours I was on the start list.

GARY:

'The decision to run in New York didn't really come as a major surprise to me. I could see that the training was coming together and I could sense that something was at the back of Paula's mind. We had watched a few TV shows

and New York seemed to always feature in some way, so there were a few cryptic messages floating about.'

There were a couple of weeks left before the race and, ideally, we would have stayed in the US for the final build-up. But my brother Martin and his family were emigrating to Australia the day before New York and I wanted to go back home to spend time with them and say goodbye. We had a big leaving party the week before the race and while it was great to get all the family together, it was also very sad. Especially as I was only just getting to know my niece Maya, who was seven months old and just starting to learn how to walk. I spent the weekend with them and then on Wednesday 3 November Gary and I headed out to New York. We also arranged for my parents to come out the day before the race. I knew that having waved off Martin, Nicole and Maya it would help take their minds off the goodbyes and cheer them up.

I was excited to be back in New York and was really looking forward to the race. I had a few runs around the reservoir in Central Park and you could sense the atmosphere building towards the coming Sunday, as people arrived from all over the world to take part in the race. I love running in Central Park: it is an unexpected oasis in the middle of such a lively and vibrant city and in the build-up to the marathon there are even more people heading to the park. It is always amazing to see so many people and nationalities coming together – everyone with their own goals and objectives but all looking forward to the race and really happy to be taking part.

I did the pre-race press conference and faced up to the habitual rehashing of my Athens experience. But I sincerely felt that this time the story would be completely different, so the journalists' scepticism just bounced off me. I was healthy and excited about the race. I knew my body was strong and I was looking forward to enjoying the day. My anticipation was growing.

Although most of the other athletes had accepted my late entry into the race I was criticised by the Dutch athlete Lornah Kiplagat, who felt that I had disrupted her race plans by entering the race at such a late stage. My answer was simple: racing is about doing precisely that. Get yourself into the best shape that you can and then go out and race whoever else you find on the start line. While I respect Lornah as a rival and an athlete I felt that her reaction only showed that she felt threatened by me.

It was also clear that a lot of people were shocked by my decision and there were a lot of discussions about whether I was ready to race, was mentally scarred from Athens, or would ever be the same again. In some ways it made me laugh – I never believed that I'd become a bad athlete in Athens or that I'd lost it all there. I do believe that maybe I tried to push too hard, that I cared too much about that Olympic race, which meant that when I broke down with injury and saw my dreams slipping away I let the worry and stress get to me, which just made everything worse. My body suffered immensely and I was forced to admit that I am human and that I can't overcome every obstacle in my path. Life isn't always fair. Sometimes we all get a bad deal or make mistakes, but I had survived, and come through. I never doubted that, with time, I would become the same person and athlete I had always been. People were asking a lot of questions about my mental state – what would happen to me if I lost? I wasn't thinking about that. I was there to win the race.

Whenever you put yourself on the line there is a risk of losing, that's what racing is about, but it is not a reason to be afraid to race. As an athlete I prepare as well as I can and then give all that I have during the race. I'm never afraid to lose. All I wish and hope for from a race is that I am able to run as well I can. I draw confidence from all the work I have done and know that people will have to work very hard to beat me. Instead of making me doubt myself, these criticisms just fired me up. I do remember being disappointed at reading some negative comments from the former 10,000 metres World Champion Liz McColgan. She was someone I looked up to very much when I was growing up, so to read her ill-informed criticism of my support team, who had done so much to help me cope, lessened my respect for her.

The build-up to the race continued. My parents and Alex arrived the day before and we agreed to have a meal together before I headed back to the hotel to get an early night. All the restaurants in the area were very busy so we didn't have much choice. At the time, I didn't think too much about the fact that our meals were cold and I had to send my spaghetti Bolognese back to be reheated. It was only when I woke about midnight with really bad acid reflux and heartburn that I became worried. Was the gastritis I had suffered earlier in the year back again? I took some Gaviscon, told myself that I would be OK, and managed to get back to sleep. In the morning I didn't feel too bad but just to make sure Gary went off to try to find some Pepto-Bismol for me while I had my breakfast and got myself ready. It's a good job New York is the city that never sleeps, as this was five in the morning!

By 6.30 a.m. all the athletes had to be on the bus which would then head out to the start on Staten Island. It takes a while to get out there from Manhattan. I was feeling good and excited to get on with the race. I also found it a little strange because I was on my own once I got on the bus – usually Gary and Alex come to the start with me, but in New York it's too hard to get back from the start so only the athletes go there. It felt a bit weird being waved off with still over two hours to go before the start. It's probably a throwback to my club roots, but I like to chat to my coach or other athletes to stay relaxed in the build-up to the start, but most of my rivals prefer to retreat into their own worlds. Luckily, I had anticipated this and treated myself to a new mini iPod the day before the race. The music helped get me through the bus journey of an hour or so. It was a beautiful morning too, with clear blue skies and the sun coming up over the city as we neared the start. As we crossed the bridge the views back to where we would soon be heading on foot were amazing. The

Statue of Liberty was really striking and I suddenly had a really good feeling about the race ahead.

The marathon got under way and I felt pretty relaxed. I ran with the pack for the first part, covering all the moves but not really concerned about making any of my own so early in the race. I wasn't concerned about times, only about winning the race, and so I scarcely looked at any of the split times. The atmosphere all along the route was amazing and the weather conditions were great too. One thing I found really interesting was that as we passed through each of the five Boroughs of New York the atmosphere changed. You could really sense the difference between each one. Also, as we passed over each of the bridges, it was almost eerie to go from loud and enthusiastic support to total silence as we ran over the bridge. But it was also useful as I could then hear my rivals and gauge things from the way they were breathing. Usually this is drowned out by the noise of the crowd.

Another factor I really had to concentrate on was the road surface. There were a lot of pot-holes and, knowing that my legs and especially my hamstrings were a little tight in places after their recent traumas, the last thing I wanted to do was tweak or wrench anything. At one point, as we came down a steep slope into the cauldron of noise of First Avenue, I did feel my left hamstring tug a bit but luckily it settled again on the flat and didn't get any worse.

Early on, the big pack included Deena Kastor, who had run a great race to take bronze in Athens and was getting a lot of support and appreciation along the route. She was struggling, though, as could be expected after such a hard run in the Olympics. She had said beforehand that she was tired and had found it hard to recover, and was only in New York because the race is so special to her. Shortly afterwards she dropped out and although she was obviously disappointed I'm sure she would be the first to say that she would rather have had her great race at the Olympics. Deena is a tough runner and a great person and I know she will bounce back.

By halfway, the leaders were down to five. I was running with Kiplagat, Susan Chepkemei, Margaret Okayo and Tegla Loroupe, and although I was starting to experience some stomach problems I was feeling pretty comfortable. I did have one annoying moment at the second drinks station when my bottle was not where it should have been. Still, this can happen and although I could have done with the drink there was nothing I could do, so I put it out of my mind. One thing that was different in New York was that I had stuck gel energy packs to some of my drinks. I don't usually need them in a marathon but after the severe depletion in Athens I had been experiencing some 'crashing' (this is where your energy reserves get really low and you feel dizzy and weak, the blood sugar drops too low to sustain the effort) on my long runs and felt that I might need the extra energy boost during the race. As I began to feel sick during the second half of the race these gels had the added advantage of settling my stomach for short periods.

As we came off the Queensboro Bridge on to First Avenue the huge roar of the massive crowd there seemed to spur on Lornah Kiplagat and she pushed the pace. Okayo and Loroupe were dropped but Kiplagat wasn't able to sustain her speed and as we went through the Bronx she fell away quickly, leaving just Susan and I together. I was still feeling sick and my legs were starting to feel a bit heavy and tired but I have raced Susan for many years, going back to the World Junior Cross-Country in 1992. I know her strengths and weaknesses and I was confident that I could finish faster and stronger than she could. It was just a case of hanging on in there until I could launch my final surge for the finish line. Over the last five or six miles we both tried, a couple of times, to inject some pace and drop the other, but neither of us could get away. We weren't bothered with the split times, we were just racing each other, which is a great way to run. The crowds were really getting into our duel and the noise got louder and louder as we approached Central Park and the finish. The couple of times that I had tried picking up the pace had only made my stomach worse and by 24 miles the acid reflux had got pretty bad. I decided to wait until we passed Columbus Circle and then make my move on the slope up into the finish (which is about 300–400 metres). That way, I knew that if I was really going to be sick then at least I would be able to finish first! I had done some strides over the final stretches a couple of days before and was confident that I could judge it right. Susan did push hard over the last couple of miles and I was digging deep to hang on, but when I finally kicked I actually felt better and stronger than when I had been running at a slower pace. I crested the hill and could see the finish and really sense the enthusiasm of the spectators. The New York crowds are always so vibrant and encouraging but there were also a lot of British voices out there.

Breaking that tape felt amazing. I had won the New York Marathon, something I had always wanted to do. It was special to me because I had also achieved my own personal goal of being a winner in New York over the three big distances – the Fifth Avenue Mile, the Mini 10k and now the New York Marathon. When I first won the mile back in 1996 I remember being really thrilled but at that stage never would have imagined how special it would feel to be back in the city eight years later winning the marathon and being part of such a wonderful event. I honestly had no thoughts of Athens or retribution at that point. I was just taking in the atmosphere and enjoying the feeling of winning the race. I gave Susan a big hug too. Not only is she a great athlete and competitor, but she is also a great person and a good friend. When you run 26 miles (and many other races) so closely together you share a bond, and although I was very happy to win and beat Susan, I also really felt for her. I know only too well what it feels like to be out-kicked after giving all that you can. It does feel slightly mean to win a race like that rather than by being out in front for a long time. Susan had lost out by just four seconds after more than 26 miles, but she had also run a great race and had herself come back from a disappointing and difficult period in her life. She seemed pleased with her run and I was happy for her.

Together we were able to jog back down the finishing stretch and thank the crowd. This is a nice touch by the organisers and something you don't usually get a chance to do in a road race. It's a little bit like a lap of honour on the track, and gave us both a chance to really take in and enjoy the atmosphere once the worst of the pain was over. After that we headed back to do the TV interviews and find our tracksuits. Fortunately, our clothes were in a tent as my stomach chose that moment to finally give up on me and I threw up violently. This was the first time I'd ever been sick after a race and I was embarrassed at making a mess in the corner of their tent. I had often seen people vomit at the end of races and it is usually just the liquid that has been consumed during the race that the stomach decides to get rid of right away. This was the case with me now. I had been feeling really green when I did the TV interviews but now I felt much better. Once again, it was a glimpse of the glamorous side of marathon running!

As we hung around for the medal presentation I was able to catch up with Gary, my parents, Alex and our friend Karl. I think they'd had a nerve-wracking time over the final few miles as they didn't have the luxury of knowing how I felt and what my plan was. As I know from my own experiences of watching Gary compete, one of the hardest parts about watching someone you care about racing is that you feel so helpless and out of control. You are really emotionally involved but you don't have the information that the person in the race has. They know how they feel, how the others sound, what they plan to do and what they have left. In the latter part of the race I knew I was OK and was just waiting for the finishing stretch, but they didn't know this. They were worried that I didn't feel good and it was only when I kicked that they knew I was OK. Still, they had enjoyed the race and we could now all relax and celebrate. After the presentation Gary and I headed off to Doping Control and the press conference before meeting up with the others back at the hotel to celebrate with champagne and chocolates. Despite my earlier sickness I now felt fine and it was great to be able to enjoy this feeling after a marathon. That evening we all went to the official post-race banquet and had a great time, although I was seriously flagging by the time we got back to the hotel. Gary and Karl headed out to celebrate further with a friend, Tony, who had also run the race having decided even later than me to take part. He had been offered a number two days before the race. I'd run faster than him during the race but he outlasted me in the evening – I was knackered!

GARY:

'Watching the race in New York, I never had any doubts, but I was concerned that we had both woken up with really bad acid indigestion and I know how this can make you feel when you are running. When I could see Paula up the pace in the last five miles and then ease off I was certain something wasn't right. The noise at the finish was deafening. I watched it on a BBC monitor with Sally Gunnell in a little tent, as it wasn't possible to see what was happening before the final turn. By the time I left the tent, they were rounding the final corner and she was clear and going further away.

It was really only after New York that we realised that people had thought that we were taking a risk with Paula's reputation, commercial value and other things, by running there. This was never about those values – it was about Paula's values and choosing to do something because you can, and not because others say perhaps you can't.'

The next morning I was up at six to do some breakfast TV shows before heading off to stuff myself on stacks of New York blueberry pancakes and syrup before the Monday press conference. Pancakes have become one of my favourite parts of a visit to New York. The press conference went well. It was nice to be sitting up on the top table with South Africa's Hendrick Ramaala, who had won the men's race. Hendrick and his girlfriend Rodica often train in Font Romeu and he had long been due a good race over the marathon distance. Afterwards we went to lunch at the Tavern on the Green, a famous restaurant in Central Park right by the marathon finish, with the race organisers. It was nice and relaxed and it was good to get the chance to thank Mary and David for letting me into the race at such short notice. Ironically, Hendrick had also been a late entrant and it had worked out well for both of us. That afternoon we did a quick appearance on the David Letterman show. It had become something of a tradition for the marathon winners to appear on the show on the Monday after the race. However, I found it really funny that we weren't actually interviewed and we didn't say a word. We just ran quickly through the back of the set! This had been brought in a few years back because the winners had not been able to speak much English, but I doubt it has done much to improve the profile of athletics in the USA.

The next day had been set aside to shoot a sunglasses advert for Nike. Photo shoots are often great fun and it gives me a chance to do something different. The funniest thing was probably the sight of me – two days after a hard marathon race – trying to look cool, while running on a treadmill wearing sunglasses. They made the whole room seem so dark that the edge of the treadmill had to be marked out in glow-sticks so I didn't fall off the end. Luckily I didn't have to run for too long at any one time. Afterwards we headed straight to the airport to catch a flight back to the UK, where I had a busy couple of weeks planned because of the launch of this book's hardcover edition and a number of book signings. It was great to be able to do all this while on a break from training but also on the back of a positive result in New York. I know I would have found it much harder to face without having had the chance to put the disappointment of Athens behind me.

I found the book signings an amazing and humbling experience. Before the first one, I remember being terrified that no one would show up and that people would find the book boring. I had been determined to be totally honest in the book, as otherwise I didn't see the point in doing it. However, there was a point during the worst of my lambasting in the press when I wondered if I really wanted to put so much of my life into the public domain. Then I realised that people were going to have an opinion whatever I did, and that this was my only real chance to write down my true feelings, emotions and experiences – and for it to reach the public unaltered. Thankfully, people did turn up to the signings. I was stunned and moved by how many people came and by their kind words and support. I want to thank all those people so much. It was great to get a chance to meet you.

19

After enjoying a refreshing and rejuvenating break in Mexico, I settled back into training in the build-up to Christmas. I had taken about four weeks' break but that had included a little bit of running after the first two weeks – partly because I wanted to take part in the Nike 'Run London' race at the end of November. I took it as a bit of fun and paced a group of runners round to their goals. This gave me a chance to take in more of the tremendous atmosphere that accompanies this event. On a dark, freezing cold night it was great to see so many thousands out taking part and enjoying and encouraging each other so much: I'll never forget the unique sight of a river of fluorescent yellow shirts flowing through the streets of London. I'm also really happy to add that two of my group ran personal bests – definitely not easy when we started at the back and had to zigzag our way through the field the whole way.

One of my memories from the pre-race press conference was of doing a television interview from the London 2012 headquarters. I remember thinking that night that there could be no better city than London to host the Olympic Games. Now, as I write this, we have already won the right to host the 2012 Games, and I have no doubts about our ability to stage a memorable Games. I'm now trying to work out how I can keep my old legs going long enough to be able to realise a dream, and be able to take part in such a momentous occasion. I'm also vowing to do all I can to help the younger generation of talent coming through to achieve all the success they can in seven years' time.

We spent Christmas in Ballygally, Northern Ireland, with Gary's family. This is always a great occasion. In a small village everyone knows everyone and doors are always open. Gary and I go for a run and before we get back everyone knows the route we have taken! With my brother and his family in Australia, my parents also came over, which made it even better. To top it all, we got a white Christmas! My favourite way to spend Christmas day would be a run in the snow followed by a great day with all my family around me, and in 2004 my wish came true. I ran 15 miles through the snow and at most points was moving a lot faster than the sliding cars. Everyone I met was in great spirits and calling out 'Merry Christmas!' The run left me nice and ravenous to tuck into my Christmas dinner, which I then burned off by building a snowman with my nephew Jack – although the turn-out for the snowball fight was a bit disappointing.

Just before leaving for our altitude stint in the US, to begin getting ready for the London Marathon that spring, I headed to Limerick for a check-up with Gerard Hartmann. My body and legs were generally in good shape but I was feeling a bit tired and lacklustre. Gerard took me to see a naturopath who tested me for food intolerances and general health. She was pretty shocked at the state of my stomach, and told me it was very inflamed and sensitive after the traumas in Athens. She advised me that I was intolerant to wheat, gluten, dairy, chicken, grapes and tomatoes, and also told me that the amoeba and parasites in my system were very strong and needed eliminating. She felt it would be best to go with a strong course of antibiotics to wipe this out and then concentrate on healing my stomach and getting it strong again. I started the new diet the day before we flew over to Albuquerque and remember thinking that it was so awkward and difficult (especially on the plane) that I would never be able to stick to it. How would I have my ice cream or scone treats after hard training sessions? However, my stomach improved so much and so quickly that I had my incentive to stick to the new regime. Suddenly runs in the afternoon were comfortable and I didn't need to take in routes with toilet stops. I was also finishing the day as I started it instead of feeling bloated. Luckily I even found a bakery with great rice breads and even gluten- and dairy-free cookies and treats. Now I wonder if I had suffered minor food intolerances for years and just never realised it, as I felt better than I had ever done in my life.

So my stomach was great – but, strangely, training-wise I was struggling to find good form. Maybe it was the antibiotics, but I was feeling really tired and heavy-legged, especially on the quicker sessions. The long runs and endurance sessions seemed fine, but for some reason my 10k sessions and tempo runs were a fair way off my best. It was getting hard to stay positive as nearly every day I seemed to be forcing myself out of the door and willing my legs to keep going, even on easy runs. It's perfectly normal in hard training blocks to have tired days where I really don't feel like going training, but motivate myself to do so by thinking about the goals ahead and the end result. Usually, though, once I get running I feel better and often end up actually enjoying the run. These days are also the exception rather than the rule. During this period, however, these days were becoming more and more frequent and it was getting much more worrying and harder to cope with. First, I worried about whether I was losing motivation or mental application, or even simply getting too old! I was also concerned that I was suppressing my immune system by pushing too much. Gary was also getting worried, as he could see me working hard but not getting the usual results or making the right progress. I was feeling vulnerable, so also had a tendency to take his concern as criticism that I wasn't trying hard enough or was even running slowly on purpose just to annoy him. I had always said that when I wasn't enjoying my life and training any more, then that would be the time to walk away. Now I mentioned as much to Gary. He turned round and said, 'Fine, do it. If that's what you want to do, then forget about athletics.' The problem was, that wasn't what I wanted at all. I felt far from ready to leave it all behind me – I still believed I had a lot more to achieve, and I still loved my athlete's life. I just needed to feel strong again, like I was firing on all cylinders. I needed to feel like me again.

GARY:

'Training blocks are never really the same, but although all of the main ingredients seemed to be there it did take a little while for them to come together. Our time in Albuquerque was pretty relaxed but we didn't really understand why things took so long to click. We got frustrated and had our days when we both seemed to be going in different directions, but the destination was the same – so we just rolled with it.'

I had some blood tests and spoke to Dr Bruce Hamilton a few times. They didn't show much, other than that my white cells were very low. We decided to take a few days' rest and cut the general volume of training down for a week or so and see if that helped. We also decided to try a change of scenery and move across to Flagstaff, Arizona for a few weeks. Sometimes a change just helps to stimulate things a little bit. I also had happy memories of our time there before New York. Something seemed to do the trick, and I began feeling a lot better. The day we left I completed a decent track session and then after the drive across to Flagstaff still felt OK on my evening run, although as it was getting dark I had extra motivation to keep moving quickly on the forest trails.

Unfortunately the weather didn't play ball. We had three or four days of good weather but then the snow arrived. At first we were able to use the indoor track for quality sessions and thought we could make do until the weather improved. Sadly the forecast was for several more big dumps of snow and the trails were already cut up pretty badly, making it especially difficult for Gary to ride the bike with me on long runs. This is pretty vital in marathon preparation as I need him to pass me drinks. So after a good hill session in deep snow we drove back to Albuquerque after just a week.

From here on things started to pick up and head in the right direction. I settled into a good training routine and was also getting good massage care from Josie Edwards Scott. Dana Paine, the masseur I had previously used in Albuquerque, was sadly having some health difficulties and put me in touch with Josie. I was able to catch up with Dana, who was his usual positive and kind self despite his worries.

Josie looked after my body really thoroughly, though we did often joke about how she was fighting a constant battle as I would leave her house feeling great and then forty-eight hours later would be back with everything stiff and tight again because of the mileage and sessions that I was doing. This is totally normal in marathon preparation, which is why I always need to be able to access good regular massage and physio care when I'm in hard training. Gary has also picked up the basics and is able to flush my legs out well every day. Another trick I use is to have an ice bath after hard workouts to cut down on muscle soreness and speed recovery.

Gerard did not come out to Albuquerque as this had been a one-off situation for a couple of years and he now needed to focus on his clinic in Ireland and his upcoming wedding. However, we headed over to Limerick for the final few weeks' preparation and he came into London with us for the marathon itself. I like to stick to routines and plans that work, and had good markers for my final key sessions in Limerick and also the peace of mind that my body was getting great care.

Before heading back, though, I had to make a difficult decision on the World Cross-Country and take in a preparatory race. Ideally I had wanted this race to be the World Cross. It is a race that is special to me and also a top quality event. I would also liked to have been part of the British team again, as I had missed the two previous World Cross races. On top of that the event was due to take place in France, a country that has a special place in my heart and where I know the atmosphere will always be great. However, the race fell five weeks before London, and usually I prefer to have a gap of just three weeks after all the hard marathon base work has been done, so my legs can be a little fresher. I had been hoping to be in shape quickly so that I could afford the luxury of easing down and racing five weeks before. However, although things were now heading in the right direction and I was happy I would be ready for London, I felt that I needed the extra edge that a couple more good long runs and sessions in Albuquerque would bring. These last few weeks went well and I decided take in a 10km road race in New Orleans before heading home. It was eight years since I had competed in and won the Crescent City Classic 10km race and I now looked forward to going back to the city. The atmosphere there is great fun, thousands line the streets and it's the only race I've ever done where beer, as well as water, is available en route. So far I've not been tempted to take any on board but it just illustrates the party atmosphere that surrounds the race.

Unfortunately I didn't get as good a result as I'd hoped for, and came away from the race disappointed. With London the priority I wanted to get my last hard 2 hours 15 run done properly and, though this went very well, with hindsight five days was probably not enough recovery time to be as sharp as I wanted to be for New Orleans. Additionally my period was due, and late, which often makes me feel heavy-legged. This is precisely what happened in the race, where I felt lethargic and flat. Isabella Ochichi was running really well after having prepared for the World Cross a few weeks before and I just wasn't sharp enough to stay with her. I was frustrated because I felt that the race hadn't really reflected the work I had done and the shape I was in. On the positive side I had still run 30.45 mins which wasn't a disastrous time. I also knew that preparations had gone well and that my menstrual cycle would be in the right place for the marathon.

And so it was on to Limerick for the final build-up to London. Here things went smoothly. I got over the jet lag and did some good final sessions. Gerard was happy with my legs and we had no last-minute panics. From there we headed back to London on the Tuesday to do the pre-race press conference and then back to Loughborough for a few days before coming back on the Thursday. I prefer to do this rather than stay in the hotel all week. Living in a hotel isn't ideal and it also means that the build-up to the race is very drawn out. I prefer to relax for a few days then come back on the Thursday and let the anticipation and excitement for the race begin to build up. If all that began earlier in the week it might be too much, and I'd be worn out come race day!

After arriving back in London on the Thursday afternoon I went straight out for my last little run – just twenty-five minutes easy, and some strides. I have fallen into a habit now of doing this run over part of the course as it winds around by the hotel, but 2005 would be different as the course had been changed to avoid the twisty bit around the hotel where runners had fallen the previous year, and also to take out the cobbled section in front of the Tower of London. I had mixed feeling about this – it might make the course easier underfoot but the section had also been a great area for atmosphere and I hoped that this wouldn't be lost. After the run Gerard worked on my legs for a bit before we headed off to the special 25th Anniversary Banquet that had been arranged for all the past winners that night. It was great to be at a dinner with so many past heroes and heroines of the distance, and amazing how little many of them seemed to have changed. Most looked like they could still run a good race! There were only a few of us there who were preparing to race on the

Sunday, so everyone else was able to really relax and enjoy the party. I got the chance to chat and catch up with a lot of the past winners, people like Catherina McKiernan, with whom I had got on well when we competed together but hadn't seen for a while. We were also seated at a table with Ingrid Kristianson and her husband, and Khalid and Sondra Khannouchi. Ingrid is someone I really looked up to when I was younger and she has always been really friendly, helpful and supportive since I first met her in 2001. Although global Championship wins are most important to me as I look to the future, it would still be a great honour and mean a lot to me to equal or surpass her achievement of four London wins. Unfortunately, because this event was just a few days before the race I didn't want to stay late, so we left just as the real party was getting started and headed back for an early night. Still, reports the next day confirmed that the organisers did a great job and it was a superb night – maybe next time we could have it *after* the race please?!

The next day was pretty relaxed; first the pre-race doping test, then a massage and then we headed to the Marathon Expo. This is always an amazing place, so many stalls and things to wander round and look at, although I didn't get too much opportunity for browsing. I went straight to the Nike stand where we did a Q & A with the crowd and then I signed autographs for an hour or so. I always enjoy this, everyone is so eager and excited about the race ahead, trying to get last-minute advice and tips for the race, and also so positive and supportive of each other. It's like a massive exhibition hall filled with hundreds of people all with one common love, passion and goal – the marathon. It must be one of the few sports where so many people with so many different goals and levels all get to take part in the same race. I always leave there buzzing and really looking forward to the race ahead.

The Saturday is always a relaxed day, one final gentle tune-up massage just to make sure everything is ready to go, and some stretching. Gerard was very happy with things generally; apart from one slightly tight hamstring at one point, we'd had no real muscular or soft tissue problems leading into the race, which is actually quite unusual for me in marathon preparation. I felt pretty laid-back and was looking forward to the Sunday. I went for a coffee and wander around outside with my friend Liz Yelling, had a short nap and my pre-race ice bath before tucking into my dinner. Because of my dietary changes I had brought a big box of food with me and cooked my own dinner in the room. I just stuck to plain salmon and lots of rice and pasta as I prefer to eat simply the night before a race. Even though the situation was totally different, I was perhaps slightly conscious of the nightmare I'd had in Athens, where I was glycogen-depleted, and I did have a lot of pasta to ensure this didn't happen again. I may have paid for this slightly the next day . . .

After that I turned in at about nine for an early night as it would be a prompt start the next morning. I don't always sleep well the night before a big race, especially when I have to be up early, but don't usually worry about this so long as I am getting rest. However, this time I did sleep soundly and woke only when the alarm went off just before 5 a.m. As soon as it got light we checked the conditions outside. Rain had been forecast but luckily the sun was out and there were blue skies which held through the day.

I was feeling relaxed as we made our way out to the start at Blackheath. I always have some nerves and butterflies, which are good because they get the adrenalin going; it also shows that the race is important to me, and I'd be worried if I felt no nerves at all. This time was especially nice as I had two good friends and clubmates from Bedford, Liz Yelling and Sharon Morris, also running. It was like old times as we laughed and joked on the bus on the way out. Later, we even won the AAA team race, even though Liz had injury problems, but sadly it didn't count as we weren't all wearing our club vests. Usually for me the bus journey is the most nervous time – once we arrive and I start warming up I am getting on with things and the nerves recede. I always enjoy the warm-up at London. I jog out along the road and you can see all the people making their way to the different starts. Everyone is excited and enthusiastic and calling out 'Good luck' to the runners. The atmosphere is great, especially when the weather is good, and it is an amazing sight seeing that many people and colours making Blackheath Common so vibrant.

At the start line there was a huge cheer when my name was announced and this gave me goosebumps and lifted me even further. What was really special about it was that a lot of the runners lined up behind me also cheered. I had only one hiccup when I realised I had left my racing gloves in the pocket of my warm-up trousers that I had given to Gary. As there was a cold wind I really wanted to wear them – Alex and Gerard ran off to try to find Gary as he was already on the press truck that goes ahead of the runners. It is a symbol of the camaraderie of runners that several people offered to lend me gloves – fortunately, though, they were able to find mine and I had them safely on my hands with two minutes to spare!

I always struggle to find the words to describe and do justice to the atmosphere of the London Marathon. It is so special and unlike anything I have ever experienced elsewhere. It is at its best on a morning such as this one: clear, crisp blue skies, yellow and green balloons everywhere and an emotional, vibrant, moving and colourful wall of support all along the route. Whistles and rattles sound out, Union Jacks and St George's flags fly proudly alongside so many others. Pubs blast out music as we run by. People race alongside at stages trying to keep abreast whilst yelling encouragement. It is as though I'm a sponge that can absorb all this energy and emotion and use it in my fuel tank to run hard and to feel great.

GARY:

'London 2005 had a different feel about it. If there was any pre-race pressure from outside, we didn't feel it. Paula was excited about the race, we knew she was in good shape and we were looking forward to it. The weather on race day

was beautiful. I was on a lead truck about 75 metres in front of the lead group, and I could hear the expectation and excitement of the crowd building as Paula approached. In a way it was quite emotional but also a little weird; watching people watching Paula and the joy it brought them.'

This year I set off with no specific pace goal in mind, I just wanted to win the race and enjoy it. Yet as I strode out through the first couple of miles I felt really good. I went with the pacemakers but the others quickly let us go. One of the pacemakers was running erratically and cutting across in front of me all the time which began to annoy me. I have never been a runner who likes to sit behind others: I much prefer to run alongside and see the road in front of me. So I began to stretch out and run my own pace. I was running fast though, and after a few miles backed off a little to try to save more for the second part of the race. Here the chasing pack began to close a little, but I never really felt threatened or too aware of them. I was locked into how I was feeling, gauging my pace and speed and taking in and enjoying all the sights and sounds. By Tower Bridge, the halfway point, I was well clear and ready to hit the second half of the race strongly. I was also on a very good pace and felt that I could maintain this before picking up the final 6 miles. Yet again the noise on Tower Bridge nearly took my breath away. My ears were ringing with the cheers, whistles and rattles, cresting the rise of the bridge feels almost like riding a wave, you've come up a small hill but hardly feel it and then you're flowing so easily down the other side.

I was now on the part of the course that had changed direction in order to avoid the cobbles. Already I could see one benefit: the crowds were really concentrated as we would pass the end of Tower Bridge twice and in some places people were nine or ten deep. Feeling good I was ready to push on harder through the second half.

Unfortunately at around 15 miles I started to experience stomach problems, and felt that I needed a bathroom stop. I tried to ignore the discomfort for as long as possible. When it subsided I was still able to run strongly, but as each wave of cramps came on I was slowing and losing time. It was also getting more and more uncomfortable! I tried to alleviate the problems without stopping but had no success. It was nothing like the problems I had had in Athens, where my stomach was in trouble well before the race. Here I didn't feel dizzy or weak, I just simply needed to go, and then I would be fine – but the question was where? I began to look around and think about options. All the Portaloos I could see were on the other side of barriers, and I knew that after twenty-odd miles of a marathon there was no way I could climb the barriers without doing damage or pulling something, and I'd also lose too much time. The crowds were really great but I had no idea how far ahead I was and so didn't know whether I had time to stop without being caught and risk losing the race. This was something I wasn't prepared to even consider. I remembered hearing stories of Steve Jones' famous pit stop in the privacy of the Blackfriars tunnel, and wanted to try to hang on until then. Unfortunately the pain was getting worse and I had to look for a more immediate solution.

Up ahead I saw a water station with some banners hanging over the tables. I had the idea of ducking under the tables out of sight and decided to do this. As I stopped, however, I discovered the banners were fixed and I couldn't duck underneath. My brain had already told my body that relief was available, though, and I had to go ahead and make the stop there. I know it was something non-runners might find hard to understand, and it is something the person that I am out of competition would be horrified and embarrassed about. However, the competitor in me was only concerned with winning the race and achieving what we'd all worked towards. In a situation like this you do what you have to do as quickly and unobtrusively as possible without risking any more than you have to. Very difficult to do when you are on your own in front of millions with a TV bike following the whole way and a press truck in front! I managed to stop just before a corner so the press truck had already turned (with the added bonus of having Gary out of sight, as I knew he would have a small heart attack if he saw me stop). By chance the BBC were not actually live on me at the time. I nearly got away with it until Steve Cram very kindly drew everyone's attention to the fact that he had seen me stop!

Thankfully I was back running quickly and feeling a lot more comfortable. Now that I felt better I was back on to a good pace and enjoying the race a lot more again.

I was now finishing the changed loop of the course and rediscovering old favourite territory – under Blackfriars tunnel and down the Embankment to Big Ben, from where it is less than a mile to the finish. Having the course the other way round through the Docklands had felt as if I was running into more of a headwind than the old course, and also as if there were more speed bumps on it, but maybe my interpretation was coloured by my discomfort at that stage of the race.

As I came through where the crowds were really thick by Tower Bridge, I was nearly deafened by the noise. Even the runners in the main race going out in the opposite direction were shouting encouragement! The contrast from that noise to the silence in the Blackfriars tunnel was eerie. My ears were ringing then suddenly everything went quiet. Momentarily I felt really disorientated and dizzy. Thankfully my senses adapted quickly and, as I hit the Embankment, I was back to normal.

As I ran the final few miles along the Embankment I was running into the wind at its strongest. I felt fine and knew I was finishing strongly. However, I also calculated that with the time I had lost before and during my stop I was now not going to be able to run in the 2 hour 16 zone I had been aiming for going into the Docklands loop. At the same time I was comfortably inside my women's-only World Best of 2 hours 18.56. Therefore I decided to maintain pace but not push myself even harder and exhaust my energy fully over the final few miles. I had the race safely won and my big goal for the year was to win the World Championships in Helsinki in August. By saving a little of my reserves now, I would help myself recover faster in time for the summer preparations.

I was in some of my favourite territory and enjoyed taking it all in as I pushed on towards Big Ben in the distance, made the turn into Birdcage Walk and towards Buckingham Palace. Again, it is so hard to do justice to the support and atmosphere; you can feel all the energy, warmth and encouragement and barely hear yourself breathe. All the colours of the rainbow brighten the sides of the route and funnel you into the Mall and the very welcome sight of the finish line. Always at the corner I see Harry Fry standing there. He works for the marathon and his job is to make sure runners follow the correct line to their respective finish lines. Like everyone at the London Marathon he is always so friendly and enthusiastic whenever you see him.

Now as I passed Harry and ran up the finishing straight I gave him and all the crowds a big smile of thanks for keeping the faith and giving me such great support. I crossed the line in 2 hours 17.42 and savoured the feeling: I was elated. I'd known I was in good shape coming into the race, but at times during the build-up after Christmas it had been tough. Part of what had kept me going through it had been imagining this amazing experience that I had enjoyed over the last few hours and was still enjoying now. I'd also had a minor crisis to deal with during the race, and knew that I was now going to have to deal with the aftermath of how I had handled that. But this was not going to overshadow for me the importance of being back running strongly and winning.

I did all the finish photos, found Gary and got a big hug, and was hustled round to do the radio and TV interviews. This kept me pretty busy and it was only mid-interview with Sue Barker that I realised I didn't know who had finished 2nd. When I asked her she laughed and said they hadn't come in yet; we looked across and saw Constantina Dita of Romania finishing in a personal best. Only then did I realise how big a gap I had had over my rivals!

Later we had the presentations, where I also got a chance to sincerely thank the crowd. This was very important to me as I truly believe nowhere can beat the London crowds. Never underestimate the energy and advantage that a great home crowd can give athletes. At a time when members of the IOC were thinking about where to award the 2012 Olympics, I could honestly imagine no better advert or showcase for the London bid.

Back at the hotel I rushed through Doping Control to the press conference and then finally got back to our room and had a chance to catch up properly with my friends and family. Gary, my parents, Grandma and Auntie Sue, Alex and Rosemary, Gerard, Karl, Alison and even Colin Jackson (enjoying his virgin London Marathon experience) were all there. While they opened the champagne, I had almond butter on toast in the ice bath! Then I had champagne, chocolates and a massage while everyone milled around. It was so nice to lie back and relax and share my happiness with everyone who meant so much to me and had helped me through the low times. Unlike many of the press and some others, we had never doubted that after Athens I would be back to winning and running fast again. I knew that in Athens I had simply had too much to fight against and had broken down and exhausted myself trying to get to the start line. Once I got healthy and wasn't glycogen-depleted I was always going to be the same athlete I was before. However, mentally we had all had a lot to deal with during the previous nine months and probably will continue to do so. In many ways this has made us all much tougher and stronger as a unit. But right now I was happy and proud that we had come through by all pulling together and were back happy with life and enjoying racing – and racing well. This was all I ever wanted.

New York had been the first step back to normality, and now after proper preparations and training I was back running near the times I wanted and know I'm capable of. I was excited and looking forward to the rest of 2005. But first I was going to relax and enjoy my post-race break.

20

As I sat in the back of the car going from the airport out to the Athletes' Village in Espoo, Helsinki, for the 2005 World Championships, my mind turned to the last occasion I'd been there. It was 1991 and my first ever international on the track — a junior match where I ran the 3,000 metres. I remember being one of the slowest in the field on paper, yet vividly recall feeling really strong down the final back straight as Dave Moorcroft, then a team coach, shouted out that I could win the race. I too felt I could, and in front of the stands full of the rest of the team I ended up winning the race by outsprinting the others in the straight. It was a great day for all of us — we won the match and many of us achieved personal bests. That night we felt we deserved to celebrate and almost the whole team snuck out of the dormitories and got a bus into the centre of Helsinki to go to a club. When we returned in the early hours we couldn't understand why the team management were so angry!

Now I remembered that experience with a smile (and sympathy for Pat Green, the team manager who had seemed such a demon at the time), and thought it a good omen for what lay ahead of me. Indeed, ten days later I would again be returning to my room in those halls of residence at four in the morning, after celebrating in a nightclub. But this time no one would be waiting to berate me and I would be the Marathon World Champion.

Getting back into training after London went smoothly. There was no rush for the summer championships so we built up gradually, and were soon up to normal volume training and sessions. This year I also felt I could fit in a trip to the Nike Prefontaine Meet in Oregon and enjoy a fun run over 1,500 metres. This is an event I had wanted to run in for a while, as it always looks like a great occasion. Knowing the story of Steve Prefontaine, the gifted US athlete who died in a car accident at the age of just 24, it also had significance in that respect. This year I would be in Oregon anyway, for a visit to Nike's Beaverton Campus to work with their designers and also to attend a surprise tribute to Phil Knight, an amazing man and truly genuine running enthusiast, who was stepping down as CEO of the company. As I had got back into training well and was even ahead of schedule for the summer, I could allow myself the luxury of a fun run. It's a distance I always enjoy but rarely get the chance to race over nowadays. I wasn't yet into top shape over the longer distances but felt I could challenge my personal best here – something I'd long wanted to do as my official best of 4 minutes 5 seconds does not reflect what I am capable of in a good, fast, honest race.

The surprise tribute worked really well – Phil Knight was truly not expecting it. He thought he was delivering the closing speech for the big annual sales conference and that all the athletes were there as part of that. Then, as he wrapped up, someone grabbed the mic and one by one we all paid our individual tributes. He is such a humble and genuine person that when you meet him you have to remind yourself also of how powerful and successful he is. I remember the first time I had the honour of being invited to meet him in his office after I had won the World Cross-Country in 2001. We were waiting outside, looking at and discussing all the old running shoes in the display cases.

I was showing Gary my first ever pair of trainers – the children's version of the famous 'Waffle' – and this guy in jeans and trainers joined us and started chatting about how shoes had changed and which were his old favourites. We didn't realise who he was and got a real shock 5 minutes later when we were shown into his office and the penny dropped. I remember being so impressed by his passion and knowledge of running – he is a highly intelligent and shrewd businessman who has achieved so much, but also just a guy who loves his running and other sports, and who wants to help athletes achieve their potential. Since joining Nike I have been very impressed and grateful for the way in which they support their athletes, and also listen to what they want. You can be totally honest in feedback to the designers and they genuinely take it into account. This isn't always the case with big companies who can often be more interested in high street sales than high performance. This ideal has been passed down directly from the man who started the company by selling running shoes to real runners from the boot of his car.

I was a little in awe at the evening function. We were surrounded by athletics icons such as Sergei Bubka, Seb Coe, Carl Lewis, Jackie Joyner-Kersee, Alberto Salazar and Justin Gatlin; and from other sports stars like Michael Jordan, Pete Sampras, Kobe Bryant and Wayne Rooney. It was a great privilege to get the chance to mix with and meet them all.

Unfortunately the 1,500m race the next day did not go according to plan. With seventeen in the race the field really needed to be strung out in order to be safe, but after a fast opening lap the pacemaker slowed drastically and in the home straight the field bunched badly. I was just trying to move wide to take it on but had decided to wait until we were round the bend and on the back straight as I would need to go out into lane four to get past. Suddenly bodies were falling all over the place in front of me. I was pushed but stayed on my feet but had nowhere to go ahead or to the side without running on top of people. I fell forwards, lost my sunglasses but jumped back up and gave chase to the lead runners who were now some 80 metres ahead. I was angry but tried to close the gap gradually. There were still about 800 metres of the race remaining. I was catching the main pack but others who had fallen were flying past me! Going through the bell I was maybe 10 metres from the pack, and those who had whizzed past were now fading. I picked them off one by one and latched on to the back of the lead pack as we came around the final bend, but I had nothing left in the straight and trailed in about 6th or 7th – although I did win the race of those who had fallen! I had run only 4 minutes 13 but had lost about 8 seconds while falling and getting back up. I was frustrated and just wanted to rerun the race (the long-distance runner in me was feeling recovered and ready to go again in 5 minutes). I was cut and bruised on my hands and knees, but at that stage felt I was not seriously hurt. Sadly, others were: Jolanda Ceplak fell badly on her hip and later missed most of the season, and several others struggled for a while after the race.

GARY:

'I couldn't believe what I was seeing. I couldn't believe that she had allowed the race to slow so much – but she didn't really have a choice. At the time we were more frustrated that she hadn't been able to run a personal best in what may have been her only 1,500m of the summer, and didn't fully appreciate the structural damage a fall like that can cause.'

Karl insisted I get checked out and I had indeed twisted and knocked my back and knees around and out of line. The chiropractors there worked on me and I felt fine in my 2-hour run the next day. However, on the plane back to Europe I must have put it out again, as after a week's training back in Font-Romeu I really wasn't feeling right at all. I put it down to jet lag and felt that I would be fine and over it by the coming weekend, when I was racing in the European Cup. Physically I was just feeling more tired than usual and my left hamstring in particular was tighter and stiffer than normal. Complicating things further I was asked to double up with the 3,000m and 5,000m after Jo Pavey pulled out. I knew that before the US trip training had been going well, I was capable of covering both events, and it would be a good workout weekend for me. It was also really important that the GB women's team get back in the Super League, where we belong. My proviso was that I get good physio cover while there, so that I could get some work done on my legs and lower back which had been really tightening up and stiffening in the ten days or so since the Portland fall.

We arrived in Lleira, Portugal on the Thursday afternoon and I headed out for an easy run. Worryingly I did feel quite tired and heavy-legged, much worse than I had done through that week in Font-Romeu. With hindsight the flight and long drive probably exacerbated the damage to my back alignment, making me feel even worse. At the time I hoped a day's rest and deep massage work would improve things – if not, the reserve would have to cover the 5,000m.

I got away with the 3,000m race on the Saturday. I ran in a controlled way to begin with then surged a bit and the field let me go. This was good because where I should normally have just been cruising at that pace I actually felt as though I was working really hard. I finished the race feeling much more tired than an 8 minute 50 race should have left me. As soon as Alison Rose, the physio, had looked at me on the Friday, she had seen how badly my sacrum (the large wedge-shaped bone in the lower back) and pelvis were twisted and out of line, and this had had a knock-on effect all the way up my back. She worked on me for about 4 hours that day and again on the Saturday before and after the race. We did get the muscles relaxed and made some adjustments, but my back can be very difficult to manipulate and we couldn't get the lower part right. I even phoned Doctor Müller-Wohlfahrt in Germany to see if he could see me on Monday, as I knew my back now needed urgent and specialist attention. I was worried about the next day as I knew I hadn't felt right at all in the 3,000m and a 5,000m race was going to be worse. To cap it all there was no distance reserve out in Portugal, so if I didn't race there would be no points for the team unless Zara Hyde Peters, the team leader, ran instead. Neither Gary nor I was happy about putting myself on the line if I wasn't right, and we agreed that if the team was clear enough ahead that we could afford not to score in the 5,000m. The team management would let me know and I wouldn't start. However, I probably wasn't clear enough about how bad I felt and as I did strides on the track before the race started, the displayed team scores showed we were not far enough ahead to be totally assured of winning. Sadly we hadn't realised that these were earlier scores and we did in fact already have the win in the bag.

GARY:

'Before the 5k in Lleira I asked Paula after warm-up if she was OK. I never heard a reply — I think I must have been talking to someone — but if I'd heard her tell me that she felt really bad she wouldn't have been on the start line. The team was important, but not as important as the World Championships in August.'

So I started, and tried to just run a controlled but decent pace; I figured I shouldn't need to run below 15 minutes in order to win and believed I could do this even if not feeling 100 per cent. I was wrong. I felt far worse than the day before, really awkward and stiff, and again as though I was running far faster than I actually was. My left leg got tighter and tighter and my right leg felt like it was doing absolutely no work. The Belorussian girl passed me and ran away from me and I was powerless to cover it. With five laps left my leg was cramping and I was genuinely worried about being able to finish at all. I desperately hoped no one else was closing on me. It took all my concentration and willpower to get through it and as I finished in a terrible time of 15 minutes 27 I was certain that I must be ill in some way. There was no way I was that unfit, and I couldn't imagine that I would run so badly simply because my back was out of alignment. Even to warm down was impossible as my left leg was so sore and the muscles so tight.

The next day I left at 4.30 in the morning to get to Munich. As soon as the doctor looked at my back he was shaking his head and telling me I should never have raced in that condition. My sacrum had been pushed back on the right side and got jammed, and my pelvis was rotated forward on the left side and backwards on the right. This meant my pelvis was twisted off to the right and I was trying to force my body to run round a track in an anti-clockwise direction. It would probably have been easier going backwards around the track! My left hamstring was also on constant stretch and my right leg was blocked and unable to do its share of the work. All this had caused knock-on disruption in my vertebrae and was affecting the neural pathways of my body, making me feel very tired. I asked if I should get blood tests to see if I was suffering from a virus or something, but he insisted that all would be OK once my back was sorted out and the muscles were able to relax and work properly. He treated my back and the chiropractor there hit my sacrum and back with all his strength to get the necessary adjustments. He was also very surprised I had run with it in such bad shape. Dr Müller was keen that I head on to Limerick to get the soft tissue around the joints worked on and make sure my back settled properly. However, Gerard was really busy and couldn't fit me in until the following week, so instead we headed to Loughborough. This actually worked out very well.

The set-up at the Loughborough High Performance Centre is light years from where it was when I first went to the university in 1992. Now athletes have no excuses not to perform well, all the support they need is available on-site and of very high quality. The rest is down to their hard work and application. Now I was able to train well and get thorough, expert treatment from my physiotherapist there, Rone Thompson, and masseurs Pipsa Rippon and Mark Edwards. I could also see my osteopath Vaughan Cooper regularly. For the time I was there I was having about 4 to 5 hours' treatment a day to ensure the muscles in my lower back released and stopped pulling the joints back out of line. My legs also needed deep work and Vaughan made sure everything settled and stayed in the right alignments. Soon I was feeling much better in my running and we headed back to Font-Romeu.

Things fell into place really quickly and suddenly I was running much better than I had been simply because my body was able to function as it is supposed to. Once I had recovered from feeling a bit tired and bruised after all the treatment, I was running personal bests in my tempo runs and track sessions. With only a few weeks to go before Helsinki I was feeling good and looking forward to the big race. While still in Loughborough we had met with Dave Collins, the new UK Athletics Performance Director. He had asked what I needed most to support my Helsinki preparations. The answer was good physio back up in my altitude training base of Font-Romeu; I needed to be there to train hard and prepare well but I also needed expert care to make sure my body didn't break down under the load. The plan worked really well, first Neil Black came out for a few intensive days then Mark Buckingham followed ten days later. This was brilliant as it enabled me to get all the necessary training done and have the confidence that my body was well looked after and supported.

The preparation was going so well that I now had a dilemma: I wanted to win the marathon in Helsinki, but training also showed that I was in pretty good shape for the 10,000 metres too. I don't get that many chances to run fast over 10,000m and probably wouldn't have many more realistic shots at World Championship success. If I could race the 10,000m without compromising the marathon, I wanted to give it a go. Gary and Alex were on the same page as me. I spoke to Dr Andy Jones, the physiologist with whom I've worked since I was 17. He felt that the eight days between races would be enough recovery time not to harm the marathon, and also that a good 10,000m race would even add to the marathon preparation both physically and mentally. Many other people weren't so supportive, but one thing I had vowed to do after Athens was not to worry too much about what others outside my immediate support circle said. I needed to be sensible and not take stupid risks, but it was also a decision that needed to take into account facts and knowledge of me as an athlete, and my ability to recover, and also what I was aiming to get out of the two races. The marathon was always the main goal and I wouldn't have done anything to compromise that. I even said that if I had a weak track session or didn't feel 100 per cent right then I would drop the 10,000m – but my last track session went better than ever! Feeling good, I completed my last hard run – a 20-mile tempo – and headed to Limerick for a few days before the trip to Helsinki.

I ended up disappointed, though, finishing 9th in the 10,000m in a time of 30 minutes 42 seconds. For some reason I didn't feel great during the race, although it's hard to say exactly why or what was wrong. I just felt as though I wasn't running smoothly or firing on all cylinders. It was a windy night, but up against the Ethiopian girls I really had only one race tactic open to me. I had to make it hard from the start and try to run away from them by the closing stages, as they are able to run much faster last laps than I am capable of (especially when preparing for a marathon). To begin with I felt OK and was trying to run a strong pace, surging slightly on the back straight where the wind was behind us and staying strong into the wind. However, after about thirteen laps I had really begun to tire. I decided to let someone else lead. The Japanese girl and a few others tried, but no one really wanted to lead in that wind and the race became very erratic. Into the home straight each time we slowed and bunched badly. The up-and-down pace probably took more out of me too, and when the final surge came with about 600 metres to go I was unable to stick with it and dropped off badly.

I wasn't consciously trying to save anything for the marathon. But maybe subconsciously I was unable to dig really deep once I realised I wasn't having a great run. Rationally, of course, the reason was probably just my legs were tuned for the marathon: everything had been planned for that race. It was also just six days since my last hard long run. Whatever the explanation, I was disappointed, not least because I had felt far better and stronger in my track session ten days before. Sometimes this can also be a reason for a poor performance, as you come down from altitude feeling great and train really well, then suddenly experience a tired lull because feeling so good has encouraged you to run a little too hard. Sometimes, too, it is possible just to have an off day without ever fully knowing the reason why. For the marathon, everything was planned to make it as perfect as possible – the 10,000m was never going to have that luxury this year. However, I honestly did believe that even with that proviso I would run far better and faster than I did.

GARY:

'I think what we have learned is that you have to make your own decisions, as you are the ones who have to live with them. I am still not sure what really happened in the 10k in Helsinki. She certainly didn't look herself or even as good as she had in the previous track sessions. She didn't feel ill, just a bit flat. Not 100 per cent. But in the end it didn't really matter, the marathon was always the main aim and it was only Paula's pride that took a bit of a beating.'

On the positive side I came out of the race feeling no ill effects and had had a good hard workout at well above marathon pace. I did a 30-minute warm-down and took an ice bath before clearing Doping Control and getting a massage. The next day I did an easy run and had a good physio session with Rone, who had now arrived into Helsinki. I then had to do a press conference before getting the chance to drive around the marathon course. After another easy run we headed out to Turku, where UK Athletics had their preparation camp.

Being in Turku gave me the chance to be in more relaxed surroundings than the village, and the food and running territory were also much better. A further advantage was that Pipsa would be there and could work thoroughly on me every day. She is a great friend as well as a superb masseuse, and also knows my body well. I was happy to be able to see her and be sure things were in great order going into the marathon. She kept saying how nice it was to work on me when I was in great condition and easing down, as opposed to when I'm banging out high mileage and quality sessions and my muscles are always tight and tired. Now she mentioned how she had never seen my body in such good condition and was able to concentrate on the really fine tuning. Another advantage was that we were cut off from the media and deliberately didn't try to read anything. In this way the heavy criticism of my 10,000m and the British team's performance in general passed me by totally.

Although I was only doing easy running and strides each day I still enjoyed exploring Turku. I ran on dirt trails in the forest and on an island off the coast. In the winters these would be cross-country skiing trails and were beautiful to run on. Pipsa's family even kindly lent Gary a bike so that I had company on the runs. Only the weather spoiled things: I got wet most days, although we didn't get the torrential rain and storms they were getting in Helsinki, and it was also a few degrees warmer than in the capital. I never really mind running in the rain when it isn't cold – you get the trails pretty much to yourself and it's quite refreshing. It felt a bit weird watching the Championships on TV each night away from the rest of the team. Only a few athletes were still in Turku and we were the last to leave and head into the city.

Back in the Athletes' Village, things continued smoothly. I had brought some black bin-liners to tape over the windows, as I had discovered that the Finns don't believe in thick curtains and it gets light very early there! This way I slept much more soundly. The food had also improved and I was able to get a few final checks with Rone.

As well as also being a good friend, she too works regularly with me and closely with Mark and Pipsa, so knows my body well. Finally she was happy with my back and we had very little to do in the last few days – on the morning of the race she said that everything was really looking 100 per cent and didn't need any final tuning at all, 'And I'm not just saying this to give you a boost!'

I spent the last days before the race just relaxing and resting. I watched the men's marathon fully to get an overview of how the course ran and an idea of which were the tough sections. I had a good sense of it after my course tour the previous week, but it's always helpful to see how people handle racing over it. The conditions for their race were actually quite humid, and after setting off at a fast pace the runners paid for this in the final 10km loop. Quite a few dropped out and many – including the winner, Gharib – seemed to be struggling in the closing stages. He had surged at about 30km and no one had been able to go with him. This reinforced my belief that I should run a decent, controlled pace in my race from the beginning and have enough left to be strong and inject pace as I needed in the closing lap. I wasn't overly concerned by the hills as I'm well used to the real hills of Font-Romeu and elsewhere, and knew I was at least as strong as anyone else on them. I had also read about how Grete Waitz, one of the great pioneers of women's marathon running and an athlete I have always admired, had won her world title there at the inaugural World Championships in 1983. I took this as another good omen.

I slept really well the night before and at 36 my pulse was nice and low on waking – always a good sign as it means I'm fit and well rested. I had my breakfast, got my bag ready and mixed up my race drinks. I relaxed by reading for a while then got ready to go. At midday we met outside the GB team block and walked over to get the bus to the start. I had a good feeling of nerves and anticipation and was looking forward to the race. I sat and chatted to Alan Storey on the bus as the other girls were quietly focusing on their own preparations. Everyone prepares differently and at this stage I always prefer to chat and relax a little rather than sit quietly. It doesn't really matter what I chat about, it's just interaction I'm after.

Once the bus arrived at the start the athletes were ushered into the call room where we were checked through and given our timing chips. There were areas for relaxation and Rone and Bruce, as medical staff, were allowed in but coaches and team managers weren't. I saw Gary and Alex outside and then sat chatting to Bruce and Rone and stretching a little until I was ready to warm up.

As I jogged in the warm-up zone in front of the start I could feel the atmosphere building. There were lots of people there already, waving flags and calling out support; many nationalities but also a good number of British people and Union Jacks. It was raining very slightly and fairly windy but not cold. Although humid, conditions were good. Wind isn't really a problem in a road race unless you are aiming for a record or fast time. It is the same for everyone and as we have the whole road to run on it is less easy to sit behind than on the track.

They lined us up. I wished the other girls good luck and we were under way. Immediately I was at the front and running a relaxed pace. I wasn't trying to get away, just feeling things out and running comfortably. I noticed that the IAAF were using as a timing car for the race a low-emission Toyota Prius, to save the athletes from inhaling fumes the whole way. This car was so far ahead of us, though, that for the most part it was impossible to see even the clock on its roof – in between us and the Toyota were all the press trucks and camera bikes belching out their fumes! I remember feeling relaxed enough to smile to myself at the irony of this.

We ran a 5km stretch before joining the main 10km loop which we would cover three and a half times. This wound along the coast and up towards the stadium and then zig-zagged back through the town, crossing a 300m long cobbled section each time. To begin with this was OK but by the last lap my feet weren't particularly enjoying those cobbles. If I didn't land just right my big toe would get crushed in the cracks between the stones. For some reason I was enjoying the uphill section of the course to the stadium more than the twisty bit back down. It wasn't that I felt bad here: rather that I felt good on the hills, and on the twisty section probably had to concentrate more in order to follow the best line and avoid the tram lines.

To begin with Yumiko Hara from Japan shadowed me, with Catherine Ndereba leading the rest of the pack a few metres back. When she dropped back Constantina Dita of Romania ran alongside me a few times and we increased the pace slightly each time. On each lap I could see my dad on the hill at the top end of the loop, and Gary was managing to get to a few points around the course. Approaching the last lap and the final 10 kilometres I got away slightly up the hill. I hadn't significantly surged; I just maintained my pace but managed to break away. From then on I just had to keep running strongly to the finish. People were shouting some time-gaps to me although I wasn't totally sure where I stood as the times varied a bit. Apparently Gary was getting information on gaps from people watching the BBC back home, and then phoning Alex and Zara out on the course so they could relay it to me. The problem was that the atmosphere on the course was so good that I only heard them once!

Up the climbs for the final time I still felt OK and knew I could increase the pace if challenged. I got a small shock as I thought someone shouted that I had a 15-second gap, which was a lot less than I thought. Luckily as I took my final drink Alan Storey shouted that I was 50 seconds ahead, and should relax and enjoy the final 2km. This I did, although being totally honest, the final short steep hill into the stadium itself felt like I was creeping up a mountain. Once I crested that, I was fine, and able to really relax and savour the entry to the stadium and the final 300m. I had noticed Gary running along the footpath as we approached the stadium and briefly wondered who would get there first. He even shouted out that I should take off my nose strip before entering the stadium.

As it was only the marathon finish and required separate tickets from the main evening session, the stadium wasn't completely full. But it was still a great atmosphere, with a huge roar as I entered and Union Jacks waving everywhere I looked. After I crossed the line I made sure to look around and take it all in, so that I would always have a good memory of that feeling. I got to Gary for a hug and picked out my parents and others including Pipsa in the stands. I waited to congratulate Catherine Ndereba as she finished, then someone handed me a Union Jack and I went around my lap of honour with the photographers all following. Someone even threw down a Union Jack umbrella and they took more pictures. I felt good, tired but very happy, and also relieved that the race had gone well and I was finally World Champion. Things had gone according to plan and I had achieved mine and everyone else's expectations. Now I had my World Championship title to go with the World Record.

GARY:
'Leading up to the marathon in Helsinki I never had any doubts. Paula was well prepared with none of the problems which had blindsided us in Athens. The race went according to plan — controlling the pace, no need for records or heroics. At the end I somehow managed to get down to track level — from experience not the best place for me to be — but I wanted to be right there on the line when she crossed it. Big smiles — job done.'

In some ways my second marathon was just beginning. I finished the race at 4.40 pm. My presentation was at 6.15, and as it turned out I would barely make it — it took me an hour and 10 minutes to get through the mixed zone where all the TV and radio crews are. I did many, many interviews in English, French and German, and apparently broke Justin Gatlin's record for the time taken to get through the zone. As I neared the end and the print media guys I suddenly felt really sick and dizzy — I hadn't eaten anything or even sat down since finishing the race, and my blood sugar had dropped. I was led into a room where I could sit for a few minutes and get myself a sugary drink and scoff a banana and some marzipan. Then it was straight into the press conference. After that I had to register in Doping Control before the hour deadline that we are given. Time was running so short, though, that I only had time to do a quick urine test and had to return to complete the blood test after the presentation ceremony. I had to be at both the team and individual award ceremonies as Great Britain had won team bronze in the World Marathon Cup, with personal bests from Mara Yamauchi and Hayley Haining – the team standings are the cumulative times of the first three runners home. This was an added bonus that I had only learned about part way through the Mixed Zone.

I arrived in the presentation area with about 2 minutes to spare. The other girls had been there a while and been able to avail themselves of the make-up facilities, and looked great; I was still covered in salty, dried sweat! Gary managed to find a wet towel so I could at least wipe my face, and I had a few seconds to use some lip gloss before we were on the rostrum. It felt really good to have a team medal as well, especially beating strong teams like Ethiopia. Kenya had won from Japan and Great Britain; we had apparently taken 6 minutes off Ethiopia over the final few kilometres. Mara and Hayley had had outstanding runs to get personal bests on a tough course. Hayley had been on my first World Cross junior team with me in 1991 and then won team World Cross bronze with me in 1998. In between she has really struggled with injury problems so it was great to be with her again in a successful team.

Next it was the individual ceremony. I knew I would feel emotional as they played 'God Save the Queen', but as the first notes rang out I was taken aback by the strength of my emotions. As the Union Jack climbed the flagpole I felt elated and euphoric, yet I also vividly felt all the emotions of the tough times, the near misses, the countless occasions I had imagined this moment and the energy and fight I had put into getting here. All of these emotions rose up in me and before I knew it I was crying as well as smiling. As the anthem finished the crowd roared and it was back to broad grins again. One of my most treasured photographs now is the one Dad took of that moment. It captures my face on the giant scoreboard below the flags being raised, and will always remind me of the emotions of that medal ceremony.

After climbing what felt like hundreds of steep steps to do further BBC TV and radio interviews I finally got my massage and ice bath. Finally at half-past nine Gary and I exited the warm-up area to find that I'd just missed a bus back to the village and had a long wait before the next one. I was still in my tracksuit and hadn't yet showered, but overriding everything else I was starving hungry and really wanted a good meal. We managed to meet my parents and found a restaurant. Soon we were all tucking into steak and chips, and I have to say that simple dish had never tasted so good. It was wonderful to be able to celebrate with them and Gary. I had also caught up briefly with Alex and later Karl joined us for some champagne. The restaurant was full of athletics fans and a table of French people kindly sent over another bottle of wine to congratulate us.

It was around 1.30 in the morning before they dropped me off back at the Athlete's Village. There I popped into the closing banquet, which was just finishing up, so that I could catch up with Rone and Pipsa and others. I even bumped into Prince Albert who was just leaving as I went up the stairs. He was really nice and congratulated me. I only intended to stay for a few minutes but Pipsa and Rone persuaded me to quickly change and go with them and a lot of the rest of the team to a nightclub. I really enjoyed it and even had the energy to show off my moves on the dancefloor. Finally at just before 4 they shut it down and we made our way back to the rooms. A long, tiring but exhilarating day had come to an end.

In becoming World Champion I had achieved my goal for 2005, and now looked forward to a holiday and a rest. It was the first time since 1990 that I'd had a holiday in August, as I'm usually busy racing or training – now I would take a few weeks off while I decided on my next aim. I didn't get too much of a lie-in the next day, though, as I discovered a message from Gary that I had to be up early in the morning to do more radio interviews!

There is certainly a lot to look forward to and work towards in the coming years. The long-term plan is tailored for Beijing and the marathon at the 2008 Olympics. Of course then there is the even longer-term plan of trying to make 2012, and live a dream by being able to run in an Olympics in my home country. By then I'll be 38, so have to hope my body will still be fit enough. I have no worries about the psychological side still being strong – what better motivation than imagining the atmosphere around the streets of London that day!

Before that, though, there is plenty to look forward to, and 2006 will be a busy year, with the Commonwealth Games, World Cross-Country and European Championships to factor in as well as the marathons. It seems strange to think about racing on the track in March before the World Cross-Country, but it could actually work out really well for both events. I'm also looking forward to racing more on the track, as in 2005 my outings there didn't work out as well as I'd hoped, due to falls and back problems. Over the next few weeks my plans and aims will fall into place and the road to Beijing and beyond will continue its winding path.

Career Record

PERSONAL BESTS

est = estimate; + timed en route to longer distance; # course or part of course not valid for official road race record

Event	Mark	Venue	Date	
400 Metres	58.6	Luton	3 May 92	
800 Metres	2:05.22	Birmingham	16 Jul 95	
1000 Metres	2:47.17	Bedford	24 Jul 93	
1500 Metres	4:05.37	Glasgow	1 Jul 01	
One Mile	4:24.94	Zürich	14 Aug 96	
2000 Metres	5:37.01+	Monaco	19 Jul 02	
	5:39.20	Sheffield	29 Aug 93	
3000 Metres	8:22.20	Monaco	19 Jul 02	Commonwealth record
Two Miles	9:17.4+ est	Bydgoszcz	20 Jun 04	Commonwealth best
	9:32.07	Loughborough	23 May 99	Commonwealth best
4000 Metres	11:35.21+	Bydgoszcz	20 Jun 04	Commonwealth best
5000 Metres	14:29.11	Hydgoszcz	20 Jun 04	Commonwealth record
6000 Metres	17:58.00+	Munich	6 Aug 02	European & Commonwealth best
7000 Metres	20:58.52+	Munich	6 Aug 02	European & Commonwealth best
8000 Metres	24:01.18+	Munich	6 Aug 02	European & Commonwealth best
9000 Metres	27:03.56+	Munich	6 Aug 02	European & Commonwealth best
10,000 Metres	30:01.09	Munich	6 Aug 02	European & Commonwealth record

Road

Event	Mark	Venue	Date	
One Mile	4:22.96	New York	27 Sep 97	British Best
5 Kilometres	14:48+	San Juan	23 Feb 03	European best
	14:51	Hyde Park	14 Sep 03	World best
4 Miles	19:51+	Balmoral	24 Apr 99	European & Commonwealth best
8 Kilometres	24:05+	San Juan	23 Feb 03	World best (unofficial time)
	24:38+	Balmoral	24 Apr 99	European & Commonwealth best (official time)
5 Miles	24:47	Balmoral	24 Apr 99	European & Commonwealth best
10 Kilometres	30:21	San Juan	23 Feb 03	World record
15 Kilometres	46:41#+	South Shields	21 Sep 03	World best
	47:44+	Bristol	7 Oct 01	
10 Miles	50:01#+	South Shields	21 Sep 03	World best
	60:06	Solihull	6 Oct 91	
20 Kilometres	62:21#+est	South Shields	21 Sep 03	World best
	63:26+	Bristol	7 Oct 01	World record
Half Marathon	65:40#	South Shields	21 Sep 03	World best
	66:47	Bristol	7 Oct 01	European record
25 Kilometres	1:20:36#+	London	13 Apr 03	World best

30 Kilometres	1:36:36#+	London	13 Apr 03	World best
20 Miles	1:43:33#+	London	13 Apr 03	World best
Marathon	2:15:25	London	13 Apr 03	World record

Indoors

| 5000 Metres | 16:16.77 | Birmingham | 22 Feb 22 | |

MAJOR CHAMPIONSHIP PLACINGS

Gold (12)
1992 World Junior Cross Country Championships
1998 European Cross Country Championships
2000 World Half Marathon Championships
2001 World Cross Country Championships (long course)
2001 World Half Marathon Championships
2002 World Cross Country Championships (long course)
2002 Commonwealth Games 5000 Metres
2002 European Championships 10,000 Metres
2003 World Half Marathon Championships
2003 European Cross Country Championships
2003 European Cross Country Championships Team
2005 World Championships Marathon

Silver (4)
1997 World Cross Country Championships
1998 World Cross Country Championships (long course)
1999 World Championships 10,000 Metres
2001 World Cross Country Championships (short course)

Bronze (2)
1998 World Cross Country Championships Team (long course)
1999 World Cross Country Championships (long course)

4th (12)
1991 World Cross Country Championships Team (juniors)
1991 European Junior Championships 3000 Metres
1992 World Cross Country Championships Team (juniors)
1992 World Junior Championships 3000 Metres
1997 World Cross Country Championships Team
1997 World Championships 5000 Metres
2000 World Cross Country Championships (short course)
2000 Olympic Games 10,000 Metres
2001 World Cross Country Championships Team (long course)
2001 World Cross Country Championships Team (short course)
2001 World Championships 10,000 Metres
2001 World Half Marathon Championships Team

5th

1995 World Championships 5000 Metres
1996 Olympic Games 5000 Metres
1998 European Championships 10,000 Metres
1998 European Cross Country Championships Team
2000 World Cross Country Championships (long course)
2002 World Cross Country Championships Team (long course)
2003 World Half Marathon Championships Team

6th

2000 World Cross Country Championships Team (long course)
2000 World Half Marathon Championships Team

7th

1993 World Cross Country Championships Team
1993 World Championships 3000 Metres
1999 World Cross Country Championships Team (long course)
2000 World Cross Country Championships Team (short course)

9th

1995 World Cross Country Championships Team
2005 World Championships 10,000 Metres

11th

1996 World Cross Country Championships Team

15th

1991 World Junior Cross Country Championships

18th

1993 World Cross Country Championships
1995 World Cross Country Championships

19th

1996 World Cross Country Championships

Did not finish

2004 Olympic Games Marathon
2004 Olympic Games 10,000 Metres

MARATHONS

Flora London Marathon winner 2002, 2003 and 2005; LaSalle Bank Chicago Marathon winner 2002; did not
finish Olympics 2004; ING New York Marathon winner 2004

OTHER MAJOR EVENTS

European Cup winner at 5000 Metres in 1998, 1999 & 2004; second in 2001; Second at 1500 Metres in 1998; Third at 3000 Metres in 1997; European Cup First League Winner at 3000 Metres & second at 5000 Metres in 2005; European Under-23 Cup winner at 3000 Metres in 1992
European Challenge 10,000 Metres winner in 1999 & 2001

NATIONAL TITLES

AAA Champion at 5000 Metres in 1996 & 2000 and Marathon in 2002, 2003 & 2005
UK Champion at 5000 Metres in 1997
English Schools Champion at 1500 Metres in 1991 and Cross Country & 3000 Metres in 1992
National Road Relay Champion (Intermediate Girls) 1990
Inter-Counties Cross Country Champion (Intermediate Girls) 1991
English National Cross Country Champion (Intermediate Girls) 1991
English National Cross Country Relay Championships (Intermediate Girls) 1991
British World Cross Country Championship Trial Winner (Junior Women) 1992
English National Cross Country Champion (Junior Women) 1992
British World Cross Country Championship Trial Winner 1994 & 1995
English National Cross Country Champion 1994
British Universities XC Champion 1996
National Road Relay Champion 1997

ANNUAL PROGRESSION

Year	Age	1500m	3000m	5000m	10,000m	Half Marathon	Marathon	British Caps
1988	14/15	4:41.0	–	–	–	–	–	1 England (Girl)
1989	15/16	4:34.9	–	–	–	–	–	1 England (Inter)
1990	16/17	4:31.3	9:41.4	–	–	–	–	2 England (1 Inter & 1 Junior)
1991	17/18	4:23.68	9:23.39	–	–	–	–	4 Junior
1992	18/19	4:16.82	8:51.28	16:16.77	–	–		3 Junior & 1 Under-23
1993	19/20	4:11.6	8:40.20	–	–	–	–	3
1994	20/21	4:23.84	–	–	–	–	–	1 England
1995	21/22	4:06.84	8:40.82	14:49.27	–	–		2
1996	22/23	4:08.42+	8:37.07	14:46.76	–	–		3
1997	23/24	4:06.93	8:35.28	14:45.51	–	–		4
1998	24/25	4:05.81	8:38.84	14:51.27	30:48.58	–		6
1999	25/26	4:06.71	8:27.40	14:43.54	30:27.13	69:37	–	5
2000	26/27	4:11.45	8:28.85	14:44.36	30:26.97	67:07	–	3
2001	27/28	4:05.37	8:26.97	14:44.21	30:55.80	66:47	–	6
2002	28/29	4:13+est	8:22.20	14:31.42	30:01.09	69:01+	2:17:18	2 + 1 England
2003	29/30	–	–	–	–	65:40	2:15:25	3
2004	30/31	–	8:39.08+	14:29.11	30:17.15	70:51+	2:23:10	2
2005	31/32	4:13.13	8:50.18	15:16.29+	30:42.75	68:27+	2:17.42	2

Total: 41 Senior British caps

OFFICIAL RECORDS SET

At 3000 Metres

8:27.40	Zürich	11 Aug 99	Commonwealth & British
8:26.97	Rome	29 Jun 01	Commonwealth & British
8:22.20	Monaco	19 Jul 02	Commonwealth & British

At 5000 Metres

14:46.76	Cologne	16 Aug 96	British
14:45.51	Brussels	22 Aug 97	British
14:43.54	London	7 Aug 99	Commonwealth & British
14:32.44	Berlin	31 Aug 01	Commonwealth & British
14:31.42	Manchester	28 Jul 02	Commonwealth & British
14:29.11	Bydgoszcz	20 Jun 04	Commonwealth & British

At 10,000 Metres

30:48.58	Lisbon	4 Apr 98	Commonwealth & British
30:40.70	Barakaldo	10 Apr 99	Commonwealth & British
30:27.13	Seville	26 Aug 99	Commonwealth & British
30:26.97	Sydney	30 Sep 00	Commonwealth & British
30:01.09	Munich	6 Aug 02	European, Commonwealth & British

At Road 10 Kilometres

30:21	San Juan	23 Feb 03	World

At Road 20 Kilometres

63:26+	Bristol	7 Oct 01	World

At Half Marathon

66:47	Bristol	7 Oct 01	European

At Marathon

2:17:18	Chicago	13 Oct 02	World
2:15:25	London	13 Apr 03	World

LIST OF COMPETITIONS

The following list does not contain every single competition Paula Radcliffe has taken part in, but does include all of her most significant performances.

Key: AAA = Amateur Athletic Association: h = heat; I = Indoor; M = mile; m = metres; pb = personal best; s = semi-final; XC = cross country

Event	Mark	Place	Meeting	Venue	Date	Note
3K XC	12.03	299	English National XC Championship (Minor Girls)	Leicester	15-2-1986	
Road	25:13	2	Southern Road Relays (Junior Girls)	Aldershot	18-10-1986	Stage 2/8:26
XC	9:51	6	Southern League XC (Junior Girls)	Bournemouth	25-10-1986	
Road	28:04	2	National Road Relays (Junior Girls)	Liverpool	8-11-1986	Stage 2/9:26

Event	Mark	Place	Meeting	Venue	Date	Note
XC		5	Southern League XC (Junior Girls)	Alexandra Palace	15-11-1986	
XC	10:28	3	Southern League XC (Junior Girls)	Welwyn Garden City	29-11-1986	
XC	9:10	2	Bedfordshire XC Championships (Junior Girls)	Leighton Buzzard	14-12-1986	
XC	8:48	14	Inter-League XC (Junior Girls)	Mansfield	28-12-1986	
XC	14:05	9	Southern Inter-Counties XC Harrow Championships (Junior Girls)		3-1-1987	
XC	13:49	5	Southern XC Championships (Junior Girls)	Epping Forest	31-1-1987	
3K XC	12:03	4	English National XC Championships (Junior Girls)	Bexley	14-2-1987	
XC	11:21	5	Inter-Counties XC Championships (Junior Girls)	Kettering	28-2-1987	
3K XC	13:23	22	English Schools XC Championships (Junior Girls)	Preston	28-3-1987	
Road	23:38	1	Southern Road Relay Championships (Junior Girls)	Aldershot	17-10-1987	Stage 1/7:45
XC	9:00	2	Southern XC League (Junior Girls)	Bournemouth	7-11-1987	
XC	12:02	1	Southern XC League (Junior Girls)	London	21-11-1987	
XC		1	Bedfordshire XC Championships (Junior Girls)	Luton	13-12-1987	
XC	15:18	1	Southern Inter-Counties XC Fleet Championships (Junior Girls)		2-1-1988	
XC	12:00	2	Inter-League XC (Junior Girls)	Barnet	10-1-1988	
XC	15:02	2	British Inter-Counties XC Championships (Junior Girls)	Nottingham	17-1-1988	
XC	13:16	2	Southern XC Championships (Junior Girls)	Swindon	6-2-1988	
XC	13:06	2	English National XC Championships (Junior Girls)	Leeds	13-2-1988	
XC	13:30	3	English Schools XC Championships (Junior Girls)	Chesterfield	5-3-1988	
3K XC	14:11	3	Home Counties Schools International XC (Junior Girls)	Irvine	26-3-1988	
1500m	4:41.0pb	8	English Schools Championships (Junior Girls)	Yeovil	9-7-1988	
Road	19:53	1	Southern Road Relay Championships (Junior Girls)	Aldershot	8-10-1988	Stage 1/6:27
XC	14:51	2	Southern XC League (Junior Girls)	Peterborough	22-10-1988	
XC	13:46	1	Bedfordshire XC Championships (Junior Girls)	Bedford	11-12-1988	
XC	15:20	1	Durham XC (Junior Girls)	Durham	31-12-1988	
3.5K XC	12:36	1	Southern Inter-Counties XC Championships (Junior Girls)	Fleet	7-1-1969	
XC	11:27	2	British Inter-Counties XC Championships (Junior Girls)	Scunthorpe	29-1-1989	

Event	Mark	Place	Meeting	Venue	Date	Note
XC	12:45	1	Southern XC Championships (Junior Girls)	Bournemouth	4-2-1989	
XC	17:12	3	English National XC Championships (Junior Girls)	Birmingham	18-2-1989	
4K XC	14:31	3	English Schools XC Championships (Intermediate Girls)	Hertford	4-3-1989	
XC	14:06	4	Home Counties Schools International XC (Intermediate Girls)	Barry	1-4-1989	
1500m	4:39.21pb	2	Southern Championships (Intermediate Girls)	Basildon	18-6-1989	
1500m	4:34.9pb	4h1	English Schools Championships (Intermediate Girls)	Wigan	7-7-1989	
1500m	4:35.0	4	English Schools Championships (Intermediate Girls)	Wigan	8-7-1989	
800m	2.15.69pb	3	CRS Dairies Games (Intermediate Girls)	Thurrock	17-9-1989	
Road	33:34	1	Southern Road Relays (Intermediate Girls)	Aldershot	21-10-1989	Stage 3/10:53 (3K)
3.5K XC	11:55	3	Southern XC League (Intermediate Girls)	Harrow	28-10-1989	
Road	32:41	3	National Road Relay Championships (Intermediate Girls)	Lincoln	11-11-1989	Stage 3/10:34
3.5K XC	13:34	2	Southern XC League (Intermediate Girls)	Bournemouth	18-11-1989	
3.5K XC	13:41	3	Southern XC League (Intermediate Girls)	Stevenage	2-12-1989	
XC	19:10	1	Bedfordshire XC Championships (Intermediate Girls)	Luton	10-12-1989	
4.5K XC	18:36	2	Southern Inter-Counties XC Championships (Intermediate Girls)	Fleet	30-12-1989	
4.6K XC	17:01	3	British Inter-Counties XC Championships (Intermediate Girls)	Bristol	14-1-1990	
4K		3	Southern XC Championships (Intermediate Girls)	Coulsdon	27-1-1990	
4.38K XC	16:20	3	English National XC Championships (Intermediate Girls)	Rickmansworth	17-2-1990	
XC	15:09	2	English Schools XC Championships (Intermediate Girls)	Wadebridge	3-3-1990	
4.23K XC	15:44	10	British World XC Trials Junior Women	Glasgow	10-3-1990	
3×2.5K XC	27:37	2	British XC Relay Championships (Intermediate Girls)	Mansfield	24-3-1990	Stage 3/8:47
4K XC	14:06	3	Home Counties Schools International XC (Intermediate Girls)	Rugby	7-4-1990	
1500m	4:41.0	1	Eastern Counties Championships	Peterborough	21-4-1990	
800m	2:15.3pb	2	British Clubs Cup First Round	Bedford	6-5-1990	
800m	2:16.1	1	Bedfordshire Championships (Intermediate Girls)	Bedford	20-5-1990	
3000m	10:04.3pb	1	Bedfordshire Championships	Bedford	20-5-1990	
1500m	4:31.3pb	3	Southern League Division 1	Bournemouth	26-5-1990	
1500m	4:45.1	1	Southern League Division 1	Chelmsford	30-6-1990	
1500m	4:36.2	3	English Schools Championships Southern League Division 1	Derby	14-7-1990	

Event	Mark	Place	Meeting	Venue	Date	Note
3000m	10:00.5pb	1	Southern League Division 1	Bedford	21-7-1990	
3000m	10:10.6	1	Southern Inter-Counties Championships (Intermediate Girls)	Horsham	11-8-1990	
800m	2:14.899pb	2	Reebok Challenge	Bromley	22-8-1990	
3000m	9:41.4pb	1	Southern League Division 1	Basildon	8-9-1990	
800m	2:14.7pb	1	Eastern Young Athletes League	Basildon	16-9-1990	
One Mile	5:00.5pb	1	General Portfolio Mile of Miles (Intermediate Girls)	Harlow	30-9-1990	
3×3K	32:23	6	Southern South Road Relay Championships	Aldershot	20-10-1990	Stage 3/9:35 (fastest of day)
XC	17:27	1	Southern XC League (Intermediate Girls)	Hayes	27-10-1990	
XC	13:17	2	Home Counties XC Intermediate (Junior Women)	Irvine	3-11-1990	
3×3K	32:16	1	National Road Relay Championships (Intermediate Girls)	Sutton Coldfield	10-11-1990	Stage 3/9:16 (fastest of day)
4K XC	14:16	1	Southern XC League (Intermediate Girls)	Bournemouth	17-11-1990	
XC	13:16	1	Southern XC League (Intermediate Girls)	Hendon	1-12-1990	
5K XC	19:04	1	Bedfordshire XC Championships (Intermediate Girls)	Luton	16-12-1990	
Road	1:45:43	7	Hawaii Young Women's Ekiden	Honolulu	5-1-1991	Stage 3/16:11
3.8K XC	12:17	1	National Inter-Counties XC Championships (Intermediate Girls)	Gateshead	13-1-1991	
XC	18:08	1	Southern XC Championships (Intermediate Girls)	Oxford	27-1-1991	Led Bedford to a fifth successive team victory
4.3K XC	15:44	1	English National XC Championships (Intermediate Girls)	Birkenhead	16-2-1991	
4.5K XC	16:39	2	English Schools XC Championships	Taunton	2-3-1991	
3×2.5K	26:25	1	English XC Relay Championships (Intermediate Girls)	Mansfield	16-3-1991	Stage 3/8:26 (fastest of day)
4.435K	14:50	15	World XC Championships	Antwerp	24-3-1991	Team 4th; 1, Lydia Cheromel KEN 13:59
1500m	4:28.5pb	1	Southern League Division 1	Bedford	27-4-1991	
3000m	9:35.5pb	1	British Clubs Cup First Round	Bedford	5-5-1991	
3000m	9:32.8pb	1	Southern League Division 1	Bedford	11-5-1991	
800m	2:11.2pb	1	Bedfordshire Championships	Luton	19-5-1991	
3000m	9:34.44	8	UK Championships	Cardiff	8-6-1991	
3000m	9:23.39pb	1	FIN v GBR v GER v URS Juniors	Espoo	15-6-1991	
800m	2:13.9	1	Southern League Division 1	Hornchurch	22-6-1991	
1500m	4:26.94pb	2	WAAA Under-20 Championships	Stoke	30-6-1991	
1500m	4:23.68pb	1	English Schools Championships	Stoke	13-7-1991	
1500m	4:25.54	3	Eight-Nations Junior International	Salamanca	20-7-1991	
3000m	9:25.80	4	European Junior Championships	Thessaloniki	11-8-1991	
10M	60:06	5	National 10 Mile Championships	Solihull	6-10-1991	Team 1st
3×2.9K	48:24	5	Southern Road Relay Championships	Aldershot	19-10-1991	Stage 3/15:31
XC	15:35	1	Southern XC League	Harrow	26-10-1991	
3×4K	47:09	17	National Road Relay Championships	Birmingham	9-11-1991	Stage 3/15:10

Event	Mark	Place	Meeting	Venue	Date	Note
4.9K XC	17:30	6	Southern XC League	Bournemouth	16-11-1991	
3.7K DC	14:26	9	Southern XC League	Hendon	30-11-1991	
5K XC	20:24	26	County Durham XC	Durham	28-12-1991	
4K XC	14:23	1	British World XC Championships Trials (Junior Women)	Basingstoke	8-2-1992	
4.71K XC	16:11	1	English National XC Championships (Junior Women)	Cheltenham	15-2-1992	
5000m	16:16.771pb	4	TSB Indoor Invitation	Birmingham	22-2-1992	1, Liz McColgan GBR 15:03.17 (world indoor record)
4.3K XC	14:43	1	English Schools XC Championships	Bristol	7-3-1992	
4.005K XC	15:30	1	World XC Championships	Boston	21-3-1992	Team 4th; 2, Wang Junxia CHN 13:35
400m	58.9pb	2	Southern League Division 1	Windsor	25-4-1992	
800m	2:10.6pb	1	Southern League Division 1	Windsor	25-4-1992	
400m	58.6pb	2	British Clubs Cup First Round	Luton	3-5-1992	
800m	2:08.7pb	1	British Clubs Cup First Round	Luton	3-5-1992	
4×400m	3:58.2	1	British Clubs Cup First Round	Luton	3-5-1992	
1500m	4:19.6pb	1	Bedfordshire Championships (Junior Women)	Bedford	17-5-1992	
400m	59.6	2	Southern League Division 1	Bedford	23-5-1992	
800m	2:07.9pb	1	Southern League Division 1	Bedford	23-5-1992	
400m	59.3	4	British Clubs Cup Second Round	Swindon	31-5-1992	
800m	2:08.2	1	British Clubs Cup Second Round	Swindon	31-5-1992	
3000m	8:57.23pb	4	AAA Championships/Olympic Trials	Birmingham	27-6-1992	
1500m	4:16.82pb	1	Southern Championships (Junior Women)	London	4-7-1992	
3000m	9:04.37	1	English Schools Championships	Hull	12-7-1992	
3000m	9:07.69	1	European Under-23 Cup	Gateshead	18-7-1992	
1500m	4:18.20	1	GBR v ESP v FRA Juniors	Horsham	29-8-1992	
3000m	9:10.77	2h2	World Junior Championships	Seoul	18-9-1992	
3000m	8:51.78pb	4	World Junior Championships	Seoul	20-9-1992	
3×4K	37:57	1	Southern Road Relay Championships	Aldershot	17-10-1992	1, Zhang Linli CHN 8:46.76 Stage 3/12:08 (fastest of day)
XC	18:33	1	Ampthill Beefeater Trophy XC	Bedford	1-11-1992	
3×4.35K	44:57	4	National Road Relay Championships	Sutton Coldfield	14-11-1992	Stage 3/13:47 (stage record)
XC	16:09	1	Southern XC League	Bedford	5-12-1992	
XC	21:52	1	Bedfordshire XC Championships	Luton	12-12-1992	
5.2K XC	16:29	2	Durham Internationa XC	Durham	2-1-1993	
4.8K XC	15:53	2	Coca-Cola International XC	Belfast	9-1-1993	
6.35K XC	20:34	18	World XC Championships (1st British senior international)	Amorebieta	28-3-1993	Team 7th; 1, Albertina Dias POR 20:00
1500m	4:25.3	1	Bedfordshire Championships	Luton	16-5-1993	

Event	Mark	Place	Meeting	Venue	Date	Note
1500m	4:13.70pb	2		Granada	29-5-1993	
3000m	9:02.42	4	UK Championships	London	13-6-1993	
1500m	4:11.6pb	1		Loughborough	20-6-1993	
1500m	4:14.53	5	GBR v USA (2)	Edinburgh	2-7-1993	
3000m	8:44.34pb	6	Bislett Games	Oslo	10-7-1993	
800m	2:06.89pb	2h1	AAA Championships	Birmingham	16-7-1993	1, Kelly Holmes GBR 2:05.74
800m	2:05.97pb	6	AAA Championships	Birmingham	17-7-1993	1, Holmes 2:02.69
1000m	2:47.17pb	5	England v World Select	Bedford	24-7-1993	
3000m	8:52.62	3h3	World Championships(3)	Stuttgart	14-8-1993	
3000m	8:40.40pb	7	World Championships	Stuttgart	16-8-1993	1, Qu Yunxia CHN 8:28.71
2000m	5:39.20pb	3	McDonald's Games	Sheffield	29-8-1993	
3×3.8K	39:03	3	Southern Road Relay Championships	Aldershot	16-10-1993	Stage 3/12:09 (fastest of day)
3×4.35K	43:34	2	National Road Relay Championships	Sutton Coldfield	13-11-1993	Stage 3/13:26 (fastest of day)
5K XC	15:37	1	Durham XC Races	Durham	1-1-1994	
4.8K XC	15:40	1	Coca-Cola International XC	Belfast	8-1-1994	
6K XC	19:27	1	British World XC Championships Trials	Alnwick	19-2-1994	
6K XC	20:51	1	English National XC Championships	Blackburn	13-3-1994	
1500m	4:23.84	1	England v Australia v Northern Ireland	Kings Lynn	9-7-1994	
1500m	4:26.5	1	Southern League Division 1	Woking	16-7-1994	
5K XC	16:04	1		Neuss	11-12-1994	
6.2K XC	23:08	3	Durham International XC	Durham	31-12-1994	
5.6K XC	17:57	4	Cross Internacional de Italica	Seville	22-1-1995	
6K XC	19:44	3	Almond Blossom XC	Açoteias	12-2-1995	
6K XC	21:46	1	British World XC Championships Trials	Ashington	5-3-1995	
6.47K XC	21:14	18	World XC Championships (4)	Durham	25-3-1995	Team 9th; 1, Derartu Tulu ETH 20:21
1500m	4:11.91	1		Dijon	28-5-1995	
5000m	15:02.87pb	1	Adriaan Paulen Memorial	Hengelo	5-6-1995	2, Derartu Tulu ETH 15:06.67
1500m	4:06.84pb	4	BUPA Games	Gateshead	2-7-1995	
5000m	14:49.27pb	2	KP Games	Crystal Palace	7-7-1995	
800m	2:06.55	3h1	AAA Championships	Birmingham	15-7-1995	1, Holmes 2:04.56
800m	2:05.22pb	5	AAA Championships	Birmingham	15-7-1995	1, Holmes 1:57.56
5000m	15:14.77	4h2	World Championships (5)	Gothenburg	10-8-1995	
5000m	14:57.02	5	World Championships	Gothenburg	12-8-1995	1, Sonia O'Sullivan IRL 14:46.47
3000m	8:40.82	4	Welfklasse	Zürich	16-8-1995	
One Mile	4:28.93pb	9	ASV	Cologne	18-8-1995	
5000m	15:00.83	4	Van Damme Memorial	Brussels	25-8-1995	

Event	Mark	Place	Meeting	Venue	Date	Note
3000m	8:49.31	4	McDonald's Games	Crystal Palace	27-8-1995	2, Yvonne Murray GBR 8:42.82 (Paula's last loss to a British woman at 3000m)
5000m	15:14.32	8	ISTAF	Berlin	1-9-1995	4, Yvonne Murray 14:57.98 (Paula's last loss to a British woman at 5000m)
3000m	8:42.55	4	IAAF Grand Prix Final	Monaco	9-9-1995	
Road Mile	4:25.8pb	2	Fifth Avenue Mile	New York	1-10-1995	
4×435K	62:22	10	National Road Relay Championships	Sutton Coldfield	28-10-1995	Stage 4/13:55 (joint fastest of day)
5.55K XC	18:15	1	Durham International XC	Durham	30-12-1995	
4.8K XC	16:02	1	Coca-Cola International XC	Belfast	6-1-1996	
XC	18:30	1	British Universities XC	Luton	3-2-1996	
6K XC	19:49	3	Almond Blossom Cross Country	Açotelas	11-2-1996	
4.8K XC	16:35	2	Eurocross	Diekrich	25-2-1996	
6.3K XC	21:13	19	World XC Championships (6)	Stellenbosch	25-3-1996	Team 11th; 1, Gete Warni ETH 20:12
1500m	4:19.48	4	AAA v Loughborough	Loughborough	19-5-1996	
5000m	15:28.46	1	AAA Championships	Birmingham	16-6-1996	Championship record
5000m	14:51.71	2	Securicor Games	Crystal Palace	12-7-1996	
5000m	15:23.90	3h2	Olympic Games (7)	Atlanta	26-7-1996	
5000m	15:13.11	5	Olympic Games	Atlanta	28-7-1996	1, Wang 14:59.88
3000m	8:37.07pb	3	Herculis	Monaco	10-8-1996	
One Mile	4:24.94pb	7	Weltklasse	Zürich	14-8-1996	4:08.42 at 1500m
5000m	14:46.76pb	5	ASV	Cologne	16-8-1996	British record
3000m	8:56.25	1	GBR v International Select (8)	Gateshead	19-8-1996	
5000m	14:59.70	4	Van Damme Memorial	Brussels	23-8-1996	
5000m	14:56.36	4	IAAF Grand Prix Final	Milan	7-9-1996	
5000m	14:09.50	2	TOTO Super Meeting	Tokyo	16-9-1996	
Road Mile	4:26.69	1	Fifth Avenue Mile	New York	28-9-1996	
5K XC	17:38	3	Durham International XC	Durham	28-12-1996	
4.8K XC	15:51	3	Coca-Cola International XC	Belfast	4-1-1997	
5.35K XC	17:20	4	Cross Auchan Lille Metropole	Tourcolng	1-2-1997	
6.6K XC	20:56	2	World Championships (9)	Turin	23-3-1997	Team 4th; 1, Tulu 20:53
10K	31:47pb	1	City Crescent Classic	New Orleans	29-3-1997	
1500m	4:08.15	5	Adriaan Paulen Memorial	Hengelo	31-5-1997	
1500m	4:06.93	3		Nuremburg	13-6-1997	
3000m	8:52.79	3	European Cup Super League (10)	Munich	22-6-1997	1, Roberta Brunet ITA 8:51.66
5000m	14:54.63	3	Securicor Games	Sheffield	29-6-1997	
5000m	15:30.36	1	UK Championships	Birmingham	13-7-1997	
5000m	15:27.25	2h1	World Championships (11)	Athens	7-8-1997	

Event	Mark	Place	Meeting	Venue	Date	Note
5000m	15:01.74	4	World Championships	Athens	9-8-1997	1, Gabriela Szabo ROM 14:57.68
3000m	8:35.28pb	2	Weltklasse	Zürich	13-8-1997	
1500m	4:07.50	1	GBR v International Select v Young Lions (12)	Crystal Palace	17-8-1997	
5000m	14:45.51pb	2	Van Damme Memorial	Brussels	22-8-1997	British record
5000m	14:50.32	3	ISTAF	Berlin	26-8-1997	
3000m	9:03.93	1	BUPA Series Final	Gateshead	7-9-1997	
5000m	15:17.02	3	IAAF Grand Prix Final	Fukuoka	13-9-1997	
Road Mile	4:22.96pb	1	Fifth Avenue Mile	New Yorkk	27-9-1997	UK best
4×4.35K	58:22	1	National Road Relay Championships	Sutton Coldfield	26-10-1997	Stage 4/13:55 (fastest of day)
Road Mile	4:32.87	5	Nike PLAY Waikiki Mile	Waikiki	13-12-1997	11, Wang 5:16.23
6K XC	20:48	2	ASLK/CGER Crosscup	Brussels	21-12-1997	
5.2K XC	(flu)	dnf	Durham International XC	Durham	13-1-1998	
4.8K XC	18:00	3	Coca-Cola International	Belfast	24-1-1998	
5.3K XC	17:29	3	Cross Auchan Lille Metropole	Tourcoing	31-1-1998	
8K XC	25:42	2	World XC Championships (13)	Marrakech	21-3-1998	Team bronze; 1 Sonia O'Sullivan IRL 25:39
10,000m	30:48.58pb	2	European Challenge (14)	Lisbon	4-4-1998	Commonwealth record; 15:22.76 at 5000m
5 Miles	24:54pb	1	Balmoral Highland Challenge	Balmoral	11-4-1998	World best; Also World best 24:45 at 8K
1500m	4:05.81pb	3	Adriaan Paulen Memorial	Hengelo	1-6-1998	
5000m	15:06.96	4	L'Humanité	St. Denis	4-6-1998	
Road Mile	4:53	4		Lisbon	23-6-1998	
5000m	15:06.87	1	European Cup Super League (15)	St. Petersburg	27-6-1998	2, Kristina da Fonseca-Wollheim GER 15:10.33
1500m	4:05.92	2	European Cup Super League	St. Petersburg	26-6-1998	1, Olga Kamyagina RUS 4:05.88
3000m	8:38.84	1	British Grand Prix	Sheffield	2-8-1998	
5000m	14:51.27	2	DN Galan	Stockholm	5-8-1998	
10,000m	31:36.51	5	European Championships (16)	Budapest	19-8-1998	1, O'Sullivan 31:29.33
One Mile	4:31.72	2	GBR v USA (17)	Glasgow	30-8-1998	1, Holmes 4:28.04
5K XC	17:47	1	Margate International XC	Margate	22-11-1998	
5.6K XC	18:07	1	European XC Championships (18)	Ferrara	13-12-1998	Team 5th; 2, Annemari Sandell FIN 18:10
6K XC	20:38	4	ASLK/CGER Crosscup	Brussels	20-12-1998	
6.5K XC	22:25	4	Durham International XC	Durham	2-1-1999	
4.8K XC	17:16	2	Coca-Cola International XC	Belfast	23-1-1999	
5.3K XC	17:53	2	Cross Auchan Lille Metropole	Tourcoing	30-1-1999	

Event	Mark	Place	Meeting	Venue	Date	Note
8.012K XC	28:12	3	World Championships (19)	Belfast	27-3-1999	Team 7th; 1, Wami 28:00
10,000m	30:40.70pb	1	European Challenge (20)	Barakaldo	10-4-1999	British record; 15:10.4 at 5000m
5 Miles	24:47pb	1	Compaq Road Races	Balmoral	24-4-1999	World best; also World best 24:38 at 8K & British best 19:51 at 4M
2 Miles	9:32.07pb	1	Loughborough v AAA	Loughborough	23-5-1999	British best
5000m	14:54.61	3	Adriaan Paulen Memorial	Hengelo	30-5-1999	
5000m	14:48.79	1	European Cup Super League (21)	Paris	20-6-1999	Cup record; 2, Irina Mikitenko GER 15:05.43
1500m	4:07.77	5	CGU Classic	Gateshead	27-6-1999	
3000m	8:34.81pb	7	Bislett Games	Oslo	30-6-1999	
3000m	8:31.61pb	4	Golden Gala	Rome	7-7-1999	
5000m	14:43.54pb	2	British Grand Prix	Crystal Palace	7-8-1999	Commonwealth record
3000m	8:27.40pb	3	Weltklasse	Zürich	11-8-1999	Commonwealth record
10,000m	30:27.13pb	2	World Championships (22)	Seville	26-8-1999	Commonwealth record; 15:25.24 at 5000m
1500m	4:06.71	3	GBR v USA (23)	Glasgow	4-9-1999	
5000m	14:59.65	8	ISTAF	Berlin	8-9-1999	
3000m	8:46.19	4	Grand Prix Final	Munich	11-9-1999	
Half Mar	69:37.pb	3	Great North Run	South Shields	10-10-1999	
4.8K XC	17:18	1	Fila International XC	Belfast	8-1-2000	
6.6K XC	21:18	3	Cross Internacional de Italica	Seville	16-1-2000	
6.5K XC	21:26	4	Great North XC	Durham	22-1-2000	
8.08K XC	26:03	5	World XC Championships (24)	Vilamoura	18-3-2000	Team 5th; 1, Tulu 25:42
4.18K XC	13:01	4	World XC Championships (24)	Vilamoura	19-3-2000	Team 4th; 1, Kutre Dulecha ETH 13:00
1500m	4:11.45	11	Adidas Ciudad de Barcelona	Barcelona	25-7-2000	
5000m	14:44.36	2	Norwich Union British Grand Prix	London	5-8-2000	
3000m	8:28.85	4	Weltklasse	Zürich	11-8-2000	
5000m	15:05.48	1	AAA Championships	Birmingham	13-8-2000	Championship record
3000m	8:36.11	3	CGU Classic	Gateshead	28-8-2000	
10,000m	32:34.73	6h2	Olympic Games (25)	Sydney	27-9-2000	
10,000m	30:26.97pb	4	Olympic Games	Sydney	30-9-2000	Commonwealth record; 15:05.70 at 5000m; 1, Tulu 30:17.49
5 Miles	25:04	1	BUPA Ireland Loughrea Run	Loughrea	15-10-2000	

Event	Mark	Place	Meeting	Venue	Date	Note
Half Mar	67:07pb	1	Great North Run	South Shields	22-10-2000	European best; British best 51:41 at 10M
Half Mar	69:07	1	World Half Mar	Veracruz	12-11-2000	Team 6th; Paula also quicker than any of the British men's team; 2, Susan Chepkemel KEN 69:40
6K XC	21:23	3	Energizer European CrossCup	Brussels	17-12-2000	
6K XC	20:21	1	Great North XC	Durham	30-12-2000	2, Tulu 21:36
6.6K XC	21:32	1	Cross International de Italica	Seville	14-1-2001	
4.8K XC	16:51	1	Fila International XC	Belfast	20-1-2001	
5.5K XC	17:54	1	Cross Auchan Lille Metropole	Tourcoing	28-2-2001	
7.7K XC	27:49	1	World XC Championships (27)	Ostend	24-3-2001	Team 4th; 2, Wami 27:52
4.1K XC	14:47	2	World XC Championships	Ostend	25-3-2001	Team 4th; 1, Wami 14:46
10,000m	30:55.80	1	European Challenge (28)	Barakaldo	7-4-2001	15:22.62 at 5000m
5 Miles	25:18	2	Compaq Women's 5M	Balmoral	14-4-2001	1, Wami 25:14
10K	30:47pb	1	New York Women's Mini Marathon	New York	9-6-2001	Second-fastest of all-time
5000m	14:49.84	2	European Cup Super League (29)	Bremen	24-6-2001	1, Yelena Zadorozhnaya RUS 14:40.47
3000m	8:26.97pb	5	Golden Gala	Rome	29-6-2001	Commonwealth record
1500m	4:05.37pb	2	GBR v RUS v USA (30)	Glasgow	1-7-2001	
5000m	14:44.21	1	Norwich Union British Grand Prix	London	22-7-2001	
10,000m	31:50.06	4	World Championships (31)	Edmonton	7-8-2001	1, Tulu 31:48.81
3000m	8:28.07	5	Weltklasse	Zürich	17-8-2001	
3000m	8:42.47	1	Norwich Union Classic	Gateshead	19-8-2001	
3000m	8:32.02	6	Van Damme Memorial	Brussels	24-8-2001	
5000m	14:32.44pb	3	ISTAF	Berlin	31-8-2001	Commonwealth record
5K	14:57	1	Flora Light Challenge for Women	London	2-9-2001	World best
4×3.851K	50:03	1	Southern Road Relay Championships	Aldershot	29-9-2001	Stage 2/11:44 (fastest of day)
Half Mar	66:47PB	1	World Half Marathon Championships (32)	Bristol	7-10-2001	Team 4th; European Best; Personal best 47:44 at 15K; World record 63:26 at 20K
6K XC	21:03	1	Campaccio Classica del Cross	San Giorgio su Legnano	5-2-2002	
10K	30:43pb	1	World's Best 10K	San Juan	17-2-2002	Second-fastest of all-time; 24:38 at 8K

Event	Mark	Place	Meeting	Venue	Date	Note
7.974K XC	26:55	1	World XC Championships (33)	Dublin	23-3-2002	Team 5th; 2, Deena Drossin USA 27:04
Mar	2:18:56pb	1	Flora London Marathon	London	14-4-2002	European best; Women-only race best; Halves of 71:04 & 67:52; 2, Svetlana Zakharova RUS 2:22:32
3000m	8:22.20pb	2	Herculis	Monaco	19-7-2002	Commonwealth record; Personal best 5:37.01 at 2000m; 1 Gabriela Szabo ROM 8:21.42
5000m	14:31.42pb	1	Commonwealth Games	Manchester	28-7-2002	Commonwealth record
10,000m	30:01.09pb	1	European Championships (34)	Munich	6-8-2002	European & Commonwealth record; 14:57.65 at 5000m; British bests 17:58.00 at 6000m; 20:58.52 at 7000m, 24:01.18 at 8000m, 27:03.56 at 9000m
10K	30:38pb	1	Nike Run London 10K	Richmond Park	22-9-2002	European best
Mar	2:17:18pb	1	LaSalle Bank Chicago Marathon	Chicago	13-10-2002	World record; Halves of 69:01 & 68:17; Commonwealth best 1:21:34 at 25K, Further world bests 1:37:40 at 30K. 1:53:45 at 35K & 2:10:08 at 40K; 2, Catherine Ndereba KEN 2:19:26
10K	30:21pb	1	World's best 10K	San Juan	23-2-2003	World record; Further world bests 14:48 at 5K & 24:05 at 8K

Event	Mark	Place	Meeting	Venue	Date	Note
Mar	2:15:25pb	1	Flora London Marathon	London	13-4-2003	World record; Halves of 68:02 & 67:23; Further world bests 1:20:36 at 25K, 1:36:36 at 30K, 1:43:33 at 20M & 2:08:29 at 40K; 2, Ndereba 2:19:55
10K	30:51	1	Nike Run London 10K	Richmond Park	7-9-2003	
5K	14:51	1	Flora Light Challenge for Women	Hyde Park	14-9-2003	World best
Half Mar	65:40pb	1	BUPA Great North Run	South Shields	21-9-2003	World best; Further world bests 50:01 at 10M, 46:41 at 15K & 62:21 at 20K
Half Mar	67:35	1	World Half Marathon Championships (35)	Vilamoura	4-10-2003	Team 5th; 2, Berhane Adere ETH 69:02
Ekiden	2:19:12	6	Hanji Aokl Cup (36)	Chiba	24-11-2003	Third on stage 1, 30:42/10K. 1, Adere 30:12; 2, Lucy Wangui KEN 30:18
6.595K XC	22:04	1	European XC Championships (37)	Edinburgh	14-12-2003	Team gold; 2, Elvan Abeylegesse TUR 22:13
10K	30:45	2	World's Best 10K	San Juan	29-2-2004	
5000m	14:29.11pb	1	European Cup Super League (38)	Bydgoszcz	20-6-2004	Commonwealth record; Estimated British best 9:17.4 at 2 miles; British best 11:35.21 at 4000m; 2, Lillya Shobukhova RUS 14:52.19
10,000m	30:17.15	1	Norwich Union British Grand Prix	Gateshead	27-6-2004	
Mar		dnf	Olympic Games (39)	Athens	22-8-2004	Dropped out at 35K after passing halfway in 74:02; 1, Mizuld Noguchi JPN 2:25:20
10,000m		dnf	Olympic Games	Athens	27-8-2004	Dropped out at 6500m after passing halfway in 15:35.5; 1, Xing Huina CHN 30:24.36

Event	Mark	Place	Meeting	Venue	Date	Note
Mar	2:23.10	1	ING New York City Marathon	New York	7-11-2004	Halves of 70:51 & 72:19; 2, Susan Chepkamel KEN 2:23:14
10K	30:45	2	Crescent City Classic 10K	New Orleans	26-3-2005	
Mar	2:17:42	1	Flora London Marathon	London	17-4-2005	Women-only race best; Halves of 68:27 & 69:15; 2, Constantina Tomescu-Dita ROM 2:22:50
1500m	4:13.13	6	Prefontaine Classic	Eugene	4-6-2005	Fell in pile-up on penultimate lap
3000m	8:50.18	1	European Cup First League (40)	Leiria	18-6-2005	2, Alesya Turova BLR 8:55.13
5000m	15:27.67	2	European Cup First League	Leiria	19-6-2005	1, Olga Kravtsova BLR 15:10.14
10,000m	30:42.75	9	World Championships (41)	Helsinki	6-8-2005	Passed halfway in 15:16.29; 1, Tirunesh Dibaba ETH 30:24.02
Mar	2:20:57	1	World Championships	Helsinki	14-8-2005	Halves of 69:49 & 71:08; 2, Ndereba 2:22:01

Edited by Mark Butler. Compiler: Tom Hurst. Thanks to Ian Hodge, Tony Miller & Peter Matthews.